THE GLORIOUS ART OF PEACE

THE GLORIOUS ART OF PEACE

FROM THE *ILIAD* TO IRAQ

JOHN GITTINGS

OXFORD
UNIVERSITY PRESS

OXFORD
UNIVERSITY PRESS

Great Clarendon Street, Oxford OX2 6DP

Oxford University Press is a department of the University of Oxford.
It furthers the University's objective of excellence in research, scholarship,
and education by publishing worldwide in

Oxford New York

Auckland Cape Town Dar es Salaam Hong Kong Karachi
Kuala Lumpur Madrid Melbourne Mexico City Nairobi
New Delhi Shanghai Taipei Toronto

With offices in

Argentina Austria Brazil Chile Czech Republic France Greece
Guatemala Hungary Italy Japan Poland Portugal Singapore
South Korea Switzerland Thailand Turkey Ukraine Vietnam

Oxford is a registered trade mark of Oxford University Press
in the UK and in certain other countries

Published in the United States
by Oxford University Press Inc., New York

British Library Cataloguing in Publication Data

Data available

Library of Congress Cataloging in Publication Data

Library of Congress Control Number: 2011939891

Typeset by SPI Publisher Services, Pondicherry, India
Printed in Great Britain on acid-free paper by
Clays Ltd, St Ives plc

ISBN 978-0-19-957576-3

1 3 5 7 9 10 8 6 4 2

She, crowned with olive green, came softly sliding
   Down through the turning sphere,
      His ready harbinger,
With turtle wing the amorous clouds dividing.
   And waving wide her myrtle wand,
She strikes a universal peace through sea and land

(John Milton, 'Nativity Ode', 1629)

Acknowledgements

Returning to the field of peace studies after several sinological decades, I have relied more than usual on the advice and support of others. My ex-*Guardian* colleague Michael Simmons read the entire draft, and so did my constant partner, Aelfthryth Gittings: both helped me enormously. April Carter, Peter van den Dungen, Helen Lackner, Linda Melvern, and Jonathan Steele read and commented on one or more chapters to my great benefit. I exchanged ideas on important issues with Ken Booth, Vijay Mehta, Mario Pianta, Phuntsog Wangyal, and Hans van Wees. I was guided to significant material by Stephanie Dalley, Scilla Elworthy, David Hart, Richard Minear, Brad Pardue, David Pritchard, Mark Selden, Gerd-Helge Vogel, and Nigel Young. I offer profound thanks to all the above who have helped me in different ways, and also to Jonathan Watts, for his enthusiasm when I first mentioned the idea. I was also encouraged by being invited to deliver the 2007 Annual Lecture of the David Davies Memorial Institute of International Studies. I owe a general debt to all those who have laboured, sometimes against hostile criticism, to develop what is now the flourishing field of international peace studies. Forty-five years after Oxford University Press published my first book on the Chinese army I am grateful for the skilled support of my editor, Matthew Cotton, and his colleagues, and for the useful comments of its anonymous readers. I would like to thank the staff of the Wychwood Library for their help in securing books: I hope that public opinion will protect the Oxfordshire Libraries service from the cuts imposed by an uncaring government. I also pay tribute to Gabriel Kolko, a historian of war quite different from all the others, whose great work has always been a source of inspiration. Finally, I offer this book to the memory of my parents: Robert Gittings, poet and biographer, who taught me how to write; and Kay (Cambell) Clay, teacher and friend of Italy, who always had confidence in me.

The poem by Kurihara Sadako (p. 243) is published by kind permission of the publishers. Its full citation is:

Kurihara Sadako, 'River's Rebirth' (part 6 of 'River'), trans. Richard H. Minear, *Black Eggs*, Michigan Monograph Series in Japanese Studies, no. 12 (Ann Arbor: Center for Japanese Studies, University of Michigan, 1994), 199–203. Copyright © 1994, Center for Japanese Studies, University of Michigan. All rights reserved.

Note from the Publisher

Whilst every effort has been made to secure permissions, we may have failed in a few cases to trace the copyright holders. We apologize for any apparent negligence. Should the copyright holders wish to contact us after publication, we would be happy to include an acknowledgement in subsequent reprints.

Contents

List of Plates   xi

Introduction   1

1. The Perception of Peace and War   15
   The language of peace and war   16
   The statistics of peace and war   20
   The benefits of peace and war   24
   The anthropology of peace and war   29
   Minoan peace? A case study   34

2. Ancient Peace: From Homer to the Warring States   39
   Peace and war in the *Iliad*   40
   Peace and war in the Chinese classics   47
   Peace and war in the city-states   53
   Peace and war in the Warring States   62

3. The Morality of Peace: From Jesus to the Crusades   73
   Pacifism in the early Christian Church   75
   St Augustine and Just War   79
   Peace and war in the Middle Ages   84
   Pax dei and the popular voice   88
   Opposition to the Crusades   91

4. The Humanist Approach: Erasmus and Shakespeare   98
   Erasmus: the peace pioneer   99
   Juan Luis Vives   106
   Erasmus and Machiavelli   108
   Shakespeare on peace and war   109
   Two problem plays   115

5. The Growth of Peace Consciousness: From the
   Enlightenment to The Hague   123
   Peace and the Enlightenment   125
   The birth of the peace societies   131
   The humanitarian impulse   136
   The Hague Conference and beyond   142

6. **Alternatives to War: The League of Nations and Non-violence** **150**
   High hopes for the League 154
   The World Disarmament Conference 158
   The Peace Ballot 161
   The 'failure' of the League 164
   The non-violent alternative 166

7. **The Misappropriation of Peace: From the UN to the Cold War** **178**
   The founding of the UN 180
   Peace as propaganda 187
   Missed opportunities 191
   Obstacles to understanding 198

8. **Giving Peace a Chance: From the Cold War to Iraq** **204**
   The peace movement revival 206
   Banning the bomb 210
   The 1990s: the missing peace dividend 218
   The 'failure' of the UN 222
   Towards the Iraq War 227

   Conclusion: Peace in the Twenty-First Century **232**

   Notes 244
   Select Bibliography 281
   Index 285

List of Plates

Plate section between pages 148 and 149

1. La Parisienne, Minoan fresco, c.1400 BC, Herakleion Museum, Crete.
© Roger Wood/Corbis.

2. Embassy to Achilles, Kleophrades (Painter), Attic red-figure hydria, c.480,
Staatliche Antikensammlungen, Munich. © Staatliche Antikensammlungen
und Glyptothek, Munich.

3. Eirene (Peace) bearing Ploutos (Wealth), Roman copy after Greek votive
statue by Kephisodotos, c.370 BC. Staatliche Antikensammlungen, Munich.
© Staatliche Antikensammlungen und Glyptothek, Munich.

4. Peaceful pursuits, Chinese stone carvings, Han dynasty, Henan. From
Chinese Rubbings (Beijing: Guoji shudian, n.d.), 147.

5. Green Tara, Tibetan-Chinese, mid-seventeenth century, Royal Ontario
Museum. With permission of the Royal Ontario Museum, © ROM.

6. St Martin Renounces his Weapons, Simone Martini, c.1320, Basilica di San
Francesco, Assisi. © The Art Archive/Alamy.

7. Minerva protects Pax from Mars ('Peace and War'), Rubens, 1629–30,
National Gallery, London. © The Art Gallery Collection/Alamy.

8. The Consequences of War ('Horrors of War'), Rubens, 1636–7, Palazzo
Pitti, Florence. © Arte & Immagini srl/Corbis.

9. Justice and Peace, Corrado Giaquinto, 1753, Museo del Prado, Madrid.
© 2011 Scala, Florence.

10. La Paix: Idylle, Henri Daumier, 1871, Musée d'Art et d'Histoire de Saint-
Denis. © http://www.daumier-register.org.

11. The Enemies of Peace, Joseph Southall, from *Fables and Illustrations*, 1918.
Reproduced with permission of the Barrow family. Photo by permission
of the British Library (LD.31.b.374).

12. Women with a Dove, Pablo Picasso, 1955, Musée national d'Art moderne/
Centre Georges Pompidou, Paris. © Succession Picasso/DACS, London
2011. Photo © Collection Centre Pompidou, Dist. RMN/All rights
reserved.

Introduction

Remember, lads, the life of old
Which Peace put in our way:
The myrtle, figs and little cakes,
The luscious fruit all day,
The violet banks and olive groves,
All things for which we sigh,
Peace has now brought back to us,
So greet her with joyous cry!

(Aristophanes, *Peace*)[1]

Peace is a strange business, a distinguished historian told me on hearing of my intention to write this book. I was already well aware of its reputation for strangeness, and of the difficulty that many people experience in understanding the word. For several years I had been part of an editorial team preparing for publication the new *Oxford International Encyclopedia of Peace*. 'That's going to be a very small encyclopedia,' remarked more than one academic colleague on hearing of the project—only half in jest. (It actually consists of four substantial volumes with 850 entries, and it could have been longer still.) Having recently retired from full-time work with *The Guardian*, I also found that answering the usual question 'what are you doing now?' was not so straightforward as it might seem. When I replied that I was helping to edit an encyclopedia of peace, my enquirers frequently looked puzzled, and failed to catch the vital 'p-word'. I took to adding, quickly, that 'by peace I mean the opposite of war'. Recognition then dawned, followed invariably by the next question: 'what exactly does that mean?'

What does peace mean? It is actually much more than the 'opposite of war' although it is seen frequently as no more than that. Nor is it just 'the absence of war' in the phrase (misattributed to Thomas Hobbes) which when used often carries the dismissive implication that while war is real and actual, peace is merely an interval between acts.[2] As Kenneth Boulding, one of the pioneers of modern peace studies, has observed, peace and war both have their own characteristic set of properties and 'neither is merely the absence of the other'.[3] Johan Galtung, the other great peace studies pioneer, has described peace as ranging from a minimum definition of the 'absence of personal violence' to a much more ample definition of the 'absence of structural violence' or, put positively, as the existence of violence-free 'social justice'. In peace studies parlance, these have come to be known respectively as 'negative peace' and 'positive peace', using Galtung's own shorthand terms.[4] Francis Beer, another modern peace theorist, suggests a similar range between 'war reduction theories' at the lower end of the scale, which concentrate on seeking to maintain the existing international system without the use of force and weapons, and 'theories of peace creation' which go beyond the status quo to focus on rebalancing and restructuring of the world system. The latter implies less emphasis on the law of war, war prevention, and peacekeeping, and greater attention to promoting a more equal share of power, wealth, and knowledge across the world.[5] Increasingly, the concept of peace these days is linked to global justice and sustainable development, and much thought is given to the building of what a UN General Assembly resolution in 1999 described as a 'culture of peace' to educate people, especially young people, in working towards 'a positive peace of justice, tolerance and plenty'. There is now an independently compiled Global Peace Index which ranks the world's nations according to their relative states of peace, based on a range of indicators from the level of military expenditure to relations with neighbouring countries and respect for human rights. This can be combined with the UN Human Development Index, which takes into account levels of health, education, income, gender equality, and many other factors, to give us a better understanding of what peace needs to consist of in a globalized and interdependent world.[6]

Another conceptual approach to peace is one which begins with its individual aspect, most fully recognized in the Buddhist and Hindu concepts of *shanti* and *ahimsa*, denoting a personal state of 'inner peace' that should expand (in theory but not always in practice) towards the 'outer peace' of the surrounding humanity for which it is a necessary condition. In the words of the Buddhist peace activist Thich Nhat

Hanh, 'without being peace, we cannot do anything for peace. If we cannot smile, we cannot help other people to smile.'[7] The concept of *ahimsa* can also be translated as 'non-violence' which, while denoting a personal state of mind, also needs to have an external aspect if it is to be effective: as its chief exponent Mohandas 'Mahatma' Gandhi constantly stressed: 'Non-violence in its dynamic condition means conscious suffering. It does not mean meek submission to the will of the evil-doer, but it means the pitting of one's whole soul against the will of the tyrant.'[8]

These different sets of ideas about peace all suggest a broad spectrum from the simple absence of violence, which still involves a high degree of oppression and inequality, and/or may be confined to the 'inner self', to a happy state of existence in which freedom from violence is only one of the freedoms enjoyed, and in which communities share with their neighbours the expectation of peace in the future as well as now. This high end of the spectrum may never be achieved more than briefly within an individual society let alone across the world: peaceful societies are not utopias and peace is a dynamic process rather than a permanent state, but it is the goal for which we strive. The concept of peace, as Galtung has observed, remains open, and no culture has a monopoly on its definition. 'We have to draw on the human experience as a whole, not only on one gender, one generation, one class, or one corner of the world.'[9]

Just as 'peace' is more complex than the absence of war, so attitudes towards peace should be placed on a much wider range than is allowed by the simple label of 'pacifism' regularly applied to those opposed to war. 'The word *pacifism*', it has been observed, 'was (and has remained) one of the most difficult and contentious to define.'[10] The term in its sense of absolute opposition to all forms of war is a relatively modern one and it was not until the 1930s that it fully acquired this restricted meaning (see Chapter 6, p. 151). We may regard pacifism in this sense as occupying the 'extreme' end—although this does not imply extremism—of a spectrum of views which peace scholars have sought to define in a number of ways. The American philosopher Duane Cady describes what he regards as a 'moral continuum' with 'warism' at one end of the scale, progressing through 'war realism' and 'just-warism' to an 'anti-war' position, and then proceeding to 'pacifism'. Even within this last category, there are several distinct versions ranging from 'pragmatic pacifism' to a position of 'extreme/absolute pacifism'.[11] The British peace scholar Martin Ceadel has proposed a similar range of positions beginning with 'militarism' and 'crusading', which then progresses to 'defencism', the majority viewpoint in which self-defence is seen as sufficient justification for fighting. Reaching the most peaceful end of the spectrum, Ceadel distinguishes between absolute 'pacifism' and a more relativistic 'pacificism'—a term which in spite of being almost unpronounceable has now been widely adopted in the peace studies field. 'Pacificism' may be regarded as a sort of 'practical pacifism' which opposes war not so much out of morality as on the grounds that it is too destructive ever to be justified rationally.[12] All of these labels are useful for analytical purposes, but they need to be used with some caution. First, they have often been—and continue to be—*misused* by states seeking to present their military action in the best possible light: this applies particularly to the doctrine of 'Just War' and to the claim of 'self-defence', both of which were employed to justify, for example, the 2003 invasion of Iraq. Second, in real life people and movements may shift from one category to another as circumstances change. Many pacifists in the late 1930s moved towards accepting the need for a defensive force against the spread of fascism. In the 1960s, many anti-war activists, though personally committed to non-violence, argued that the Vietnamese people had the right to resist US military intervention by force.

The definition of peace may be complicated, but it is a condition of life without which we would not continue to exist. As the Greek historian Thucydides put it long ago, peace brings its own 'honours and splendours and countless other advantages, which are free from danger and would take as many words to enumerate as when we describe the evils of war'.[13] These honours and splendours are not accompanied by the sound of cannons or the exulting cries of the victor, but they are more substantial and longer lasting: indeed, humanity could not have developed at all unless it had enjoyed long periods of creative peace. Most people, most of the time, simply wish that they, their families and friends, and the larger community around them should live in peace, and that this state of affairs should extend to future generations. Nor does peace merely allow the enjoyment of life until one dies in one's bed at home. It has also offered, over past millennia, the space and time for the development of settled agriculture, which, as many populations know from bitter experience, cannot be sustained, far less advanced, through the continual disruptions of war. Similarly, peace has been the prerequisite for the growth of culture, education, and the values of a

humane society: we know this instinctively when we talk of the dehu-
manizing effect of war. Far from being a breathing space between wars,
peace has been a restorative period, after the affliction of war, when
humanity can recover its balance and resume its onward path. Without
peace, we would not be here today.

Of course there have been many wars, terrible wars, and it is understandable that looking back on our history we see them emerging
as promontories on which our predecessors have wrecked their lives
and their well-being at all too frequent intervals. Yet war is rarely a
solution and is likely to lead to unforeseen consequences. As the leading historian of war Gabriel Kolko has observed, looking back on
a century of modern warfare, 'the theory and the reality of warfare
conflict immensely, for the results of wars can never be known in
advance. Blind men and women have been the motor of modern history and the source of endless misery and destruction.'[14] Wars can be
prevented and, contrary to loose statistical claims, there have been
more 'peaces' than 'wars' in human history. Humanity has not been
continually at war (attempts to show this to be so rely on aggregating
different forms of conflict and assuming that these affected entire populations). If that had been the case then the human species would have
risked a counter-Darwinian self-destruction. As put eloquently by the
American educationalist Robert Maynard Hutchins (1899–1977):

The goal toward which all history tends is peace, not peace through the
medium of war, not peace through a process of universal intimidation, not
peace through a program of mutual impoverishment, not peace by any means
that leaves the world too frightened or too weak to go on fighting, but peace
pure and simple, based on that will to peace which has animated the overwhelming majority of mankind through countless ages. This will to peace
does not arise out of a cowardly desire to preserve one's life and property, but
out of a conviction that the fullest development of the highest powers of men
can be achieved only in a world of peace.[15]

If peace is so important, why is the concept of a book about peace so
hard to grasp, and why is it so hard to find such books on the shelves,
in spite of what is now an abundant literature on the subject? Foyles
in London, which describes itself as the largest bookshop in Europe,
has 280 shelves on military history and related subjects such as air and
naval warfare; titles relating to peace are scattered over a much smaller
section of fewer than thirty shelves covering strategy, military thought,
and conflict resolution. There are eight different editions of the text of

Clausewitz, several of Machiavelli and of Sunzi's *Art of War*, but none of the essay by Erasmus which describes the 'Arts of Peace'.[16] Other bookshops display a similar lack of choice: one is much more likely to find Azar Gat's study of *War in Human Civilization* (2006) than David Cortright's *Peace: A History of Movements and Ideas* (2008), or Lawrence Freedman's Oxford reader *War* (1994), than David Barash's Oxford reader *Approaches to Peace* (2000). (It is very rare to find a bookshop which devotes a separate marked section of shelving to 'peace', such as the one at the Friends' Meeting House in London.) The situation is similar online, where a search of the *Encyclopaedia Britannica* produces more than 120 entries on war and warfare, but only 20 related to peace. The encyclopedia's entry on 'war' consists of a 7,000-word article which concludes with a brief discussion of peace and disarmament. There is no separate entry in the encyclopedia for 'peace'.

These contrasts cannot be fully explained by a disparity between the volume of war and peace studies and the literature which they generate. Thanks to the efforts of a number of dedicated scholars— and against the opposition of influential figures including, at one stage, British prime minister Margaret Thatcher[17]—peace studies has developed as a recognized academic discipline in the last half-century on a scale not far short of more traditional war studies, with a corresponding increase in books and journals. UNESCO's *World Directory of Peace Research and Training Institutions* (2000) lists more than 1,200 organizations, either in academic institutions or as separate research bodies, located in more than 80 countries across the world. There are now more than 80 journals of peace and conflict studies in the English language alone. Nor is there such a dearth of peace literature from earlier times as the bookshop preference for Sunzi and Machiavelli would suggest. The monumental project of the Garland Library of War and Peace (1971–9) assembled and reprinted 360 titles of significant works on 'the causes of war and the necessity of peace' dating from the Renaissance to the Second World War. My 'Select Bibliography' offers a list of works which every central library should try to stock. They include a number of excellent histories of peace in general or in specific areas (to which I owe a considerable debt), and a number of very useful peace readers and bibliographies.[18] There is also a growing quantity of important new academic work, especially in the fields of classical and early medieval studies, and of research into the role of peace advocacy from the mid-nineteenth to mid-twentieth century.

The study of peace can be as exciting as the study of war and, far from there being little to say about it, it is an engrossing subject. We need to start by identifying the perception, and frequently misperceptions, surrounding the subject of peace which so often results in its advocacy or pursuit being regarded as utopian or naive. I suggest instead that from ancient times onwards there has been a rich discourse about the meaning of peace and how to secure it which has often come to eminently *realistic* conclusions. (Throughout my text, I use this word, in its various forms, without quotation marks when I wish to indicate what I regard as *real* realism, and within quotation marks when I am referring to the 'Realist' school of analysis in the study of international relations. Modern 'Realism', we should remember, is an intellectual product of the early cold war, and the principles on which it is based are as open to challenge and debate as those of any other political theory.)[19] From this peace discourse, which I describe from ancient times to today, several themes of an entirely realistic nature emerge:

i. That on a sober calculation of the long-term costs as well as the short-term advantages, war is rarely worth the price which will be paid, and that if war-leaders were not swayed by emotion and self-delusion, they would understand this.

ii. That in consequence, it will usually be more sensible to settle for less than the maximum goal peacefully than to strive for it through war: compromise also requires paying a (lesser) price.

iii. That where the temper of disputes is raised beyond the ability of the participants to resolve them, recourse should be had to external conciliation and arbitration (in modern times, by the United Nations).

iv. Such outside intervention should also seek a peaceful outcome by all possible methods, and should only resort to military means as the very last resort to prevent a catastrophe which would have worse results than the consequences of war.

v. That the determination of peace and war is not the exclusive prerogative of the gods, nor of potentates and princes, nor the product of the impersonal contention between states, but that the outcome can be swayed by rational argument, and that there is therefore a place for the endeavours of human individuals in the interests of peace.

vi. That the prerequisite for peace, beyond all else, is the well-being— both material and in terms of equality and justice—of society,

not only one's own society but that of the wider world including that of one's potential enemies. In modern terms, this may be
described as 'globalization'—but (as the British peace scholar Ken
Booth argues) what this really means is that the economic forces of
globalization should be 'harmonized' in the global human interest
rather than working against it.[20]

This book has been written with the general reader in mind, to provide an overview of the way that peace has been perceived (and mis-
perceived) from ancient times to today, and to bring to life at least a
small portion of the wealth of peace advocacy and imagery, in philosophy and political argument, in literature and art, which has accumu-
lated over several millennia. I begin in Chapter 1 by examining some
common assumptions about the historical appeal and prevalence of
war, the benefits which it has allegedly bestowed on civilization, and its
supposed character as an irrevocable 'part of human nature'. These are
partly due to the undoubted appeal of what has been called 'the culture of war', which in spite of some aspects of warfare having become
deglamorized in the past century, still has a sizeable fan club in academic circles as well as among games enthusiasts (and at times of war
among sections of the media). In addition, there is a tendency at times
among self-avowedly hard-headed 'Realists' to show a strangely emotive dislike of the arguments for peace. The anthropologist Douglas Fry
has observed 'what seems like a puzzling phenomenon: A substantial
number of people do not like the idea that peaceful societies exist. It is
interesting to ponder why this is the case.'[21] The prejudice, exacerbated
by the cold war, against the very word 'peace' led to a degree of defen-
siveness even among those engaged in peace studies about using the
'p-word'. Thus in 1956, when Kenneth Boulding and his colleagues set
up the Center for Research on Conflict Resolution at Michigan, they
'deliberately avoided the use of the word "peace" in the title because
of the misunderstandings which might arise'.[22]

Chapter 2 looks at some key episodes of ancient Greek and Chinese
history, as reflected in well-known historical and literary texts. It might
seem an uphill task to discern a peaceful narrative in Homer's *Iliad*,
alongside the more familiar themes of rage and war, or to identify the
advocates of peace in fifth-century Greece at a time of incessant city-
state warfare. However, looking more carefully we will find an alternative scenario deeply embedded in Homer's narrative, and expressed

visually in his remarkable description of the Shield of Achilles.[23] Modern scholarship also shows that attitudes towards peace and war in classical Greece are much more complex than might be inferred from the Thucydidean approach, while critical attitudes on the Greek stage can be identified not only in the *Peace* and other familiar works of Aristophanes, but in many of the surviving plays of the great tragedians. The chronicles of the Spring and Autumn and subsequent Warring States periods of pre-imperial China, with their endless tales of battle and intrigue, might also seem poor material for a peace-oriented study, while the triumph of the first Chinese (Qin) emperor might appear to vindicate the pro-war arguments of the Legalist philosophers in China's 'Hundred Schools'. Yet we can reconstruct rational arguments giving preference to peace rather than war in the counsel offered by ministers and advisers in the historical annals, and by the main schools of political thought from Kongzi (Confucius) onwards. The popular voice of the farmers who had to abandon their fields to fight on remote frontiers is rarely heard, but we should also note the anti-war sentiment in many of the folk songs recorded in the *Shijing* (*Book of Songs*).

Chapters 3 and 4 take what must inevitably be a selective look at the history of peace-oriented thought from the beginning of the Christian era through to the Renaissance. This formative period in our imagined past is most often rendered as a history dominated by war, frequently in its most horrific forms. While not denying the brutality of the times, we should not minimize the countervailing narrative of opposition to war and the search for humane resolution to conflict, and of ignoring altogether the mostly silent voices of the rank and file led by compulsion or obligation into battle. Chapter 3 opens by examining early Christian attitudes towards peace and war, which raised questions—still relevant today—about the real meaning of the injunctions of Jesus Christ, and the balance to be struck between temporal and spiritual obligations. In the conventional account, these questions were answered by the doctrine of Just War as first formulated by St Augustine. Yet this doctrine was in reality a later construct, and Augustine himself was concerned much more with peace than war: even when compelled to wage the latter, he maintained, one should 'cherish the spirit of a peacemaker'.[24] The first half of the eleventh century saw efforts to restrict warfare by new rules, expressed in the *pax dei* (peace of god) and *treuga dei* (truce of god) movements: the decrees which limited the seasons for

warfare and excluded civilians and their means of production from
being targets of attack might even be viewed as an embryonic Geneva
Convention. In the next two centuries the Crusades provided an alternative outlet for military zeal, yet the extent to which they enjoyed
support after the first burst of popular enthusiasm remains controversial. There is evidence of criticism voiced at the court or in the
monastery: the opinions of the rank and file called on to serve in the
Crusades remain largely out of reach.

Chapter 4 explores the humanist sentiment of the Renaissance, a
precursor to the liberal ideas of the Enlightenment, so often over-
shadowed by the realpolitik attributed to Machiavelli and by its long
chronicle of wars. We focus first on Erasmus, the great humanist scholar
and theologian of the age whose eloquent advocacy of peace continues to be undervalued today. Yet with Thomas More and other fellow humanists he spoke directly to kings and princes at a time when,
however briefly, the peaceful settlement of disputes between states still
seemed within reach. We then turn to consider Shakespeare, whose
plays never glorified war unambiguously, and who shifted in his later
years towards a distinctly pacific outlook. Of particular relevance here
is *Henry V*, a play which—in spite of the two martial speeches which
everyone remembers—poses questions about Shakespeare's real attitude towards his subject which have been a matter for debate ever
since they were first raised by the essayist William Hazlitt in the early
nineteenth century. Within three years, Shakespeare was staging *Troilus
and Cressida*, a play whose unremitting cynicism towards war is more
widely recognized. Both plays may be regarded as falling in the category of 'problem plays'. As with Homer, Shakespeare is too great an
artist, and his genius is too finely tuned to the human predicament, for
us to attach either pro- or anti- labels to his work, but our understanding is enriched by the breadth of his view.

With the rise of the nation-state and the accompanying revolution
in military technique, peace thinkers of the Enlightenment took the
first steps towards serious consideration of an international approach
to the limitation of war. Chapter 5 pursues the argument which developed among intellectual circles in the seventeenth and eighteenth
centuries to reach its fullest expression with Immanuel Kant's essay
Perpetual Peace. Although often dismissed as an idealist, Kant addressed
in realistic terms many issues which we now regard as of global concern, including the universality of human rights and the need for

international agreement to prevent war. The peace societies which began to emerge after the Napoleonic Wars, drawing on a wider social and geographical basis, and driven by the horrors of modern conflict, made 'peace' for the first time the concern of millions rather than thousands. Although they suffered drastic reversals and were easily silenced by the shrill sound of patriotism whenever a new war broke out, they quickly came back to life when the costs of such a war were reckoned up. By the end of the century they could even lay claim to the support—however equivocal—of a Russian tsar and a multitude of European government ministers. It is easy to dismiss the nineteenth-century peace movement for placing too much faith in the power of persuasion and for underestimating the strength of militarism. Yet the First Hague Peace Conference of 1899 did achieve practical results in the fields of arbitration and the regulation of rules of war, while peace and disarmament were placed on the international agenda, where they have remained ever since.

After the First World War the goal of universal peace was linked for the first time to that of social justice, through the International Labour Organization and other agencies of the League of Nations, laying the foundation for the humanitarian work two decades later of the UN. The issue of disarmament dominated public perception, leading eventually—after what proved to be a fatal delay—to the World Disarmament Conference of 1932. In Chapter 6 it is suggested that the conference should not be written off so easily, and that it might have achieved positive results if it had been held earlier (a view shared at the time by Anthony Eden). We also consider the British 'Peace Ballot' in 1934—often dismissed as a 'pacifist' exercise—yet which was characterized by Winston Churchill as expressing a 'positive and courageous policy' to contemplate war under the League's authority. The ultimate failure of the League in the 1930s is not a reason for dismissing the efforts made by its supporters to prevent war, and they remain a significant example of popular mobilization.

This chapter concludes by looking at the legacy of Tolstoy and Gandhi towards the emergence in the twentieth century of a coherent doctrine and practice of non-violent protest. Although Tolstoy's ideas are often regarded as idiosyncratic, they inspired Gandhi and many activists in the peace—and particularly the pacifist—movement in following decades. Gandhi's own philosophy and example offer what for most people was an entirely new technique of peaceful protest by individuals within states. In reality passive resistance, public protest, and non-cooperation had always been a weapon of those without a voice—in many episodes which have been barely recorded, or not at all, in history. Today the voices of those protesting peacefully resonate around the world and present a practical alternative to war as the means of remedying injustice and oppression.

The half-century and more since the end of the Second World War presents a mixed record in the pursuit of peace (Chapters 7 and 8). The United Nations built on the lessons of the League to provide what has proved—in spite of much denigration—a more effective international organization promoting peace and development. However, from the crucial early days of the UN's establishment, there has always been a tension between the desire of the great powers to dictate its decisions—or else to ignore them—and the principle of universality and democratic decision-making. The world has avoided, though often as much by good luck as by intention, a descent into a third world war, but it has paid a heavy price for doing so. For many countries in the developing world, where the two superpowers fought a surrogate battle, the cold war was a real war. By the end of it, nearly all of the 20 million and more people killed in conflicts since 1945 had died in Asia, Africa, and Latin America.[25] The pressure of the two blocs also undermined efforts by newly independent countries to achieve democracy and remain non-aligned. Finally, the acquisition of nuclear weapons, which to a certain (but very risky) degree restrained the superpowers from direct conflict, has left a Faustian legacy of nuclear proliferation for which the world community still has no solution.

The cold war illustrated a continuing inability of world leaders and advisers to escape from the traditional mind-set in which war or its threat is the default mechanism, rather than—to use the protesters' slogan—'giving peace a chance'. In the triumphalist victors' view of the cold war, no lessons need to be learnt from its history: Chapter 7 discusses the contrary view (now beginning to be looked at more seriously by some scholars) that there were significant moments when a greater willingness to explore the possibility of peace might have led to meaningful détente at an earlier date. On both sides, to advocate peaceful exploration was more dangerous than to cling to the status quo of armed confrontation. On the side of peace advocacy, the threat of nuclear annihilation combined with the politicization of the 'p-word' by both superpowers led to a narrowing of focus on 'the Bomb'. The anti-nuclear movement with the backing of public opinion did succeed in imposing constraints upon the world powers, nudging them in the direction of limited gains such as the Test-Ban and Nuclear Non-Proliferation Treaties—and would influence the 'new thinking' of Mikhail Gorbachev. Yet the movement failed to produce a more comprehensive view of what peace means and requires in the contemporary world, and which was needed even more when the cold war ended.

A new global discourse on the linkage of peace and development and the need for UN reform—two key elements in any re-formulation of peace for the next century—did begin to emerge in the early 1990s. However, as is shown in Chapter 8, initiatives on both these tracks petered out, while the much-promised 'peace dividend' which would have underpinned them, and helped to achieve ambitious targets to reduce global inequality and deprivation, failed to materialize. New thinking on these issues was unable to effectively challenge orthodox strategic doctrines which survived the cold war. When the threat of global terrorism was dramatized and magnified by Al Qaida, the orthodoxy of a 'new war (on terror)' prevailed, leading to the disaster of the Iraq War. The leaders of the Western 'coalition' in that conflict drew an explicit analogy between the previous cold war and the new war on terror: both were presumed to be 'generational' and likely to extend far into the future. Just as the cold war was seen as having been 'inevitable' in both its extent and its duration, so there was a presumed inevitability about the continuing clash between the presumed values of democracy and of 'Islamic extremism'. The emergence of a doctrine of humanitarian responsibility, although justified in principle, could also be applied in such a way as to undermine the UN's authority and provide a dangerous rationale for counter-productive military intervention. The democracy movements of 2011 in the Middle East underline the truth that 'regime change' can and should only be brought about by the populations concerned.

In my Conclusion I suggest an alternative agenda for peace, bringing together efforts to solve the four separate challenges facing the world: nuclear proliferation, long-standing injustices such as the issue of Palestine, an out-of-control financial system which nurtures poverty and inequality, and environmental degradation which threatens the poor more than the rich. While the superficial trappings of war have been deglamorized, it is still seen as the ultimate arbiter. We need to

recapture some of the idealism and the enthusiasm of the peace thinkers and movements of the past. We need to see a vision of the future, as
the young Alfred Tennyson did so presciently, which has survived the
thunderstorms of war by land and air to become one truly globalized
and peaceful world. But before that can even begin to happen, we
need to regard peace, not war, as the Glorious Art which demands our
attention in the challenging and dangerous century ahead.

> For I dipt into the future, far as human eye could see,
> Saw the Vision of the world, and all the wonder that would be;
> Saw the heavens fill with commerce, argosies of magic sails,
> Pilots of the purple twilight, dropping down with costly bales;
> Heard the heavens fill with shouting, and there rain'd a ghastly dew
> From the nations' airy navies grappling in the central blue;
> Far along the world-wide whisper of the south-wind rushing warm,
> With the standards of the peoples plunging thro' the thunder-storm;
> Till the war-drum throbb'd no longer, and the battle-flags were furl'd
> In the Parliament of man, the Federation of the world.
> There the common sense of most shall hold a fretful realm in awe,
> And the kindly earth shall slumber, lapt in universal law.
>
> (Alfred Tennyson, 'Locksley Hall', 1837–8)[26]

I

The Perception of Peace and War

Peace is ploughing and sowing and reaping and making things and being on television and getting married and raising a family and dancing and singing and opera....

(Kenneth Boulding, 1987)[1]

Wars are exhilarating when fought elsewhere and by other people. Perhaps they are most exhilarating of all when over and done with; and historians of all civilizations had traditionally regarded them as the most interesting topic in their field.

(Arnold Toynbee, 1954)[2]

There are four prevailing views of war versus peace: (i) that war, however horrible, is intrinsically more interesting than peace, and that the history of war, if not its current reality, is still a glamorous subject, (ii) that historically and statistically war has been the default mode of human civilization, while peace has been the interval between war, (iii) that war until recent times has been satisfying and beneficial to progress, and even today there are positive benefits from war preparedness, and finally (iv) that however much we may wish for a world at peace, war is in some sense 'natural', even perhaps 'in our genes', and that this can be demonstrated by looking at primitive society (and indeed at the social organization of other primates). The conclusion from these received truths is that war, like the poor, is always with us and always will be so. These views are still widespread in spite of the impressive growth of peace studies in the past half-century, which has led to alternative and more credible ways of looking at conflict and conflict prevention, and has explored fuller and more 'positive' forms of peace which could deliver social and economic justice in a globalized world. This revolution in peace-oriented scholarship has had only a modest influence on mainstream academic defence studies, a limited effect on the media and on public opinion, and a marginal impact upon the strategic policies of governments. Yet although the field of war studies professes to be much more realistic than that of peace scholarship, it is often prone to make glib and sweeping judgements which reveal a hidden subjectivity. In this chapter we shall explore some of these misperceptions.

The language of peace and war

War is 'the deadliest of sins, and unfortunately sin fascinates while good deeds bore', we are told by Professor Lawrence Freedman in his introduction to the Oxford reader on *War*, and he supports his point by quoting Thomas Hardy: 'War makes rattling good history but Peace is poor reading.'[3] The same quotation appears in many books on modern war including recent studies of the Peninsular War and the American Civil War, and it appears in most dictionaries of war quotations. Yet this was not Hardy's own opinion, but a cynical comment which he puts in the mouth of the aptly named Spirit Sinister in *The Dynasts*, his epic verse drama on the war with Napoleon. Alone among the other spirits who watch the events unfold from Hardy's imagined 'over-world', this malign spirit sees 'good sport' in war and looks forward to 'pleasing slaughter'—quite contrary to Hardy's own view. For *The Dynasts*, as one early critic commented, 'encourages no glorification of war... [but stresses] its horror, waste and futility, and the foul obscenities of carnage'.[4]

If war appears to be more interesting than peace, this is also because customary linguistic usage is richer and more vivid in relation to war than to peace. Since the rise of the modern nation-state, notes the philosopher William Gay, 'almost all societies have coupled the aim of maintaining national sovereignty with the capacity to wage war. Not surprisingly, then, discourse about war is much more deeply ensconced in the languages of the world than is discourse about peace.'[5] Rhetorical metaphors and myths also help to mobilize support for military action: at home the purpose of such language is 'to promote unity and patriotism'; abroad, 'it binds allies and deters enemies', writes Francis Beer, author of another study of the semantics of war, suggesting that 'our progress away from war and toward peace depends on our ability to decode this language' and to 'elaborate less warlike scripts'.[6]

The phrases 'glorious warfare', 'death or glory', and 'deathless glory' have for so long been part of the vocabulary of war (and extended figuratively to the language of religion) that we can no longer easily trace their origin. Shakespeare's *Othello* is often cited for the early use of the phrase 'glorious war', found in the passage where Othello invokes—and bids farewell to—the 'pride, pomp and circumstance of glorious war!' Yet this comes at the psychological crux of the play when Othello has been convinced by Iago that Desdemona is false to him. It is a lament, not a celebration, from a man whose simplistic martial values leave him unequipped to cope with the complexity of real life, and whose mind is already infected by delusion (see further below, p. 114).

Two quotations from early English poets are also often taken out of context. Edward Young is cited for one of the first invocations of the 'glorious art' of war, in his seventh *Satire* (1725–8) dedicated to Sir Robert Walpole. The sentiment may then be contrasted with an earlier reference by Andrew Marvell, in his *Ode on Cromwell's Return from Ireland* (1650), to 'the inglorious arts of peace'. Young in his poem is actually extolling Walpole's successful efforts under King George I to keep Britain at peace and avoid war in Europe. He praises at length the 'blessings' of peace, denounces those seeking glory on the battlefield, and concludes that war is legalized murder:

> When men extol a wild destroyer's name,
> Earth's builder and preserver they blaspheme.
> One to destroy is murder by the law,
> And gibbets keep the lifted hand in awe;
> To murder thousands takes a specious name,
> War's glorious art, and gives immortal fame.

Marvell's Horatian *Ode* offers a psychologically profound portrait of a man of great talents and ambitions who is increasingly driven to defend his power by his sword—eventually through the regicide of Charles I (Marvell's sympathy here lies on the side of the king).

> So restless Cromwell could not cease
> In the inglorious arts of peace,
> But through adventurous war
> Urgèd his active star;
> ...
> Then burning through the air he went,
> And palaces and temples rent;
> And Cæsar's head at last
> Did through his laurels blast.

And so it will continue, Marvell predicts in his closing lines, for 'The same arts that did gain | A power, must it maintain'. It is not the poet but the politician who sees the path of war as unending, and the arts of peace as inglorious—and this will not be the last time that poets and politicians have disagreed.

Today after a century of global conflict which has resulted in more than a hundred million deaths, such phrases no longer sound appropriate to describe actual warfare—although our warriors still merit the heroic epithets of earlier times—but the language of glorious war still supplies the titles, with variations, for many computer war-games.

If war is glorious, can we not say the same about peace? In past centuries there were many occasions when 'glorious peace' was celebrated, but usually only as the conclusion to a war—and by the victors in that war. It was peace as in the *pax romana*, the glorious peace of the days of Trajan and Hadrian as portrayed by Gibbon and other historians of the Enlightenment which the rulers of nation-states in the modern age saw as the supreme achievement of glorious Rome. Thus Napoleon wrote to his brother Joseph after the Battle of Austerlitz, pouring scorn on overtures for peace from the defeated enemy: 'Peace cannot be secured by shouting for it.... The word "peace" means nothing. It is a particular kind of peace that we want—peace with glory.'[7] And in his proclamation to the French soldiers after the Battle of Friedland (1807) he declared:

Frenchmen: You have been worthy of yourselves and of me. You will return to France covered with laurels, having obtained a glorious peace, which carries with it a guarantee of its duration. It is time for our country to live in repose, sheltered from the malignant influences of England. My bounties shall prove to you my gratitude, and the full extent of the love which I feel for you.[8]

However it was the 'malignant' English who would celebrate a glorious (though short-lived) peace seven years later in London, after the fall of Paris and Napoleon's exile to Elba. The Grand Jubilee to celebrate 'the present Glorious Peace'—combined with the centenary of Hanoverian rule—was followed by a visit from the rulers of Russia and Prussia. Its attractions included a Temple of Concorde which was erected in Green Park, and a re-enactment of the Battle of the Nile on the canal in St James's Park. (The bridge over the canal was embellished by a seven-storey Chinese pagoda which unfortunately caught fire during the battle, killing two men and a number of royal swans.)[9]

The restoration of the 'blessings of peace' was regularly invoked in treaties which brought hostilities to an end. The Paris Peace Treaty (1783) which gave independence to the United States was signed 'in a spirit of conciliation...on the return of the blessings of peace'. In the preamble to the Treaty of Portsmouth (1905) the emperors of Japan and Russia declared that they were 'animated by a desire to restore the blessings of peace'. The news of the end of the Boer War (1902) was announced in St Paul's Cathedral, London, by the Bishop of Stepney, who told the congregation that 'God has been pleased to answer our prayers and to give us the blessings of peace.' South Africa, the congregation was told, had become 'a land rich in memories of sacrifice and heroism [by the British forces], and able to provide a worthy environment for a manly and high-minded society'.[10]

However, there has long existed a very different discourse of peace and its blessings, which does not depend on the end of war, but rather assumes a condition in which war has no place. In literature it has long been expressed in the bucolic tradition, reflecting the deep desire of rural communities for a tranquil life so necessary for the natural cycle of agriculture. In religion it also has a long history of expression in the morality of personal peace, but extended to the sphere of social behaviour. In political theory it is grounded in the concept of good government whose purpose is to ensure a peaceful environment for its people to prosper. In the terminology of modern peace scholars, the goal is not merely a 'negative' peace—the fortunate but perhaps temporary absence of war—but a 'positive' peace in which people may enjoy both material plenty and social harmony. The artistic language of peace is also rich and evocative, expressed by images of beauty, serenity, and a wide range of pacific human behaviour which vastly outnumber the works where the artist has addressed themes of conflict and war. Here we may start by contemplating one of its most beautiful literary expressions, which survives in a fragment of verse by the fourth-century BC Greek playwright Philemon:

> Philosophers engage in lengthy quest
> To know the good and where it may be found.
> Virtue, reason and much else they say.
> I learned it digging up the ground.
> Peace it is, born of kindliest goddess,
> Bestower, dearest Zeus, of every treasure;
> Weddings, kindred, children, friends,

> Wealth, health, wheat, wine and pleasure.
> These are the things which, if they should be lost,
> The life of all that's living pays the cost.[11]

The statistics of peace and war

'From earliest times to the present, man has always fought and has always had weapons, both natural and artificial, with which to decide his conflicts.' This confident assertion by M. R. Davie, the very first sentence in a popular book published between the two world wars reflecting the convictions of Social Darwinism (see below pp. 152–3), has been echoed many times since then by those who believe that warfare is and always has been endemic to mankind.[12] In the familiar phrase, 'there always have been wars and always will be'. Christians who take this view, and believe that only the second coming will bring an end to war, often quote from the Gospel of Matthew:'You will hear of wars and rumours of wars, but see to it that you are not alarmed. Such things must happen, but the end is still to come.'[13]

The concept of endless and inevitable war grew more firmly entrenched in the twentieth century, nurtured by the protracted ordeal of the trenches in the First World War. As Paul Fussell has noted in his study of *The Great War and Modern Memory*, this idea seems to have become 'seriously available to the imagination around 1916'. When Edmund Blunden arrived in the trenches, he soon grasped 'the prevailing sense of the endlessness of war. No one here appeared to conceive any end of it.' After visiting the front in 1916 and meeting General Haig, George Bernard Shaw wrote that 'he made me feel that the war would last thirty years, and that he would carry it on irreproachably until he was superannuated'.[14] When the Great War did conclude, the new hope of 'a world set free from military force'—to which the *Manchester Guardian* aspired in its leader on the first day of peace[15]—was always burdened by memories. Pessimism would quickly reassert itself in the succession of wars which began with China, Abyssinia, and Spain. Opinion surveys throughout the Second World War showed that though people hoped for a better world at the end of the war, they were gloomy about the chances that such a world would come about. A nationwide US poll conducted in January 1943 showed a two-thirds majority in favour of establishing a post-war 'world union' in the interests of peace. Yet asked to choose whether, after the war,'we will be able to end all wars between nations', or whether 'there will always be big wars', only 27 per cent thought that all wars could be ended, while 57 per cent thought there would always be wars.[16]

The argument is supported by what appear, at first sight, to be compelling statistics on the frequency and incidence of war. Sometimes these are put forward by those advocating a 'realistic' acceptance of war, but they are also advanced by those wishing to shock us into taking action against it. This often takes the form of estimating the number of major and minor wars which have occurred since ancient times (the starting point varies from 3600 BC—roughly the beginning of the Bronze Age—to around 1500 BC at the dawn of 'Western civilization'), and calculating the number of deaths from war or violent conflict in the same period (figures here range between 1 and 3.6 billion people), and/or the numbers of years when no war has been recorded anywhere in the world. In a typical example an independent commission on the humanitarian challenge posed by modern war, set up through a UN initiative in 1981, asserted that 'The history of humanity is one long succession of war and conflicts...In over 3,400 years of documented human history, only 250 have been years of peace. War is thus the normal state of relations between man.'[17]

Many of these calculations can be traced back to a piece of semi-fiction. In 1953–4, the US novelist and peace campaigner Norman Cousins wrote two articles referring to the sorts of figures on the incidence of war which 'could be expected' if systematic research were done. Cousins suggested these might show that since 3600 BC the world had known less than 300 years of peace, and that during this period there had been more than 14,500 small and large wars in which 3.64 billion people had died. He added the colourful notion that the value of the destruction inflicted in these wars would pay for a golden belt around the earth 156 kilometres in width and 10 metres thick. The first article by Cousins, in December 1953, was subtitled 'A report of an imaginary experiment'; the second four months later began with the sentence 'The following editorial is of course fanciful.' Later Cousins incorporated the material into his book *In Place of Folly* (1961) but reduced the figure of casualties to 1.24 billions killed either in war or by disease produced by war.[18]

Questioned much later, Cousins could not recall whether his figures had any factual basis, but two Danish war historians have found several similar examples of statistics dating back into the nineteenth century, one of which may have been adapted by Cousins. The earliest example was a work published in 1864 by the now obscure French philosopher Odysse Barot asserting that since the year 1496 BC nearly 8,400 peace treaties had been concluded, but that during the same period there had only been 227 years of peace.[19] Almost identical figures reappear in a recent edition of the *Encyclopedia of the United Nations*.[20] Figures of this kind have provided the basis for recalculating the number of wars over the same period, and then for extrapolating them over an even longer period of time. The recalculation begins with the dubious assumption that all peace treaties in history (a) were the result of war, and (b) were 'broken' by the outbreak of another war. Then it can be claimed that (a) more than 8,000 peace treaties have been 'made and broken' in recorded history, and (b) that there have been more than 8,000 wars since 1496 BC and, by mathematical inference, more than 14,500 over the longer period starting in 3600 BC.

Such calculations are highly speculative but, even if broadly accurate, they would not bear out the conclusion that war is 'the normal state of relations between man'. While there may be very few 'warless' days for the entire world, this does not tell us what percentage of the world's population is actually at war during the year or years in question. Humanity as a whole cannot be judged to be in a 'normal state' of war simply because of one or even several ongoing conflicts in one or several particular areas of the world. The fallacy is exacerbated today when modern news reporting can bring the remotest war close to us—we may even feel as if we are involved in it—even though most of the global population is not experiencing any form of warfare.

The quantity of fatal casualties as a result of war is also less overwhelming than would at first sight appear from the large numbers involved. Against a suggested range of 1–3.6 billion deaths through war since 3600 BC (see above) we should set an estimated figure for total population deaths (i.e. everyone who has been born and has died in this 5,500-year period), which is probably not less than 100 billion.[21] Fatalities from war would therefore amount, at the highest, to 36 per thousand, a significant but not overwhelming proportion. Focusing on the twentieth century, Kenneth Boulding has calculated that the overall number of human deaths must have been about 1.5–2 billion, while deaths through war totalled about 80 million—or about 4 per cent of total deaths.[22] Most humans since ancient times, we may conclude, died—and would expect to die—from accident, disease, or old age, not from war.

More scholarly research exists on the number of wars in relatively recent times—since the Napoleonic period or even since the Middle Ages. Pioneering work in the quantitative study of war was carried out from the 1930s through to the 1950s separately by Lewis Fry Richardson, Pitirim Sorokin, and Quincy Wright.[23] The compilation of such data was not performed for its own sake, but to provide the evidence on which further questions could be asked, such as: would it be possible on the basis of this evidence to predict the risk of future war, and could one determine whether war was becoming more or less frequent? Even the attempt to compile the raw data of war was beset by problems of definition: for example, Richardson's *Statistics of Deadly Quarrels* included lesser episodes of violence in addition to warfare, but excluded deaths from famine and disease associated with war. However, by classifying wars and other quarrels by their magnitude, he was able to provide a survey of 'the entire spectrum of human violence' which remains useful to this day. (Not surprisingly the two world wars occupy the top of the scale and together account for about 60 per cent of all statistics of violence compiled by Richardson in the period 1820–1950.)

Attempts have been made to extrapolate from this data backwards in time: one such effort actually comes up with a figure for major and minor wars since 3600 BC which is close to Cousins's fantasy.[24] As well as being statistically suspect, to calculate the incidence of 'wars' in a given time can only serve some purpose if compared to the number of 'peaces' over the same period. Boulding has tackled this by an attempt to define war and peace as 'proportions of human activity' through measuring the proportion of GDP spent on the war industry (defined very widely) in the USA and other major countries. War figures prominently in history, he concludes, because it is 'so dramatic and visible', but it is doubtful whether over time 'it has averaged more than 5 or at most 10 per cent of human activity'.[25]

Many societies at various times in world history have known long periods of peace—contrary to the general view that 'periods of peace are in fact neither more nor less than oases in a desert of perpetual war'.[26] Attempts have been made to identify specific periods of peace, where these are thought to be noteworthy because of their unusually long duration. A study of peace in the ancient world by Matthew

Melko and Richard Weigel challenges the view of its history as a tale
of sieges, charges, gallant Greeks, and victories against odds. Surely,
they maintain, 'there were times of peace when trade could be carried
out, when crops could be harvested, when games could be held, poets
could write and philosophers could convene at the *agora*'.[27] After establishing a set of fairly rigorous criteria, the authors identify ten ancient
'world periods of peace' starting with the Middle Kingdom in Egypt
(1991–1720 BC) and concluding with the Hispanic-Roman period on
the Iberian Peninsula (19 BC to AD 409). In all these cases peace was the
general state of affairs, with minor interruptions, for an area of considerable size over a duration of a century or more. The authors could
have included, by the same criteria, long periods of peace and stability
in imperial Chinese history interrupted by relatively short periods of
war, either through dynastic breakdown or as a result of foreign invasion. There was also a relative absence of warfare in East Asia, with
only two major wars between states in almost 500 years from the mid-
fourteenth to mid-nineteenth centuries. Long periods of peace can be
identified too for large populations under Islamic rule from the ninth
to seventeenth centuries AD. Applying the term 'peace' in these cases
implies no moral judgement: the regime in question may be fighting
a war at its borders to defend itself, or a war for offensive purposes
elsewhere. Those who believe that real peace requires the absence of
war abroad as well as at home will, quite rightly, regard the *pax romana*
and other examples, from Egypt to China, of imperially imposed peace
as seriously defective. Yet those who insist that human history is one
of 'perpetual war' have to reckon with the fact that millions of people
within these territories enjoyed what they regarded as the benefits of
peace over long periods of time.

The benefits of peace and war

Is war really such a bad thing? Not everyone has always thought so.
The cloud of war has often in the past, and even in recent times, been
presented as offering more than one silver lining: war, it is argued, has
served as a valuable means of promoting a sense of nationhood and of
social cohesion; it has provided a necessary stimulus to the economy;
and it has been a source of inspiration and creativity. Such thinking
might seem wholly out of place today in the twenty-first century,

yet politicians and strategists continue to apply what they regard as legitimate criteria of cost–benefit analysis to war. Western policy in the cold war, with its 'hot' appendages, is widely judged to have been a good thing inasmuch as it destroyed the rival appeal of communism, dissolved the Soviet empire, and brought democratic values (in varying degrees) to Eastern Europe. The consequences of 11 September 2001, and the resulting 'war on terror', have served as a 'wake-up call' about the existential threat posed to democratic values by extremism, and should also—the war's defenders insist—promote a new sense of unity, all the more necessary because such a war is likely to last 'for decades'.

Might we not, in some sense, even 'need' war? In 1967 a secret government report on the problems which might occur if the USA entered a state of lasting peace was published by a freelance journalist, Leonard Lewin, to whom it had apparently been leaked. Its conclusion stated that war, or a credible substitute for war, is necessary for governments to maintain power, and that a prolonged peace is not in the interests of a stable society. War, it argued, 'is the basic social system, within which other secondary modes of social organization conflict or conspire'. It showed that military spending performed an essential stabilizing role in the economies of modern societies. In political terms war had become virtually synonymous with the existence of the nation-state. War also served as a mobilizing and unifying force in society, encouraging a sense of patriotism. Finally, war had been the chief evolutionary mechanism for maintaining a proper balance of population and resources.

The publication of this 'leaked report' caused a sensation: it was on the *New York Times* best-seller list and was translated into fifteen languages. The report had allegedly been compiled by a government-sponsored study group which met once a month over two years: the first and last meetings were held in an underground nuclear shelter inside Iron Mountain in upstate New York, hence the title as published: *Report from Iron Mountain*, subtitled 'On the possibility and desirability of peace'.[28] The location was said to be not far from the conservative Hudson Institute think-tank (set up by Herman Kahn, nuclear strategist, author of *On Thermonuclear War* (1960) and reputedly the model for Dr Strangelove in the film of the same name by Stanley Kubrick). Many—but not all—readers and reviewers concluded that it was probably an extended satire on the prevailing strategic orthodoxy which took for granted the need for a permanent war economy and regarded the danger of nuclear war as an acceptable risk. The report was indeed a hoax, as Mr Lewin (who had previously edited a book of political humour) would confirm five years later in the *New York Review of Books*. Yet it was a sign of the accuracy of the satire that until his admission few commentators felt entirely sure. As a group of distinguished US sociologists observed in a symposium on the report convened by *Transaction* magazine, 'The fact is that the Report could have been compiled entirely from authentic sources. There are many social scientists doing this kind of investigation; there are members of the Defense Department who think like this.'[29]

It has long been argued that war, and preparations for war, have had a constructive effect on economic and social development. The medieval knight was an early example of the specialization of labour, according to the German economist Werner Sombart (1863–1941). Later, the cost of war led to the expansion of credit, and the need of modern armies for uniform products on a large scale encouraged the development of mass production. Similarly, the American historian of technology Lewis Mumford (1895–1990) argued that the invention of gunpowder had stimulated the production of iron while the military engineer was the prototype of the industrial director.[30] A letter to Mumford from the Scottish biologist Patrick Geddes—whom Mumford greatly admired—sets out the broader argument:

Agriculture—indeed peaceful industry of all kinds—is dispersive: each man to his own field or job. War *must* concentrate, the warrior *must* mobilise, control, command. The old folks of authority & influence (male & female) in the peaceful peasant world have no choice but to accept this dictatorial command....

But war needs weapons, defensive and offensive, shields, spears & swords, bows, by & by guns! Thus a new impulse to industry, the Smith in power![31]

Such arguments were challenged by economic historians such as Professor John Nef who, in his *War and Human Progress*, while not denying some linkage between military and industrial innovation, showed in detail a much more complicated picture. Indeed, 'when, after 1640, England became more heavily engaged in wars, there was a notable slackening in the rate of industrial and commercial growth'.[32] The scientific revolution of the eighteenth and nineteenth centuries was fostered in a relatively peaceful atmosphere, encouraged by a belief in the rational powers of the mind and in human improvement which had little military connotation. Advances in production of the means for modern war were driven by advances in the natural sciences, not the other way around. If we look at the Napoleonic Wars, we find that wars 'contributed less than nothing, while the preparations for war contributed relatively little, to the economic progress of those nations on the Continent which bore the brunt of the destruction'. By the mid-nineteenth century 'commerce, with its concrete objects of exchange, seemed in fact to be replacing war as a means of satisfying human desires'.[33] Arnold Toynbee has also shown in broader terms that war and militarism, far from being the driving force of human change, have always been 'the most potent cause of the breakdown of a society'.[34]

Yet though few today would express this view of the beneficial economic effects of war as crudely as Geddes, in a modern version it is still one of the arguments advanced by those defending the arms industry which provides the resources for war. Particularly during the post-Second World War arms race, armament manufacture was defended and justified on the grounds that it continued to contribute to economic development, as it had during the formation of the modern state. Discoveries in arms technology were said to have proved 'increasingly relevant to the problems of "civilian" industries' with many advanced technologies being 'transferred from the aerospace industries into general industrial use, at great benefit to the economy'.[35] A recent book on the subject which argues on the same lines is provocatively titled *Is War Necessary for Economic Growth?* The author, Vernon Ruttan, an expert on innovation, concludes that the American and technological landscape today would be very different 'in the absence of military and defense-related contributions to commercial technology development' and that the technology of nuclear power might not have developed at all in the absence of military procurement.[36]

To say that there has been a considerable spin-off of military to civilian technology is not necessarily to endorse war preparations or the arms industry. However, the argument easily shades into justification of their existence and can also be deployed to argue against proposals for the conversion of military to civilian production. The 'Micro Uninhabited Aerial Vehicle' (MUAV)—miniature drone—is under development to identify targets for full-sized drones such as the Predator which have been controversially used to 'take-out' alleged terrorists in remote areas of Pakistan, Afghanistan, and the Yemen. The manufacturers British

Aerospace claimed in 2002 that the MUAV will have 'significant commercial applications, including traffic monitoring and border surveillance...[and] could be ideal for detecting trapped people in burning
buildings'.[37] The Israeli government claimed more broadly in 2000
a considerable civilian spin-off for its defence industry: many high-
technology products are said to have been subsequently applied in
areas such as the internet, medical electronics, and robotics—including
even the invention of a 'robot lawn-mower'.[38] The 'spin-off' argument
has been effectively challenged in a detailed study published in 2008
which concluded that 'military R&D is not an important factor for
economic growth'.[39] Indeed, it may constitute a net loss, by diverting
vast resources of money, material, and human effort away from areas of
much greater contemporary need such as combating climate change.
Yet the development of 'smart' military technology (such as Stealth
aircraft), battlefield robotics, and space surveillance equipment still has
its allure in the media and in countless films, TV programmes, and
electronic games.

Beyond economic calculation, has not war had an inspirational and
creative effect on human existence, and while peace is undoubtedly
a good thing, may not too much of it be stultifying? Peace 'leads to
enervation', wrote Jacob Burckhardt (1818–97), while 'war restores
real ability to honour'—adding that war might also dispose of those
'wretched lives' who flourish in times of peace and 'as a whole degrade
the nation's blood'.[40] We may discount this unpleasant assertion by
the famous art historian of the Renaissance, who was perhaps overly
impressed by the martial trappings of that time (when, he suggested,
war itself could be seen as 'a work of art').[41] Yet we should note that
John Ruskin, Burckhardt's contemporary and no lover of war himself, could still assert that 'all the pure and noble arts of peace are
founded on war; no great art ever yet rose on earth, but among a
nation of soldiers'. He was, it is true, lecturing to the cadets of the
Royal Military Academy at Woolwich, yet he does appear to have been
genuinely seduced by the romantic appearance of war, at least in times
past. (He was opposed to the 'scientific' and 'chemical and mechanic'
nature of modern war, but he had nothing but praise for the 'great
composure and a subdued strength' of the ancient Spartan warrior.)[42]
Even the pioneering psychologist and pacifist William James (brother
of Henry James), while calling in 1906 for a 'war against [the prospect
of European] war' described militarism as 'the great preserver of our

ideals of hardihood'. It was only in the modern age, he argued, that 'the martial type of character can be bred without war'.[43]

We may reasonably suppose that, after a century of total war and with the threat of nuclear devastation still ever present, there is less belief in the glamour of war and its ennobling effect on those who make it. There were no cheering crowds in the streets on the 1914 pattern when the Second World War broke out; only a minority during the cold war expressed the preference to be Dead rather than Red. As the scene of war has shifted to the less developed world, the link between war and poverty is better understood: images of war from these battle fields (usually involving civilian death and suffering) are transmitted the same day to our TV screens. Yet while few would advocate a war in the years ahead, war in the past—including the recent past—continues to be glamorized and its participants uniformly portrayed as heroes in a way that weakens criticism. War's inspirational character is still vigorously asserted by some historians, as by Martin van Creveld in his recent (2008) study of *The Culture of War*. The purpose of this book, we learn, is to put 'firmly in their place' various types of people, including 'the more maudlin kind of pacifists, and feminists', by showing that 'not only does a culture of war exist, but much of it is magnificent and well worth studying'. (Van Creveld has asserted elsewhere that 'the real reason why we have wars is that men like fighting, and women like those men who are prepared to fight on their behalf'.)[44] Pacifists, maudlin or otherwise, and all those who believe that the study of peace should receive at least as much attention as the study of war, still need to elaborate and explain more fully the superior attractions of a 'culture of peace' to both men and women (as I shall seek to do in my Conclusion).

The anthropology of peace and war

Is war/aggression irrevocably part of human nature which we have inherited from the animal world? It is striking how often this assertion is made by historians and other social scientists in terms which are unscientific and based on little or no evidence. The French philosopher Raymond Aron (1905–83), whose judgement on war is generally restrained, compares humankind to the mouse who bites when his tail is pinched, and the stickleback who defends his nest. Such examples support his conclusion that 'The human race is situated on the upper part of the aggressiveness scale among primates. Man, as an animal, is relatively combative—in other words, a slight stimulus is enough to release aggression.'[45] Julius Fraser (1923–2010), distinguished scholar of the nature of time, tells us that 'Early tribal hostilities were surely the continuation of animal competitions and combat, demanding brawn and fortitude, to which the leaven of human imagination, skills, and restlessness were added.'[46] The argument that the instinct for combat is not only part of human nature but has been inherited from the animal world was popularized more recently by the anthropologist Robert Ardrey, in *The Territorial Imperative* (1967), where he argued that 'if we defend the title to our land or the sovereignty of our country, we do it for reasons no different, no less innate, no less ineradicable, than do lower animals'. Attachment to territory and the need to defend it by war satisfied the three basic human needs—for identity, stimulation, and security. This was as true for the Venetian, the Scotsman, and 'the man from La Crosse, Wisconsin' as it was for the albatross, the three-spined stickleback, the lungfish, and the lion. 'Several hundred million years of biological evolution have altered not at all the psychological tie between proprietor and property.'[47] Another influential writer on animal and human aggression from the 1960s was Konrad Lorenz, the Austrian zoologist (and former Nazi enthusiast). 'To the humble seeker after biological truth', he wrote in *On Aggression*, 'there cannot be the slightest doubt that human militant enthusiasm evolved out of a communal defence response of our pre-human ancestors.'[48]

Arguments of this kind are typically overstated, focusing only on one aspect of human behaviour (aggression), while ignoring the complementary aspect of human cooperation, and often attributing its origins to a single cause—in Ardrey's case the so-called 'territorial imperative' and for Lorenz animals being biologically programmed to fight for resources. Such arguments often claim to reflect a Darwinist view of savage competition as the driving force in nature, but they should more correctly be labelled as pseudo-Darwinist. For Darwin, as the philosopher Mary Midgley has noted, did not share Hobbes's belief that all human action springs from selfish calculation, but maintained in *The Descent of Man* that cooperation becomes more noticeable among species as one moves further up the evolutionary scale.[49] Darwin did not take such a low view of human nature as claimed for him by 'reductionists and determinists speaking in his name', writes the Darwinian scholar David Crook, but preferred a more cheerful view which echoed the optimistic ethos of his time. His picture of human progress, although dark and violent in its origins, became more positive as communities grew larger and the benefits of cooperation more evident. In Darwin's own words, 'The simplest reason would tell each individual that he ought to extend his social instincts and sympa- thies to all the members of the same nation...This point being once reached, there is only an artificial barrier to prevent his sympathies extending to the men of all nations and races.'[50]

Even when confined to the animal world, the pseudo-Darwinian approach proves to be shakier than is often claimed. Field observa- tions of animal behaviour have displayed a much greater variabil- ity, both between and within species, than the view of 'nature red in tooth and claw' would suggest, and some observations have been modified over time. The British anthropologist Jane Goodall attracted much attention for her earlier work which appeared to show high levels of aggression and violence among chimpanzee troops. However, after over twenty-five years of study in Tanzania, she concluded that 'Aggression...is vivid and attention catching, and it is easy to get the impression that chimpanzees are more aggressive than they really are. In actuality, peaceful interactions are far more frequent than aggres- sive ones.'[51] Biologists, according to the behavioural biologist Frans de Waal, have come a long way since the 1960s:

Despite the continuing popularity of the 'struggle for life' metaphor, it is increasingly recognized that there are important costs associated with open competition, hence that there exist sound evolutionary reasons for constraints on the expression of competitive tendencies.[52]

Independent of any perceived link between animal and human behav- iour, there is still a widespread view that human beings have always been incorrigibly violent, and that the earliest archaeological evidence for prehistoric man incontestably demonstrates the prevalence of war. The argument is often coupled with a rejection of the myth of the 'peace- ful' or 'noble' savage, attributed (incorrectly) to Jean-Jacques Rousseau. The same phrase has been used in the subtitles of two books by pro- ponents of the case for prehistoric violence—Lawrence Keeley ('the myth of the peaceful savage', 1997) and Steven LeBlanc and Katherine Register ('the myth of the peaceful, noble savage', 2003). Primitive and prehistoric warfare was 'just as terrible and effective as the historic and

civilized version', writes Keeley, while LeBlanc and Register argue that
there is a popular bias among anthropologists to 'sanitize and ignore
warfare' among the ancient people they are studying. Extending this
argument to more recent times, the authors maintain that such ideas
still dominate our view of the past: 'For example, [we say that] it was
the "cowboys" who decimated the Indians. (True, but the Indians
fought fiercely among themselves long before the encroaching Euro-
Americans arrived.)' There is nothing value free, it appears, about
anthropological judgement of our prehistory, as the publisher's blurb
to this book indicates: 'With armed conflict in the Persian Gulf now
upon us, [the authors take] a long-term view of the nature and roots
of war...'[53]

This view has been challenged by other modern anthropologists,
and most forcefully by a leading authority on conflict and aggression,
Douglas Fry: the subtitles of his recent books indicate a completely
opposite approach ('An anthropological challenge to assumptions
about war and violence', 2005, and 'The human potential for peace',
2007). Attacking what he calls the 'me the warrior' approach to aggression, Fry sets out to reveal 'how the human potential for conflict resolution tends to be under-appreciated, whereas warfare and other forms
of violence tend to be emphasized, exaggerated, and naturalized'. Fry
believes that the evidence shows that while periodic violence of a
ritualized nature occurred among early hunter-gatherers, such societies showed a good deal of restraint. Warfare has spread and intensified
'only in the most recent millennia, the period corresponding with a
multitude of major changes in human social life following the agricultural revolution'. Fry's conclusion also brings the anthropological
study of the remote past uncomfortably close to the present day. Why
does the 'man the warrior' outlook resonate so powerfully for us, he
asks? Because it retells a current-day tale, in a world where a war is
always raging somewhere, that is 'familiar and easy to accept'.[54]

A small number of case studies among modern-day 'primitive'
societies have become controversial in this debate: if such societies
are found to be violent or war-prone, are we entitled to draw infer-
ences from their conduct about the remote human past? One of the
best-known cases, that of the Yanomami of Venezuela and Brazil, has
led to sharply opposed conclusions. A study by the American anthropologist Napoleon Chagnon—again with a significant subtitle ('The
Fierce People')—appeared to show that the Yanomami were engaged in

endless conflict over women, status, and revenge, and became a standard college textbook widely interpreted as illustrating the age-old human propensity for violence. This interpretation has been challenged by other anthropologists including Brian Ferguson, who argues instead that the Yanomami have been affected by European incursions since the eighteenth century, that recent conflicts including those described by Chagnon may have been fought over goods supplied by outsiders, and therefore that such warfare cannot be taken as typical of prehistoric tribal societies.[55]

However the questions considered above—whether or not prehistoric societies were as violent as those of recorded history, and whether or not aggression is a common feature of the natural world—may be answered, the issue of war and peace in more recent times should still be considered separately. No one can deny that human society has evolved since we were hunter-gatherers (and more so 'since we were apes'), and it is probably true that greater social complexity and competition for resources have led to more frequent incidents of warfare. Yet unless we regard anger as the only human emotion, and war as the only salient feature of human history—both difficult propositions to sustain—there is clearly much more to discuss. Throughout this chapter, we have been looking at a common—perhaps understandable—tendency, in the face of our apparent inability to achieve lasting peace, to take refuge in judgements (often no more than aphorisms) about the history, culture, and natural origins of humanity which provide, so to speak, an alibi for the prevalence of war. We should at least pay equal attention to the prevalence of peace, and to the very different human emotions and aspirations which engender and seek to extend peace. Here for the time being let us conclude with these words of Anatol Rapoport, from his classic study of the psychology of conflict and cooperation:

It is almost a folk saying that there will always be wars because human beings are aggressive by nature. There is no lack of evidence of 'man's inhumanity to man'. Reading some accounts of human events, we can easily get the impression that murder and massacre, torture and enslavement, robbery and rape are the principal activities of human beings. It is hardly worth mentioning that this evidence by itself does not warrant the conclusion that the dominant ingredient of 'human nature' is violence. Another list could be compiled of instances of altruism and cooperation, passionate quests for knowledge and wisdom, celebrations of love and friendship. In spite of the seemingly ubiquitous propensity of boys to fight, the very young human child seems to be a gentle creature, readily reaching out to other small living creatures, human and non-human, with gestures of affection rather than with threats of violence.[56]

Minoan peace? A case study

The controversy over the character, peaceful or otherwise, of the remote and still obscure Minoan civilization offers a revealing insight into how we perceive peace and war in the ancient world—and how such a perception can change over time.

The palace of Knossos, centre of the Bronze Age Minoan civiliza- tion on Crete for 600 years or more (c.2000–c.1400 BC), is approached by a shallow curving valley now, as then, from the harbour and beaches of the island's northern coast some three miles away. There are no natural defences to the north, from which a seaborne attack might be launched, or to the east where the land rises quickly to higher ground. The palace sprawls across a large area with a maze of rooms, levels, and courts, and is impressive for its complexity and horizontal spread: it lacks any dominant vertical feature. The central court, where some believe the celebrated Bull Games may have been staged, lies at the heart of the palace but is overlooked by two upper storeys. A smaller court where significant ceremonies probably took place (possibly dancing on a floor traced with the pattern of a labyrinth), the so-called Theatral Area, is located near the western entrance, easily accessible to the inhabitants of the adjacent town. The whole position is ill suited for fortification, and yet, as the art historian Friedrich Matz observed, 'for six centuries, life flourished in this palace, and despite the fact that it was frequently destroyed by fire and earthquake, it was repeatedly rebuilt without the protection that fortifications could afford'.[57]

When the Mycenaean invaders whom we now call Greek overthrew the Minoan rulers at the end of the fifteenth century BC (or perhaps later), they would have faced no bastion or rampart at Knossos, merely the retaining wall of the western court. Of the three other great palaces so far discovered on Crete, only Phaistos occupies an elevated site but like Knossos shows no sign of fortification. Mallia lies on the northern coastal plain while Zakros is close to the shore on the south-east of the island, with steep hills immediately behind. 'The dangers of war seem distant; neither towns or palaces are fortified,' observes Walter Burkert, the German scholar of Greek mythology.[58] The contrast with the famous mainland acropoli of the Mycenaeans—most famously at Mycenae itself—is striking. Heavily fortified, they are guarded by circuit walls with stones of enormous size. Their layout is rigid, inward-looking, and focused on defence, unlike the extensive sprawl of the Cretan palaces, with the *megaron* or large hall, the exclusive precinct of the ruling lord, at its heart and at its highest point. Standing on their windy heights, one can easily be transported in imagination to the rough world of Agamemnon, Menelaus, and fellow warlords of the *Iliad*.

There are also striking contrasts in style and subject matter between Minoan and Mycenaean art, which seem to illustrate more profound cultural differences. Minoan art is described by one historian of ancient Greece as 'a delirious dance of colour and the senses, [a] fascination with plant and animal life, with sex and social intercourse and religious ritual, with the stylised dangers of boxing and bull-vaulting, [which] reveals a life-style clear outside the mainstream of European history'.[59] We may catch a sense of the vivacity of Cretan art from the fragment of fresco named by its finders 'La Parisienne' (Plate 1), often described as the most charming of surviving paintings: though usually identified as a dancing-girl, the subject may be a goddess presiding at a ritual scene of dance.[60] Cretan artisans either transmitted their skills to Mycenaean craftsmen or were themselves imported by the Mycenaeans to paint frescoes, carve ivory, cast bronze, and fashion gold and silver objects with the most vivid detail. Though the Minoan source can be easily recognized, much of the resulting art took on a harsher aspect. Mycenaean fresco-painting 'owed everything technically, and almost everything stylistically, to Crete', but it lacked the 'gay and spontaneous quality' of the Cretan model, and the 'scenes of war and the chase' which the Mycenaeans preferred were rarely found on Cretan frescoes.[61]

Many aspects of Minoan Crete remain obscure to us: unlike contemporary civilizations of Egypt and Mesopotamia there are no available written records. The Linear B tablets brilliantly deciphered in the 1950s belong to the subsequent period of Mycenaean domination—and perhaps to the very end of that period.[62] The distant memories transmitted by classical Greek historians have to be treated with great caution. We must therefore rely almost entirely on the interpretation of existing artefacts and on fresh discoveries to infer the character of what was certainly a long-lasting, powerful, and brilliant civilization.

Early on in the rediscovery of this civilization, archaeologists con-curred that it was not only new and exciting, but also a notable example of a predominantly peaceful society. Their view while supported by striking evidence of the kind outlined above also reflected a tendency, particularly on the part of Sir Arthur Evans, who first excavated Knossos (and applied the term 'Minoan' to its rulers), to enhance its appeal by investing the Minoans with exceptional qualities. The concept of a peace-loving Minoan culture—that of a people secure on their island and defended by their sea-power—was first put forward by Evans in 1900, early on in his excavations. This has been interpreted critically as an attempt by Evans to demonstrate 'Minoan Crete's importance as a historical precedent for Victorian Britain's pre-eminence'.[63] Another critic has suggested unkindly that for Evans 'the lithe body of the bull leapers reflect[ed] the British sporting aesthete' of the current time.[64] The fact remained that on the basis of the archaeological evidence, as compared with the contemporaneous Bronze Age cultures of Egypt and the Near East empires, Minoan Crete offered little evidence of militarism. One did not have to be a defender of the British empire to support the view of a relatively pacific Minoan civilization, as expressed by Martin Nilsson in his great work on Minoan-Mycenaean religion: 'Crete was peaceful: the palaces were not fortified, and weapons and representations of warriors and fights have little prominence.'[65]

Some new finds have been made in recent years which may, it is argued, cast a different light on the traditional picture of a peaceful Minoan Crete, while some of the earlier evidence has been reassessed. However, a sceptical bias has also emerged which has led some inter-pretations to the opposite extreme. If in the end the case for a 'pacific' Minoan culture relied too much on supposition, then the opposing case, that it was as bloody as anywhere else in the Bronze Age, may lean just as heavily—or more so—upon inference from slender contrary evidence. Typical of this new approach is the argument by Azar Gat in his study of *War in Human Civilization*. In all societies such as that of Minoan Crete, Gat insists, it is a simple and 'almost self-evident' fact that 'armed force was a major, and sometimes the major, factor' in the accumulation of power and that, once secured, such power could not be maintained 'without the underpinning of superior, covert or overt, coercive force'. Quoting Thucydides and Herodotus (who wrote almost a millennium after the heyday of Minoan culture) Gat writes that this was achieved abroad by a powerful Minoan naval force while, on the island itself, the peaceful appearance of the luxurious palace economy and its wealthy residents must have been secured early on by intra-island warfare, which could then only be maintained by 'elite dominance in all its aspects'. Finally, Gat along with several other modern writers attaches great significance to 'the remains of sacrificed people [which] have been excavated in several locations in Crete, casting a darker shadow on the earlier bright image of Minoan religion'.[66]

This last evidence consists of two comparatively recent finds. (i) In the ruins of a sanctuary at Anemospilia, four human skeletons were found of whom one, that of a young man, lay in a contracted position suggesting that he may have been trussed up for sacrifice: a bronze dagger was also found among his bones. The other three persons, it was surmised, had just completed the sacrifice when they were surprised by an earthquake and crushed in the collapse of the building. (ii) In the 'North House' at Knossos, the bones of four or more children were unearthed bearing signs of knife marks comparable to butchery marks on animal bones, also said to indicate that they had been sacrificed, possibly for the purpose of ritual cannibalism. It is also suggested by Gat that there may be a 'faint echo' of this 'grim reality' in the later legend of Theseus and the Minotaur in which young men and women from Greece were supplied as annual tribute to Crete, to meet their deaths in the monster's labyrinth.

The evidence is plausible but not as conclusive as is claimed for it by those determined to demolish the peaceful Minoan 'myth'. Some Aegean scholars have questioned whether the building at Anemospilia was a temple; and they suggest that the contracted position of the young man's skeleton may result from his death agony in the earthquake, while the bronze dagger could have fallen on him or been carried by him. The children's bones at Knossos could indicate a 'secondary burial'—the well-known practice of re-interring a body at a later stage—while the bones may have been cut to remove the flesh for that purpose.[67] Yet if the more sinister interpretation of these finds is justified, we may still ask how much they tell us about a society lasting over many centuries where the archaeology, compared with others of the same period, reveals so little sign of warlike disposition. As for the legend of Theseus' triumph over the tyrannical King Minos, this may dimly echo the victors' version of history—a tale told by the Mycenaeans who conquered Crete to present the defeated Minoan rulers in the worst possible light. The subsequent abandonment by

Theseus of Ariadne—the daughter of King Minos without whose aid he could not have defeated the Minotaur (and with whom he then slept)—would also fit this interpretation: the Cretan people had effectively been raped for the sake of the Mycenaean empire. As has been said of a later legendary abandonment—that of Dido by Aeneas, famously recorded in Virgil's *Aeneid*—'the price of empire is the loss of human love'.[68]

In the last analysis, the evidence for a more warlike Minoan Crete remains inconclusive, as was shown in several papers at an international conference in 1998 called to discuss the issue of war in the Bronze Age Aegean.[69] We should heed the warning of the British Aegean scholar Oliver Dickinson not to succumb to 'the recurrent temptation to create an ideal Minoan society in terms that reflect modern preoccupations'.[70] Yet for various geographical and cultural reasons which we can only surmise (its island location and trading strength, perhaps even the survival of a matriarchal culture), Minoan Crete may well have been comparatively less conflict-prone for long periods of time, and may have possessed a more pacific society. Thus it would offer evidence to strengthen the case—which is after all quite a modest one—that some ancient communities at some times were more peaceful than others.

2

Ancient Peace

From Homer to the Warring States

For I believe nothing can be compared to the value of life—
Neither Troy's wealth in times of peace before we Greeks came,
Nor all the riches piled up at Delphi on Apollo's threshold.
Plump sheep and cattle can always be seized by force;
Tripods and fine bay horses can always be got hold of;
But a man's life can never return or be won back,
Once indeed the spirit has passed out through his lips.

(speech by Achilles, *Iliad*)[1]

I have heard that one can win the support of the people by policies which are just but I have never heard of anyone doing so by
disrupting their lives. To try to do so would be like tangling silken
threads instead of straightening them out... As for using armed force,
that is like lighting a fire: unless it is kept under control one will be
consumed by the flames.

(speech by Zhong Zhong, *Chronicle of Zuo*)[2]

The ancient and classical history of the two oldest world civilizations still extant today, those of the Greek and the Chinese peoples,
appears dominated by chronic warfare and by martial values, stretching
over the first millennium BC—from Mycenaean Greece and the Shang
dynasty of China to Greek city-states and the Chinese Warring States
period. Homer's *Iliad* is described by one recent editor 'as a glorification
of war and as the definition of a man as a skilled fighting machine'.[3]
A textbook on warfare in ancient Greece tells us that 'a hostile
relationship was assumed to be the norm between Greek states' while
peace was 'an abnormal state that could not be expected to last indefinitely'.[4] The whole of the recorded history of early China, from the

'Spring and Autumn' period (722–403 BC) to the unification of
China at the end of the 'Warring States' (403–221 BC), is described
in another recent textbook as 'a violent age, at a time when victors presented the cut-off ears of enemies at their ancestral temples,
when the blood of captives was spread on ceremonial drums, when
thieves had their feet cut off, and when rulers ran a considerable risk
of assassination'.[5] Many historical and literary records of both cultures are best known for their portrayal of battlefield heroism, strategic cunning, political manoeuvre, treachery, and death. We might
suppose that there is very little to learn about peace rather than war
from an epoch which was characterized by fierce struggle and conflict. Yet we will find in the surviving works of Greek and Chinese
history and literature—if we choose to look—a rather more complex narrative, in which the values of peace as well as war are argued
and asserted in terms which we can recognize today.

Peace and war in the *Iliad*

When Achilles, hero of heroes, responds (in the speech quoted above)
to Odysseus' attempt to persuade him to resume fighting, he does not
just reiterate his grievance against Agamemnon, the Achaean (Greek)
commander-in-chief, but muses on the pointlessness of risking one's
life in war. At this critical turning point one-third of the way through
the *Iliad*, the classical Greek vase-painters showed the hero neither
as wrathful nor as sulking, but wrapped in his cloak and pondering
deeply (see Plate 2).[6] Achilles' speech has been described as 'one of
the greater glories of the *Iliad*', and as the hinge on which the entire
story depends.[7] His severely wounded pride has led him to question
the whole basis of the conflict before the walls of Troy, and to declare
his resolve to take his ships home. It is only for a moment: Achilles will
stay and by doing so carry forward the tale told by Homer of his wrath
to its bloody and tragic consequence. Yet while it would be a mistake
to crudely reinterpret the *Iliad* as an anti-war poem, the *Iliad*, like all
supremely great works, offers a complete perspective on human life
which includes peace as much as war.

It has often been claimed that the *Iliad* provides epic evidence for
the primacy of martial over pacific values in ancient society. Homer
is said to be 'absorbed with battles and the warlike qualities of his

protagonists',[8] and to show that 'the essence of the human condition is strife'.[9] Of the *Iliad*'s 15,000 lines, it has been calculated that 'battle takes up some 5,500, made up of three hundred encounters'.[10] Dozens of violent deaths are described in gruesome detail: an eyeball is spitted by a spear; a severed head hangs to the neck by a flap of skin; blood spurts out through mouth and nostrils; and a sharp spear quivers in the entrails.[11] Homer as the chronicler of war had a special appeal for great generals. Alexander the Great is said to have slept on his campaigns with the *Iliad* by his side, and Napoleon read it on St Helena to while away the time, declaring that Homer must have been a warrior himself.[12]

Yet Homer never celebrates war in the uncomplicated way that might be expected in a martial epic (and was probably characteristic of other less distinguished Greek epics which have not survived). Homer's central ambiguity on the question of violence was powerfully illustrated by the French philosopher Simone Weil in her essay 'War and the *Iliad*', written in the shadow of the Second World War. 'The true hero, the true subject, the centre of the *Iliad*,' Weil wrote, 'is force. Force employed by man, force that enslaves man, force before which man's flesh shrinks away.' And yet, Weil concludes, nowhere does Homer celebrate force. 'The cold brutality of the deeds of war is left undisguised; neither victors or vanquished are admired, scorned, or hated.'[13] Successive editors of the Penguin Classics editions of the *Iliad* have also reflected on Homer's ambivalence towards war: E. V. Rieu, Penguin's first translator, noted that while Homer generally respects the gods, there is one exception.

He gives the war-god many terrible and bloody attributes, but he takes no pains to make us feel that he is much more than a bully. It is possible that the reason why he persistently degrades and ridicules Ares in a poem which is much concerned with battle, is that the Iliad was written not to glorify war (though it admits its fascination) but to emphasize its tragic futility.[14]

In an updated edition of the Rieu translation, editor Peter Jones has expressed a similarly tentative view: 'if...we were to ask what is the moral of the *Iliad*, or what Homer really wanted us to think about Achilles, or war, or life, we would struggle to produce a definitive answer'.[15] Finally Robert Graves, poet, novelist, and amateur classicist, had no doubt in the preface to his translation that 'an inveterate hatred of war appears throughout the *Iliad*' and that Homer treated his heroes, even Achilles, the greatest of them all, with irony.[16] Other modern commentators agree that the *Iliad* is by no means an uncomplicated narrative of war: this is particularly true if—as I shall suggest here— we recognize that Homer has woven into his story a thread of events pointing to the possibility of an alternative peaceful outcome.

The thread of peace

(1) (Book 2) After nine years spent laying siege to Troy, the Greek army en masse are frustrated by their failure and anxious to go home. Agamemnon decides to test the resolve of his forces by telling them that he has been instructed by Zeus to give up the struggle. The trick works all too well, and the whole army rushes down towards their ships, yelling loudly, and prepare to launch them. Even the resourceful Odysseus is shaken and stands watching in silence until the goddess Athena rouses him to action. The men are herded back to the assembly, where (after a blustering intervention by barrack-room lawyer Thersites in favour of retreat) Odysseus pitches his counter-appeal: would it not be humiliating to go home empty-handed? Why not wait a little longer and find out whether the prophecy of victory for the Greeks in the tenth year is right or wrong? The men are won over, but only through a patently un-heroic argument.

(2) (Book 3) Within hours the two armies are facing each other prepared for battle, yet before a blow has been struck it looks as if the dispute may be solved by agreement between the two sides. Paris (Helen's seducer) offers to engage in single combat with Menelaus (Helen's husband). Whoever wins will have possession of Helen, while the opposing Trojans and Greeks will swear solemn oaths of friendship. In a significant aside, Homer informs us that Priam's senior advisers, watching with the king from the walls of Troy, would much prefer Helen to return home on the Greek ships, observing

> How terribly she resembles one of the immortal goddesses!
> Yet however fair she may look, we should surely let her go home,
> Lest she stay here to bring disaster to us and our children to come.

However, they only murmur their doubts to themselves, unwilling to sound defeatist.[17] In any case a solution appears in sight, because no one opposes the proposal to settle by duel, even though if Menelaus loses the Greeks will go home empty-handed, while if Paris loses, the Trojans will have to pay substantial compensation as well as surrendering Helen. The duel commences and Paris is on the point of being slain when he is whisked away to safety (actually into bed with Helen) by his protector, the goddess Aphrodite: Menelaus can now claim to have won by default. The war is, or should be, over.

(3) (Book 4) For a teasing moment, Zeus himself seems prepared to accept the result of the duel, but when his wife, Hera, and daughter Athena protest, he grudgingly agrees that they may restart the war. Athena persuades one of the Trojan warriors to break the truce by firing an arrow at Menelaus. Battle is joined and within a short while Greeks and Trojans lie dead on the ground, stretched out side by side 'in their multitudes'. A day of fierce fighting follows (Books 5 and 6), to end with another tantalizing hint of settlement by single combat between Hector and Ajax (Book 7). However, their fight to the death is interrupted by heralds—acting as umpires—who judge both equally brave and point out that it is getting dark.

(4) Even now, peace is not out of the question. Both sides are deeply shaken by the bloodshed of the day and uncertain that they will prevail. The Greeks decide instead to ask for a truce, and to build a defensive ditch around their ships. The Trojans, in a heated assembly, consider a proposal to return Helen to the Greeks, but decide only to offer to return the property which she brought with her when abducted by Paris. The offer is rejected but the truce is observed during the next day (Book 8) while the dead are buried: in the following night Zeus raises an ominous storm which causes all the fighters to shake with fear.

(5) (Book 9) The definitive battle is launched which will rage over the next two days, yet peace is still not entirely ruled out. At the end of the first of these two days, in which the Trojans have the upper hand, Agamemnon proposes to his council—this time in earnest—that they should board ship and return to their homes. He is persuaded instead to send a delegation to offer Achilles everything he wishes, and more, if he will return to battle. The result, as we have seen above, is that Achilles not only rejects the offer but threatens in his turn to sail home the next day—and advises the rest of the Greek camp to do the same.

(6) Achilles does not carry out his threat and the war resumes (Books 10–17), culminating after two days of battle in the death of Patroclus, clad in Achilles' armour, at the hand of Hector, who then

despoils his victim of the armour. We now arrive at the third and final act of the *Iliad*, beginning in Book 18 with the terrible grief of Achilles at the death of his dearest friend. Even in his grief Achilles is capable of a brief moment of deeper insight into the futility of war before he swears vengeance. Would that strife were banished from gods and men, he says despairingly, and with it the anger which is so tempting even to the wisest—the same anger which provoked him to defy Agamemnon and thus led to the loss of Patroclus. Again, the moment of introspection passes, and he resolves to seek out and kill Hector, knowing that this will lead to his own predicted death. Yet before this can happen, Achilles will need a new suit of armour.

The Shield of Achilles

Achilles' mother, Thetis, the immortal nymph, cannot dissuade him from his intention, but urges patience while she persuades Hephaestus, the craftsman god, to make him a new suit of armour, helmet for the head, corselet for the body, guards for the legs—and a great and sturdy shield. Homer focuses our attention on the famous Shield of Achilles, and particularly on its decoration, in a vivid ekphrasis (extended visual description) which concludes Book 18. At 130 lines, nearly one-fifth of the book, it is the longest passage of sustained description in the whole of the *Iliad*.

The shield of the greatest warrior in the Greek camp might be expected to carry images designed to shock and awe. Such was the shield of Agamemnon, previously described by Homer as bearing the fearsome face of the Gorgon and the images of Terror and Rout.[18] Depictions of the Shield of Achilles found on vases of the archaic and classical periods also show the Gorgon's head and similar images.[19] Yet the Shield of Achilles, as described by Homer, is covered mainly by images of peace, plenty, and normal life rather than of war. Its intricate decoration, presented in concentric circles, some subdivided into separate scenes, includes festivals and dancing, ploughing and harvest, the gathering of grapes and the herding of cattle, all described in warm and vivid detail.

> Next he placed on the shield a broad field with rich soil
> To be ploughed three times, and many ploughmen
> Drove their teams up and down, going round and about.
> And every time they reached the end of the furrow

A man would place in their hands a beaker of honey-sweet wine
Which they drained, turning eagerly to reach the other end,
While the golden field grew black as if it had been really ploughed—
A miracle of art from the hand of Hephaestus.[20]

If we reconstruct the most likely design of the shield, we may conclude that only half of one circle is devoted to human conflict, and this is a circle which portrays two cities in contrast—the city of war and the city of peace.

The Shield serves a crucial purpose at this turning point in the narrative of the *Iliad*. On the verge of the epic's bloody finale, Homer has imposed a critical pause on the action, skilfully setting the expectation of renewed war against the greater, and more valued, reality of peace. Just as the surface of the Shield gives Hephaestus ample space to display the subtle intricacies of his art, so its description allows Homer broad scope to describe in some detail the life which should be desired yet which is rendered impossible by conflict. It is here, as we feel ourselves being drawn inexorably forward into further bloodshed and vengeance, that we are most clearly invited to reach a moral judgement on the rival merits of peace and war.[21] The peaceful images on the shield have much in common stylistically with Homer's famous similes found throughout the *Iliad*—word-pictures each as vivid and sharp as a painted miniature. It has been suggested in an academic study of these similes that 'Homer repeatedly and deliberately jars us by the clashing juxtaposition of the lovely with the ugly, the productive with the destructive, the gentle with the violent, the peaceful with the warlike.'[22] They may also be compared to the scenes of settled life in Homer's *Odyssey*, and especially the happy world of Phaeacia which Odysseus visits at the end of his wanderings. What humans really aspire to, Homer is telling us, is not blood and violence, but the 'easy hedonistic existence spent in feasting with the pastimes of conversation, song and dance, making love—in fact a life such as the gods lead', even if they only achieve such happiness in brief snatches.[23] (W. H. Auden grasped Homer's meaning completely, offering in his own 'Shield of Achilles' a dystopic contrast in which the dancing floor is choked with weeds and all of Homer's other peaceful images are similarly blighted by the devastation of twentieth-century war.)[24]

The most significant design on the shield is its second circular band of decoration depicting the 'two fine cities of mortal men', one at peace and one at war. The second city is under siege: the besieging army has

threatened to lay waste to it unless they are given half of all it possesses.
The besieged reject the offer and—led on by divine intervention—
plan a surprise ambush on the besiegers, but the ambush goes wrong. A
pitched battle ensues, typical of those described elsewhere in the *Iliad*,
in which Strife and Uproar get to work and the dreadful goddess of
death, wearing a cloak 'stained red with blood', kills off the wounded.
However, in the city at peace, there are weddings and feasts, with a
procession of the brides at night time by the light of blazing torches.
Young men whirl in the dance and women gather at their doorsteps
to watch. Here too there is the potential for conflict: two men are in
dispute over compensation for a man who has been killed (presumably
in a private quarrel). But the conflict has been submitted to arbitration
by the city elders, and both disputants have agreed to accept the result.
The contrast between the two cities is clear: how much better it would
be, with the Trojan War now in its tenth bitter year, to settle the dispute
by negotiation rather than to resort to war.

Summing up the *Iliad*

There could of course be no negotiated settlement, no Greek retreat
across the sea, and no Trojan surrender of Helen, without doing violence to the legend well known both to Homer and his listeners. Yet
it is only the middle section of the *Iliad* (the two days of battle, Books
9–17) which might be said to express 'the values of an elite warrior
society'[25] or justify the comment that the poem is 'saturated in blood'
and that the poet and his audience 'lingered lovingly over every act of
slaughter'.[26] Much of this material is repetitive and many individual
episodes could be shortened or deleted without damage to the main
story. These may include passages from earlier versions of the Trojan
War which reflected a more straightforward martial ethic dating back
to the Mycenaean age. Gerardo Zampaglione, in his pioneering study
of the idea of peace in antiquity, has suggested that the material used by
Homer is likely to have undergone 'a process of refinement', moving
away from the unrelieved violence of earlier epic narrative.[27] Thus the
Iliad contained a stratum of 'heroic' celebration of war, overlaid with
a more 'humane' view of its horrors as seen in retrospect from a less
martial age. Perhaps a more complex approach to war only developed
as Greece emerged from the Dark Ages, as the city-states expanded
through trade and colonization, allowing more room for diversity of
opinion, as the art of writing was rediscovered and art departed from

its rigid geometric patterns. Epic poetry too then broke free from its traditional constraints to become much more than a bare chronicle of heroes, battles, and bloodshed.[28]

By the eighth century BC the popular argument for peace could be heard as well as the elite argument for war. The barrack-room lawyer Thersites, who early on in the *Iliad* makes a rational case that the Greeks should pack up and go home, may be seen as the prototype of the man from the masses who objects to being bossed around by city aristocrats.[29] Robert Graves has suggested that Homer had to present Thersites in an unflattering manner—Thersites is 'horrible-looking, and a general nuisance'—in order to dissociate the narrator in front of his aristocratic audience from an argument which was in fact 'sensible and telling'.[30] This may be speculative, but it is only when Thersites speaks that we hear the voice of the ordinary Achaean squaddie.

In the *Iliad*, war prevails over peace as it so often does in real life, and yet its narrative still holds out another possibility. Homer's unfulfilled alternatives have been described as 'contra-factual hypotheticals',[31] devices through which the poet prolongs his story and defers its out-comes, but they also suggest a view in which other options could be rationally considered. The imagery of the Shield of Achilles, laid out for us at a critical moment in the narrative, strongly reinforces this view. Jean Giraudoux captured this essential truth in his anti-war play (written as the clouds were gathering for the Second World War) *La Guerre de Troie n'aura pas lieu* (*The Trojan War will not take place*), where a peaceful outcome is frustrated at the very last moment by a single action. Hector has done a deal with Odysseus for the peaceful return of Helen, but he is denounced by his fellow Trojan Demokos, who is bent on war. Hector wounds Demokos fatally to stop him rousing the Trojans to combat. However Demokos, as he lies dying, pretends that he has been killed by the Greek commander Ajax—thus ensuring that war will, after all, break out. *La guerre aura lieu.*[32]

Peace and war in the Chinese classics

The *Chronicle of Zuo*

The Spring and Autumn (*Qunqiu*) period (conventionally dated 722–403 BC) covers China's turbulent transition as the imperial rule of the Eastern Zhou dynasty was undermined by the contention of its

nominally vassal states. The historical annals for this period—principally the *Zuo Zhuan* (*Chronicle of Zuo*), hereafter referred to as the
Chronicle—seem at first sight to offer unpromising material for an
enquiry into the perception of peace in ancient China. China in the
seventh and sixth centuries BC, we are told in a recent account, 'was
dominated by a warrior aristocracy whose privileged status was marked
by its monopoly of ritually directed violence', and whose ancestral rites
consisted of 'sanctioned killing' in the forms of sacrifice, warfare, and
hunting.[33] The *Chronicle* is certainly a record of chronic wars and violent coups d'état, intrigues and political upheavals, during this turbulent period of city-state rivalry and shifting alliances, as the authority
of the Zhou dynasty—always limited to a relatively small area of the
north China plain—waned and its feudal lords contended for power.
Yet it also reveals a wide range of thought and argument in which rulers and their advisers considered seriously questions of both morality
and expediency in the exercise of power, weighing up the benefits of
peace against the advantages of war.

The *Chronicle* appears to have been put together in the state of
Lu some time after the death of Confucius (479 BC) as an extended
commentary on an earlier document, the *Qunqiu* (*Spring and Autumn
Annals*), covering the same period, supposedly compiled by Confucius
himself. However, the *Chronicle* drew on much fuller records, not only
from Lu but from many of the other contending states, to provide a
narrative history going far beyond the limited entries of the *Annals*.
Much of this material consisted of policy debates and arguments, some
recorded in direct speech, between state rulers and their ministers as
they deliberated a course of action or reflected on its consequences.
Though the compiler of the *Chronicle* (traditionally identified as Zuo
Qiuming) may have reshaped or embellished some of his material it
still provides an important guide to the intellectual thought of the
Spring and Autumn period, with many arguments bearing directly on
issues of peace and war.[34]

Some of the advice given to rulers by their ministers was based
on realpolitik, regarding treaties as temporary and military force as
primary, but there are also arguments grounded in morality. Decisions
taken on principle sometimes result in defeat at the hands of the
unprincipled, but at other times it is the unprincipled course of conduct which leads to disaster, while in yet other cases virtuous conduct

can bring its own reward. The *Chronicle* offers a range of different scenarios:

(a) The duke of Song goes to war when a dependent state is invaded by the much more powerful southern state of Chu, but he refuses to gain the advantage by attacking while the Chu army is crossing a river. The duke defends his decision on the grounds that in ancient times it was a rule never to mount a surprise attack on the enemy. His minister of war (who had advised against taking on Chu in the first place) objects that the most important rule is to 'slay the enemy' and to seize any opportunity to do so. The Song army is routed and the duke's people blame him for the defeat.

(b) The brother of the Chu ruler objects to breaking a treaty with the state of Jin. The minister of war, Zifan, replies: 'When the enemy offers us an advantage we should advance; what use is a treaty then?' Shen Shushi, a retired minister, comments that 'Zifan will come to a bad end! Proper behaviour [*li*] depends on keeping good faith; and self-preservation depends on proper behaviour.' After a day-long battle between Chu and Jin, the Chu forces are put to flight and Zifan commits suicide.

(c) The state of Jin suffers famine and begs for grain from the duke of Qin. The Jin ruler is a tyrant, and a defector from his court urges the duke to take advantage of Jin's plight and invade, but the duke prefers the advice of his minister: 'Natural calamities come round in turn to one state after another: to have pity for one's neighbours in trouble and provide disaster relief is the right way [*dao*].' Next year it is Qin's turn to suffer famine and ask for aid—which the detestable duke of Jin refuses, rejecting advice from his officials. Qin survives the famine and a year later intervenes in Jin and overthrows its ruler.[35]

Although treaties are often broken, some treaties are signed in good faith and incorporate explicit pledges of cooperation, such as agreement to provide famine relief when needed, to extradite traitors and criminals, to support the nominal rule of the royal house of Zhou, and not to attack each other's allies. The *Chronicle* records at length a remarkable, although ultimately unsuccessful, attempt in 547–546 BC to conclude a grand peace treaty between all the states, and particularly the four dominant states of that time (Jin, Chu, Qi, and Qin), proposed by Song Xu, prime minister of the smaller state of Song

which was on good terms with both Jin and Chu. Jin responded to
the proposal favourably, persuaded by the argument of one of its ministers which presents a typical mix of principle and expediency:

War is a disaster for the people, like an insect that eats up their wealth, and an
even greater calamity for small States. If any one is opposed to it, even though
we think his plan is unfeasible, we simply must approve it. Otherwise Chu
will do so, and then call a meeting of the States together, and we shall lose our
position as leader of the alliances [*meng*].[36]

Chu followed suit but there was resistance in Qi until a minister
warned that to refuse would have a negative effect: 'Since Jin and Chu
have agreed, how can we refuse? For *people will say* [my italics] that we
refused to approve of opposing war, and that will certainly make our
people disaffected.' The treaty was signed, and although Qin refused
to take part it was partially successful: there was no war for the next
forty years between Jin and Chu and the north was generally peaceful
although a new round of conflict began in the south.[37] The *Chronicle*
concludes with the pessimistic verdict of the duke of Song: 'Who
can abolish war? It has been around for too long!' Nevertheless, the
attempt was significant both for being made and because it indicates
the importance of what 'people will say'—which we would now call
public opinion.

The world of thought reflected in the *Chronicle* 'belongs mostly to
the male aristocrats of the Central Plain'.[38] We catch only an occasional glimpse of the way in which their subjects' lives were affected by
the demands of warfare. Male adults were obliged to provide military
service when required although in some cases this might be avoided
by substitution or paying higher taxes. However, military discipline
had its limits: we hear of peoples who 'flee and desert their ruler' in the
face of the enemy.[39] Wise ministers routinely advised their rulers that
no policy would succeed—and least of all going to war—unless they
exercised good government and ensured that their people did not suffer from the consequences of natural disaster (especially drought and
famine). In a revealing passage, the viscount of Chu exempts his people
from military service for a period of five years while he takes measures
to improve their lot:

to comfort the people, to give aid and support to the poor; to look after
orphans and the young; to improve life for the old and the sick; to pick out
the deserving; to relieve those hit by natural disasters; to ease the burden on

orphans and widows; to remit punishments on [some] offenders; to keep a check on immorality; to lift up those whose path has been blocked; to treat properly those who are newly arrived while taking care of long-term residents; to reward those with merit and keep families together; to appoint honest and capable officials.[40]

The futility of ritual and sacrifice to the gods unless the ruler practises good government is also a recurring theme. 'If a ruler does not behave in a principled way [de]', the lord of Yu is told, 'the people will not be in harmony with him and the spirits will not enjoy his offerings.'[41] When the marquis of Sui claims that he is bound to succeed in battle because his offerings to the gods have been rich and ample, he is rebuked by a minister with an almost revolutionary thought: 'The common people are the master of the spirits.' Offerings of rich and fat animals, he goes on to argue, will only be acceptable if they signify that the people's livelihood is secure, while offerings of clean and abundant millet must denote that the people's crops are not suffering from blight or insects. If these assumptions are not true, then the acts of worship will be meaningless.[42] For further insight into the feelings of the 'common people', we must turn to our second text from the Chinese classics.

The Book of Songs

> My husband is on the campaign,
> I know not for how long
> When, oh when, will he return?
> The fowls are roosting in their nook,
> The sun is already setting,
> The sheep and cows have come down,
> But my husband is on the campaign
> How can I not be melancholy?
>
> ('A Wife's Lament', *Book of Songs*)[43]

Ancient China had no epics on the scale of ancient Greece, yet music and poetry played a significant role in the courts of the king and his feudal lords, both for ritual and for entertainment. The *Book of Songs* (*Shijing*) is the world's earliest anthology of verse and is based on material compiled by court musicians and historians during the Spring and Autumn period (the same period as is covered by the *Chronicle*). The *Book of Songs* can be divided into two roughly equal halves, (a) the Lyrics of the States (*guofeng*) and the Small Odes (*xiaoya*), and (b) the Big Odes (*daya*) and Hymns (*song*). The Big Odes record historic deeds

and the lives of the rulers, while the Hymns sing the praises of the
rulers' ancestors and celebrate their achievements, going back as far as
the previous semi-mythological Shang dynasty. However, most of the
Lyrics, and some of the Small Odes, consist of popular songs and dit-
ties, gathered in fourteen of the emerging city-states as well as in the
royal capital. The purpose seems to have been to keep a finger on the
pulse of popular sentiment: the Han historian Ban Gu would explain
that 'In ancient times, there were officials who were responsible for
collecting poems (or folk songs) for Kings so that they could understand the customs, yearnings, and lives of commoners.'[44]

Performed in the courts of the state rulers, these songs became part
of the literary equipment of courtiers and ministers, and would be
quoted in argument or diplomacy to make or illustrate a point by
poetic analogy. The orthodox interpretation of these poems as moral
homilies was compared by Arthur Waley, the great translator of classical Chinese poetry, to the traditional biblical view of the Song of
Solomon.[45] In reality many were simple songs of courtship, marriage,
work, and leisure, marking the seasons, expressing joys and sadnesses,
voicing contempt for the ruling elite, and lamenting the hardships of
war. As one of the Small Odes laments:

> Small are the people's hovels and their food is coarse.
> No blessings for them as Heaven strikes them hard.
> The rich can manage, but pity the poor and lonely!
> The rich may get through, but alas for the helpless and solitary![46]

Soldiers in these songs complain bitterly about physical hardship: the
march is long and they are thirsty and hungry but no one listens to their
complaints; they must climb steep mountains and cross deep rivers with
no time to rest. Are we buffaloes or tigers that our home should be in
the desolate wilds? ask others. Just as wild geese have trouble alighting
on trees, the peasant-soldiers are out of place far away from their fields:
without their labour to tend the land, how can their parents get food?
No one is in doubt as to why they are compelled to be soldiers: the
king's service brings many hardships and the king's business never ends.
Some complain that 'those fine gentlemen' at home have not joined
them at the front. One song pokes fun at a well-dressed officer clad in
leopard furs and lambswool, while another mocks a general for staging
empty manoeuvres.[47] More than one soldier will return home to find

that his wife has left him to marry again: wild creepers have invaded the empty house, there are woodlice in the bedroom, cobwebs at the door, and the rain pours down outside.[48]

While the soldiers at the front lament separation from their families, the wives at home complain of loneliness, and the parents fear they will never see their sons again. 'Alas,' cries a mother, 'my son is serving far away and cannot sleep night or day. Be careful! Come back! Don't be taken captive there.'[49]

Through the *Book of Songs* we glimpse the reality of military service and corvée labour imposed on the common people by their feudal rulers, in a time of growing instability with shifting alliances and inter-state intrigues, which would pave the way for the subsequent two centuries (403–221 BC) known as the period of the Warring States. Such poems are the forerunners of the genre of 'frontier poetry' (*biansaishi*) which would develop in the Han dynasty (206 BC to AD 220) when soldiers were sent to the far reaches of the empire, and achieve its highest expression in the Tang dynasty (AD 618–907).[50]

Peace and war in the city-states

It is rash to assert, as has been done by some, that war was the permanent characteristic of all Greek communities. If peace was worth attaining, it was worth preserving and common interests were likely to encourage a continuance of relations in time of peace. In early times often a period was fixed during which peace should endure, but it could be argued that such a practice did not so much limit as confirm the durability of inter-state agreements.

(Frank Adcock, 1975)[51]

The goddess Eirene—Peace—is an ample figure, wearing a full, belted gown of wool and depicted in a posture which expresses abundance, dignity, and calm (see Plate 3). In this famous statue made by the sculptor Kephisodotos, and erected in or after 375 BC at the Altar of Peace in Athens, she is carrying Ploutos the god of wealth, shown as a plump boy reaching up trustingly to his mother. The erection of the altar, to celebrate what seemed at the time to be the achievement of peace after decades of war, inaugurated an annual festival of Eirene in Athens. As so often before, there were more wars to come but there is no reason to doubt that most Greeks desired to see, in the words of an anonymous poet, the appearance of 'sweet Eirene, wealth-giver to mortals'.[52]

The emphasis on war in our perception of classical Greece derives from a limited period of time—from the outset of war with Persia (492 BC), through the Peloponnesian and Corinthian Wars, to the peace settlement which ended the supremacy of Thebes (362 BC)—the period covered in detail through the writings of Herodotus, Thucydides, and Xenophon. The picture changes if we look at a broader historical stretch. While less is known about warfare in the preceding archaic age (the seventh and sixth centuries BC) there seems to have been 'a predominance of relatively limited warfare, both in the frequency of wars and in their scope'.[53] Athens did not have a publicly run army or a mechanism for mobilizing soldiers till late in the sixth century. War 'does not seem to have dominated public life in sixth-century Athens. What campaigns there were usually had a limited goal.'[54] At the other end of this period, the 'King's Peace' which ended the Corinthian War (395–387 BC) launched a series of 'common peace' (κοινη ειρηνη) treaties, ranging over the next fifty years, providing a more permanent guarantee than the truces (σπονδαι) which had been made—and broken—so often before. The new treaties became more elaborate and refined, and constituted 'the first great diplomatic movement in the history of Greece to organize peace on a general level'.[55]

Rather than attribute the high incidence of wars in the long fifth century to an inveterate militarism among the Greeks, we can more usefully identify a set of specific causes. On the Greek mainland, a large number of city-states had emerged, which rubbed shoulders with one another in a relatively restricted area but possessed no tradition or myth of pan-Hellenic unity to encourage movement towards federation. A shift from hereditary kingship to wider political participation led to internal contention, typically between aristocratic and popular parties, which also made it harder to pursue consistent or long-term peaceful goals in foreign policy. The establishment of colonies along the Ionian coast collided with the emerging power of the Persian empire following the rise of Cyrus the Great (559–530 BC).[56] To resist and ultimately defeat Persian power required the Greek city-states to find a measure of unity, but in the process this led to the assumption of hegemony by Athens. The city-states soon faced the choice of accepting Athenian dominance or seeking another patron—most often in Sparta, the only serious military contender for hegemony.

This unstable skein of dependent relationships was the root cause of the Peloponnesian War.

The history of Thucydides

The accounts of this period which have survived come mostly from Athens—the arch-imperial power—and particularly from the historian Thucydides. As Simon Hornblower points out critically, our view of international relations in classical Greece has long been dominated by Thucydides' 'relentlessly war-based approach' which says little about periods of peace and, for example, does not even mention the successful peace diplomacy of the mid-fifth century with Persia.[57] Some modern historians—as Hans van Wees argues—'have often gone beyond even Thucydides' realism' in such a way as to 'turn the history of Greek international relations into a caricature' dominated solely by the ruthless pursuit of self-interest.[58] Thucydides' descriptions of acts of war, while narrated with apparent dispassion, often convey a powerful though repressed sense of horror. Thus, commenting on the civil war in Corcyra he observes that 'there was death in every shape and form. As it usually happens in such situations, people went to every extreme and beyond it.' War, he continues, is a 'stern teacher' which leads to savagery unthinkable in conditions of peacetime. Moderation becomes dangerous and thoughtless aggression is regarded as an act of courage in a climate of opinion where 'words [have] to change their usual meanings'.[59] Thucydides himself had first-hand experience of war, having served as a general during the early part of the Peloponnesian War.[60]

We should also bear in mind that while there were always 'young men impatiently waiting for war to break out' there were many other Greeks who 'lamented the miseries of war'.[61] The fifth-century sophist Gorgias describes how even the sight of battle can cause such terror that men 'fall victim to useless labour and dread diseases and hardly curable madnesses'.[62] War was described in the words of a Larisaean pamphleteer (400 BC) as 'the greatest of all evils by as much as peace is the greatest of all blessings'.[63] And Xenophon puts in the mouth of an Athenian peace negotiator in 371 BC the persuasive argument, that 'if it is indeed ordered of the gods that wars should come among men, then we ought to begin war as tardily as we can, and, when it has come, to bring it to an end as speedily as possible'.[64]

Diplomacy and debate

If peace had been regarded by the Greeks as only an interval in the natural state of war, it would be hard to explain the elaborate institutions
of inter-state diplomacy, the various diplomatic methods employed,
and the considerable expenditure of time and effort by leading citizens
in the hope of averting war. Heralds, whose calling dates back to the
society described by Homer, enjoyed diplomatic immunity and were
exchanged between parties seeking peace or truce. Envoys negotiated
treaties with detailed stipulations carefully recorded on stone, with a
time duration of anything between one and thirty years. Few treaties
survived to the end of their term, yet there are exceptions. The treaties
between Sparta and Argos (451/50) and between Sparta and Mantinea
(418/17) lasted for the full term of thirty years. Treaties were vulnerable because it was tempting, in a fragmented world of rival states, to
switch horses for short-term advantage, but they could still inhibit the
resumption of hostilities.[65] We may note the reluctance of the Spartan
king Archidamus to initiate the Peloponnesian War, after a truce with
Athens which had lasted for fourteen years. Although their assembly
had voted for war, the Spartans sent three missions to Athens over a
period of almost a year, influenced by the 'cautious and sober arguments' of Archidamus, before negotiations finally broke down.[66]

Every declaration of war or conclusion of a peace treaty or an alliance was decided after debate by the Athenian assembly, and similarly
by deliberative councils in the other city-states. Most assembly speeches
were not written down and only a small number survive from the
fourth century, so that for all the crucial debates of the Peloponnesian
War we must rely on the selective reporting of the historians. While
Thucydides gives us in full his version of the speech by Pericles advocating war with Sparta (432 BC) he summarizes in half a sentence
the argument of those urging compromise. In describing the peace
eventually concluded a decade later (the Peace of Nicias) Thucydides
barely mentions war weariness as a factor. It is only in Plutarch's much
later life of Nicias that, in a vivid passage based on a source no longer
available to us, we gain a flavour of the strong desire for peace in 'militaristic' Athens.

The two sides had previously arranged a kind of armistice for a year, during
which they had held meetings and once again tasted the pleasures of security,
leisure, and the company of guest-friends and relatives, and so had come to

miss a life without the stain of war and were happy to hear choruses singing lines such as 'May my spear be laid aside for spiders to weave their webs
around', and to remember the saying that in times of peace men are woken by
cocks, not trumpets. So they denounced and censured those who said that the
war was fated to last thrice nine years, and in this frame of mind they met for
thorough discussions and concluded a peace treaty. Most people [in Athens]
took this to mean that their troubles were definitely over, and Nicias was a
frequent topic of conversation. They described him as a favourite of the gods,
and said that the gods had rewarded his piety by attaching his name to an
unparalleled and exceptional blessing. They really did regard the peace as the
work of Nicias, just as they considered the war the work of Pericles. The one
was held to have involved the Greeks in calamitous disasters, for no very good
reason, while the other managed to persuade them to forget all their terrible
injuries and become friends.[67]

A total of only nineteen speeches, fifteen delivered in the Athenian
assembly and four in the law courts, survives from the fourth century:
they include two notable examples of peace advocacy, both known
by the title 'On the Peace', by the Attic orators Andocides (392) and
Isocrates (355). Andocides, arguing for the acceptance of Spartan proposals, appeals to history to show that previous peace agreements
made Athens stronger, not weaker, and did not undermine her system
of democracy. He reminds the assembly of the disastrous consequence
of rejecting an offer of peace from Syracuse in 416, when the assembly chose instead to launch the Sicilian expedition. 'The result was
the loss of a large part of the Athenian and allied forces, the bravest
being the first to fall; a reckless waste of ships, money, and resources:
and the return of the survivors in disgrace.'[68] Isocrates was speaking at
a time when the three traditional Greek powers, Athens, Sparta, and
Thebes, had in 362/1 accepted a 'common peace' of the Greek states,
and were faced with the rise of Macedonian power under Philip of
Macedon—father of Alexander: Athens was again discussing war to
keep in line its reluctant allies. Isocrates denounced imperialism and
those 'depraved orators and demagogues' who sought to revive its
flickering flame. War had robbed Athens of security and of its good
reputation among the Greeks, whereas if Athens made peace and
observed its treaties, then its people would 'dwell in our city in great
security, delivered from wars and perils and the turmoil in which we
are now involved amongst ourselves, and we shall advance day by day
in prosperity'. It is reasonable to suppose that he was not alone in
this view.[69]

The revived threat of Persia in the fourth century encouraged a new emphasis on pan-Hellenic unity—the goal which had been so disastrously lacking in the internecine wars of the fifth century. The Attic orators of the fourth century were by no means pacifist but they were opposed to the irrationality of most wars. In a recent study of their surviving speeches, Peter Hunt finds that there was never any dispute that peace was preferable to war—indeed, the same sentiment can be found in many speeches in Thucydides—and that the ideal of pan-Hellenic unity did come close to providing 'a compelling moral argument against war'.[70]

Peace advocacy on the Greek stage

It was not always easy to argue for peace against the demagogic voices of the pro-war party—except on the stage. As Isocrates observed, 'I know that it is hazardous to oppose your views and that, although this is a free government, there exists no "freedom of speech" except that which is enjoyed in this Assembly by the most reckless [pro-war] orators, who care nothing for your welfare, and in the theatre by the comic poets.'[71] The writers of comedy enjoyed a special licence to satirize the powerful and to challenge conventional belief, and the tragic dramatists were also able to address, though less directly, issues of peace and war through their treatment of stories from the mythical canon. The power of drama to influence public opinion in Athens had been evident from its origins. The citizens of Athens came to the theatre 'not merely for entertainment or for intellectual and emotional stimulus, but for instruction', writes Philip Vellacott, translator of Euripides, although having received such instruction, 'if they did not like it, they might well be hostile to the man who offered it'.[72]

The surviving plays of Aristophanes (c.446–386) bear witness to the latitude given to Greek comedy to criticize the argument for war: three out of the nine which have come down to us have peace as their central theme.

- *The Acharnians* was performed in 425 when Athens had been at war—as a result of Pericles' oratory—for six years, during which the countryside was ravaged by Spartan marauders while the city, its population swollen by rural refugees, was stricken by plague. 'The play is one of those that are extremely well composed, and it appeals for peace in every possible way,' comments the unknown author of an ancient summary attached to the play.[73] How to obtain peace with Sparta is not a complicated matter: the play's hero, Dikaiopolis (honest citizen) simply enlists the help of an immortal to obtain it.

- *Peace* came at a more hopeful time in 421, a fortnight before the conclusion of the Peace of Nicias, yet it followed a bloody war lasting for ten years. In this play it takes a harder struggle for the hero Trygaeus—another ordinary Athenian with more common sense than the generals—to win. First he has to ascend to heaven on a flying dung beetle, then he has to liberate the goddess Peace from the cave into which she has been thrown by War. Trygaeus also brings back one of Peace's handmaidens, Harvest, and the play ends with a wedding ceremony. 'Oh thrice happy man, who so well deserve your good fortune', sings the leader of the chorus, adding in less elevated vein, 'The bridegroom's fig is great and thick, the bride's very soft and tender.' The message of Make Love Not War could not be more explicit.

- In the *Lysistrata,* the message becomes Make War and you won't Make Love. The play was performed in 411 when the peace had broken down, and thousands of young Athenians had died in the disaster of the Sicilian campaign.[74] The heroine of the title persuades not only the women of Athens but those of the other Greek states to deny sex to their men. Forced to conclude peace, both sides party on the Akropolis and the Athenians find, to their surprise, that the Spartans are really quite fun. Perhaps we should always be drunk when we go to Sparta on diplomatic missions, says one. We could not do worse than when we were sober. This comic coda points up the message of the play: peace by negotiation is always preferable to war.[75]

Tragedy

All three of the great writers of tragedy whose works have partially survived, Aeschylus (*c.*526–456), Sophocles (496–406), and Euripides (*c.*480–406), had direct experience of war at close quarters.[76] Of the three, Euripides is most visibly preoccupied with the morality of war and its effect on society—the underlying theme of most of his seventeen extant works—and the consensus of opinion regards him as generally 'anti-war'. The smaller number of surviving plays by Aeschylus (7 out of 90) and Sophocles (7 out of 120) makes it harder to gauge their stance, and there is considerable disagreement regarding Aeschylus' attitude to war in his *Persians* (472), which describes the impact on the Persian capital of the news of the defeat of Xerxes' fleet at Salamis.[77] A clearer indication may be found in his *Seven against Thebes*, a drama which has been described as 'rich in the imagery of war and the consequences of violence'.[78] Eteocles and Polynices, the sons of Oedipus, have agreed to rule Thebes in turn year by year, but Eteocles refuses to step down. Aeschylus gives the voice of the chorus to the women of Thebes who, in vain, urge Eteocles not to resist the siege laid against the city by Polynices. And at the end of the play, when the two brothers have killed each other in battle (thus fulfilling Oedipus' prophecy)—the chorus bewails the fate of the rank and file caught up in their fratricide, of the 'many in their city [who] were marshalled into the bloody ranks of death, many who lie full-length in the fields outside'.[79]

Among the surviving plays of Sophocles, his *Ajax* reveals most clearly a penetrating view of the human consequences of war. In this moving psycho-drama, the eponymous hero of the Trojan War, giant in stature and renowned for bravery, is driven to madness because the arms of the fallen Achilles (whose body he and Odysseus have rescued from the Trojan forces) have been awarded to Odysseus instead of to him. His first, wildly disproportionate, reaction is to seek revenge on his Greek comrades-in-arms but, blinded by the goddess Athena, he slaughters a flock of sheep and cattle instead. Coming to his senses, Ajax—a warrior who has always said that crying is a sign of weakness in a man—bursts into uncontrollable tears. He contemplates suicide but is apparently dissuaded by his wife, Tecmessa, announcing that he will bury his prize sword (a gift to him from the Trojan prince Hector), with a deeply cynical comment on the futility of war: 'I've newly come to understand, the enemy we're bound to hate today will one day be our friend; and while I hope to serve and help my friend, I know he'll not remain my friend forever.'[80] Then in another devastating mood-swing, Ajax reappears alone on the stage to make a final speech filled with anger against his comrades and fall on his sword. Lawrence Tritle, himself a Vietnam veteran, has argued that Ajax should be seen as 'an ancient Greek equivalent to the traumatized veteran from Vietnam' who, numbed by combat and betrayed by his own comrades, loses control and 'strikes out at whoever or whatever is nearest to hand. Afterwards nothing is left but suicide.'[81]

Euripides, the third of the great tragedians, wrote most of his ninety-odd plays in the years leading up to and during the Peloponnesian War. According to the translator Philip Vellacott, fifteen of his extant complete plays, and about twenty only known to us by surviving fragments, either address the subject of war directly or 'contain clear comments on such topics as the difference between a just and an unjustified war, the treatment of refugees, the concept of sacrifice, the principle of reprisal, the fate of the defeated'.[82]

One of his best-known plays today, the *Trojan Women* (performed in 415), was written in the shadow of a notorious war crime committed by Athens—the massacre at Melos in which all the able-bodied men on the island were slaughtered while the rest of the population was enslaved.[83] Set in the immediate aftermath of the sack of Troy, the play shows the Trojan women at the mercy of their Greek captors, waiting to hear their fate: it has been described as 'one of the most telling anti-war plays ever written'.[84] In the course of the play the young son of Hector's widow Andromache is seized from her and hurled to his death over the city wall while Hecuba, widow of King Priam, learns that her daughter Polyxena has been sacrificed on the tomb of the Greek hero Achilles. The play vividly depicts the brutality of war, and particularly the bloodlust which follows capture, but it is also notable for Euripides' apparent premonition, through the voice of Cassandra, Hecuba's other daughter, of disaster ahead for Athens. (Plans were already under way for the calamitous Sicilian expedition which was launched within months of the play being staged.)[85]

Less attention has been paid to another remarkable play by Euripides, *Herakles* (also known as *Herakles Mainomenos*, or 'The Madness of Herakles'), which was staged in 416. While Herakles is performing one of his labours in the underworld, his father, wife, and children are sentenced to death by the tyrant of Thebes. Herakles returns home in the nick of time to kill the tyrant and save them. Then, inexplicably, he is seized by madness and kills his wife and children himself in a wild frenzy. The play has been criticized for a supposed lack of unity between the two episodes, and Euripides offers no explication—except to blame the gods—for the shocking descent of its hero into madness. This play may be seen too as a psycho-drama, like the *Ajax* of Sophocles, which shows the devastating consequences of battle strain upon the surviving 'heroes'. Today we might say (as the play's translator

Robert Meagher has suggested) that Herakles was suffering from post-traumatic stress disorder.[86]

Peace and war in the Warring States

> In wars to win land, the dead fill the fields; in wars to seize cities, the
> dead fill their streets. This is what we mean by 'teaching the earth
> how to eat human flesh'. (Mengzi)[87]

Warfare in the Warring States period of Chinese history (403–221 BC) was no longer a seasonal pursuit led by the nobility and restrained to some extent by custom and ritual. The states which had survived from the previous Spring and Autumn period now commanded larger populations which could be recruited for larger armies, supported by improvements in agricultural techniques as the use of iron spread. We have a vivid picture of the everyday existence of the great majority of the rural-based Chinese people two millennia ago recorded in brick reliefs from the subsequent Han dynasty. Planting rice, tending sheep, feeding the ox, hoeing, dyeing, preparing meals, holding village festivals with dragon dances, and (as in Plate 4) carrying produce for sale into town.

This was the life increasingly disturbed by chronic warfare between a diminishing number of rival states, which would lead to the first great unification by the state of Qin (*Chin*, hence 'China'). The conventional history of the Warring States has been dominated by incessant rivalry, by shifting alliances and devious statecraft, by guile and deception on and off the battlefield, as recorded in semi-fictional annals such as the *Zhanguo Ce* (*Stratagems of the Warring States*) and later by the Han historian Sima Qian. Yet it was also a time of intense and lively discussion on war and peace, both from a moral and practical perspective, in which the plight of the common people was not forgotten. The main lines of argument may be reconstructed from the texts which survived the infamous 'burning of the books' by the first Qin emperor, and they raise issues which we can interpret in terms still current today.

With the break-up of the feudalistic and ritualized state system, a new breed of scholar-gentry (*shi*) had emerged enjoying more autonomy than the court retainers and hereditary officials of the past: in an age of social mobility, some were able to rise from humble origins. Some rulers became known for their patronage of argument and debate. King

Xuan of Qi (ruled 319–301 BC) was famous not only for his pleasure palaces and hunting parks, but for setting up the Jixia Academy which hosted, it was later said by Sima Qian, as many as a thousand scholars from all the rival schools. Traditionally, they were said to have gathered 'at the gate': we may imagine them staying at hostels and drinking in tea-houses just inside the main gate of the typical walled city.

The various schools of philosophy and military and political thinking which emerged in the course of two and a half centuries became known as the 'Hundred Schools of Thought' (they are usually divided into ten or twelve schools, though they also numbered free-thinkers who adhered to no particular school). These include the School of Strategists (*bingjia*), with Sunzi, supposed author of the *Art of War*, as its illustrious predecessor. Much of this military thinking was incorporated into the political philosophy of the Legalists (*fajia*) who viewed agriculture and war under rigorously authoritarian rule as the essential basis for a successful state. Legalist advisers served the ruler of the state of Qin who in 221 BC defeated his rivals and became the first Qin emperor.[88] Sunzi's *Art of War* can be easily found today in translation— there are at least five or six English versions in print at any time— and is said to have influenced the military strategies of Napoleon, the Japanese naval command in the Russo-Japanese War, the German High Command in the Second World War, North Vietnamese General Giap in the Vietnam War, and senior US commanders in the Gulf War. Mao Zedong applied the principles set out by Sunzi during the anti-Japanese and Civil Wars of 1937–49; Chinese military leaders today continue to regard it as a fundamental text, which is 'a valuable asset for the Chinese people and will remain so in any future war against aggression'.[89]

Yet the Strategists and Legalists were not unchallenged: our obsession with the *Art of War* can lead us to overlook the vigorous views on peace and war of the other main schools, the Confucians, Mohists, and Daoists, which directly criticized the militarism of the time. While differing among themselves, they all sought to blunt the rulers' appetite for war, to counter the influence of their military advisers, and to redirect their attention to the primary purpose of government—to ensure the well-being of their own people. They also offered vivid descriptions of the impact of war on the common people: 'Thorns and brambles will grow where armies have camped,' says Laozi. 'After a great war there will be years of terrible hardship.'[90] Wars to capture cities or territory, says Mengzi, are a way of 'teaching the earth how to eat human flesh'.[91] If the peasants are taken from the fields to fight and cannot till the land, says Mozi, 'the common people will freeze to death and die of starvation'.[92] This constant topic of the peasants 'freezing and starving', a recent study of the Warring States suggests, 'cannot be dismissed as pure propaganda: it evidently reflects the real empathy of the ruling elite for those they ruled'.[93]

The Confucian School

Living at the end of the previous Spring and Autumn period, Kongzi (Confucius, 551–479 BC) set the model for future generations of itinerant scholars, lending his services to the ruler whom he judged capable of good things, but packing his bags if the task seemed hopeless. When asked by the ruler of Wei to offer advice on military matters, he declined and left the court, saying, 'A bird may choose its tree, but how on earth can a tree choose its bird?'[94]

Kongzi was a conservative who sought to maintain, or revive, the values of the remote founders of the Zhou dynasty by strict observance of the ancient rituals. He stressed the need for 'reverence' (jing), the concept traditionally applied to one's state of mind when making sacrifice, but which for Kongzi—as his biographer D. C. Lau has observed—meant 'the awareness of the immensity of one's responsibilities to promote the welfare of the common people'.[95] Such a responsibility was especially great for the ruler, and in Kongzi's moral scheme of government, it was unlikely to be achieved through the use of force. When questioned by a disciple about the purpose of government, he replied, 'Give the people enough to eat, and enough soldiers to defend them, and they will have confidence in you.' To the follow-up question—which of the two, if one is obliged to, should be given up first?—he responded simply, 'Give up the soldiers.'[96] On another occasion he summed up the essence of good government with this advice:

Where goods are evenly distributed no one will be poor, where there is social harmony a small population does not matter [i.e. the population will unite in resisting aggression by a larger state], and where there is stability the state will not be overthrown.[97]

Mengzi (Mencius, 372–289 BC), the second founder of what would become known as Confucianism, lived in the increasingly violent age of the Warring States, and made no secret of his loathing for the Strategists. 'The so-called good ministers of today [who advise their prince to go to war] would have been called robbers of the people in olden days,' he remarked.[98] Mengzi believed that the ruler had been installed by heaven solely for the benefit of his people, and that human nature tends towards goodness, just as it is the natural tendency for a forest to grow. Mengzi found himself obliged more than once during the chaotic struggles of the Warring States to weigh up the morality of what we would now call 'humanitarian intervention'. The truly good ruler would be looked up to even by the people of neighbouring states, who will 'turn to him like water flowing downwards with a tremendous force'. To wage an expedition (zheng) for the sake of people who wished to have their lives improved (zheng, literally 'rectified'—a play on two words with the same sound) was not the same thing as war.[99] However, Mengzi was soon disappointed by King Xuan of Qi who, having liberated the state of Yan, inflicted a new oppressive regime upon its people. Humanitarian intervention, Mengzi discovered—and as we know very well—can turn out very differently in practice.

Far from taking an idealistic position. Mengzi had to recognize, as his modern translator W. A. C. H. Dobson has noted, that 'the world of the fourth century BC...was a very different place from the world of his ideals'.[100] His ultimate view remained one of extreme scepticism towards, and disapproval of, war, as reflected in his judgement that 'In the *Spring and Autumn Annals* [see above p. 48], there are no just (yi, 'righteous') wars. They merely show that some wars are not so bad as another.'[101]

Xunzi (Hsun Tzu, c. 312–? BC), the third great early Confucian thinker, lived half a century or so after Mengzi, witnessing the final decades of inter-state struggle leading up to the victory of the Qin. While Mengzi had believed that people have an intrinsic tendency towards goodness, Xunzi believed instead that human nature has an intrinsic tendency towards evil. As his translator Burton Watson has remarked, this was not a surprising conclusion considering the 'cutthroat age' in which he lived.[102] These contrasting world views of Mengzi and Xunzi do not greatly affect their attitudes towards war and peace, where Xunzi's approach to a large extent builds on that of his predecessor.

Xunzi's contempt for the military strategists, who by this time were playing an ever larger role, is even more pronounced than Mengzi's. Stratagems and ruses are only useful, he says, against a state in which the relationship between ruler and subjects has completely broken down. Asked by the ruler of his native state what was the best way for a king to manage his army, Xunzi replied dismissively that 'such detailed matters are of minor importance to Your Majesty, and may be left to the generals'.[103] Xunzi shared Mengzi's insistence that what was of real importance was to rule with humanity and justice, and that unity between the ruler and the people was the best way to resist aggression. 'For a tyrant to try to overthrow a good ruler by force would be like throwing eggs at a rock or stirring boiling water with your finger.'[104] Again following Mengzi, Xunzi approved of humanitarian intervention, but added the important requirement that if there is strong resistance then the ruler should not persist in attack.

A true king may be compelled to intervene, but he does not go to war. When a city is well guarded, he does not lay siege; when the opposing soldiers are in good shape, he does not attack them. When the ruler and his people in another state have a happy relationship, he congratulates them.[105]

The Mohist School

Mozi (Mo Tzu, c.460–390 BC) was born in the early years of the Warring States period, at about at the same time as the death of Kongzi, with whom he ranks as equal in influence among the ancient political thinkers. While Kongzi and his followers are described as *ru* (a word conventionally translated as 'scholar') the Mohists were known after the name of their founder and had more humble origins.[106] Collectively, the *Ru-Mo* came to represent a humanist, non-military strand of Chinese political thought which was denounced by the Legalists and banned by the first Qin emperor, but while both tendencies deplored war and its consequences, they disagreed sharply on how to achieve peace. The Confucians believed in what might now be called 'peace in one state': a ruler could ensure the survival of his state by practising humane policies which won the support of his people. Mozi advocated a more internationalist policy, arguing that the rulers of all states had a common interest in peace and stability and should practice, in effect, peaceful coexistence.

Mozi's argument is based on the concept of *jian ai*—usually translated as 'universal love'—though in the fuller phrase *jian xiang ai*, also used by Mozi, this conveys the wider sense of 'mutual' (*xiang*) responsibility. No one will attack anyone else if they all regard themselves as part of the same big (international) family. If the rulers love the states of others as if they were their own, no one will commit aggression.[107] Mozi also appeals for a state ruler to take the initiative (as we might say, to act unilaterally) to break the cycle of violence.

The world has been beset by aggression and war for too long, and it is as weary of it as a school boy who is tired of playing horse. If only one of the feudal rulers could convince the others of his sincerity by an act of unilateral benefit to them! When a large state behaved improperly, he would share the sorrow of those who suffered; when another large state attacked a small one he would join in its rescue; when the defensive walls of the city of a small state were defective he would help to repair them; to those who ran out of food and clothing he would supply them; when they were short of money and silk he would share his own.[108]

Although Mozi would be fiercely criticized by Mengzi and Xunzi, the universalizing aspect of Mohism was incorporated by the later Confucians into their core principle of humane behaviour (*ren*, 'benevolence').[109] Conversely, Mohist contemporaries of Mengzi and Xunzi shared their view that punitive action was acceptable if undertaken to punish an evil ruler and to rescue his people. Some became adept in the art of military defence against armed attack, particularly in devising techniques to resist a siege. Itinerant Mohist siege experts offered their services to the rulers of states under threat—as portrayed today in popular Chinese films such as *Battle of Wits* (2006), with the martial arts star Andy Lau in the leading role. This aspect of later Mohism would obscure the original thrust of Mozi's doctrine, and his skill in translating pacifist principle into coherent political thought.

The Daoist School

Laozi lived, according to the traditional view, at the time of Kongzi: however, the 'Sayings' attributed to him in the book known as the *Classic of the Way and Virtue* (*Daodejing*) are a composite work probably put together in the fourth century BC, reflecting a deep distaste for the conflict-ridden world of Warring States, and a desire to rediscover the roots of harmonious existence. Only by following the Way (*Dao*) would conflict be avoided—as put in a vivid phrase from the *Daodejing*: 'When the Way prevails, horses are used to pull dung-carts. When the Way is absent, they breed war-horses at the frontier.'[110] The early Daoists did not reject the society in which they lived, although

Daoism would develop in later times in a more mystical and reclusive direction. Their famous concept of *wu wei*, 'doing nothing' or 'inaction', was not an injunction to withdraw from society but rather to 'do nothing' which did not conform with what was spontaneous and harmonious in life. They were interested, writes one modern scholar, 'in convincing the ruler in power that policies which are aggressive, authoritarian, rigid, and violent will not succeed in achieving the goal they have set themselves—namely, political control'.[111] In this context Daoism disapproved deeply of war but, recognizing its reality, did not condemn it solely from a pacifist perspective.

The *Daodejing* warns against the unforeseen consequences of war and cautions those who give advice to the ruler not to 'encourage him to use force to dominate the world'. Doing so will only result in 'retribution' (*huan*). It is better to keep a low profile and avoid war if possible. 'He who is skilful in martial arts, will not be aggressive; he who does fight well, will never do so in anger; he who can conquer the enemy, will avoid giving battle; he who can command men, will put himself beneath them.'[112] The ideal relationship between states is one in which they are so close that they can hear their neighbour's chickens squawk and dogs bark, and yet they leave each other alone.[113]

In addition to the Daoists, there are individual pacifist thinkers of considerable interest but only known to us indirectly, such as Song Xing and Yin Wen (both active in the late fourth century BC) who are loosely associated with Mohism and appear to have advocated total pacifism. The final chapter of the Daoist work attributed to Zhuangzi (*c.*300 BC)—probably added during the early Han dynasty—describes them as peripatetic scholars seeking to persuade all who would listen (and some who would not) of the benefits of peace.

They were not ashamed to suffer insult in their efforts to save the people from conflict; they sought to deter aggression and to stop fighting, in their efforts to save the world from war. Roaming over the whole land with this purpose, they argued with rulers and preached to the people, and even though their ideas were not taken up, they pressed the case loudly and would not be silent. It was said of them that 'High and low were tired of seeing them but they insisted on showing up.'[114]

The Strategists

We come finally to the *Art of War*, a text which has attracted many commentaries—unlike those examined above—in relation to issues of peace and war. Sunzi's text summed up the military tactics and strategy of the Warring States which built in turn on ideas already formulated in the preceding Spring and Autumn period. (Whether Sunzi was a historical person is no clearer than in the case of Laozi.) The text is not a political treatise but starts at the point where the necessity of conflict is assumed, without considering the alternatives to war. However, the exercise of force is predicated on the assumption that the ruler who is making war benefits from a 'moral law' which 'causes the people to be in complete accord with their ruler, so that they will follow him regardless of their lives, undismayed by any danger'. An immoral ruler who does not satisfy his people's interests will fail regardless of his skill in the art of war.[115] It has been argued that underlying Sunzi's work is the recognition that 'warfare is an evil', and that 'the resort to military means is a political failure', but this may be reading too much into the text.[116] It remains true that the military classics attributed to Sunzi and to Wuzi, another leading strategist of the Warring States period, generally prefer a non-violent alternative where possible and attach more importance to defence than offence.

To conclude, none of the major schools of thinking in the Hundred Schools, except for the Legalists, endorsed war unequivocally as an instrument of state or approved of militarism; they believed rather that victory through violent means was more likely than not to destroy the order it sought to impose. Overall, war was a contested issue during the period of the Warring States. As one study on the ethics of warfare during this time has concluded, China produced 'both moralists and Machiavellians. If the moralists never persuaded rulers to follow their teachings, the Machiavellians never extinguished peoples' drive to place kindness or, at least, utilitarianism above the wild brutality of war.'[117] The legacy of this for future history was that unity of the Chinese nation became prized above all because it ensured domestic peace. Warfare, in the judgement of the great historian of China John King Fairbank, was 'disesteemed' and the values of the civil (*wen*) triumphed over the military (*wu*)—those of 'literate culture over brute force'. For the emperor to resort to war was an admission that he had failed to deliver good government.[118]

Conclusion

The early Chinese and Greek classics considered above suggest an evolution towards a more considered view of whether war is inevitable or indeed desirable. There is a shift over time from a single-minded

focus on the martial virtues—*wu*—under the Shang dynasty to view-
ing these as complementary to the civil virtues—*wen*—as the rulers
of the Zhou kingdoms wrestle with problems of statehood. This dual-
ity of *wen* and *wu* will become central to later Chinese philosophical
thinking on peace and war.[119] We may also detect a corresponding
shift in the Greek experience from an uncomplicated emphasis on the
achievement of fame (*kleos*) by feats of arms in the Mycenaean age,
which probably survives in some of the battle scenes of the *Iliad*, to a
greater appreciation of the dire effects of war, as conveyed in Homer's
more nuanced elaboration of the Troy myth.

The Chinese and the Greek texts also suggest a growth of scepticism towards the operational reality of the gods, whose intervention
comes to be seen as of less consequence than human activity. By the
middle of the Spring and Autumn period, heaven is still invoked, but
on a pragmatic basis. Yuri Pines has noted that 'if a leader succeeds,
then that must mean he is backed by heaven, not that he will only succeed if he is backed by heaven'. Rulers are seen as needing to 'concentrate on human affairs rather than seeking deities' support'.[120] The role
of the gods in the Homeric epics is also problematic: when Athena and
Apollo agree to halt the bloodshed temporarily by suggesting a duel
(*Iliad*, Book 7), Hector issues a challenge which is accepted by Ajax. Yet
the two gods have not told anyone to organize the duel! Homer merely
says that one of Priam's sons was able to 'divine what the gods have
agreed' and hence encouraged Hector to issue his challenge. We need
to ask, it has been suggested, 'at what level of seriousness or acceptance
the Homeric deities were understood. Did the Greeks believe in the
Gods of their myths?'[121] If war can no longer be simply attributed to,
or blamed upon, the gods, this will require a higher degree of human
responsibility for the choice between war and peace.

By the time of the Chinese Warring States and the Greek city-states,
the decision to go to war had been to some extent democratized or
at least opened up to a degree of debate. The so-called philosophers
of the Hundred Schools function more as political advisers, ready to
give an opinion (and presumably rewarded for it) when consulted by
the contending rulers. Today we might regard their schools as political think-tanks. In Greece we know that there were both peace and
war parties in the assemblies of the city-states, though the surviving
records (principally Thucydides) obscure the record of debate by giving preference to the argument for war. The debate was also carried

on, less directly but often more powerfully, on the stage of comedy and tragedy, as we can tell even from the very small number of surviving plays. It is less clear to what extent the Greek philosophers took part in that debate. It is likely that if we possessed texts from the school of Cynics, these would provide more evidence of their opposition to the institution of war, which conflicted with their desire for brotherhood and peace, and with the cosmopolitan ideal first attributed to Diogenes (c.404–323 BC).[122] While war is in the background of Plato's writings, he says little explicitly about it perhaps, it has been suggested, 'because he wants to turn his readers' attention to the requirements of peace'. While he was not a pacifist and believed that the city or polis should be prepared for war, he believed that 'The best…is neither war nor civil war—the necessity for these things is to be regretted—but rather peace and at the same time goodwill towards one another.'[123] Aristotle's views on war have been more influential in the centuries since his death than during his life. He believed that war should only be made for a moral purpose, and saw the propensity for making war as one of the inherent dangers of tyranny. Most military states fail when they have acquired their empire, he wrote, 'and for this the legislator is to blame, he never having taught them how to lead the life of peace'.[124] (He does not appear to have instructed Alexander the Great very successfully on this subject.)

The discussions on war and peace which I have described above may be phrased in a remote Greek or Chinese idiom, but they address issues which ring true today. As we have seen, many modern scholars now take a less simplistic view of the role of war in ancient Greek culture. One striking development has been the reappraisal of the *Iliad* and of many Greek plays in the light of our experience of modern combat—particularly that of the Vietnam War which, through the new medium of television, played so vividly on our consciousness. Works such as Jonathan Shay's *Achilles in Vietnam*, a study of the psychological devastation of war which compares the soldiers of the *Iliad* with Vietnam veterans suffering from post-traumatic stress disorder, and those by Lawrence Tritle and Robert Meagher (discussed above), have opened up this new ground.[125]

The view that there was a 'pacifist bias' in the Chinese tradition of government, as suggested by Fairbank and Joseph Needham, is a matter of academic controversy today with a contemporary political edge.[126] Although Mao Zedong in his later years extolled the Legalist approach and condemned the Confucians, China's rulers in the twenty-first century advocate building a 'harmonious' society at home, and a peaceful world abroad, in terms which appeal explicitly to this presumed tradition of 'peace and harmony' in Chinese history. Chinese Buddhism has also regained popularity in many parts of China— although in Tibetan areas it still suffers from restriction because of its association with the exiled Dalai Lama. Temples have been rebuilt and images and posters of bodhisattvas ('enlightened beings') are often seen. These include the widely venerated Guan Yin, who conveys the spirit of compassion, and Tara, 'the one who saves', who offers peace and prosperity (Plate 5). Official pronouncements have invoked both Buddhism and Confucianism as evidence of China's commitment since ancient times to a 'harmonious world'.[127] How far this is true, or relevent today, is a matter for debate between China's friends and critics in assessing the current and future trajectory of Chinese foreign policy.

Modern-day scholars of classical Greece have also extended their argument to reflect more generally about the nature of peace in the wider ancient world. The voices of those who called for peace are now hard to discern, it is suggested, sometimes because the evidence has not survived but in other cases 'because the extant evidence reflects only the perspective of the mighty elites'.[128] It is argued too that while wars were very common in antiquity, relations between the ancient 'society of states' from the Mediterranean to Mesopotamia featured a wide range of devices, from treaties to kinship bonds, designed to inhibit and avoid violence: it could even be said that '"natural" peace, not a war of all against all, was widely regarded as the default state of international relations'.[129]

3

The Morality of Peace

From Jesus to the Crusades

The rambling vine is held in check with Saturn's pruning shears,
and the overgrown land is tended and grows tame.
The spear rejoices to become a scythe,
the sword to become a plough.
Peace brings riches to the lowly
and despoils the mighty.
Hail, high Father, grant perfect salvation
to all who love the quiet of peace.

(Fulbert of Chartres, 'Hymn', eleventh century)[1]

Martin, born in AD 316 during the rule of Emperor Constantine, was compelled to join the Roman army at the age of 15 because his father was already a military tribune. One bitter winter's day, he came across a poor man completely destitute of clothing, and, himself wearing no outer clothing except his cloak, divided the garment in two and gave one part to the wretched man. That night he had a vision of Jesus, clad in the same half-cloak which he had given away: Martin hastened to be baptized and sought to retire from military service, but before he did so the army was assembled to prepare for a battle with the Gauls. The emperor (by now Julian Caesar) distributed largesse, as was customary, to the soldiers to encourage their fighting spirit: when it came to Martin's turn he refused to accept the money, saying: 'I am the soldier of Christ; it is not lawful for me to fight.' Accused by the emperor of cowardice, Martin offered to 'stand unarmed before the line of battle' and place his trust in the protection of Jesus. In the fresco by Simone Martini (c.1317–19), we see the Emperor Julian looking uncomprehendingly at Martin, with his treasurer behind him

distributing money. Martin looks back at Julian and, in the act of blessing, walks towards the fierce Gauls (see Plate 6).

Martin was thrown into jail to await the battle, but the very next
day the enemy sent ambassadors to sue for peace. Though Jesus could
have saved the unarmed Martin from death in the front line, explains
the chronicler (and personal friend) Sulpicius Severus, he did not
wish his eyes to be pained 'by witnessing the death of others, [and
so] he removed all necessity of fighting'. Thus no one suffered death.[2]
Whatever the truth of this tale, it illustrates how even after the historic compromise between the Church and Constantine (272–337), in
which the Roman emperor embraced Christianity, some Christians still
believed that serving as a soldier was incompatible with being received
into the faith. It was one of several examples of conscientious objection
to military service recorded as occurring in the fourth century.[3] Thus
we are told of Victricius (330–407), the son of a Roman legionary
who, after becoming a Christian, refused to serve in the legions and
was sentenced to death, but managed to avoid execution—presumably
with divine assistance. Victricius was a friend of Martin, and both were
subsequently beatified.

It is not, however, as a war resister that Martin is remembered today:
in his saintly role he has a number of patronages including those of
horses, innkeepers, tailors, and wine-makers, but he is known above all
as the patron saint of soldiers. This ironic role reversal is explained on
the grounds that he left the army of men and joined the army of God:
his performance as a 'soldier of Christ' thus becomes an exemplar for
those who are soldiers at war. Accounts of his life usually describe his
division of the cloak in full, but often abbreviate the story of his refusal
to fight to the simple statement that he was 'freed' or 'discharged' from
the army.[4] It seems a remarkable transposition for a saint who from the
beginning, we are told, did not want to join the army and once baptized was prepared to die rather than remain a soldier. Yet it is not really
so surprising for a religion which has wrestled constantly over the
ethics of war. For almost two millennia, as Peter Brock, the historian
of pacifism, has observed, Christians 'have sought confirmation in the
books of the New Testament for either a pacifist or an anti-pacifist
stand, for war has been too ever-present a social reality for Christians
to have been able to escape making a judgement'.[5] The story of St
Martin and its subsequent treatment is a reminder of how often the
Sword of Christ has been transformed into the Sword of Caesar.

Pacifism in the early Christian Church

Mahatma Gandhi observed during the First World War that 'the fright-ful outrage that is just going on in Europe, perhaps shows that the message of Jesus of Nazareth, the Son of Peace, had been little under-stood in Europe'.[6] (This may be the basis for the apocryphal quota-tion attributed to him that 'the only people who do not know that Jesus was non-violent are Christians'.) Gandhi's criticism certainly did not apply to the early Christian fathers, who were closer to the spirit of the Gospels and the New Testament than many theologians of sub-sequent ages. The evidence for a pacifist outlook within the Christian Church is most widespread in the earliest period preceding its rap-prochement with Constantine, although the subject remains contro-versial among many religious historians. Roland Bainton, author of a classic study of Christian attitudes towards war and peace, maintains that 'the age of persecution down to the time [of] Constantine was the age of pacifism to the degree that during this period no Christian author to our knowledge approved of Christian participation in bat-tle'.[7] This spirit of rejection is vividly conveyed by Justin Martyr (c.100–c.165), one of the earliest Christian apologists, who wrote, 'we [Christians] who were filled with war, and mutual slaughter, and every wickedness, have each through the whole earth changed our warlike weapons—our swords into ploughshares, and our spears into imple-ments of tillage, and we cultivate piety, righteousness, philanthropy, faith, and hope ...'[8]

Those pronouncements of Jesus which spoke against violence, and the smaller number which might be interpreted as countenancing it, have always been crucial to the discussion. The sixth commandment was less significant than the moment in the garden of Gethsemane when Jesus, betrayed by Judas, told Peter and his other disciples not to resist. 'Put up your sword. All who take the sword die by the sword,' he said, according the Gospel of Matthew (and more briefly in John: 'sheathe your sword', and in Luke, 'let them have their way').[9] For Tertullian (c.160–c.220), the conclusion was beyond doubt. Jesus had 'unbelted every soldier' by disarming Peter after he had struck off a soldier's ear: 'How will a Christian man [behave in] war, nay, how will he serve even in peace, without a sword, which the Lord has taken away?'[10] The ambiguous comment 'It is enough' made by Jesus at the

Last Supper (and recorded only in Luke) when the disciples showed him 'two swords' apparently in their possession, was made much of by later commentators opposed to Christian pacifism but was not even mentioned by Tertullian or by Origen (see below).[11]

Tertullian was a brilliant polemicist, a Berber African converted after watching Christian slaves courageously facing death in the amphi-theatre, who has been called the father of Latin Christianity. His most significant work on the issue of peace was the treatise *De Corona Militis* (AD 211), written in defence of a Christian soldier who had refused to wear a garland on the emperor's birthday. Critics who seek to mini-mize the pacifist outlook of the early Church have described this work as merely concerned with the issue of idolatry (the wearing of the garland or crown). In fact Tertullian explicitly goes beyond this to con-sider the prior and larger question—should a Christian be a soldier at all—writing with his customary energy and wit:

Will it be lawful for him to occupy himself with the sword, when the Lord declares that he who uses the sword will perish by the sword? And shall the son of peace, for whom it will be unfitting even to go to law, be engaged in a battle? And shall he, who is not the avenger even of his own wrongs, admin-ister chains and imprisonment and tortures and executions?...And shall he carry a flag, too, that is a rival to Christ? And shall he ask for a watchword from his chief, when he has already received one from God? And when he is dead, shall he be disturbed by the bugler's trumpet—he who expects to be roused by the trumpet of the angel?[12]

A Christian should not serve in the army at all. The case is different, Tertullian acknowledges, for those who are converted when they are already performing military service: they then face a difficult choice—either to quit at once or stay but refuse to take part in any unchristian action, and thus face martyrdom. We know of one later example: the centurion Marcellus who was martyred in AD 298 after he had refused to celebrate the emperor's birthday and cast his military belt to the ground. In this case the objection to taking part in a non-Christian ritual seems to have prompted a more thorough rejection of the act of arms. Marcellus is supposed to have told the judge who sentenced him to death that 'it is not seemly that a Christian man, who renders military service to the Lord Christ, should render it [also] by [inflict-ing] earthly injuries'.[13] These and similar stories may be no more than legends built on slender fact, but they evoke a real issue of life and death importance facing the early Christians.

The argument against Christian engagement in war was carried further by the scholar and theologian Origen (c.185–254), particularly in his refutation of an anti-Christian tract by Celsus (a Greek opponent of Christianity of whom is nothing else is known). Origen saw that it was necessary to address Celsus' argument that Christians were weakening society as a whole by refusing to serve the state. Celsus had urged Christians to help the emperor with all their strength, and if necessary to 'fight for him and serve as soldiers', and warned that if all were to follow the Christian example and abstain from politics, the affairs of the world would fall into the hands of 'wild and lawless barbarians'.[14] This may well be the first recorded example of the argument against conscientious objection which has been repeated in one form or another up to modern times (for 'barbarians' read, in the context of the Second World War, 'Nazis'). Origen agreed that Christians had a duty to serve the state, but argued that 'Christians benefit their countries more than the rest of men', citing two forms of service: (a) through prayer in support of the emperor and against all hostile forces, and (b) through setting a good example, educating the citizens, and teaching them to be devout. Whether or not this was a sufficient answer, Origen in making it sought to address the issue rather than reject altogether the claim of emperor and state.

As noted above, the extent of pacifism in the early Church—and even the true perspective of its leading exponents Tertullian and Origen—has always been a matter of controversy. Bainton's own account acknowledges that while, for example, there is no evidence of Christians serving in the Roman army until the late second century, we do not know whether this is because they were averse to service or because they were barred from it. He also notes that pacifism was 'less prevalent in the frontier provinces menaced by the barbarians'. However, the complaint from Celsus quoted above certainly indicates that Christian conscientious objection could be a serious issue—we do not know from what part of the Roman empire Celsus was writing. And in northern Africa, there is evidence both of acceptance of military service by Christians and rejection of it.[15] Both aspects are recorded in the story of Maximilian, the 21-year-old son of a Roman legionary, who refused to be recruited in Numidia (now Algeria) because he was a Christian. When it was pointed out to him that there were Christians serving as imperial bodyguards, he replied, 'That is their business. I am a Christian too, and I cannot serve.'[16] Critics argue that the apparent

pacifism of the early fathers really reflects their opposition not to warfare as such but to the idolatrous practices of emperor worship in the
Roman army. A second argument from the critics (at odds with the
first) is that pacifism was an expression of eschatology—the belief that
the end of the world was nigh and that therefore it was pointless to
engage in such worldly pursuits as warfare. There are scattered remarks
in both Tertullian and Origen which admit, and seem to approve of,
the presence of Christians in the army—though not their participation in bloodshed. (Since many civilian posts were filled by military
officers in the Roman empire, and local garrisons might act more as
a police force than as combatants, this is not so strange as it might
sound.) It is sensible to conclude that 'on the momentous issues of war
and peace ... we should not be surprised to find uncertainties, inconsistencies, and changes of outlook among Christians as the centuries
progressed'.[17]

Views on early Christian pacifism have differed over time not only
for scholarly reasons but because of more general changes in attitudes
towards peace and war. For many Christian theologians and historians
of the late nineteenth and twentieth centuries, the pacifism of the
early Church could be invoked to argue, amidst the horrors of modern
war, for a return to basic principles. Thus the distinguished Mennonite
theologian John Howard Yoder (1927–97) argued that 'Christians
today cannot be faithful to the teachings of the early Church without
being pacifists'.[18] During the cold war, the subject was often argued
around the issue of the legitimacy or otherwise of a nuclear deterrent
policy which, if it failed, might obliterate millions of human lives. In
the current age, where the danger of nuclear obliteration has receded
but the Gulf, Iraq, and Afghan wars have sharply polarized opinion,
views on the early Church's position have again become divided.
This division may be illustrated by the contrasting titles of two recent
books by American religious historians: *Love your Enemies: Discipleship,
Pacifism and Just War Theory* (Lisa Cahill, 1994), and *When God says War
is Right: The Christian's Perspective on When and How to Fight* (Darrell
Cole, 2002). Outside the scholarly literature, the pacifism of the early
Church is often mentioned only in passing if at all. The opening chapter on early Christian communities in the *Oxford Illustrated History of
Christianity* (1990) does not touch on the subject, nor is it discussed
in two other recent histories of Christianity.[19] What was perhaps a
bias towards an over-enthusiastic view of early Christian pacifism in

the work of leading early or mid-twentieth-century scholars has now been corrected even to the point of omission.

St Augustine and Just War

During the cold war, questions about warfare concentrated mostly on the morality of the use or retention of nuclear weapons, or else on the strategic calculations behind deterrence theory. There was little room here for application of the Just War theory: the doctrine of deterrence meant, as the political scientist Michael Walzer put it in his study of the subject, that 'against the threat of an immoral attack, they [the nuclear states] have put the threat of an immoral response'.[20] Such debates either transcended the traditional argument of the justification for war, or did not go so far, although the Vietnam War—a relatively limited conflict which it soon became clear would not lead to global conflagration—did trigger some debate in traditional Just War theory. However, the end of the cold war largely removed the threat that any localized conflict could have such incalculable consequences, while allowing more room for concern about humanitarian issues which might require (or provide the pretext for) military intervention. As a result there has been an explosion of interest in Just War theory, with intense argument on issues of justification, proportionality, and pre-emption among others. This interest has been intensified by the invasions of Afghanistan and Iraq following the 11 September terrorist attack on the USA. And in this context the writings of the Christian father St Augustine (AD 354–430), to whom the origins of the Just War theory are often attributed, have received renewed attention. Augustine has been invoked almost as a patron saint of the Just War—but would he recognize, or approve of, the use which is made of his doctrine?

This is not the first age to have approached Augustine with urgent questions as to whether war can be justified, and for some to have found the answers in the saint's voluminous writings. (He was one of the most prolific writers in terms of what has survived: the extant corpus totals more than five million words and the list of his works contains more than one hundred titles.) Yet as the Augustinian scholar James O'Donnell emphasizes, 'it must be asserted and constantly held in mind that it was not to answer the questions of other ages that Augustine wrote'.[21] Nowhere does Augustine spell out such a thing as a Theory of Just War. This has to be pieced together from scattered passages in writings over a period of forty years: nine principal sources have been identified ranging from *De Libero Arbitrio* (*On Free Choice*) which dates from early in his career to one of the last of his more than two hundred dated letters (*To Darius*, No. 229).[22]

The relationship of the Christian Church to the Roman empire had been placed in a very different context by the accession of Constantine and his embracing of the faith. The bishops were no longer outside the imperial power structure, addressing a congregation of individual Christians who had to reconcile their faith with the demands and exactions of that power. Increasingly they operated within the political system, and spoke directly with the local ruling elite and on occasion with the emperor and his entourage. As Constantine consolidated his own power, 'so too did those urban bishops upon whom he increasingly relied as ad hoc administrators of welfare and justice'. Throughout the fourth century, except for a brief interruption during the reign of Constantine's pagan nephew Julian, 'imperial and ecclesiastical politics grew increasingly intertwined'.[23] By restoring the *pax romana*, Constantine was seen to have 'pacified the world…and made possible the proclamation of the gospel to all nations'.[24] Eusebius, bishop of Caesarea (263–339), was a prominent participant in the Council of Nicaea (325), called by Constantine to promote unity in the Church. 'Thus, by the express appointment of the same God,' wrote Eusebius, 'two roots of blessing, the Roman empire, and the doctrine of Christian piety, sprang up together for the benefit of men.' One universal empire prevailed; and the human race, 'subdued by the controlling power of peace and concord, received one another as brethren'.[25]

By the year 335, according to a recent study of Constantine's relationship with the bishops, the emperor saw them as 'players in the game of empire' who represented a community of some six million persons, nearly 10 per cent of the empire's entire population.[26] The issue for the bishops was no longer how to measure individual Christian conscience against the demands of military service by a hostile regime: it was how to regard the military actions of a regime now working in concert with the Church, and defending it against the 'pagan' threat of those peoples beyond the Roman frontiers. St Ambrose (*c.*339–97), whose observations on war are often seen as a precursor for those of Augustine, was himself a Roman governor who had been persuaded with some reluctance to become the bishop of

Milan—although he was not even baptized at the time. War was permissible, he argued, if it was undertaken for defence or to protect the empire against barbarian heresy. 'No military eagles, no flight of birds', wrote Ambrose to the Emperor Gratian, 'here lead the van of our army, but Thy Name, Lord Jesus, and Thy worship. This is no land of unbelievers, but the land whose custom it is to send forth confessors—Italy.'[27] (This linkage of war to religious orthodoxy has been rightly described as an 'ominous development' for the future, taking the first step down the road towards justification of holy war against heathens and infidels.)[28]

Augustine, who was deeply influenced by Ambrose while working in Milan as a relatively young man, dealt with these issues more explicitly and more frequently in his long career of writing and argument. However, as already noted, nowhere did he address war as his central theme. His arguments were almost forgotten until they were taken up by the twelfth-century jurist Gratian and amplified by St Thomas Aquinas: as the leading Just War scholar James Turner Johnson has written, '[there] is no just war tradition prior to its coalescence in the Middle Ages around concepts drawn from canon law, theology, secular law, chivalric morality, and the habits of relations among princes'.[29] It would be especially anachronistic to regard Augustine as concerning himself with the relationship between states, when such a relationship in the modern sense did not exist. Augustine's remarks on the morality of warfare are made in the context of the two issues which seemed relevant then: the principles to be observed in the course of the Roman empire's efforts to defend itself against 'barbarian' attack, and how far the instances of war in the Old Testament, undertaken in the name of God, could be justified. The 'Just War theory' which has been inferred from his writings can be summarized as follows: (i) there must be a just cause (in self-defence or to punish aggression), (ii) war must be undertaken with the right intention (not for revenge), (iii) it may only be undertaken by a competent authority (the state), (iv) it should only be undertaken as a last resort, and (v) peace is the ultimate objective (the warrior should be a peacemaker). Discussion of the theory attributed to Augustine often focuses on the first four principles, yet if we turn to the original we find that he writes with most conviction on the last—on peace. As has been shown by John Mattox, author of the most recent study of Augustine and Just War, 'Both Cicero and Ambrose recognise the desirability of peace. However, Augustine, far beyond merely recognizing its desirability, considers peace to be the indisputable end to which all wars are fought.'[30]

Augustine's *City of God*, written after the sack of Rome by the Visigoths in AD 410, is often cited as the fullest source for his views on Just War. Yet its most eloquent and lengthy passage is not concerned with war but with peace—occupying two-thirds of the much-quoted Book 19. A principal purpose of Augustine's work was to provide consolation in this time of uncertainty and defeat. Even if the peace of the earthly city of Rome—the city of man—was threatened, the true believer could find eternal peace in the city of God. This was not however an eschatological message promising peace only in the hereafter, for the city of God, or at least a portion of it, exists on earth (represented naturally by Christian life and the Church). What is more, even in the city of man there is a desire for peace and, however defective, a measure of peace in reality. Peace in Augustine's eyes is 'a good so great, that even in this earthly and mortal life there is no word we hear with such pleasure, nothing we desire with such zest, or find to be more thoroughly gratifying'. Man may have fallen from grace but peace is still preserved by the law of nature at every level, from the peace between man and God, to the peace between man and man, and then to the peace of the family—while civil peace is a similar concord between citizens. Peace may be unequally distributed but it will always exist in some measure. Those who are miserable are less so than if they had no peace. In one of several moving passages, Augustine writes:

[God has] imparted to men some good things adapted to this life, to wit, temporal peace, such as we can enjoy in this life from health and safety and human fellowship, and all things needful for the preservation and recovery of this peace, such as the objects which are accommodated to our outward senses, light, night, the air, and waters suitable for us, and everything the body requires to sustain, shelter, heal, or beautify it: and all under this most equitable condition, that every man who made a good use of these advantages suited to the peace of this mortal condition, should receive ampler and better blessings, namely, the peace of immortality, accompanied by glory and honour...[31]

We may find in these words of Augustine a pre-Darwinian view that peace (not war) is the essential requirement for the continuation of the human race, for if animals protect their own species, how much more powerfully does man's nature move him to 'maintain peace with all men so far as in him lies'. Indeed even those who do make war do so (by implication, should do so) for no other purpose than to secure peace, for 'every man seeks peace by waging war, but no man seeks war by making peace'. Nor can we postpone peace to the life hereafter while neglecting it in the here and now. Augustine carefully explores the relationship between the two peaces—immortal and temporal. The city of God does not scorn the temporal peace but makes the best use it can of it and obeys the laws of the earthly city. Even the heavenly city 'avails itself of the peace of earth' which is not to be lightly esteemed. Indeed it is in the interest of Christians 'to enjoy this peace meanwhile on this earth, for as long as the two cities are commingled, we shall also enjoy the peace of Babylon'.

By contrast with Augustine's extended discussion of peace, only one passage in his entire works attempts to define the meaning of 'Just War'. It occurs in his *Questions on the Heptateuch*, in which Augustine addresses more than 650 questions suggested to him by a close reading of the first seven books of the Old Testament. Question No. 10 out of 30 which he poses on the Book of Joshua is headed 'When is War Just?' The question is raised for Augustine by that part of the text (Joshua 8: 2) where Joshua has been instructed by God to set an ambush against the enemy (the city and people of Ai). Augustine concludes that the issue is not whether an ambush is legitimate but whether a war is just—in which case any tactic would be justified. He goes on to define Just Wars as

those which avenge wrongs, if some nation or state against whom one is waging war has neglected to remedy the injustices committed by its own side, or has failed to return something which was wrongfully taken. It is [also] evident that one should consider a war which has been ordered by God as a Just War...[32]

It is also evident, one might add, that this is a rather perfunctory answer dictated by the specific nature of the question: since God ordered this particular war there is no need for Augustine to provide a more lengthy definition of the Just War. Elsewhere Augustine calls on combatants to exercise mercy and forbearance and, in *Against Faustus*, says that 'the real evils in war are love of violence, revengeful cruelty, fierce and implacable enmity, wild resistance, and the lust of power'. He is also at pains to show that even in the biblical cases of war which God has commanded, this is not through a divine whim but because the opposing side has put itself into the wrong.[33]

In several of his letters towards the end of his life, Augustine did address the issue of military service, which he pronounced not to be

contrary to Christian doctrine. This was no abstract statement, for
Roman rule in Africa was collapsing and Augustine would die in the
city of Hippo while it was under siege from the Vandals. One such
statement was in a letter urging Count Boniface, whose wife had just
died, to stay at his post in southern Numidia, resisting nomadic raids,
rather than resign and enter a monastery.[34] Even in this case, Augustine
urged peace wherever possible as preferable to war: 'Peace should be
the object of your desire; war should be waged only as a necessity, and
waged only that God may by it deliver men from the necessity and
preserve them in peace.'

In the year before his death, and in almost the last letter that
Augustine wrote, he offered the same advice to the imperial envoy
Count Darius who had been sent to negotiate with Boniface. Those
warriors who establish peace through force of arms should be admired
for their bravery, said Augustine, but

it is a higher glory still to stay war itself with a word, than to slay men with the
sword, and to procure or maintain peace by peace, not by war. For those who
fight, if they are good men, doubtless seek for peace; nevertheless it is through
blood. Your mission, however, is to prevent the shedding of blood.[35]

If one sentence conveys the dominant view of war held by the alleged
'father of the Just War', it is Augustine's judgement in the *City of God*
that if anyone can contemplate warfare 'without heartfelt grief', then
such a person has 'lost all human feeling'.[36]

Peace and war in the Middle Ages

In the fourteenth-century Palazzo Pubblico (town hall) overlooking
the great square of Siena, a remarkable fresco by Ambrogio Lorenzetti,
completed in 1340, depicts in vivid detail the contrasting fates of a
city at war and a city at peace. On the one side, below the flying
figure of Fear, we see a city with empty streets and rough soldiers,
houses in disrepair, women being raped, and, outside the city gates,
abandoned fields, buildings set alight, and looters at work. The horned
figure of Tyranny rules over the scene, with Justice bound at his feet.
In the city on the other side, the population throngs in the streets but
there are no soldiers in sight, the houses are well kept with flower-
pots in their windows; there are craftsmen at work, a tailor, a cobbler,

a goldsmith, and a wine shop with people playing chess, while the fields outside are well cultivated, with a watermill, sheaves ready for threshing, farmers driving in their pigs to market, and a hunting party out with their dogs. These contrasting scenes are presided over on the centre wall by the crowned figure of the Common Good, symbolizing the Commune of Siena, flanked by Justice with her scales and by a sequence of the Virtues. Peace (see the jacket of this book) is the most prominent among these—and also the most relaxed, half reclining on one elbow, and wearing a white dress (contemporary for her time) which emphasizes her attractive form. While the frescoes have come to be described as an allegory of 'good and bad government', in medieval times they were known more directly under the simple title of 'Peace and War'.[37]

Lorenzetti's composition had been commissioned by the Noveschi, the Council of Nine drawn from the merchant guilds, who ruled by rotation every two months over the Commune under a system which lasted nearly seventy years (1287 to 1355). To the Nine as they sat in their council chamber, and to the citizens of Siena who would attend assemblies there, the allegory was an everyday reminder of the superiority of peace. Through a system of fair taxation the Nine rebuilt their city, stimulated commerce by raising public debt, improved agriculture in the surrounding countryside, and to a greater extent than most other contemporary city-states avoided war. Their rule succeeded in keeping neighbouring Florence at bay, in resisting papal interference, and pacifying internal dissent, but was finally overthrown by the effects of the Black Death and foreign intrigues.[38] By the standards of the time the Nine were unusually successful in pursuing the ideals, witnessed daily in the allegory on their walls, of Justice, Beauty, and Peace. Occupying the central point on the central fresco of the hall, Peace continues to stand out today, a reminder that she was still the aspiration, and sometimes the reality, in an epoch more usually known for its wars.

The prevailing view of the Middle Ages (in whatever time frame this very loose historical period is to be defined) is of an age of warfare, in which images of nobility and chivalry coexist uneasily with those of slaughter and massacre. And while the term 'chivalry' came to denote a set of values applicable to civilian life which included 'justice, modesty, loyalty to superiors, courtesy to equals, compassion to weakness and devotedness to the Church', the value which came first (in the classic account of the age of chivalry by Thomas Bulfinch) was that of 'invincible strength and valour'.[39] The chivalrous knight, in its original meaning, was the mounted warrior entitled to bear arms and use them, in the feudal service of his king or patron—a role comparable to that of the samurai warrior under Japanese feudalism. The rules of chivalry at first sought to impose limits upon the unrestrained violence of warring lords and chieftains in an age when the central authority of popes and emperors had declined. As political power began to coalesce around secular states in the later medieval period, chivalry imbued what would now be called the military profession with status and glamour: as the *Penguin History of Medieval Europe* describes it, 'the military calling was held to be noble: to follow arms was in itself to "live nobly"'.[40]

For rural dwellers during long stretches of restless times, serfs or peasants or cottagers struggling to till the land and keep a roof of sorts over their heads, chivalrous war had a very different reality. Their livelihood and safety might be threatened by the lawless behaviour of the armed retainers of local lords, by the plunder and rape committed by invading armies, or even by the scorched earth policies of their own rulers seeking to deny land to the enemy. Thus did King Jean of France in 1355 burn and carry off provisions from the countryside around Amiens when King Edward of England invaded. 'Left to face a hungry winter robbed of their hard-earned harvests,' Barbara Tuchman observes, 'the people experienced their own warrior class not as protectors but ravagers.'[41]

For those who lived in the medieval towns, where a more settled life had begun to provide greater security, the threat of war took other forms. It could cause serious shortages of food for the general populace, who also risked impressment into military service. The emerging merchant class saw their commercial activities disrupted, and could be faced with special levies to fund the armies. Urban communities not infrequently faced two even greater dangers: they might find themselves under siege—with a fearfully uncertain future if the town fell to the enemy—and they might be struck by disease and pestilence during the siege, or in the chaotic aftermath of war. Siege followed by massacre was a frequent phenomenon in the Crusades where victory for the invading forces, in a generally hostile environment, was defined by the capture and plunder of urban centres, such as the dreadful brutality which followed the fall of Jerusalem in the First Crusade.[42]

The Middle Ages is also the period when, it is generally agreed, both the theory and practice of modern war began to develop. The scattered thoughts of St Augustine, which had for centuries made little impact, formed the basis for a new formulation on Just War by the twelfth-century jurist Gratian, in his *Decretum* (*c*.1148), which would become a standard text for several centuries. Developed by his followers, the Decretists, his doctrine would legitimize the Crusades as a Just War authorized by the Church. St Thomas Aquinas (1225–74) addressed the same issue in his *Summa Theologica*, refining the three conditions for a Just War: right authority, just cause, and right intention, although he was more equivocal on the legitimate status of the Crusades. The later Middle Ages is also seen as the period in which the practice of warfare began to develop in ways which would lead into the so-called 'military revolution' of the early modern period (from the sixteenth century onwards). Though armies were still small compared to more modern times, they became better drilled and equipped, with such weapons as the pike and crossbow. The role of infantry became more significant and use was also made increasingly of mercenaries. Firearms and artillery were introduced, and the art of siege and of corresponding fortification against it was improved further.[43]

By the early Renaissance, the accepted picture is that 'war was constant. And not only war—so was treason, murder, and plot'.[44] In Italy, regret for the relatively peaceful Quattrocento was accompanied by acceptance that war was inevitable. The Church helped to rally support in Florence for the militia, and pictures of St Barbara, associated with the use of guns (because her father had been killed by explosive thunder), became common—gunners at the school of artillery in Sicily were instructed to invoke the saint's aid every time they loaded. Looking back we associate the military ethos which the Renaissance would bequeath to future centuries with the ideas of Machiavelli, particularly as set out in *The Prince* and *The Art of War*. Whether or not our current use of the term 'Machiavellian' fully expresses his approach, it is certainly the case that the necessity of war for Machiavelli was dictated by the logic of power rather than, as in the Augustinian view, by the desire for peace, and that in the cycle proposed by Machiavelli, peace led to idleness and disorder, and could only be restored again by military valour.[45]

The dominant narrative on matters of war and peace from the Middle Ages into the Renaissance is therefore one of conflict, violence, and

militarism based on realpolitik. Yet there is a countervailing narrative of
demands for peace, criticism of war, and pacific humanism which has
been under-researched except for a few outstanding studies, and fails
to make much impact on our general perception of the times. As one
medieval historian has observed, 'medieval war fascinates modern scholars. Learned studies continue to appear on the crusades, just war, military tactics, war financing, and nobles. But peace has fared less well.'[46]

Pax dei and the popular voice

By the late tenth century, both the clergy and the general populace
in many parts of Western Europe were suffering grievously from
the lawlessness of local lords and knights, and their retainers, following the collapse of Charlemagne's imperial administration. At a time
when the greed of the powerful was no longer restrained by temporal
authority, the bishops took action to defend their own interests and
those of the people, defined as farmers, peasants, and villagers.[47] Thus
there arose a movement, organized by the Church but depending on
popular backing, to compel the feudal elite to swear their commitment to peace, which became known as the Peace of God (pax dei).
The warlords were invited to attended an open council—we would
now call it a rally—held in a large open space, attended by crowds of
the common people, to which senior members of the Church had
brought the most precious and sacred relics. Threatened with divine
retribution, the nobility was urged to pledge its support for a policy
of pacific restraint. Typically this would include a commitment not to
attack the clergy or the unarmed populace, not to rob church property
or seize the livestock of the peasants or the goods of passing merchants,
and often to limit military activities of all kinds to a specified period
of time which excluded a portion of the week and religious holidays.
Such an agreement to limit the duration of conflict became known as
a Truce of God (treuga dei).

   One of the first recorded instances of pax dei was proclaimed in 989
at the Synod of Charroux, held at the Benedictine abbey on the borders
of Aquitaine and attended by a large crowd of people from surrounding regions. It declared, in the name of the archbishop of Bordeaux,
anathema against those who broke into churches, who robbed the
poor, or who injured clergymen.[48] In an example of the more elaborate

treuga dei, dated 1063, Drogo bishop of Terouanne and Count Baldwin of Hainault proclaimed the peace to be established 'with the cooperation of the clergy and people of the land' and to last from 'sunset on Wednesday till sunrise on Monday'—and every day of the week from Lent to Easter and at other specified times in the church calendar:

1. During those four days and five nights no man or woman shall assault, wound, or slay another, or attack, seize, or destroy a castle, burg, or villa, by craft or by violence.

2. If anyone violates this peace and disobeys these commands of ours, he shall be exiled for thirty years as a penance, and before he leaves the bishopric he shall make compensation for the injury which he committed. Otherwise he shall be excommunicated by the Lord God and excluded from all Christian fellowship.

   ...

5. In addition, brethren, you should observe the peace in regard to lands and animals and all things that can be possessed. If anyone takes from another an animal, a coin, or a garment, during the days of the truce, he shall be excommunicated unless he makes satisfaction....

6. During the days of the peace, no one shall make a hostile expedition on horseback, except when summoned by the count; and all who go with the count shall take for their support only as much as is necessary for themselves and their horses.

7. All merchants and other men who pass through your territory from other lands shall have peace from you.[49]

The voice of the common people may only be heard dimly, as one would expect, in the accounts of these assemblies compiled by the monastic historians. The most famous example comes from Aquitaine in 1033 when the desire for peace was raised to an even greater height by millennial expectations that, a thousand years exactly after the death of Christ, the world would enter a time of heaven-inspired peace and abundance. As described by the chronicler Ralph Glaber (985–1047), the bishops and magnates of the entire region held councils to re-establish peace and consolidate the holy faith:

Then were innumerable sick folk healed in those conclaves of Holy men.... At this all were inflamed with such ardour that through the hands of their bishops they raised the pastoral staff to heaven, while themselves with out-spread palms and with one voice cried to God: Peace, peace, peace! that this might be a sign of perpetual covenant for that which they had promised between themselves and God; on condition that, after the lapse of five years, the same covenant should marvellously be repeated by all men in the world in confirmation of that peace.[50]

This great shout, notes the modern historian of this period Richard Landes, represented 'the first popular millennial voice recorded favour-ably by clerical writers who, since Augustine, had expressed enormous hostility to millennialism'.[51] In an early study of the popular aspect of this eleventh-century peace movement, Loren MacKinney concluded that 'the attendance of the common folk not only served as an additional guarantee of strict fulfilment of the agreements, but also greatly stimu-lated public interest and paved the way for more active participation in the peace movement'. The popular role could be a cause for worry to the ruling class. In 1041, writes MacKinney, 'Emperor Henry III had viewed with concern the Council of Montriond, at which under clerical auspices some ten thousand people were said to have convened for the adoption of a French Truce programme.' Two years later the emperor himself took the lead in claiming to establish peace through-out his realm—an early example of the tendency for the authorities to seek to co-opt the popular movement with the support of the bishops who had brought the movement to life in the first place.[52] For while the clergy and populace (or *rustici*) had originally a shared interest in curbing the lawless behaviour of the knights, and religious enthusiasm was harnessed to that end, their interests now diverged and the Church was wary of undermining the secular authority of dukes and kings.[53]

The clamour of the populace for peace and justice fades from the record and the great shout is no longer heard in the chronicles, although it finds an occasional echo in medieval French literature. Several poems in the late twelfth century urge the king to put peace with his neighbours in first place since, whoever wins, the people will suffer. A rare study of this spirit of protest, compiled almost a century ago by the American scholar Mary Morton Wood, gives some striking examples. Étienne de Fougères (d. 1178), bishop of Rennes, urges the following advice to his ruler (Henry II of England whom he served as chaplain) in his *Livre des manières*:

A king ought to love peace and concord, justice with mercy; he who causes war and dissension ought to be hanged with a rope.

Let no king desire to seize the land of another or to conquer it unjustly; for in this way he often starts a war which brings men to exile and death.

Several decades later, Guillaume le Clerc, a Norman cleric, makes the argument even more vividly in a passage of his allegorical poem *Le Besant de Dieu:*

...if one king injures the other, the peasant, who is on the soil, pays for the wrong some day so dearly that he has not where to sleep at night; nay, even the cottage that he had low and small is burned and his oxen and sheep are seized, his sons and daughters bound, and he himself led away a wretched prisoner so that he is sorry to be alive .... God! how shall a Christian king send forth from his kingdom thirty thousand fighting men, who must leave their bereaved wives and children at home, when they go into mortal combats in which a thousand shall soon be slain and never again see their country, and as many men on the other side.[54]

Although medieval poets did not write in the simple vernacular of the oppressed peasantry, they could as these passages show be conscious of their plight. In another example of medieval literary responses to warfare, the late twelfth-century Flemish poet Jean Bodel expresses a strong anti-war message in a charming *pastourelle*, a genre that typically describes the encounter of a young man with a shepherdess. The shepherdess in this poem is not interested in love, but in calling a plague on the houses of both warring Flemish and French.

In the sweet springtime, when the grass is fresh and the days clear and bright, I came across a shepherdess wearing a garland of leaves and a belt of roses ....
I said 'Pretty one, I'll be your lover if you're willing.'
'Sir, I have given my heart to Perrin and mean to marry him, but we are overrun in this country. The French have been here, and have devastated it too much. Sir, are you one of those [Flemish] wretches who have passed the river, who gathered across the Lys? Traitors and rebels and perjurers—they will all be made landless and their shame revealed.'[55]

Opposition to the Crusades

By the second half of the eleventh century, it is clear that the authentic force of the Peace and Truce of God was losing its drive: 'the direct involvement of clergy and populace was on the wane, and the control of violence was devolving upon public institutions headed, at first, by the Holy See'.[56] The Church was edging towards the acceptance of

'sanctified violence', in part because as Rome became a more substantial force on the world stage it would need 'some form of material
military power with which to enforce its political will'.[57] In 1095, after
receiving an appeal from the Byzantine emperor requesting military
assistance against the Seljuk Turks, Pope Urban II called a grand ecclesiastical council at Clermont. From one perspective, the council was
the climax to a series of French peace councils at which Pope Urban
had fully committed himself to the peace movement. At the same time,
the pope while condemning domestic war used the same doctrine to
justify foreign war against the infidels, calling on clergy and laity alike
to support what would become known as the Crusades. The peace
movement, writes MacKinney, 'paradoxically and yet quite naturally,
had become the pledged ally of warfare'.[58] According to Fulbert of
Chartres, chronicler of the First Crusade, the pope exhorted his bishops gathered at the council with these words:

Although, O sons of God, you have promised more firmly than ever to keep
the peace among yourselves and to preserve the rights of the church, there
remains still an important work for you to do.... For your brethren who live
in the east are in urgent need of your help, and you must hasten to give them
the aid which has often been promised them.[59]

From this time on throughout the Crusades, turbulent knights and
troublemakers at home would be urged to direct their energies
against the foreign infidel, and win indulgence by so doing. Thus the
Cistercian abbot Bernard of Clairvaux, commissioned by a later pope
to preach the Second Crusade in 1146, would call on the citizens of
Genoa (in conflict with Pisa) to divert their efforts away from war with
their neighbours and friends to 'work off your warlike spirit by subdu-
ing the enemies of the Church'.[60]

Many scholars have stressed the popular character of the early
Crusades—particularly the first—and there is an extensive literature
discussing the reasons for this. Contemporary figures were wildly
exaggerated, but a recent study estimates that a horde of unarmed
followers, numbering between 20,000 and 60,000, accompanied the
first army in 1096, itself composed of some 7,000 knights with perhaps
35,000 armed infantry.[61] What drove both armed and unarmed crusaders to embark on a perilous journey of 3,000 kilometres has long
been debated. Historians from the late nineteenth century onwards
often emphasized material causes such as population pressure at home,

and this factor was referred to by Urban II in his famous speech at Clermont, according to Robert the Monk, chronicler of the First Crusade (though writing twenty-one years after the council was held): 'This land in which you live, surrounded on one side by the sea and on the other side by mountain peaks, can scarcely contain so many of you,' the pope is supposed to have said.[62] Other reasons given are the number of younger sons with no prospect of inheritance, the provision of subsidies to the crusaders, and hopes or dreams of fantastic booty. More recent scholarship has placed greater weight on spiritual concerns: the quest for personal salvation through the indulgences granted to the crusaders, the atmosphere of penitence which accompanied the call for a crusade, and the close connection between monastic institutions and the knightly aristocracy. The materialist view of the Crusades as in effect forerunners of the age of imperial expansion has come under attack, sometimes with less academic dispassion than might be expected. One contemporary scholar refers to those offering such a view of the Crusades as the 'anti-crusaders'.[63] Another argues that 'crusades to the East were in every way defensive wars', and condemns the classic three-volume history by Steven Runciman as 'terrible history', on the grounds that it regards the crusaders as 'proto-imperialists'.[64]

The motivation of the tens of thousands of poorer participants in the Crusades for whom no direct first-hand records survive is even harder to assess—as are the diverse feelings of the greater number of the European populace who would have heard the call to join but refused to do so.[65] Opposition within sections of the Church and nobility, and in emerging urban society, whether on theological or practical grounds, can often only be discerned through the counter-arguments which advocates of the Crusades deployed against them. The situation is similar to that facing the modern student of the Cathar and Waldensian sects who faced persecution in the later Middle Ages for heresies, including some which might be labelled as anti-war. As the pacifist scholar Peter Brock has observed, we depend for our knowledge of the two sects 'almost exclusively upon the accounts left by their opponents, with all the possibilities of omission and distortion to which ignorance or prejudice on the part of the official church could give rise'.[66] However, it is clear from the canonical arguments in favour of the Crusades, writes one scholar of the Holy War, 'that the defences for a morally justifying war were hammered out in a debate where the minority view always had supporters'.[67] An example was the doubt expressed by the late twelfth-century writer Ralph Niger about the propriety of offering papal indulgences to the crusaders, which allowed their sins to be expiated by the shedding of blood. Another scholar in this field has concluded that 'criticism of the Crusades in the thirteenth century was even more widespread than in Ralph Niger's day and created some problems for the papacy in pursuit of its crusading goals'.[68]

A full-length study of criticism of the Crusades during this period was published by Palmer Throop in 1940 and this single monograph remained our main secondary source on the subject for nearly fifty years, until the publication of a significant study by Elizabeth Siberry.[69] The primary material for this period comes from a number of treatises written in the late thirteenth and early fourteenth centuries addressing what had become an urgent question; how and indeed whether to save the remnants of the Latin Kingdom of Jerusalem, established by previous Crusades, from being destroyed by Muslim forces. Opinion in Europe was not ignorant of their plight, Throop observes. During and after the papal rule of Gregory X (1271–76) there is abundant evidence that 'all Europe was acutely conscious of the losses in the Holy Land', and yet the response was surprisingly half-hearted. The pope was especially alarmed by the failure and sought to revive the original crusading fervour: some of the reports describing the situation on the ground in Palestine, and the treatises seeking to explain the reasons for popular apathy at home, were commissioned by papal authority, at first by Innocent III and later by Gregory. These reports cannot have made pleasant reading. 'Every one of them indicates in some manner disapproval of a new general crusade to recover the Holy Sepulchre,' writes Throop. One response, from Humbert of Romans, actually uses the term 'public (or general) opinion' in discussing opposition to the Holy War.[70]

Criticism covered a very wide spectrum, from the opinions of those who reproached the popes for failing to prosecute the Crusades efficiently, and accused their envoys of mismanagement and corruption, to those who believed that it was contrary to Christian doctrine to spill blood—even the blood of an infidel. There was also deep resentment in the French-speaking provinces, expressed in Old French and Provençal poetry, at the diversion of the anti-heathen crusade to pursue domestic (and Christian) heretics in the Albigensian Crusades.

When it was proposed to consider Simon de Montfort, the crusading leader killed during the siege of Toulouse, for sainthood, the anonymous author of the *Chanson de la croisade contre les Albigeois* responded in satirical fury:

And I have heard it said that it may well be so: if by killing men, by shedding blood, by destroying souls, by consenting to murders, by following evil counsels, by starting conflagrations, by destroying barons, by bringing the nobility to shame, by seizing lands, by advancing the wicked, by kindling evil, by extinguishing good, by killing women and destroying children, one can gain Jesus Christ in this world, one should wear [a saint's] crown and shine in heaven![71]

The sharpest criticism among the memoranda submitted to Gregory X was directed at the abuses of clerical authority, including taxation of the poor to raise funds for the crusade, and the forced redemption of crusader vows by which crusader volunteers bought exemption from actually taking part. Appropriately called the *Collectio de Scandalis Ecclesiae*, this lengthy document according to Throop 'reflects admirably the state of public opinion so far as a crusade is concerned': 'I will tell you how behave those who once exhorted the faithful to take the cross,' complains the contemporary troubadour Raimon Gaucelm de Béziers. 'For a sum of money they permit most to rid themselves of it.' The crusader vow could also be imposed as a punishment by a secular court—and then redeemed for cash. Other criticism suggests that crusaders soon acquired a bad reputation for lawless behaviour. Few went on the Second Crusade, one critical cleric argued, for religious reasons: they went out of curiosity, to escape their debts or punishment of crime. Some were described as 'ravishing wolves'. The author of the *Collectio* does not advocate abandoning Christian control of Jerusalem, but he advises employing mercenaries to do the job, and urges crusade supporters at home to rely on the force of prayer.[72]

Some tracts written in response to Gregory's call were written in the field: among these the *De Statu Saracenorum* is of particular interest. The author, William of Tripoli, a Dominican monk living in Acre, argues that the recovery of the Holy Land is more likely to succeed if carried out by missionaries rather than by soldiers, and he insists that common ground can be found between the Muslim faith and Christianity. Franciscans also argued in favour of peaceful conversion, inspired no doubt by the example of St Francis. Some modern scholars have cast doubt on the traditional view that he expressed opposition to the armed crusade during his famous mission to the sultan at Damietta in 1219. A contemporary account by Thomas of Celano states that 'the holy man [Francis] therefore arose and approached the Christians [crusaders] with salutary warnings, forbidding the war, denouncing the reason for it'. However Celano goes on to explain that Francis had foretold the crusaders' defeat at Damietta, claiming that 'The Lord has showed me that if the battle takes place on such a day, it will not go well with the Christians.'[73] Less ambiguously, the English Franciscan Roger Bacon condemned utterly the waging of war against non-believers, on the grounds that those of them who were killed by definition would not have been converted and would go to hell, while those who survived would only become more embittered against Christianity.[74]

The clearest evidence for opposition to the Crusades in the late thirteenth century, for a variety of reasons ranging from a preference for staying at home (with one's lady-love) to a principled belief that the Christian should not shed blood, comes in the memorandum of Humbert of Romans, the senior Dominican who passionately supported the crusade and sought to demolish the arguments of its opponents. Humbert cited in detail eight 'hindrances' to the crusade, and seven types of men who objected to it: first in the latter list were those who believed that the Crusades were not compatible with Christianity. Among other objectors were those who declared that they would defend themselves if the Saracens invaded but otherwise preferred to leave them alone. (This was short-sighted, Humbert argued, for if the Christians did not attack the enemy in the East they would eventually have to face him in the West—an argument which has been heard more recently by defenders of the US-led war in Afghanistan.)[75]

Throop's work only deals with the late thirteenth century: a more recent study by John Derksen suggests that objections in principle to the Crusades appear as early as 1130, although 'their arguments survive only in the words of crusade apologists.... it seems that pacifists insisted that other ways could be found to prevent Muslims from oppressing Christians, that killing them was worse than letting their iniquity spread, and that soldiers who killed to defend the faith were no different from those who killed for profane reasons'.[76] The subject remains controversial, and another modern scholar (Elizabeth Siberry) maintains that 'In the Central Middle Ages most critics were concerned with abuses or with particular aspects of the crusading movement, rather than with the concept itself.'[77] However, writing more broadly about attitudes to pacifism in medieval Europe, Keith Haines concludes that while the medieval period was turbulent, brutal, and bellicose, 'there were those who found the taking of human life to be objectionable and sinful, and who openly and outrightly refused to fight, even in defence of their own towns and possessions. They clung strictly and tenaciously to the pacifist ideal; theirs was a passive plea, yet a distinct one, for peace and Christian brotherhood.'[78]

4

The Humanist Approach

Erasmus and Shakespeare

Would it not be best, oh noble soldiers,
Not to commit such a dreadful heap of crimes,
But to lay down your weapons and live well at home,
With your faithful and lovely wife in your arms,
To see your little children playing at her breast,
And clinging to your neck with their baby hands,
Ruffling your beard and tugging at your locks,
Calling you papa with a thousand little games?
Better surely than to live in camp and sleep on the ground,
Suffering from the summer heat and the winter cold,
Better to die old surrounded by your family
Than to find your tomb in the stomach of a dog.

(Pierre Ronsard, *Exhortation pour la paix*, 1558)[1]

War/Mars in person has burst out of the Temple of Janus, in the *Consequences of War* (or *Horrors of War*) by Rubens (1637–8) (Plate 8). Peace/Venus, with streaming hair and desperate gaze, seeks to restrain him, but he is urged forward with puckish excitement by the Fury Alekto. Amid a swirl of war-clouds lurk the two monsters of Pestilence and Famine. Behind the figure of Peace, with despairing upraised arms, is another female figure, whom Rubens described in a letter to the patron who commissioned the painting: 'That grief-stricken woman clothed in black, with torn veil, robbed of all her jewels and other adornments, is the unfortunate Europe, who for so many years now has suffered plunder, outrage and misery, which are so injurious to everyone that it is unnecessary to go into detail.'[2] Rubens was referring to the destruction and death (much of it caused by

Pestilence and Famine) of what would become known as the Thirty Years War (1618–48).

Yet Rubens had produced a very different allegory of Peace and War less than ten years before—his *Minerva Protects Pax from Mars* (1629–30) (Plate 7). Here too Peace is a Venus-like figure, shown not in despair but as maternally serene, feeding at her breast the young child Ploutos, god of wealth. A helmeted Minerva, goddess of wisdom, protects Peace/Venus from Mars, behind whom the Fury Alekto is retreating in defeat. Among a host of symbols indicating the joys of peace, two young girls are led forward to gather fruits from a cornucopia proffered by a kindly satyr. (Charmingly, they were modelled on the children of Rubens's host in London at the time.) Rubens had been acting as an unpaid diplomat, using his contacts with kings and ministers to promote reconciliation between Spain and England. In 1629, he was sent to London, where he painted this picture, and helped to bring about the Anglo-Spanish Treaty signed in the following year. Even in the midst of the worst war to affect Europe so far, peace was striven for and at times achieved.[3]

These two contrasting paintings by Rubens are a reminder that throughout the Renaissance, in philosophy and politics as well as art, there was a discourse of peace alongside that of war, which is often overlooked. In this chapter, I shall examine the peace advocacy of Erasmus, the great humanist of the early sixteenth century, and his fellow humanists, in contrast to the war advocacy of Machiavelli, before moving to the end of the century to reflect on Shakespeare's complex attitude to war and peace.

Erasmus: the peace pioneer

> Although the writers of antiquity divided the whole theory of state government into two sections, war and peace, the first and most important objective is the instruction of the prince in the matter of ruling wisely during times of peace, in which he should strive his utmost to preclude any future need for the science of war.
>
> (Erasmus, 'Arts of Peace', 1516)[4]

'Few people now read Erasmus; he has become for the world in general a somewhat vague name,' wrote the Oxford classical scholar J. W. Mackail a century ago. 'Only by some effort of the historical imagination is it possible for those who are not professed scholars and students to realize the enormous force which he was at a critical period in the history of civilization.'[5] Today this great humanist scholar and theologian of the Renaissance—one of the most eloquent advocates of peace in the history of the modern world—remains poorly known or understood outside academic circles. Writing at the same time as Machiavelli, Erasmus (1466–1536) addressed the problems of princely power and the resort to force from the diametrically opposite perspective. Admired for his intellect and his integrity, Erasmus was invited to the courts of kings and popes—he received handwritten invitations from Henry VIII and François I—and his numerous works circulated throughout Europe in the relatively new form of printed books. 'No man laboured so arduously to bring learning abreast of technology,' his biographer Ronald Bainton has written. 'His incense was the odour of printer's ink.'[6] Apart from his writings on theology and education, his essays and letters, and extensive notes on language and idioms, those on matters of peace and war amount to nearly 400 pages in modern translation.[7] Yet academic bookshops today, while ensuring that they keep in stock one or more editions of Machiavelli's *Art of War* (1521), are very unlikely to have a copy of Erasmus' *Education of a Christian Prince* (1516) which contains his reflections on the 'Arts of Peace', nor his full-length essay on the same subject, the *Complaint of Peace* (1517). Only one work by Erasmus is likely to be found: *The Praise of Folly* (1510), a *jeu d'esprit* which he wrote to amuse his friend and fellow humanist Thomas More, which has been published in the Penguin Classics series.[8] And while the adjective 'Machiavellian' has become a familiar term applied to political philosophy and strategy, 'Erasmian' is rarely used except with reference to ancient Greek pronunciation (a topic on which his work is still relevant today).

Erasmus has been dismissed by the war historian Michael Howard as the first of a long line of humanitarian thinkers for whom, Howard claims, 'it was enough to chronicle the horrors of war in order to condemn it' and who 'provide little constructive advice as to how to deal with the phenomenon which they find so abhorrent to nature and reason'.[9] Even a sympathetic biographer, Johan Huizinga, observed in connection with Erasmus' writings on peace that he had 'a wholly non-political mind... and thought too naively of the corrigibility of mankind'.[10] Peter van den Dungen, a leading Erasmian scholar today, provides a more balanced view. While Erasmus' works were largely moral appeals and exhortations to the Christian rulers of his day, they were not devoid of political insights and practical suggestions. Erasmus 'frequently made clear the connections between the internal structure of a state and its external behaviour', and he also recommended arbitration as an alternative to war, both of which features anticipated the peace projects of Immanuel Kant and the Enlightenment (see below, Chapter 5). We may also see him as preparing the ground for the seventeenth-century Dutch jurist Hugo Grotius who laid the foundations of international law, and who greatly admired Erasmus.[11]

Erasmus was the most eloquent as well as the most prolific of a group of Renaissance humanists who, in the early sixteenth century, sought to convince the rulers of the emerging European nation-state system that the interests of potentate and populace alike were best served by peace, not war, and who for a short while believed that their arguments might prevail. The optimism of Erasmus, of Sir Thomas More, of John Colet and of Juan Luis Vives, was not entirely unfounded. Though Europe had been racked by wars throughout the fifteenth century, there was a comparative lull in warfare in the early sixteenth century. The force of the Inquisition had waned as the heresies which it pursued had been suppressed or gone underground: the bitter conflicts and new religious wars of the Reformation still lay ahead. In England the Wars of the Roses had come to an end with the accession of Henry VII, whose peace policies were at first confirmed by Henry VIII. Continental warfare was relatively small-scale and professional diplomats negotiated with their counterparts seeking to conclude peace in a more lasting form.

Erasmus and his fellow humanists of the Renaissance wrote in an intellectual climate stimulated by the rediscovery of the classical world, and particularly the world of Roman history and literature, through texts which were being circulated by means of the new art of printing. They looked back to a Golden Age of peace through the works of Cicero and the Roman Stoics, including particularly those of Plutarch and Seneca. 'We are mad, not only individually, but nationally,' Seneca had written with a passion which Erasmus would echo: 'We check manslaughter and isolated murders; but what of war and the much-vaunted crime of slaughtering whole peoples? There are no limits to our greed, none to our cruelty. ... Deeds that would be punished by loss of life when committed in secret, are praised by us because uniformed generals have carried them out.'[12] The humanists, however, also invested Rome itself with some of the characteristics whose loss had been lamented by the Stoics, taking what may seem an unduly rosy view of the *pax romana*. As Robert Adams (author of the definitive study of the Erasmian age) has observed, ancient Rome, glittering through its ruins, seemed to present 'an age of universal peace, almost the only season of widely extended freedom from war which civilized mankind had ever known in recorded history'.[13] Cicero's views on war expressed in his *De Officiis* may be regarded today as providing 'an ethic of empire', in approving of war to the death against the barbarians and indeed in justifying on these grounds the destruction of Carthage.[14] Erasmus attached more weight to those passages of Cicero which cast doubt on military heroics and condemned wars fought for empty glory. 'Cruelty can never be of advantage,' Cicero had also written (referring to an atrocity committed by the Athenians against the people of Aegina), 'seeing how inimical this is to nature, with which our actions have to be in harmony.'[15]

The humanists were also exploring new limits in the world of ideas at a time when new frontiers in the living world were being discovered across the seas in the Renaissance voyages of exploration. It was not by chance that Thomas More, in his famous essay *Utopia* (1516), claimed that the traveller who describes the island of this name was a sailor who had accompanied Amerigo Vespucci on three of his voyages.[16] More's perspective on war and peace in this work is complex, and our understanding of it is further complicated by the satire and irony which pervades this work. The essence of it has been summarized by Adams: 'The Utopians, when war is unavoidable, employ it to protect or to enhance, first, the good life in the island, second, Utopian justice and the rights of common humanity as opposed to the interests of tyrants and their equally criminal supporters abroad.'[17] Yet because they regard the art of war—like the art of hunting—as cruel and perverse, they will not engage in it themselves, when it is unavoidable, but employ mercenaries to do the deed. If these professional soldiers should be killed, that is no loss to humanity, but if they survive, then they will be richly rewarded. The Utopians will also use their wealth to purchase the assassination of enemy leaders (by definition tyrants), and thereby will save further bloodshed. On the face of it, this is not a very pacific approach, but the key to understanding More's approach to war is that his Utopia is not a blueprint for the perfect society but a fanciful escape from the very imperfect one in which he lives, sketching an alternative society which could not possibly exist. We may find an artistic analogy in Hieronymus Bosch's *Garden of Earthly Delights* (1480–90), from more or less the same period (Bosch died in the year that More's *Utopia* was published). The artist presents the world both as earthly paradise, with a wealth of charming but fantastical imagery, and as a hell in which gamblers are nailed to the playing table and sinners are crucified on a giant harp or lute.[18]

We may also refer to Sandro Botticelli's *Mystical Nativity* (*c.*1500), which conveys, through a very idiosyncratic depiction of the birth of Jesus, the idea of the arrival of peace at the end of the world (under the influence, it has been suggested, of the apocalyptic Florentine preacher Girolamo Savonarola). Here, hell has been vanquished and angels and mortals alike bear the olive branch, symbol of peace, while a few devils lie on the ground, bound to poles.[19] The iconography of peace was also enlarged at about the same time by Giovanni Bellini in his depiction of *Orpheus Charming the Animals* (1513), and the harmonious coexistence of beasts of prey with their former victims would became a familiar image—contrasting with the realities of contemporary war—over the next century.[20]

However idealized their view of the past, the humanists had some grounds for hopes of peace in the present age, and their voices were at times influential. According to Adams, the English humanists were in the unusual position of being listened to by those rather then merely talking to themselves. Erasmus' *Complaint of Peace* would appear over the next dozen years in twenty-four editions including translations into French, German, and Spanish.[21] Colet preached two sermons in 1512–13 in the presence of Henry VIII, counselling against war with France, and arguing that an unjust peace was preferable to a just war.[22] The alliance of 1513 between England, Aragon, and the emperor was followed by the Peace of Paris two years later, by the Treaties of Noyon (1516) and London (1518). The humanists' hopes rose and fell in a rapidly changing international scene: the high point came in 1518 when Cardinal Wolsey appeared to have secured in the Treaty of London 'a basis for universal peace not only between England and France but among all the European powers'.[23] The ground was now set for the Treaty of Universal Peace (1520) concluded at the famous encounter between Henry VIII of England and François I of France on the Field of the Cloth of Gold.

The power of Erasmus' anti-war rhetoric may be illustrated in the following two passages of his *Antipolemus* (*Against War*) (1507)—an essay which would provide much of the material for his better known *Bellum* (*War*) (1513–15, itself an extended entry in his immense collection of *Adages*).

[On war] Now then view, with the eyes of your imagination, savage troops of men, horrible in their very visages and voices; men, clad in steel, drawn up on every side in battle array, armed with weapons, frightful in their crash and their very glitter; mark the horrid murmur of the confused multitude, their threatening eye-balls, the harsh jarring din of drums and clarions, the terrific sound of the trumpet, the thunder of the cannon, a noise not less formidable than the real thunder of heaven, and more hurtful; a mad shout like that of the shrieks of bedlamites, a furious onset, a cruel butchering of each other!—See the slaughtered and the slaughtering!—heaps of dead bodies, fields flowing with blood, rivers reddened with human gore!—It sometimes happens that a brother falls by the hand of a brother, a kinsman upon his nearest kindred, a friend upon his friend, who, while both are actuated by this fit of insanity, plunges the sword into the heart of one by whom he was never offended, not even by a word of his mouth!—So deep is the tragedy, that the bosom shudders even at the feeble description of it, and the hand of humanity drops the pencil while it paints the scene.
[On peace] Now amidst all the good this world affords, what is more delightful to the heart of man, what more beneficial to society, than love and amity? Nothing, surely. ... Peace is, indeed, at once the mother and the nurse of all that is good for man: War, on a sudden, and at one stroke, overwhelms, extinguishes, abolishes, whatever is cheerful, whatever is happy and beautiful, and pours a foul torrent of disasters on the life of mortals. Peace shines upon human affairs like the vernal sun. The fields are cultivated, the gardens bloom, the cattle are fed upon a thousand hills, new buildings arise, ancient edifices are repaired, riches flow, pleasures smile, laws retain their vigour, the discipline of the police prevails, religion glows with ardour, justice bears sway, humanity and charity increase, arts and manufactures feel the genial warmth of encouragement, the gains of the poor are more plentiful, the opulence of the rich displays itself with additional splendour, liberal studies flourish, the young are well educated, the old enjoy their ease, marriages are happy, good men thrive, and the bad are kept under control.[24]

The *Bellum* (confusingly often described as 'Erasmus against War') was followed by his *Complaint of Peace*, in which the personified figure of Peace insists that there is a feasible alternative to war, appealing to the rational self-interest and Christian conscience of both the rulers and the ruled. Erasmus had reached the age of 50 when he wrote the *Bellum*, but the essential lines of his argument for peace had been developed when he was still in his twenties, in an *Oration of Peace and Discord* which, though unpublished at the time, prefigures his later work. 'The fields of our land are rich with harvests, the meadows with cattle, the nearby sea with fish, and affluence abounds. Why does this not suffice us? Tears start as one views the calamities of our time,' he had written then, concluding with an appeal for concord to replace discord: 'The one builds cities, the other demolishes.'[25]

The Education of a Christian Prince (1516) was written at the suggestion of Jean Le Sauvage, chancellor of Brabant, after Erasmus had been appointed counsellor to the young Prince Charles of Castile, ruler of the Netherlands and soon to become Holy Roman Emperor. Erasmus seized the chance: at the age of 16 Charles might still be receptive to instruction in the moral qualities befitting a prince who will one day be king, those of 'wisdom, justice, moderation, foresight, and zeal for the public welfare', and he should become the sort of person who 'loves .peace, tries to arrange peace, and holds steadily to it'. The *Education* sets out a comprehensive programme of such qualities, particularly in its third section ('The Arts of Peace') and its final section ('On Starting War') which I paraphrase below:

'The Arts of Peace'
- The prince's first and most important objective is to 'strive his utmost to preclude any future need for the science of war'.
- He should regard his people as he would his family, and regard their welfare as dearer than his own life.
- He should have good advisers who are themselves approved of by the people.
- He should ideally be born and raised among his own people, but if he does come from outside should take pains to learn their ways.
- He should ensure that the people are governed by just laws, and that the youth are well educated.

'On Starting War' (which might better be entitled 'On Not Starting War').
- The effects of war are so damaging that the wise prince will 'sometimes prefer to lose a thing [by not fighting] than to gain it [through war]'.
- War is unchristian even when it is legitimized as a Just War: why should we attach more attention to St Augustine's approval—'in one or two places'—of war, than to the disapproval of Jesus Christ?

- War is too often the means by which princes and nobles stir up hostilities on trumped-up grounds so as to 'reduce still more the power of the people'.

- Even war against the infidels—the Turks—should not be rashly undertaken: the faith is spread not by force of arms but by the example of martyrs. Let us only attack the Turks once we are sure that we are genuine Christians (here Erasmus' argument tilts against even this kind of war).

Erasmus returned to the subject a year later in his best-known work of peaceful advocacy: *The Complaint of Peace* (1517). The personified figure of Peace complains that while she is praised both by men and gods she is rejected by them in their actions, and she elaborates the Erasmian case for peace in its fullest version, appealing both on rational and Christian grounds. The essay has been described as 'a direct effort to induce men to see a crucial truth—that they were the victims of the tyranny of unsound ideas and corrupt men, and that practical alternatives did indeed exist'.[26] It was an eloquent restatement of Erasmus' previous arguments, but with significant elaboration. Erasmus conceded that war might be necessary for the purpose of self-defence 'against barbarian hordes, or to defend the commonwealth, at risk of life and limb, against unprovoked attack'. But he also expanded his view that it is worth making sacrifices for peace to include—at least two centuries ahead of his time—the concept of arbitration:

There are laws, there are scholars, venerable abbots, reverend bishops, by whose prudent counsel the matter can be composed. Why not try these arbiters, who can hardly create more problems and are likely to cause many fewer than if recourse were had to the battlefield? Hardly any peace is so bad that it isn't preferable to the most justifiable war.[27]

Juan Luis Vives

Erasmus' fellow humanist the Catalan philosopher and social theorist Juan Luis Vives (1493–1540) also advocated peaceful conciliation as the means of settling disputes between Europe's warring princes, risking his own safety to do so. After Erasmus, Vives was one of the most widely read authors in the sixteenth century, and during his lifetime more than one hundred editions of his works were published.[28] Invited to England in 1523 to act as tutor to the Princess Mary, he was given a readership at Corpus Christi College, Oxford, recently founded by Bishop Fox of Winchester and already a centre of humanistic thought. In the following year he wrote his essay *De Consultatione* which argued for compromise based on mutual self-interest as the best way of resolving differences. In March 1525 he sent a memorandum directly to Henry VIII, urging Henry to make a magnanimous peace with the French king (François I) and with the French people—who were not to blame for their king's reckless behaviour.[29] Vives argued that war disturbed what we would now call the international community—then, the known European world—and that peace should be the common aim. 'My anxiety is great', he wrote to Henry, 'in seeing the Christian world divided by dissensions and wars, and it seems that a perturbation cannot be caused in any part of the world without affecting all the rest.'[30]

In a second letter, he warned the king that peace was almost always preferable in the end to war: 'How many have repented of starting a war even under the most auspicious circumstances! And how nobody has regretted peace though secured at a cost!'[31] Instead Henry, and his chief counsellor Cardinal Wolsey, tempted by the vision of regaining England's old possessions in France, planned a new war in alliance with the Holy Roman Emperor Charles V. A year later, after a wave of popular opposition to taxes for a new war, the plan had metamorphosed into the contrary intrigue of seeking an Anglo-French alliance against Charles. In both cases, humanist criticism was not welcome: Vives was deprived of his readership and had to return to his home in Bruges. Vives would develop his thoughts on cooperation between the European powers in his long essay *De Concordia et Discordia in Humano Genere*, which he dedicated hopefully to Charles. Concord or harmony, he argued, was both natural and essential to human progress, whereas discord/war was destructive, materially and spiritually, of all that made life worthwhile. Vives's proposal for promoting European concord has been described as a precursor of the concept of the League of Nations.[32] Even if the damage done by the recent wars could be remedied, he told Charles in his dedicatory preface, there would be no lasting improvement without a new spirit of 'Peace and Concord' between the princes.

We see the fields destroyed and devastated, the buildings toppled, some towns levelled to the ground and others empty and abandoned, provisions in scarce supply and at the highest of prices, studies interrupted and almost abandoned, social behaviour completely degenerated, the capacity of justice so corrupted that crimes receive the approval due to good deeds....Yet even if [these features of society] can be revalued and restored exactly to the level from which they have fallen, they certainly will not remain there for any length of time if they are not protected and supported by Peace and Concord, since they were brought down by dissension not only between the Princes but between individuals, and will be brought down again as often as dissension breaks out between them.[33]

Erasmus and Machiavelli

Erasmus and Niccolò Machiavelli (1469–1527) reflected opposite facets of this unstable time of transition from the feudal and theocratic Middle Ages to a Europe which prefigures the modern age of competing states. The Erasmian case for a humanist peace could take some comfort from the repeated though short-lived peace initiatives of the time. There were many disappointments and Erasmus had few illusions, but he, and especially Thomas More, saw their role as that of peace missionaries at the courts of princes.[34] Machiavelli, on the other hand, while growing up with a humanist education, began his career as a Florentine diplomat at a time when Italy was becoming the focus of foreign contention, and Florence and the other city-states lost their republican freedom amid bloody conflict. This period, known as that of the 'Wars of Italy', is seen to have begun in 1494 with the French invasion leading to the conquest of Naples: it is variously calculated as lasting for thirty-six—or sixty-five—years. 'Peace and war, war and peace, | These two rule the world today,' wrote an anonymous poet of this age.[35] Machiavelli's ten years' diplomatic service ended with the capitulation of Florence, which had taken the French side, to the forces of the Holy League between Pope Julius (known as the 'Warrior Pope') and Spain. He then survived imprisonment to offer his advice to the new Medici rulers of Florence in *The Prince* (1513). 'In this mathematically clear text-book of the ruthless exercise of power and conquest in the realm of politics,' writes Stefan Zweig in his biography of Erasmus, 'we find the counterpoise to Erasmus's teaching plainly set forth and formulated as if in a catechism.'[36]

Machiavelli's famous essay stands in direct opposition both as moral and practical advice to Erasmus' *Education of a Christian Prince*. Good laws and good armies, Machiavelli argued, were the principal foundation of all states—but good armies were the more important. Cruelty, not mercy, commanded respect and, in the much-quoted phrase, 'it is much safer for a prince to be feared than loved'. Although war was to prevail over peace, the ideas of both Machiavelli and Erasmus should be ranked on the same level for their significance and influence on future thought. While the realpolitik of Machiavelli would influence authoritarian statesmen up to Bismarck and beyond—to the huge detriment of European peace—the humane outlook of Erasmus, based on practical as well as moral argument, would inspire Locke, Voltaire, and other thinkers of the Enlightenment. The dialectical struggle between these two opposed views of humanity and its significance for peace remains alive to this day.

Shakespeare on peace and war

> ... in the temple of great Jupiter
> Our peace we'll ratify; seal it with feasts.
> Set on there! Never was a war did cease,
> Ere bloody hands were wash'd, with such a peace.
> (*Cymbeline*, Act 5, Scene 5)

War and peace, between states, kings, nobles, and the people, are woven into the fabric—the comedies aside—of the Shakespearian dramatic canon. The two words are among the most frequent significant nouns to appear in his works (even after allowing for the use of 'peace' as an exhortation). Foreign wars and civil conflict, and the various attempts to kindle, exploit, or resolve them, are central themes in the two sets of historical plays (*Richard II, 1* and *2 Henry IV, Henry V*; and *1–3 Henry VI, Richard III*), which came relatively early in his writing career (they have been staged more than once under the generic title 'Wars of the Roses'). The most famous war in literature is the Trojan War which dominates *Troilus and Cressida* from first to last line. Acts of war bring the plots of *Julius Caesar, Macbeth, Timon of Athens*, and *Coriolanus* to their dramatic conclusions. Shakespeare concludes his own writing life, and his last three plays, in a more mellow mood of peace: the last word of *Cymbeline*, the last speech of *Henry VIII*, and the peaceful resolution of life's storms in *The Tempest*.

The scholar Paul Jorgensen, writing in 1953 on Shakespeare's varying approaches to war and peace, expressed surprise that 'this distinction has been almost ignored in the main body of Shakespearean criticism'. More attention has been paid in recent years to the way that Renaissance thinking on war and peace is reflected in Shakespeare's plays, but it remains true, as Jorgensen pointed out, that much of this critical work centres on a single play, *Henry V*.[37] Even less work has been done on the evolution of Shakespeare's own thinking: the peaceful conclusion of *The Tempest* is usually treated in personal terms as signalling the playwright's more mellow mood as he reached retirement.[38] On the stage, there is a tendency to treat his plays as capable of infinite interpretation, and as mirrors held up to reflect the present age. In a study of the treatment of Shakespeare's history plays up to the mid-twentieth century, Harold Jenkins observed that for Victorian Britain, in the age of industrial and imperialist expansion, 'the most obvious thing about Shakespeare's history plays was their expression of a national spirit. Together they formed an "immortal epic" of which England was the true protagonist.' Again, a popular account of Shakespeare published during the Second World War—*The Olive and the Sword* (1944) by the well-known critic G. Wilson Knight—has been described as 'less a study of the histories than an exploitation of them to provide a "gospel" for Britain at war'.[39] The contrast has often been noted between Laurence Olivier's film of *Henry V* (1944), which struck a positive and patriotic note during the dark days of the war, and Kenneth Branagh's more equivocal approach in his film of 1989 (see further below, pp. 116–19).[40] *Troilus and Cressida*, with its overwhelmingly cynical approach to war, was almost forgotten for three centuries, but has become 'one of the great reclaimed plays of the last [twentieth] century' which now seems 'suited to our sorry, dangerous times', as theatre-goers to a 2006 production by the Royal Shakespeare Company were told in their programme notes.[41]

Although the humanist ideals of Erasmus were in retreat after the religious conflicts of the earlier sixteenth century, Queen Elizabeth began her rule in 1558 seeking and proclaiming a middle way between the extremes of Protestantism and Catholicism—which also conveyed a balanced approach to the merits of war and peace. Her purpose was clearly expressed in the opening speech to her first parliament in January 1559 by Nicholas Bacon, Lord Keeper of the Privy Seal, proclaiming the goal of a united, prosperous, and peaceful England. Twelve years later, on 2 April 1571, Bacon again delivered the queen's speech on her behalf, looking back on a largely peaceful decade. The first benefit to the nation of Elizabeth's accession, he loyally declared, was the restoration of 'God's holy [i.e. Protestant] Word'; the second was 'the inestimable benefit of Peace'—the peace which England now enjoyed while its European neighbours were still immersed in war (the three 'long wars'—civil war in France, the seven years Baltic War, and the Spanish conflict in the Netherlands).

...what is Peace? is it not the richest and most wished for Ornament that pertains to any publick Weal? Is not Peace the mark and end that all good Governments direct their actions unto? Nay, is there any benefit, be it never so great, that a man may take the whole Commodity of, without the benefit of Peace? Is there any so little Commodity, but through Peace a man may have the full fruition of it? By this we generally and joyfully possess all; and without this generally and joyfully we possess nothing. A man that would sufficiently consider all the Commodities of Peace, ought to call to remembrance all the miseries of War; for in reason it seems as great a benefit in being delivered of the one, as in the possessing of the other. Yet if there were nothing, the common and lamentable Calamities and Miseries of our Neighbours round about us, for want of Peace, may give us to understand what blessedness we be in that possess it.[42]

Elizabeth, though no pacifist, was cautious by temperament and necessity, and her essentially defensive foreign policy kept Protestant England out of major conflict with the Catholic powers of Europe. War with Spain was postponed for more than twenty years till she felt obliged to intervene in the Netherlands to counter the ambitions of Philip II. She still sought to counter the risk of invasion by diplomacy: the negotiations failed, but so in 1588 did the Spanish Armada. After a bad beginning with the abortive occupation of Le Havre in 1562, she would take care to stay on reasonable terms, amounting at times to a defensive alliance, with France. However, Elizabeth's policy of war avoidance was essentially pragmatic (and driven partly by concern over the expense of war). The arguments of war and peace parties were in contention at her court, and those of war often spoke louder. Ancient wars and warlike virtues were celebrated in literature and plays; sermons and tracts warned against the dangers of letting down the island nation's military guard. In England as elsewhere in Europe, the climate of opinion in the late sixteenth century favoured the Machiavellian view of statecraft. 'Machiavel' in person utters the prologue to Christopher Marlowe's *Jew of Malta*: 'Might first made kings', he declares, 'and laws were then most sure when... they were writ in blood.'

Shakespeare reflects both sides of the argument in the plays of his early and middle periods, yet although these contain many bloody episodes of war, it is never a subject for glorification or praise. War is 'all-abhorred' (*1 Henry IV*) and 'cruel' (*Troilus* and *Coriolanus*), it is 'none-sparing' (*All's Well*) and 'mortal-staring' (*Richard III*), it is 'dreadful' (*3 Henry VI*), 'fierce and bloody' (*King John*), 'mad-brained' (*Timon*), and 'hungry' for men's blood (*Richard III*); it is a 'hideous god' which has a 'harsh and boist'rous tongue' (*2 Henry IV*).

Some scholars have made much of Shakespeare's references to the stock militarist views of the time, but none is conveyed in such a way as to demand our agreement. In the most significant example, from *Henry V*, Shakespeare acknowledges the prevailing doctrine of Just War—the obligation for a would-be belligerent to ascertain that his cause is just. But when the king seeks the advice of the archbishop of Canterbury as to whether he has just cause to go to war with France, we already know that the Church wishes to encourage him to do so—in order to divert his attention from taxing them at home. In *Richard III*, the future Henry VII appears vindicated by results when, preparing for the Battle of Bosworth which will overthrow Richard III, he proclaims that 'God and our good cause fight upon our side'. However, Richard II similarly claimed that 'heaven still guards the right', and proved to be mistaken. In his perceptive study of Shakespeare's views on war and peace, Theodor Meron has concluded that 'whether Shakespeare actually believed that fighting a just war increases the probability of victory is unclear. He did know that each party would claim to have God and justice on its side, and that some of those who invoke God and justice would lose, like Richard II.'[43]

Other references to prevailing war doctrine are less substantial: there is a single mention in *Coriolanus* of war's role to reduce the 'musty superfluity' of population. In *2 Henry IV* war is described as a political device to divert attention from domestic issues—to 'busy giddy minds with foreign quarrels'. The chivalric concept of war as a kind of medicine, needed from time to time to correct the excesses of a society at peace, appears in the same play: 'fearful war' will 'diet rank minds, sick of happiness'. In *Macbeth*, war is prescribed as a 'purge' for the sickness affecting the country—but they were after all exceptional times. The doctrine that war and peace form a recurring cycle occurs in *Timon of Athens*: 'Make war breed peace, make peace stint war, make each prescribe to other, as each other's leech,' but the idea that peace will 'stint' war—rather than in its turn 'breed' it—weakens the argument.

Another stock theme of Elizabethan 'alarmist' literature was that too much peace renders a society ill prepared for war, and in *Troilus and*

Cressida Hector seems to agree with this, observing that 'The wound of peace is surety, | Surety secure.' However he immediately goes on to argue that Helen is not worth a single death and should be surrendered to the Greeks! In *Henry V* the French dauphin observes that 'Peace should not so dull a kingdom' that its defences are not properly 'maintain'd, assembled and collected'—but he fails to take his own advice to prepare against the English threat. Shakespeare's strongest statement of the case for war as social therapy is put so cynically as to negate its value, in a passage of dark humour from *Coriolanus*. The servants of the Volscian leader Tullus Aufidius have just learned that Coriolanus, the Roman war hero, has defected to their side after being driven out of Rome by a plot, and they now look forward to Coriolanus joining in a war of revenge against his own people.

SECOND SERVINGMAN: Why, then we shall have a stirring world again. This peace is nothing, but to rust iron, increase tailors, and breed ballad-makers.

FIRST SERVINGMAN: Let me have war, say I; it exceeds peace as far as day does night; it's spritely, waking, audible, and full of vent. Peace is a very apoplexy, lethargy; mulled, deaf, sleepy, insensible; a getter of more bastard children than war's a destroyer of men.

SECOND SERVINGMAN: 'Tis so: and as war, in some sort, may be said to be a ravisher, so it cannot be denied but peace is a great maker of cuckolds.

FIRST SERVINGMAN: Ay, and it makes men hate one another.

THIRD SERVINGMAN: Reason; because they then less need one another. The wars for my money. I hope to see Romans as cheap as Volscians.

This coarse and satirical view of the superiority of war to peace (which has something in common with that of the Sinister Spirit in Thomas Hardy's *The Dynasts*—see above p. 16) can hardly be counted as serious argument. In the same way, the most pejorative description of peace anywhere in Shakespeare's works is provided by the arch-villain Richard III in his opening soliloquy. While others, more favoured in physique, may enjoy the 'merry meetings', the 'delightful measures', and 'caper[ing] nimbly in a lady's chamber', he, duke of York, takes no delight in 'this weak piping time of peace'.

There are passages in Shakespeare's plays which celebrate the heroic face of war and the heroic (though bloody) deeds of warriors, though they are less frequent than might be expected in a body of work which contains so many wars. Kings (even a queen), Romans and Goths, princes, nobles, and the spirits of leaders past are approved of as 'warlike'. Coriolanus himself, before being driven out of Rome, is praised extravagantly for his successful slaughter of the enemy: in battle after battle, we are told, he was 'a thing of blood, whose every motion was timed with dying cries'. In *1 Henry IV* the valiant Harry Hotspur is roused to jealousy by the description of his rival Henry Prince of Wales (the future Henry V) as leaping from the ground like a 'feather'd Mercury' to mount his steed and bewitch the world 'with noble horsemanship'. And yet, the most vivid word picture ever painted by Shakespeare of 'glorious war'—and the only time that he uses the phrase—comes from *Othello* at the tragic turning point of the plot, when Othello is convinced (falsely) by Iago that he has been betrayed by Desdemona.

> I had been happy, if the general camp,
> Pioners and all, had tasted her sweet body,
> So I had nothing known. O, now, for ever
> Farewell the tranquil mind! farewell content!
> Farewell the plumed troop, and the big wars,
> That make ambition virtue! O, farewell!
> Farewell the neighing steed, and the shrill trump,
> The spirit-stirring drum, the ear-piercing fife,
> The royal banner, and all quality,
> Pride, pomp and circumstance of glorious war!
> And, O you mortal engines, whose rude throats
> The immortal Jove's dead clamours counterfeit,
> Farewell! Othello's occupation's gone!

This is hardly an untroubled hymn to war, but the desperate cry of a man whose mind is already gripped by delusion—horribly conveyed in the notion that Desdemona might be capable of sleeping with his entire army. The grandiloquent images of this speech should be seen rather as a flight of nostalgia for the supposed simplicities of martial life which may be no more real than the phantoms bred by Othello's jealousy. When this speech is understood in its proper context, the title of *Pomp and Circumstance* which Elgar chose from it for his set of military marches looks wildly inappropriate. (Elgar's uncomplicated mood of Edwardian optimism was better expressed in the patriotic poem 'The March of Glory' by Baron de Tabley which he inscribed as a motto on his original score.)

While the noble aspects of war are depicted ambiguously by Shakespeare, its futility and horrors are set out without equivocation in several passages. The most extended and elaborate, though not the most subtle, occurs in *3 Henry VI*, where the king, having withdrawn to a peaceful corner of the battlefield, observes a son lamenting that he has killed his father. Immediately afterwards, he sees a father making the same dreadful discovery that he has killed his son. What a 'miserable age', the father exclaims, and how 'unnatural' the result of this 'deadly quarrel'. In a soliloquy Henry muses on the attraction, for a king beset as he is by dissent, of a peaceful life—here personified in his imagination by a shepherd's tranquil existence.:

> Ah, what a life were this! how sweet! how lovely!
> Gives not the hawthorn-bush a sweeter shade
> To shepherds looking on their silly sheep,
> Than doth a rich embroider'd canopy
> To kings that fear their subjects' treachery?

The starkest statement of the futility of war is found in *Hamlet*, when the prince, wrestling with his own lack of resolution to avenge his father's death, encounters the Norwegian army marching to engage with the Poles over some trivial border dispute. As a captain in the army explains to him, the disputed territory is 'a little patch of ground | That hath in it no profit but the name', not even worth the effort to cultivate. Hamlet reflects:

> How stand I then,
> That have a father kill'd, a mother stain'd,
> Excitements of my reason and my blood,
> And let all sleep, while to my shame I see
> The imminent death of twenty thousand men
> That for a fantasy and trick of fame
> Go to their graves like beds, fight for a plot
> Whereon the numbers cannot try the cause,
> Which is not tomb enough and continent
> To hide the slain?

Two problem plays

We come now to two plays with war as central to the plot, *Henry V* and *Troilus and Cressida*, both written by Shakespeare in mid-career and within two or three years of each other, yet presenting the subject in sharply contrasting ways. The militaristic ring of *Henry V* (although capable of more than one interpretation) is far removed from the deep and unremitting cynicism towards war sustained throughout *Troilus*. Yet *Henry V* still deserves to be regarded, almost as much as *Troilus*, as a 'problem play' which is characterized by moral ambiguity.[44]

Henry V

The address of King Henry to his troops at the storming of Harfleur— 'once more into the breach, dear friends'—and his tribute to 'we happy few, we band of brothers' before the Battle of Agincourt have become part of the mythology of war in its most heroic, patriotic, and self-sacrificial guise, and continue to be invoked at times of British national crisis. The critic J. Dover Wilson, in an edition published soon after the Second World War, drew an explicit parallel between the 'few' of Henry's speech and Churchill's famous epitaph to the 'few' of the Battle of Britain to whom so much was owed. Both came, Dover Wilson said, from the same 'national mint'.[45] Soon after the 1991 Gulf War had resulted in overwhelming victory for President George Bush, *Forbes* magazine published a celebratory article headlined 'Miracle in the Desert'. To understand 'the full miraculous measure of the US victory in the Gulf', readers were told, 'you have to go back and read Shakespeare's *Henry V*'.[46] More recently, an address to British soldiers in the Royal Irish battle-group by Colonel Tim Collins, on the eve of battle in the 2003 Iraq War, was hailed in the British press as the embodiment of Henry V. Five years later Kenneth Branagh, the actor-director of the 1989 film of the play, would act the part of Colonel Collins in a BBC Television docudrama on the war—broadcast on the anniversary of his speech.

Of all Shakespeare's plays *Henry V* has war most central to its theme and offers the fullest account of it: 'its causes, the ritual of embassies and ultimata, the mobilising and the strategy, the discipline, heroism, and horror', as the editor of the Penguin Shakespeare edition of the play has described it.[47] It is also the only play through which Shakespeare's attitude to war has been analysed extensively over nearly two centuries of conflicting argument. At one end of the critical spectrum, *Henry V* has been seen as a play of epic spirit, telling the story of an ideal and heroic war which, when it was performed, resonated for its audience with England's recent victory over the Spanish Armada. The words of Shakespeare and his historical sources, wrote J. H. Walter, editor of the Arden Shakespeare, may be English but they convey 'the note of epic heroism that sounded at Thermopylae and in a pass by Roncesvalles'.[48] Shakespeare in this view was faithfully reflecting, and approving, the 'Tudor myth' that the civil wars of the fifteenth century had been resolved by the glorious reign of the Tudor dynasty, culminating in Henry V as hero in a patriotic war against England's traditional enemy. A play with such a message, it is argued, staged with the memory of the defeat of the Armada still fresh, would naturally please an audience living under the rule of Elizabeth I, last of the Tudors. And for the same reason, it was inconceivable that Shakespeare should seek, even indirectly, to denigrate Henry or his war. True, the blessings of peace are invoked eloquently in the final scene of the play by the duke of Burgundy who asks the kings of both England and France

> Why that the naked, poor and mangled Peace,
> Dear nurse of arts, plenties, and joyful births,
> Should not in this best garden of the world,
> Our fertile France, put up her lovely visage?

But it is a peace on English terms, achieved as the result of an English victory, against an enemy who had refused Henry's call to capitulate peacefully and had paid the price for it. Henry's offer, in this view, conformed exactly to the Elizabethan preference for peace but determination to go to war, if necessary, in a just cause.[49]

This uncomplicated view of Henry V was questioned early on by the essayist William Hazlitt, in his study of Shakespeare's characters published in 1817, for whom the king 'seemed to have no idea of any rule of right or wrong, but brute force, glossed over with a little religious hypocrisy and archiepiscopal advice [as to the just nature of the war]'. Because Henry's own title to the crown was doubtful, 'he laid claim to that of France'. Henry is an appealing character, Hazlitt acknowledged, but it is the appeal of 'a panther or a young lion in their cages in the Tower', and we can enjoy his boastful and patriotic speeches all the more because 'no blood follows the stroke that wounds our ears....no dead men's bodies are found piled on heaps and festering the next morning—in the orchestra!'[50] This sterner judgement on Henry has been echoed by several modern commentators. 'Many critics have seen the play as a celebratory epic that uncomplicatedly praises Henry as the perfect warrior-king,' notes one recent editor, 'But the play is darker and more ambiguous than that.'[51] In a new age of wars, it is harder for both audience and directors to see King Harry in quite such a heroic light as before.

The question posed by two English Shakespearian scholars—'[Was] Henry V [a] war criminal?'—is intentionally provocative but makes a serious case based on one of several problematic episodes in the play.[52] Briefly, when the fight at Agincourt is almost won, Henry comes on stage with his escort and (according to the original stage directions) 'with prisoners'. Seeing that the French have reinforced their 'scattered men', he gives the order 'that every soldier kill his prisoners', and prepares for further battle. Meanwhile—although Henry at this stage is unaware of this—the retreating French have passed through the English baggage-park and killed the unarmed attendants there. When Henry discovers this in the next scene, he declares his anger and his intention to 'cut the throats of those we have'. As Dr Johnson observed, Henry is so enraged that 'having cut his prisoners' throats once he orders that they shall be cut again'.

The execution of innocent prisoners was, according to the chronicler Holinshed whom Shakespeare followed closely, a historical fact. Holinshed gives a vivid account of the 'pitiful' scene when 'some Frenchmen were suddenly sticked with daggers, some were brained with pollaxes, some slaine with malls, other had their throats cut, and some their bellies panched'. The sequence of events in Shakespeare's version remains unclear. Perhaps we should not examine the text too rigorously for consistency but recognize that it is based upon 'protean scripts' that might be performed differently in separate performances.[53] Yet the whole episode is sufficiently worrying for some productions to omit altogether Henry's first order to kill the prisoners. Both Olivier and Branagh dodged the issue in their films by omitting any reference to prisoners being killed, whether before or after the deaths of the English baggage followers.

The question remains to be asked: was Shakespeare using this episode to distance himself from the heroic image of war, and did he intend his audience to do likewise, or were such incidents regarded as normal and therefore not detracting from Henry's martial glory? Or did Shakespeare, as suggested by the American scholar Norman Rabkin, never settle on a single viewpoint towards war, but intend to leave an insoluble doubt in the audience's mind? The ultimate power of the play, wrote Rabkin, is precisely 'the fact that it points in two opposite directions, virtually daring us to choose one of the two opposed interpretations it requires of us'.[54] Henry's insistence that he must have proof that this is a just cause before going to war is subverted by the self-serving and devious justification provided by the archbishop of Canterbury. His concern for the welfare of the non-combatant citizens of Harfleur, when the city has surrendered, comes after he has threatened to let loose his soldiers to rape, pillage, and slaughter innocent children. The heroic tone of Henry's speeches and the play's choruses contrasts with the bombastic talk and cowardly behaviour of Henry's former friends from the Eastcheap tavern. When the king explores his own lines in disguise, in the early dawn before the Battle of Agincourt, he finds soldiers who are willing to fight but remain sceptical about his own outward display of courage. (They may have their throats cut, says one, but the king if captured will consent to be ransomed.) And behind the chivalric tone of Henry's courtship of the French princess lies a harsher note of compulsion when he demands a kiss against 'the nice fashion of your country'.

Troilus and Cressida

The underlying philosophy of *Troilus and Cressida*, a love story set in the midst of the Trojan War (although largely invented by Boccaccio and other medieval authors), is so unremittingly cynical that it might illustrate the adage that 'all is fair in love and war'—a sentiment already common, in one form or another, in Elizabethan times. Before the action has begun, war is described by the actor delivering the prologue to be as fickle as the audience's approval:

> Like, or find fault: do as your pleasures are;
> Now good, or bad, 'tis but the chance of war.

Cressida, daughter of the Trojan priest Calchas, and Troilus, one of the sons of Trojan King Priam, fall in love, with her uncle Pandarus as a bawdy go-between. After they have enjoyed one night of passion, Cressida is sent to the Greek camp (to which her father has defected) in exchange for a captured Trojan prince. On her first night of captivity, observed without her knowledge by Troilus, she transfers her affections to the Greek commander Diomedes. The battle which is joined the next day is confused and inconclusive: Troilus fights furiously for revenge, slaying many Greeks, and remains alive—but those in the audience familiar with the story know that he will soon die. His brother, the great Trojan warrior Hector, chivalrously spares the life of Achilles after the Greek has lost his weapons, but our respect for Hector's chivalry is quickly undermined: he pursues another Greek warrior solely to acquire his fine armour. Exhausted after stripping the dead man, he takes off his own armour and is surprised by the return of Achilles with his Myrmidons. Rejecting Hector's plea for a reciprocal act of chivalry, Achilles commands his men to strike him down. Troilus, doubly enraged by Cressida's betrayal and Hector's death, vows to continue fighting but predicts the destruction of Troy.

Disease of one kind or another, relating both to love and to war, is a recurring metaphor in the play. When Hector strips the dead Greek of his armour he discovers that the man's body had—contrary to nature—already decomposed—a warning of his own imminent death. On the Greek side, the cowardly Thersites has matched Pandarus in providing his own cynical commentary on events. Earlier in the play, as the Greek commanders are seeking to persuade Achilles to return to the fight, Thersites mocks the argument with another image of decay: 'Now the dry serpigo [a creeping skin disease] on the subject, and war and lechery confound all!' The play itself ends with a venomous closing speech from Pandarus: apparently dying from syphilis, he wishes his illness upon the audience—who, he suggests, is composed of prostitutes and fellow panders!

What should we make of *Troilus and Cressida*, with its deliberately anti-heroic narrative and bitter conclusion, and what did its audiences make of it? They may have had little chance: the foreword ('Epistle') to the second Quarto edition implies that it had not yet played in a public theatre (though it was probably performed at an Inn of Court), and there is no record of it being staged subsequently for nearly three centuries, until it was revived in 1907. Steven Marx in a study of Shakespearian pacifism describes *Troilus* as a counter-companion piece to *Henry V*: 'Instead of glorifying, it condemns war and those who make it. In the earlier play, Shakespeare counters pacifist objections to war with militarist rationales; here, he counters militarist rationales with pacifist objections.'[55] In contrast to the long discussion by the king and his councillors in *Henry V* over the legitimacy of Henry's claim to France, the Trojan council's deliberation—can war be justified in defence of the abduction of Helen?—is perfunctory and contradictory. Concluding the debate, Hector insists that the Trojans should hand her back to the Greeks—then reverses his position on the grounds that Trojan honour is at stake:

> If Helen then be wife to Sparta's king,
> As it is known she is, these moral laws
> Of nature and of nations speak aloud

> To have her back return'd: thus to persist
> In doing wrong extenuates not wrong,
> But makes it much more heavy. Hector's opinion
> Is this in way of truth; yet ne'ertheless,
> My spritely brethren, I propend to you
> In resolution to keep Helen still,
> For 'tis a cause that hath no mean dependence
> Upon our joint and several dignities.

Troilus may have been completed in 1603, the year in which the unwarlike James I succeeded Elizabeth. From now on, Shakespeare's treatment of war becomes increasingly critical: his martial tragedies of the later period (*Othello*, *Macbeth*, *Antony and Cleopatra*, and *Coriolanus*) all have as their subject a general of great military prowess whose character is fatally flawed—by jealousy, ambition, sexual weakness, or pride. In *Cymbeline* (also classed as a tragedy although it has a romantic theme and ending), war has assumed a negative character. It is the loutish and lecherous Cloten who calls for war to the death against the invading Romans. Instead the British king Cymbeline resolves to end the war, although victorious in it, and to resume payment of tribute to the Roman empire in the interests of harmony and peace. In its resolution both of personal and political conflict, *Cymbeline* may be seen—the Arden Shakespeare editor of the play suggests—as 'a vision of perfect tranquillity, a partial comprehension of that Peace which passeth all understanding'.[56]

Some scholars have argued that the pro-peace orientation of the later Shakespeare was merely in deference to Jacobean pacifism, and that it was only natural that Shakespeare 'should have paid tactful heed to one of his sovereign's most deeply felt convictions'.[57] While Shakespeare clearly gauged the royal and public mood throughout his career, this is to reduce him to a mere sounding board, and to ignore the progression of his own thought. In his final plays, *The Tempest* (1611) and— possibly written jointly with another playwright—*Henry VIII* (1613), Shakespeare has arrived at a compassionate outlook on life in keeping both with the irenic tone of Jacobean rule and with his personal transition from the turbulence of the earlier plays to a more pacific and mellow view. *The Tempest* concludes with Prospero's emergence as merciful ruler of his domain, pardoning those who have wronged him, and promising them 'calm seas, auspicious gales' to convey them home. The epilogue which he addresses to the audience ('Now my charms are all o'erthrown...') has often been interpreted as a personal metaphor for

Shakespeare's own retirement from the theatre, although some critics take a more restrictive view.[58] Scholarly opinion is even more divided on the subject of *Henry VIII* which, it has been suggested, Shakespeare came out of retirement to write—perhaps because he quickly tired of life in Stratford-on-Avon![59] The majority view that the play was written jointly with John Fletcher is disputed by R. A. Foakes, the Arden Shakespeare editor: the reason which points most strongly to the Shakespearian unity of the play, he argues, is 'the similarity in compassionate tone and outlook between *Henry VIII* and the other late plays'.[60] The play ends on a note which is both pacific and valedictory, with the king-figure no longer a warrior as in *Henry IV* or *V*, but a peacemaker: 'Rather than busying giddy minds with foreign quarrels, this Henry is committed to peace in international relations'— the same goal which Erasmus and his fellow humanists believed for a time that Henry VIII would deliver.[61] It concludes with Archbishop Cranmer's prediction of the golden age to come under Elizabeth and her successor.

> In her days every man shall eat in safety,
> Under his own vine, what he plants; and sing
> The merry songs of peace to all his neighbours:
> God shall be truly known; and those about her
> From her shall read the perfect ways of honour,
> And by those claim their greatness, not by blood.

The speech has been criticized as over-effusive, and it was certainly intended as a compliment to James I at whose court it was probably performed. Yet we may still note that the blessings of peace were the theme of what might be described as Shakespeare's last speech.[62]

5

The Growth of Peace Consciousness

From the Enlightenment to The Hague

When glory leads the way, you'll be madly rushing on,
Never thinking if they kill you that my happiness is gone.
If you win the day perhaps, a general you'll be;
Though I'm proud to think of that, what will become of me!
Oh, if I were Queen of France—or, still better, Pope of Rome,
I would have no fighting men abroad—no weeping maids at home.
All the world should be at peace, or if kings must show their might,
Why, let them who make the quarrel be the only men to fight.

('Jeannette's Song', *c.*1848)[1]

Justice and Peace, accompanied by charming cherubs, recline on a billowing cloud in elegant embrace; the vestiges of past war are symbolized by a dead youth sprawled in the foreground, a broken pillar, and a sword. A cornucopia of fruit overflows at the feet of Peace; the lion lies down with the lamb, and other cherubs gather the fruits of harvest. *The Allegory of Justice and Peace* (1753; Plate 9) by Corrado Giaquinto is in high baroque style, suffused with warm shades of gold, green, pink, and melon; the dove of peace emerges from the last clouds of war as they are dissipated by the sun's rays. Giaquinto, who had just taken up his position as first painter at the Spanish royal court, presented in this allegory the virtues of Fernando (Ferdinand) VI, portrayed in the literature of the time as a just and peaceful king who avoided war and preferred conciliation.[2] This was not so far from the truth: the Spanish peace followed a series of disastrous wars fought by previous Bourbon rulers. Fernando would pursue a policy of strict neutrality in the conflict about to break

out between France and Britain (the Seven Years War, 1756–63), rejecting offers from both sides to support them in the war—a policy reversed
by his successor Charles III, who allied Spain with France.

The Seven Years War was a major conflict involving the European
powers and their colonies to the extent that it is often referred to as
the first 'global war'. Over a million deaths were caused by it either
through direct combat or through subsequent famine and other
upheavals—roughly a half of these consisting of civilians. It came
midway through the eighteenth century, during the transition from
relatively small-scale dynastic warfare to conflicts between nations
with a much heavier impact on their peoples.[3] It was a time of imperial expansion and of accelerating change in military technology and
organization: the main European powers established standing armies,
staffed by a professional officer corps and maintained by substantial
peacetime expenditure, resulting in wars that had a greater impact on
non-combatant populations, and paving the way for the even more
substantial military revolution ushered in by the Napoleonic Wars. War
in the eighteenth century was 'central to the history of the period and
to the experience of its peoples', in a tangled web of conflicts between
shifting alliances which began at the start of the century with the War
of the Spanish Succession.[4] Formed in the name of securing the balance of power, such alliances were inherently unstable, trust and good
faith were in short supply, and the advantages of going to war were
often baffling. As the poet Robert Southey would write, looking back
from the end of the century on the Battle of Blenheim (1704)—one of
the first major battles in the conflict over the Spanish Succession—

> 'It was the English,' Kaspar cried,
> 'Who put the French to rout;
> But what they fought each other for,
> I could not well make out;
> But everybody said,' quoth he,
> 'That 'twas a famous victory.'
>   ('The Battle of Blenheim', 1798)

As war became more of a profession, the number of those with a vested
interest in making war grew and those rulers who, like Fernando VI,
sought to stay neutral were vulnerable to criticism. Their dilemma was
eloquently described in the entry for 'Peace' in the first great intellectual project of the Enlightenment, Diderot's *Encyclopédie*, written while
Fernando was on his throne.

The sovereign has need of unalterable firmness, and an invincible love of order and the public good, to resist the clamour of those warriors who surround him. Their tumultuous voice constantly stifles the cry of the nation whose sole interest lies in tranquillity. The partisans of war have no shortage of pretexts with which to stir up disorder and make their own self-interested wishes known: 'it is through war', they claim, 'that the state affirms itself... a nation grows soft and degrades itself through peace. Its glory requires it to take part in the quarrels of its neighbours; only the feeble will abstain.' Tricked by these specious reasons, rulers are forced to yield: they sacrifice to fear, and to a chimerical view, the peace, the blood and the treasure of their subjects.[5]

Peace and the Enlightenment

Free-minded thinkers in the age of Enlightenment identified clearly the threat posed by the shifting alliances of nations led by wilful rulers and grappled to devise systems of law and regulation. Their efforts constituted the first steps towards serious thinking on an international approach to the limitation of war and began a critique of narrow state interest. The peace theorists of the Enlightenment did not work in isolation: their thinking was linked by a loose but coherent thread, referring back to earlier advocacy from Erasmus (whose works enjoyed a revival) onwards. Among their forerunners the French monk Émeric Crucé (1590–1648) stands out: in the *Nouveau Cynée* he proposed a permanent Council of Ambassadors to resolve disputes between states, to be located in Venice. In a stroke of internationalism far ahead of its time, Crucé said that it should include not only the European states but 'the Emperor of the Turks, the Jews, the Kings of Persia and China, the Grand Duke of Moscovy (Russia) and monarchs from India and Africa', insisting that 'the distance of places, the separation of domicile does not lessen the relationship of blood. It cannot either take away the similarity of nature, true base of amity and human society.'[6]

The Quaker scholar and founder of Pennsylvania William Penn (1644–1718) also made a significant contribution to early ideas on peace organization in his *Essay Towards the Present and Future Peace of Europe* (1693), in which he set out a more detailed structure for the pan-European council vaguely sketched by Crucé. Penn took as his starting point a different plan for 'perpetual peace' known as the Grand Design, attributed to Henri IV of France (1589–1610) but actually drawn up by his finance minister the duc de Sully. Described by Penn as a European 'Diet, Parliament, or Estates', this structure amounted to a permanent international tribunal, in which the European countries were represented by delegates in numbers corresponding to their economic power—thus 12 for Germany, 10 for France, 6 for England, and so on. Penn laid down the proportion of votes needed to secure a decision (75 per cent) to be cast in a secret ballot. Those states refusing to accept or implement decisions which had been properly reached would be subject to collective enforcement. Penn even anticipated modern conference procedure by setting out rules for the layout of the council chamber: 'to avoid quarrel for Precedency, the Room may be Round, and have divers Doors to come in and go out at, to prevent Exceptions [being taken].' Accurate records of the proceedings would be taken by clerks and then kept under lock and key so that there could be no dispute over what had been agreed. There should be a common language (Latin or French) and no one would be allowed to leave before the session was over. Finally, although this was to be a European assembly, it would be only 'fit and just' if the 'Turks and Muscovites' also took part—with ten delegates for each. Penn's essay began with the psychologically astute observation that the blessings of peace were, too often, only fully realized after the experience of war. It was as though 'we could not taste the benefit of health, but by the help of sickness'. If only the princes of Europe could see the benefit of one without the other, it would be to the advantage of all. And freed from the necessity to make matrimonial alliances for political advantage, he added later, those same princes would then be able to marry for love![7]

The French rationalist and early Enlightenment thinker the Abbé de Saint-Pierre (1658–1743) drew on the works of Sully, Penn, and probably Crucé for his own *Project for Perpetual Peace*, first published in 1712 (and more generally known through an abridged version of 1729). As secretary to one of the French negotiators at the peace negotiations in Utrecht which ended the War of the Spanish Succession, he saw at first hand the defects and impermanence of a treaty brought about merely through the exhaustion of the combatants. His *Project*, more detailed and extensive than those of his predecessors, set out his plan for a League of European States with a permanent Congress of Representatives, and a Senate with powers to arbitrate disputes and enforce its decisions if necessary by military sanctions, while all peacetime armies were to be reduced in size to no more than 6,000 personnel. An indefatigable writer with an eclectic mind, Saint-Pierre proposed a variety of other *projets* including the standardization of weights and measures, improvement of roads, suppression of duelling, and an end to priestly celibacy.[8]

Jean-Jacques Rousseau (1712–78) would edit Saint-Pierre's *Project*, adding a 'judgement' or commentary of his own which made some critical points. Saint-Pierre was mistaken, Rousseau said, in suggesting that the princes who made war would be attracted by the argument that peace was less costly. 'The degree of power they have in mind is not counted by the millions they possess. The prince always makes his schemes rotate: he wants to command to be rich, and to be rich to command.' Likewise the prince's ministers would not be easily swayed by rational argument against war, because '[they] need war to make themselves necessary, to put the prince in difficulties which he cannot get out of without them, to lose the state, if necessary, rather than their position'. The abbé's plan, Rousseau concluded, was as it stood 'too good to be adopted'. It would only work if the congress which he proposed was run by the citizens of the member states rather than by their rulers, since 'the former bore the costs of war while the latter reaped the glory'.[9] (Here we encounter, in an earlier form, the argument—still persuasive today—that ruling elites may have a vested interest in maintaining the mechanism and perceptions of war.)

The discourse of peace which began in the early Enlightenment, already influenced by previous humanist thought, reaches its peak with Immanuel Kant (1724–1804), whose essay on 'perpetual peace' has received more attention than its predecessors. Kant's plan for a League of Nations (he was the first to use the term), although conceived in a restricted sense, would have a practical influence on the Versailles negotiations a century later, and there has been a much more recent revival of interest in his work among proponents of 'democratic peace theory'. Kant was spurred to write his essay by the conclusion in March 1795 of the Treaty of Basel between Prussia and the First French Republic—yet another example of the divisions of spoils in the name of making peace (France acquired all territory west of the Rhine while acquiescing in Prussia's division of Poland). It was precisely the sort of treaty which Kant condemns, in the first section of his essay, as 'a suspension of hostilities but not peace': Prussia became France's ally against Britain in the subsequent war but changed sides again when the Third Coalition was formed against Napoleon in 1805.

Although treaties of this period were routinely described as 'definitive' and pledged both sides to 'peace for the future' or 'perfect harmony', the reality was very different, as Kant wryly noted in his preamble:

Whether this satirical inscription ['Perpetual Peace'] on a Dutch innkeeper's sign upon which a burial ground was painted had for its object mankind in general, or the rulers of states in particular, who are insatiable of war, or merely the philosophers who dream this sweet dream, it is not for us to decide.[10]

Kant begins his essay with a set of preliminary articles—amounting to aspirations or ideals that would govern the condition of real and lasting peace, invoked in vivid and compelling language. (a) No treaty is valid if a party to it secretly intends, once it has recovered its strength, to find a pretext for a new war by digging around in 'dusty documents'. (b) Rulers have no right either to dispose of their states or add to their territory over the heads of their people, nor should they supply troops as mercenaries so that their soldiers are 'manipulated at pleasure, are used and also used up'. (c) Standing armies should in time be totally abolished: they are often the cause of war since they incite states 'to compete with each other in the number of armed men'. (d) Wars should not be financed by increasing the national debt—an 'ingenious invention' which Kant attributes to 'a commercial people'—i.e. English. (e) No state should interfere by force with the constitution or government of another state, however reprehensible such may be. And (f) if war does take place, proper restraint should be observed in its conduct so that mutual confidence in an eventual peace is not destroyed in advance.

Kant then proceeds to define and elaborate on three 'definitive articles' for the establishment of perpetual peace between states. The first is that 'the civil constitution of every state should be republican'. As long as states are governed by despotic rulers, he argues, they are at liberty to go to war on a whim and leave their diplomats to justify it. Only under a republican form of government, where executive authority is separated from the legislative, and power is not monopolized either by individual or mass despotism, can peace be assured. The second definitive article is that 'the law of nations shall be founded on a federation of free states'. Here Kant begins to explore the relationship between individual states and the community of nations which in our current world, after six decades of the United Nations, is still incompletely defined.

What Kant has to say is challenging and not entirely clear: we can see his mind searching for the solution to a double paradox: first, that all states claim to be acting justly when they go to war, even invoking the support of international law, and second, that all states belong to a community of nations but will not accept the discipline which citizens are bound to accept within the community of a state. Kant proposes the establishment of

... a league of peace (*foedus pacificum*) ... which would be distinguished from a treaty of peace (*pactum pacis*) by the fact that the latter terminates only one war, while the former seeks to make an end of all wars forever. This league does not tend to any dominion over the power of the state but only to the maintenance and security of the freedom of the state itself and of other states in league with it, without there being any need for them to submit to civil laws and their compulsion, as men in a state of nature must submit.

Such a 'federation' of states (although, as the passage implies, it is not subject to any super-national authority) should 'lead to perpetual peace', Kant says hopefully, 'under the idea of the law of nations'. Kant then seems to undercut his own argument by pointing out that, under this presumed law, states are 'subject to no external judicial constraint', and may still destroy each other if they feel so inclined. The solution in theory is that states, like human beings, should 'give up their savage (lawless) freedom, adjust themselves to the constraints of public [i.e. international] law, and thus establish a continuously growing state consisting of various nations, which will ultimately include all the nations of the world'. However, this is not going to happen, and in place of such an ideal—a 'world republic'—we must settle for 'the negative surrogate of an alliance which averts war, endures, spreads, and holds back the stream of those hostile passions'. Not surprisingly, there has been much argument over Kant's meaning here, and it is unlikely that he was entirely clear in his own mind. However, he does perceive that the maintenance of world peace has to be a joint endeavour, and he does identify the lack of what we would now call 'enforcement' as a major problem.

The third definitive article of Kant's hypothetical treaty also antici-pates an issue which has become more evident in our modern glo-balized world: 'The law of world citizenship', he states, 'shall be limited to conditions of universal hospitality.' Originally, humans had no spe-cial right to occupy a particular part of the earth: today, those who inhabit the earth still have the right to travel on it freely. While it is no longer realistic for such a right to entitle one to permanent residence in another state, there is 'a right of temporary sojourn, a right to associate, which all men have'. This right may not be asserted by force or lead to unjust demands—here Kant presciently denounces the evils of emerging colonialism. 'The injustice which they [the supposedly civilized states of Europe] show to lands and peoples they visit (which is equivalent to conquering them) is carried by them to terrifying lengths.' The violation of human rights through the 'outrages' which have been committed—Kant mentions slavery, the promotion of internal wars, the spread of 'famine, rebellion, perfidy and the whole litany of evils which afflict mankind'—only illustrates the need for peaceful relations on equal terms which will bring the world closer to 'a constitution establishing world citizenship'. Opposition to colonialism, support for open borders, and the goal of world citizenship—Kant anticipated many modern concerns, and in his conclusion he even invoked the effect of what we would now call globalization:

Since the narrower or wider community of the peoples of the earth has developed so far that a violation of rights in one place is felt throughout the world, the idea of a law of world citizenship is no high-flown or exaggerated notion.

Kant's plan for perpetual peace is underpinned by a supplement setting out his view on the history of human development which deserves our equal attention. Kant is no idealist: he has already asserted that 'the state of peace among men living side by side is not the natural state: the natural state is one of war.' The paradox which he now explores at length is that war—whether against the environment, the animal world, or among themselves—has driven humanity forward to occupy the world. Internal war, or the threat of internal discord, has then forced settled peoples to formulate and abide by the laws of society and states. And humanity has now reached the stage where the danger of external war, and the desire for economic progress, will lead a world composed of independent but neighbouring states to formulate and abide by international law, which will in time lead to global harmony and agreement. Thus in a dialectical process which anticipates Darwin in the role it assigns to the force of 'nature', war will lead eventually to peace. At least we may reasonably hope this will be the case, for Kant concludes that peace is achievable but not inevitable.

In this manner nature guarantees perpetual peace by the mechanism of human passions. Certainly she does not do so with sufficient certainty for us to predict the future in any theoretical sense, but adequately from a practical point of view, making it our duty to work toward this end, which is not just a chimerical one.

Bertrand Russell praised Kant's *Perpetual Peace* for its display of the philosopher's 'vigour and freshness of mind in old age', but others expounding his work have not always taken the essay so seriously.[11] Kant's arguments are sometimes ignored altogether, or else he is accused of advocating an unrealizable utopia.[12] However, peace historians accurately describe Kant as 'amazingly prescient in identifying the fundamental political and economic conditions of peace', for making 'the first major effort to focus specifically on the dangers of armaments', and for his influence on all projects for international peace up to and including the UN.[13] We can today share both his commitment to the peace ideal and his realistic view that the forces driving humanity towards peace will only succeed if they are supported by our own considerable effort.

The birth of the peace societies

The period—almost exactly a century—from the end of the Napoleonic Wars to the outbreak of the Great War saw the birth and development of the modern peace movement in a story of high hopes alternating with deep disillusion. The effects of war, increasingly mechanized and bloody, were a powerful stimulus to voluntary organization and to imaginative proposals for peaceful alternatives. Such enterprises could even win the approval of kings, princes, and heads of states. Yet when these efforts failed and a new war broke out, the organization was seriously damaged, and the peace cause submerged by tides of patriotic and nationalist fervour. The perennial optimism of the peace enthusiasts was open to satire and ridicule. The caricaturist Honoré Daumier, in a set of cartoons mocking their high-flown sentiments, showed Victor Hugo addressing the 1849 Paris Peace Congress with a bridal wreath of roses on his over-sized head: Hugo had shown, according to Daumier's caption, 'the worthlessness of military glory and has proved by example that the crown of laurels can be replaced to advantage by the crown of roses'. Nevertheless, Hugo's speech predicted a time when Europe would be united and 'war will seem as absurd and impossible between Paris and London, between [St] Petersburg and Berlin, between Vienna and Turin, as it...would seem absurd today between Rouen and Amiens, between Boston and Philadelphia'. Today, in the world of the European Union linked to Russia with a partnership agreement, Hugo's forecast appears more prescient than naive— though it would take much longer to fulfil than he had predicted. As a whole, the nineteenth-century peace movement, though often over-idealistic and self-deceiving while subject to drastic ups and downs, represents a significant advance, which made peace the concern of millions rather than thousands and laid the basis for more tangible steps towards international peacekeeping in the following century.[14]

The idea that peace could be—and must be—achieved on a lasting and international basis became for the first time a widely accepted goal after the devastation of the Napoleonic Wars. In their own interests, the great powers who formed the Congress of Vienna sought to create a 'federating bond' to 'unite all the states collectively', appearing to legitimize the quest for peace. Among concerned citizens of their countries, a collective view began to emerge that peace was achievable and that organized pressure upon rulers and governments might help to achieve it. Noah Worcester, one of the founding fathers of the American peace movement, could credibly pose the question in his essay *The Custom of War* (1815) which became one of the most widely distributed works of early peace literature:

Isn't it possible to produce such a change in the state of society, and the views of Christian nations, that every ruler shall feel that his honour, safety, and happiness depend on his displaying a pacific spirit, and forbearing to engage in offensive wars? Can't peace societies be extended to every nation of Christendom, to support governments and make the nations safe from war?[15]

The London (later British) Peace Society and the American Peace Society were formed almost simultaneously but through independent initiatives: the movement was at first mainly Anglo-American and the first peace society on the European continent only emerged in 1830. Members of the societies came mostly from the liberal middle and upper classes which generated similar advocacy movements for free trade, social and political reform, and opposition to slavery and other forms of exploitation, and for philanthropic initiatives such as prison reform and temperance. The movement brought together

Christian evangelists, Quakers with a previous history of peace commitment, and secular humanitarians in seeking a more peaceful world. They were driven not only by considerations of morality and compassion, but increasingly by rational arguments as to the harmful socio-economic effects of war and military preparation. In an age of industrial revolution, liberal economists including Jean-Paul Say and utopian social reformers such as Charles Fourier and Henri de Saint-Simon looked forward to a new world order where economic cooperation would become a substitute for war. Geneva's long association with peace was begun by the Swiss philanthropist and pacifist Jean-Jacques de Sellon who campaigned against slavery and the death penalty and founded the Société de la Paix de Genève in 1830. Sellon argued that the warlike and monarchical spirit of the past was being replaced by 'a beneficial revolution of...industrialism and economics'. Savings on military expenditure would allow investment in public works, projects to relieve poverty, and other worthy causes including the restoration of crumbling churches, the establishment of chairs of political economy—and construction of what would later be known as the Suez Canal![16] (In the first recorded example of modern peace architecture, Sellon had a Temple of Friendship and Peace constructed on his country estate, with an obelisk also dedicated to peace.)

In 1843 the British society followed the example of the World Anti-Slavery Convention (1840) and held the first international peace congress (with a modest thirty-two foreign delegates out of a total of more than ten times that number). The British approach by this time was influenced by the free-trade thinking of Richard Cobden, whose crusade against the Corn Laws had already set the example for a successful campaign to win over political opinion. Although pacifists and Quakers still played an important role, the main thrust of argument emphasized the economic irrationality of war and the possibility of resolving disputes by peaceful means—in particular by international arbitration. In 1846 the American peace activist Elihu Burritt, known as the 'learned blacksmith', arrived in England as US consul in Birmingham, and encouraged the English movement to work for a new congress. (Burritt had been apprenticed as a blacksmith: he was self-educated in history and philosophy, and had mastered several languages.) Hopes of meeting in Paris in 1848 were frustrated by the revolution there and a congress, officially known as the First International Congress of the Friends of Peace, was held in Brussels. Its proceedings had a

strong flavour of free-trade economics and proposed the arbitration of
disputes in greater detail. With Henry Richard, the new secretary of
the British society, Burritt succeeded in holding the Second General
Peace Congress in Paris a year later, with full-scale European participation. With some 600 delegates, and with the republican French poet
and novelist Victor Hugo and the radical British politician Richard
Cobden among many eminent participants, it was the high point of
the peace movement's international strategy and would become 'a rich
source of peace-movement lore and legend in future decades'.[17] In his
opening address, Hugo made a prescient appeal for European unity,
and argued that modern progress would make war obsolete: their task
was to speed up the process.

How distances become less and less; and this rapid approach, what is it but
the commencement of fraternity? Thanks to railroads, Europe will soon be
no larger than France was in the middle ages. Thanks to steam-ships, we now
traverse the mighty ocean more easily than the Mediterranean was formerly
crossed. Before long, men will traverse the earth, as the gods of Homer did the
sky, in three paces! But yet a little time, and the electric wire of concord shall
encircle the globe and embrace the world.[18]

The conference resolutions included one proposed by Cobden, stating that 'the Congress condemns all loans and taxes intended for the
prosecution of wars of ambition and conquest'. (Daumier poked fun
at Cobden too, in a cartoon showing him having his shoes shone by
a general in uniform while another senior officer carried his luggage.
'Universal peace having been decreed,' read the caption, 'the honourable
Sir Cobden finds a practical use for generals who are out of a job.') The
delegates were given an official welcome in Paris, and treated to free
entry to all museums, a special display of the fountains at Versailles, and
an audience with the French president Louis Napoleon, to whom Hugo
presented a set of the conference resolutions. However, the president,
while concurring with the views of the congress on the need to reduce
military expenditure and rely on peaceful diplomacy, said that 'their execution must be deferred to some more seasonable opportunity'. Three
years later Louis Napoleon would seize power and proclaim himself
Emperor Napoleon III. Peace acquired a different meaning as he sought
to calm public apprehension by declaring 'L'Empire, c'est la paix.'
    Encouraged by the successful atmosphere of the Paris congress
and the abundant—though mixed—publicity which it attracted, the

international activists went on to organize conferences in Frankfurt
(1850) and London (1851) in what was intended to be a series of annual
events. However, pressures both internal—disagreement between those
who opposed all war and those who believed it was justified in certain
circumstances—and external—the challenge of war-threatening crises
and of actual new wars—were already beginning to be felt: plans for
an 1852 congress were scrapped and the initiative petered out with two
smaller congresses, both confined to British members, in Manchester
and Edinburgh in 1853.

At a time of revolutionary turmoil, when Italy had been swept by the
struggle for independence, there was support for the view as expressed
by one French delegate to the Paris congress that force was still necessary to defend national independence; that peace should be 'founded
on justice and liberty' (M. De Gueroult). The Frankfurt congress
adopted a resolution urging a 'system of international disarmament
without prejudice to such measures as may be considered necessary
for the maintenance of the security of their citizens'—a victory for the
internationalists, led by Cobden, over the pacifists.[19] There was a deep
gulf between the US and British peace campaigners, and the European
democrats 'who considered European peace as the last stage of national
liberation, inseparable from human rights and justice'.[20]

The London Peace Congress benefited from the generally pacific
and internationalist mood of the Great Exhibition with which it coin-
cided; it was extensively reported and enjoyed a mixed but on the whole
favourable press. Peace hopes rose to unprecedented heights, but it
proved to be 'the pinnacle of the nineteenth-century peace movement',
only to be followed by 'a decade and a half of adversity'.[21] In Britain,
the movement struggled to retain unity and even to survive against the
patriotic fervour for the Crimean War. The war was a classic proof of
the two basic principles which the peace advocates had insisted on: that
one almost always paid a higher price for war than for peace, and that
the failure to avoid war through intelligent compromise was likely to
lead to immense human suffering. The British foreign secretary, the earl
of Clarendon, regarded its prospect as a 'horrible calamity', while his
Russian counterpart Count Nesselrode predicted that it would be 'the
least justifiable war ever undertaken', and yet the two sides drifted into
a war which, once begun, stifled opposition.[22] In November 1854 the
London Peace Congress Committee decided that 'any attempt to hold
public meetings in the midst of the present warlike excitement would

be productive of more harm than good', although it still resolved to distribute tracts and placards against the war.[23] As Cobden observed, it was futile to 'set up our standard and begin preaching for peace while the bells are ringing for victory'.[24] At the Paris conference which ended the war, a peace deputation led by Cobden persuaded the delegates of the great powers to include in the treaty a protocol expressing the 'desire' for recourse to mediation in future disputes: it was a very modest victory for a movement in decline. In England the critics of Britain's aggressive posture in China (leading up to the Second Opium War) lost ground to its advocate Lord Palmerston in the 1857 general election: Cobden and his ally John Bright were both defeated. In America, where the issue of slavery was also beginning to weaken the unity of the peace movement, the Civil War had a similar paralysing effect. Although the American Peace Society urged a peaceful solution, once the war had broken out its official view was that 'our laws should be enforced against those [i.e. the secessionist South] who violate them'. This led to a split in the society, with Quakers and other non-resisters seceding to form the Universal Peace Union in 1866.[25]

The humanitarian impulse

By the mid-century, in spite of these setbacks, public opinion was beginning to respond more actively to a wide range of humanitarian issues, from working conditions and treatment of the poor to prison reform and women's rights. Improvements in modern communications, including the more rapid dispatch of news and the growing circulation of newspapers in more literate populations, also meant that the horrors of war could be more vividly and widely reported. One of the first tracts to be published (1818) by the London Peace Society was titled 'Sketches of the Horrors of War' and contained extracts from an account of Napoleon's campaign in Russia, written by the military engineer Eugène Labaume, with painful descriptions of the suffering of ordinary soldiers and camp followers during the winter retreat from Moscow, 'pale, emaciated, dying with hunger and cold'. Labaume also described the suffering of the Russian population as Moscow burned during the French retreat:

At that moment, about the dawn of day, I witnessed a spectacle, at once affecting and terrible, namely, a crowd of the miserable inhabitants drawing upon some mean vehicles all that they had been able to save from the conflagration. The soldiers, having robbed them of their horses, the men and women were slowly and painfully dragging along their little carts, some of which contained an infirm mother, others a paralytic old man, and others the miserable wrecks of half-consumed furniture. Children, half naked, followed these interesting groups...[26]

The Napoleonic Wars, by virtue of their military scale, geographical spread, and duration, dramatized the human cost of war. The Battle of Leipzig—the so-called Battle of Nations which led to Napoleon's abdication—involved the largest number of troops in any battle until the First World War: one in six of the 600,000 taking part were killed or wounded. A generation later, the war would be treated in a decidedly anti-heroic way in works such as Stendhal's *The Charterhouse of Parma* (1839) and Thackeray's *Vanity Fair* (1848). (Thackeray's earlier novel *Barry Lyndon* (1844) had already presented a picaresque view of the Seven Years War through the eyes of his eponymous anti-hero.) Stendhal was praised by Balzac for his treatment of the chaos at Waterloo and Tolstoy would acknowledge the novel's influence on his own account of the Battle of Borodino in *War and Peace*. A series of conflicts, beginning with the Crimean War (1853–6), and followed by the Franco-Austrian War (1859) and the Franco-Prussian War (1870–1), now had a greater impact, generating popular support for measures to alleviate the consequences of war and for the first steps towards an international humanitarian law.

The Crimean War is often described as the first modern war, observed by professional reporters whose dispatches reached the home country speedily and had a significant influence on public opinion. William Howard Russell of *The Times* witnessed all the main conflicts with the Russian defenders of Sebastopol during its siege by British, French, and Turkish troops. Russell's reports on the mismanagement, poor provision, and lack of adequate medical facilities for the British forces are credited with causing the public outrage which led to Florence Nightingale's mission to the front. Public opinion was aroused not only by the inadequacy of medical services in the Crimea but by the bungled conduct of the war, dramatized by the disastrous Charge of the Light Brigade which Russell observed at first hand. Tennyson's famous poem was being recited by soldiers at the front within weeks of its publication.[27] Thanks to telegraphy, events from a war in progress were now being reported soon after they occurred, linking the home and the battlefront to an extent impossible before. Initial popular enthusiasm for the war, which had led Lord Aberdeen's government into it against his own judgement, quickly turned into middle-class disenchantment and the government's fall in January 1855.

The key (12 and 13 October 1854) dispatches describing conditions on the hospital ships bringing the sick and wounded from Sebastopol to Scutari, and lack of medical equipment in the hospital there, were written by Thomas Cheney, another *Times* correspondent, but Russell provided the most extensive coverage of the war, later published in a thousand-page edition in two volumes under the terse title of *The War.* Russell's reports included a vivid description from Varna in August 1854 of a hospital overwhelmed by an epidemic of cholera (which together with dysentery killed more soldiers than actual combat): 'Men sent in there with fevers and other disorders were frequently attacked with the cholera in its worst form, and died with unusual rapidity, in spite of all that could be done to save them.' By January the epidemics had abated but the cold weather which reduced them wreaked its own havoc: soldiers exhausted by 'constant fatigue, inces-sant wet, insufficient food, want of clothing and of cover from the weather, now die away in their tents night after night, many of these men are too far gone to recover'. On 23 January Russell observed the sick being evacuated from their camps to Balaclava by mule litter or on horseback:

They formed one of the most ghastly processions that ever poet imagined. Many of these men were all but dead. With closed eyes, open mouths, and ghastly attenuated faces, they were borne along two and two, the thin stream of breath, visible in the frosty air, alone showing they were still alive. One figure was a horror—a corpse, stone dead, strapped upright in its seat, its legs hanging stiffly down, the eyes staring wide open, the teeth set on the pro-truding tongue, the head and body nodding with frightful mockery of life at each stride of the mule over the broken road. No doubt the man had died on his way down to the harbour. As the apparition passed, the only remarks the soldiers made were such as this,—'There's one poor fellow out of pain, any way!'[28]

Meanwhile on the other side of the siege lines, the 26-year-old Leo Tolstoy was observing the conflict as a staff officer: he had applied for a transfer from the Caucasus to the Crimean front to 'see the war'. Tolstoy reported back home not as a journalist but as a budding writer. The first of his three long sketches from Sebastopol, covering the period December 1854 to August 1855, was commented on favourably by Tsar Alexander II; but passages in his second and third instalments describing the blood and carnage of the siege were suppressed by the Russian censor as 'anti-patriotic'. Private letters and extracts of journals kept by soldiers at the front also circulated widely, criticizing senior officers for tactical blunders and lack of bravery. As the Crimean struggle dragged on, complaints grew of military incompetence and of the financial burden imposed by the war, and satires and denunciations in prose and verse circulated in hundreds of copies. In spite of censorship, public opinion in Russia too had an effect: as one newspaper commented, 'We have to thank the war for opening our eyes to the dark sides of our political and social organisation, and it is now our duty to profit by the lesson.'[29]

The Battle of Solferino (1859) between the French army under Napoleon III allied to the Sardinian army under Victor Emmanuel II, and the Austrian army under Franz Joseph I, marked a decisive stage in the struggle for Italian unification—and was the last battle in world history where the rival armies were directly commanded by their monarchs. It was also one of the most bloody conflicts of the nineteenth century, witnessed by chance by a Swiss businessman, Henri Dunant (who had come to the front to seek Napoleon's backing for an agribusiness project in Algeria). Out of 300,000 troops engaged in a fifteen-hour battle, about 40,000 were left dead or seriously wounded on the battlefield with little or no medical provision, and the final death toll would rise to 80,000. Dunant helped local civilians to organize help for the injured and also persuaded the victorious French to release some captured Austrian doctors. After returning to Geneva, he wrote *Un souvenir de Solferino* (1862) which described what he had witnessed in vivid terms.

Here is a hand-to-hand struggle in all its horror and frightfulness; Austrians and Allies trampling each other under foot, killing one another on piles of bleeding corpses, felling their enemies with their rifle butts, crushing skulls, ripping bellies open with sabre and bayonet. No quarter is given; it is a sheer butchery; a struggle between savage beasts, maddened with blood and fury. Even the wounded fight to the last gasp. When they have no weapon left, they seize their enemies by the throat and tear them with their teeth.[30]

After the battle the local villages were overwhelmed with casualties which filled their churches and chapels: the casualties lay on the bare flagstone floors so close together that they had no room to move. Dunant was particularly impressed by the commitment of the local people in the town of Castiglione to help whomever they could regardless of nationality: 'tutti fratelli' (they are all brothers), said the women as they brought water to the wounded and linen for bandages. Foreign spectators and tourists passing by were also enlisted as helpers. The improvised and voluntary nature of these efforts led Dunant to reflect, at the very end of his small book, on the need for a permanent organization to provide such aid. Significantly, he prefaced his proposal by expressing regrets that the dreams of the Abbé de Saint-Pierre and of the peace societies for permanent peace could not be realized and that 'new and terrible methods of destruction' were invented daily. 'Would it not be possible,' Dunant asked, 'in time of peace and quiet, to form relief societies for the purpose of having care given to the wounded in wartime by zealous, devoted and thoroughly qualified volunteers?' It would need proper organization, transport, and professional skills: the 'lovely girls and kind women' of Castiglione had only been able to bring temporary relief to those who were going to die.

Dunant and his friends set up the Geneva Society for Public Welfare and prepared to convene an international conference to translate his plan into reality. At his own expense, Dunant distributed copies of his book to heads of state and other prominent figures around Europe. At a second meeting held in August 1864, twelve states agreed to sign the First Geneva Convention for the Amelioration of the Condition of the Wounded and Sick in Armed Forces in the Field; thus laying the foundation for the International Committee of the Red Cross (the name which was adopted in 1876).

The Franco-Prussian War (1870–1) was the first test for the new movement. At the decisive Battle of Sedan, in one day's fighting, the French suffered over 17,000 casualties and the Prussians lost 2,320 killed and 5,980 wounded. Daumier's cartoons in the *Charivari* magazine provide a bitter commentary on the build-up to this unnecessary war and its terrible toll. In 1867, the year of the World Fair in Paris, Daumier produced his own proposal for the 'statue of Peace' to be exhibited there: it showed Peace, with pack and forage cap, sword and bayonet, standing on a plinth before a mounted cannon, while France, armed with chisel and mallet, finished the last details on a pile of cannon balls. In 1869 Peace plays at shuttlecock with War, using the head of Europe as the shuttle. After Napoleon III's disastrous defeat and capture at Sedan, Daumier sketches a scene of devastation, above the ironic title 'L'Empire c'est la paix.' Finally, in March 1871, in the most famous of Daumier's Peace cartoons—'La Paix: Idylle'—Peace is shown as an eviscerated skeleton, sitting on the battlefield and playing the double pipes (Plate 10).[31] Zola and his fellow writers have also left a devastatingly ironic picture of the war in their short stories first published in 1880 as *Les Soirées de Médan*. These include Guy de Maupassant's well-known 'Boule de suif', and Zola's 'L'Attaque du moulin'—which ends with a French officer crying 'Victoire! Victoire!' after a skirmish with the Prussians, while the miller's daughter mourns over the bodies of her father and her lover, both killed during the episode. Zola returned to the horrors of this war in *La Débâcle* (1892), the penultimate work in his series of novels about the life of a family in the Second Empire.

During the war, nineteen national Red Cross societies helped to alleviate the soldiers' suffering, including the British Red Cross, founded in response to a letter in *The Times* by Colonel Robert Loyd-Lindsay. Within two months, there were more than 100 British surgeons, nurses, and other workers in the field, cooperating with both the German and French relief societies. The first British volunteer died in October 1870. 'As the war is prolonged so its horrors increase,' said *The Times* in an editorial, noting how many wounded soldiers were 'left to perish of cold on the spot where they fell' (29 December 1870). As bystanders in the conflict, the British could more easily show compassion: the Red Cross Society observed that it was 'fortunate' that Britain had been neutral and that its forces had not been engaged: 'We were working in aid of foreign armies, and not with the weight of the responsibility of having an army of our own in the field' (*The Times*, 29 August 1871).

There was from the start an element of ambiguity in a humanitarian intervention which, if successful, restored soldiers to be able to fight again. Prussia was very much in favour of the Red Cross: the crown prince sent a letter expressing 'heart-felt gratitude' to the British society—the volunteers' efforts could be seen as helping to protect Prussia's investment in troops: the prominent American volunteer Clara Barton was even awarded the Iron Cross of Merit by the Prussian emperor for her efforts. When war broke out between Turkey and Serbia in August 1876, the argument was put with brutal logic in another letter to *The Times* entitled 'Philanthropy in War'. The effect would be, the writer argued, 'to prevent the lessening of the number of effective fighting men, and to leave them free at once for continuing the fight, and for killing and wounding another crop at the earliest possible moment' (19 August 1876).

The Hague Conference and beyond

The final decades of the nineteenth century saw the advance of the peace movement to an apparent triumph in 1899 at the Hague Peace Conference—inspired by no less a figure than the tsar of Russia—but it rapidly slumped to virtual non-existence with the outbreak of the First World War. While the Red Cross initiative led to the expanding definition—never attempted before—of international humanitarian law, the peace movement successfully placed what would now be called concepts of 'conflict resolution by other means than war' on the diplomatic agenda. By the end of the century there had emerged a shared vision of a liberal internationalism which might create 'a set of organisations which would provide international security without force of violence'.[32] Peace activists could claim a share of credit for dozens of bilateral treaties and agreements between states with provisions for the peaceful arbitration of disputes. Plans for obligatory arbitration on a wider international scale, and for the creation of a real international judiciary, began to be discussed. Though optimism was already fading by the time of the second Hague Peace Conference in 1907, the peace societies had sown the seeds for a society of nations which, after the war, would germinate into the League of Nations. Overall, these were significant gains.

A second stage in the peace society movement began in the late 1860s with the formation of the Ligue Internationale et Permanente de la Paix (LPP) in Paris (1867) and in the same year the Ligue Internationale de la Paix et de la Liberté (LPL) in Geneva. As in the 1850s, the issue of national liberation divided the movement. The LPP, led by Frederic Passy, later to win the Nobel Peace Prize, took the moderate view that if only military spending were curbed and there were no more wars, then society could begin to be transformed for the better. The LPL took the opposite view, supported by Victor Hugo, that national liberation and democracy were the prerequisites for ending war and oppression.[33] (Its opening congress was presided over by Garibaldi—who left it still in progress to return to Italy and launch his attack against the papacy in Rome.) The European peace movement was brought once more to a halt by conflict, with the outbreak of the Franco-Prussian War (1870–1). In an illustration of the movement's weakness, a plan by activists in Paris to send a peace appeal to the German

soldiers surrounding the city was blocked by the French commander.[34]
In the United States too, the peace movement was checked and divided
by the Civil War. Yet in the longer term, the outcome of these wars, and
the growing rivalry between the imperial powers which promised more
wars, would lead to a new revival of peace advocacy in the 1880s and
'90s which almost amounted to a world peace movement.

The campaign to promote international arbitration as the way to
settle disputes by peaceful means rather than by war was boosted by
a provision in the 1871 Treaty of Washington between Great Britain
and the United States in which a contentious issue (the 'Alabama dispute') was referred to an arbitration committee in Geneva. In Britain
Henry Richard, secretary of the Peace Society and a Liberal MP, scored
a notable victory by proposing a parliamentary motion in favour of
arbitration, and winning an unexpected majority. Europe's military
expenditure had doubled in the past thirty years, argued Richard, and
there was no reason why it should not do so again:

Is the combined statesmanship of Europe equal to nothing better, as international policy, than playing on a more and more gigantic scale this miserable
game of 'beggar my neighbour,' by which they exhaust their resources, embar-
rass their finances, and oppress their peoples, while they leave themselves at
the end of the process comparatively and proportionally just where they were
at the beginning? While spending so much of time, thought, skill, and money
in organizing war, is it not worth while to bestow some forethought and care
in trying to organize peace, by making some provision beforehand for solving
by peaceable means those difficulties and complications that arise to disturb
the relations of States, instead of leaving them to the excited passions and
hazardous accidents of the moment? (*Hansard*, 8 July 1873)

Prime Minister William Gladstone praised the motion—but asked
the House of Commons to reject it: Richard's cause was admirable
but they must be 'content to proceed step by step'. Instead, it was
passed by ten votes, and the initiative was followed in the legislatures
of Italy, Belgium, Sweden, Denmark, Holland, the USA, and Canada,
beginning a process of cooperation leading eventually to the first
Inter-Parliamentary Conference (IPC), held in Paris in 1889, which
announced the peaceful resolution of differences by arbitration as its
main aim.[35] The first Universal Peace Congress (UPC), also held in
Paris in the same year, revived something of the spirit of the earlier
Peace Congresses of 1848–51. Some one hundred peace societies were
registered at the International Peace Bureau, set up in Berne by the

UPC. Both organizations would now meet annually while the national societies became more vocal, and it seemed as if peace advocacy was at last becoming 'universalized'.[36]

One day in August 1898, during a particularly troubled period of international diplomacy, the Russian foreign minister Count Mikhail Muraviev sprang a surprise on the foreign ambassadors in St Petersburg as they gathered in his office for a regular weekly meeting. He handed each one in turn a paper from his desk signed by him on behalf of Tsar Nicholas II. It began in splendid style:

The maintenance of universal peace and a possible reduction of the excessive armaments which weigh upon all nations represent, in the present conditions of affairs all over the world, the ideal towards which the efforts of all Governments should be directed. This view fully corresponds with the humane and magnanimous intentions of His Majesty the Emperor, my august Master.

and concluded with the most worthy of aspirations:

...the constant danger involved in this accumulation of war material renders the armed peace of to-day a crushing burden more and more difficult for the nations to bear. It consequently seems evident that if this situation be prolonged, it will inevitably lead to that very disaster which it is desired to avoid, and the horrors of which make every humane mind shudder by anticipation. It is the supreme duty, therefore, at the present moment of all States to put some limit to these unceasing armaments, and to find means of averting the calamities which threaten the whole world.

The tsar's initiative stemmed from a mixture of military-economic calculation and of genuine response to arguments for peace. Russia faced a new arms race, as the other powers improved their modern weaponry (and particularly artillery), from a position of serious financial weakness: the minister of finance had warned that the arms bill must be curbed if bankruptcy and famine were to be avoided.[37] An easing of tension among the European powers would also leave Russia free to devote more resources to the eastern end of the empire. But Nicholas was also influenced by a book referred to him by his censors—*The War of the Future* by the Polish industrialist Jean de Bloch—which argued that war in the future would lead to economic collapse accompanied by famine, disease, and the break-up of society—and by his own conversations with Bloch. The tsar was also impressed by the proceedings of the 1896 meetings in Budapest of the IPC and UPC, transmitted to him by his consul-general there, which set out the dire consequences of unrestrained arms expenditure.

The tsar's proposal that the great powers should meet for an 'international discussion' on the 'grave problem' of the arms race came as a shock to the diplomatic world but as a delight to the world of peace advocacy. The prominent Austrian pacifist and novelist Bertha von Suttner wrote in her diary that 'from this time on [our] movement is incalculably nearer its goal; new ways are opening before it'. In a letter to her, Henry Dunant said that the tsar's move was 'a gigantic step, and, whatever may happen, the world will not shriek, "Utopia". Disdain of our ideas is no longer possible.'[38] Few shared the scornful view of Leo Tolstoy that 'he [the tsar] proposes a childish, silly and hypocritical project of universal peace, while at the same time ordering an increase in the army—and there are no limits to the laudations of his wisdom and virtue'.[39] Within days of the announcement by Muraviev, the British Peace Society had passed a resolution expressing its deep gratitude to 'Almighty God that, at length ... its ideals should be recognized as practicable, and such a proposal be made to carry them into effect by one of the greatest potentates in the world'.[40] While others were more sceptical about the tsar's motives, the opportunity for peace leaders to engage fully with great power diplomacy and argue the cause from within was too tempting to be missed. The peace societies organized campaigns of support with rallies and petitions, publishing pamphlets (300,000 were distributed in Britain), and lobbying their governments.

There was much greater scepticism among the governments addressed by the tsar. The general approach was to respond to the proposal with positive but vague approbation, although in the end the invitation could not be refused. Two months before the conference opened a British deputation from the International Crusade of Peace—led by the Liberal peer the earl of Aberdeen—presented, on behalf of meetings held up and down the country, a memorial calling on the government to support 'all practical proposals which will tend to lessen the burden of armaments, to diminish the horrors of war, and to extend the use of the principle of arbitration in the adjustment of international disputes'. They were received by the First Lord of the Treasury, Arthur Balfour, who expressed the government's 'heartiest sympathy' for their cause. He shared their hope that the conference would produce practical results, but said that even if it failed to do so, the movement inspired by the emperor of Russia in which they were taking part should be regarded as 'a great landmark in the progress of mankind' (*The Times*, 30 March 1899). As the conference approached, some of the excitement abated—a development welcomed by *The Times* editorially: the tsar's proposals were 'estimable', but 'extravagant expectations would have been certain to lead to disappointment' (19 April 1899).

The tsar's aim had already been narrowed down in a second statement from his foreign minister—the Muraviev Circular—which no longer spoke of 'universal peace' but sought only to restrict 'for a fixed period' the current armed forces levels and military budgets. The most important addition, which turned out to be the only practical consequence of the conference, was the proposal that it should establish 'a uniform practice' of arbitration to settle disputes by peaceful means. A hundred delegates from twenty-six countries (including China and Japan) gathered for the conference from 18 May to 29 July 1899 at The Hague, in the Oranjezaal of the Huis ten Bosch, the palace placed at its disposal by the queen of Holland. In the frescoes decorating the hall, the Angel of Peace was shown conferring her benediction on Frederik Hendrik—riding in his chariot—the Prince of Orange whose victories led to the end of the Eighty Years War with Spain at the Peace of Munster (1648). It was an appropriate allegory for a conference with an agenda devoted to peace but offset for many participants by considerations of war.

However, although no progress was made on the proposals for disarmament—the conference merely referred the question to the respective governments for further study—two of the four main sections in the resulting Hague Convention would have important consequences. The section on Laws and Customs of War on Land provided the basis for the development of modern laws of war over the coming century, while that on the Pacific Development of Disputes resulted in the establishment of the Permanent Court of Arbitration. Housed in the Peace Palace at The Hague, it continues to this day to adjudicate on disputes referred to it by states, intergovernmental bodies, and private parties. In addition, one of the declarations adopted by the conference on the use of asphyxiating gases paved the way for the 1925 Geneva Protocol banning the use of gas in war (although it did nothing to prevent its use in the First World War).

The evident failure of the first Hague Peace Conference to modify significantly the behaviour of the powers was demonstrated within months when Britain went to war with the Boer Republic in South Africa, refusing a proposal from US President McKinley that the dispute should be submitted to arbitration (on the specious grounds that the Republic was not a party to the Hague Convention). In Britain the Boer War seriously weakened and divided the established peace movement: the Peace Society refused to join the Stop the War movement led by the crusading journalist and peace activist William Stead. In the following year, all the major powers would join in a punitive war against China, and Russia's pacific credentials were finally demolished in the Russo-Japanese War of 1904–5. However, these disappointments led to a new initiative, begun by the American Peace Society, and taken up by the IPC, for a second peace conference. Sponsored by President Theodore Roosevelt, this finally met at The Hague in 1907. Though attended by more governments, it achieved even fewer results than that of 1899. Its most positive achievement was a declaration 'Respecting the Laws and Customs of War on Land' which built on the work begun at the first conference. The second conference agreed, under American pressure, to call for a third conference to be held within another seven or eight years: it was finally held at The Hague in 1999, as a centennial celebration of the first conference.

The Hague Peace Conferences have not featured prominently in most accounts of modern history and war: they were not mentioned in the classic study of *The Struggle for Mastery in Europe 1848–1918* (1954) by the Oxford historian A. J. P. Taylor. More than fifty years elapsed between the first comprehensive study of the two conferences by Merze Tate (1942) and the monographs of Arthur Eyffinger (1999 and 2007). It has always been easy to mock the enthusiasm of the peace advocates, their willingness to believe the best of their governments, and the meagre results which were shown. Yet there were real achievements in placing issues of peace on the diplomatic agenda which would be developed further. As the US secretary of state Elihu Root argued in 1907, the question was not merely what the conference had accomplished but also what it had begun and moved forward.[41] The two conferences also obliged those governments to pay more attention to public opinion—however much they might sneer at it in private. As summed up by Tate, 'the fact that the question of peace was no longer discussed merely by philosophers, jurists and Utopians, but by responsible governments also, was proof of the enormous strides forward that had been made in the sphere of international politics'.[42]

The contradictions exposed at The Hague, writes Eyffinger, were a reflection of a new contradictory reality in the world outside: 'a world of jingoism and pacifism, of blood and iron on the one hand, and the dawning inklings of human rights on the other'.[43]

This narrative of the pre-1914 peace movement would not be complete without consideration of another basic contradiction of that period—and one which would persist into the inter-war years—the contradiction between socialism and pacifism (using the latter term in the sense which it then possessed of broad but not necessarily absolute opposition to war). In the uncompromising view associated above all with Lenin, the wars of the current age were inevitable under the capitalist system, manifesting the international contradictions of that system, and the resulting militarism could, as Rosa Luxemburg put it, 'only be abolished from the world with the destruction of the capitalist class state'. The wars were quite different too from civil war, which, in Lenin's words, when waged 'by an oppressed class against the oppressor class' should be regarded as 'fully legitimate, progressive and necessary'. To call for peace and oppose militarism under these circumstances was like asking wolves and lions to cease from fighting: Luxemburg criticized 'the bourgeois friends of peace' and Lenin, once the war did break out, warned that 'we must not let ourselves get mixed up with the sentimental liberals'.[44]

War had not at first been a major problem for socialists in the second half of the nineteenth century, when the conflict between classes seemed of much greater importance than the conflict between states. 'Even the most anti-militarist Socialists', it has been suggested, 'rarely saw war as such as the problem; indeed it was almost invariably a particular war or kind of war to which they objected.'[45] The gathering clouds at the turn of the century, however, encouraged a narrowing of the gap between socialist views on war and those of the peace movement. On the socialist side there was a shift towards a less hard-line stance, which acknowledged that the working class might better further its interests by supporting the forces of peace rather than by standing on one side. Peace theorists began to move away from opposition to war based entirely on morality and, in an approach which came to be known as that of 'scientific pacifism', they recognized that the most effective arguments for peace were based on calculations on the economic and social costs of war.[46] The French socialist leader Jean Jaurès, a committed anti-militarist, argued eloquently that the working class

1. La Parisienne, Minoan fresco, *c.* 1400 BC.

2. Embassy to Achilles, Kleophrades Painter, Attic red-figure hydria, *c.* 480 BC.

3. Eirene (Peace) bearing Ploutos (Wealth), Roman copy after Greek votive statue by Kephisodotos, (*c.*370 BC).

4. Peaceful pursuits, Chinese stone carvings, Han dynasty, Henan.

5. Green Tara, Tibetan–Chinese, mid-seventeenth century.

6. 'St Martin renounces his weapons', Simone Martini, *c.* 1320.

7. Minerva protects Pax from Mars ('Peace and War'), Rubens, 1629–30.

8. The Consequences of War ('Horrors of War'), Rubens, 1636–7.

9. Justice and Peace, Corrado Giaquinto, 1753.

10. La Paix: Idylle, Henri Daumier, 1871.

11. 'The Enemies of Peace', Joseph Southall, 1918.

12. Women with a Dove, Pablo Picasso, 1955.

should actively enter into a militia system where they would receive a military education, practising manoeuvres in the open air (instead of performing 'sterile exercises' in military barracks), thus showing

> by their cheerful activity that it is not out of timid egotism or servile cowardice or bourgeois indolence that they are fighting militarism and war, but that they are as resolved and ready to secure the full working of a thoroughly popular and defensive army system as they are to topple the warmongers.[47]

At the Stuttgart Congress of the Second Socialist International in 1907—attended by Jaurès leading its French Section—a resolution against 'militarism and imperialism' sought to bridge the gap between the socialist and pacifist visions. It called for a 'democratic reorganization' of the army in line with Jaurès's proposal, urged the working class to take strike action against the threat of war, and endorsed the arbitration of disputes between governments which had previously been seen as a futile bourgeois half-measure. Revolution would only appear on the agenda if these and other actions failed to prevent war—a compromise wording proposed by Luxemburg. The resolution of the Stuttgart congress has been described as representing 'the first serious democratic attempts to create a strategy of public action to prevent war' by bringing together a range of proposals for civil anti-militarist action.[48] In a more sceptical view, 'the pleasure with which [the Resolution] was greeted obscured the imprecision of its terms'.[49] In any case, it was not accompanied by any mechanism for the international coordination of anti-war forces, and the left would be plunged into confusion again by the outbreak of war in 1914.

6

Alternatives to War

The League of Nations and Non-violence

By the hundred thousand, young men have died for the hope of a
better world. They have opened for us the way. If, as a people, we can
be wise and tolerant and just in peace as we have been resolute in
war, we shall build them the memorial that they have earned in the
form of a world set free from military force, national tyrannies and
class oppression, for the pursuit of a wider justice in the spirit of a
deeper and more human religion.

(*Manchester Guardian*, 12 November 1918)

The First World War presents historians of peace and war with a
bitter paradox. In the preceding decades the demand for peace
had been internationalized on an entirely new scale, with vocal support ranging from citizens to national leaders. The decade leading up
to 1914, writes M. S. Anderson in his textbook on European history,
'probably saw a more widespread belief in the possibility of international cooperation and a more general optimism as to the possibility
of achieving permanent peace between the great powers than had ever
been known before' (and, we might add, than has ever been known
since).[1] According to the military historian Michael Howard, 'the
abolition of war, that dream of the eighteenth-century philosophers,
seemed almost within reach' for many peace advocates.[2] The peace
movement reached 'the apogee of its public influence and support
in the years immediately preceding World War I', suggests the peace
historian David Cortright.[3] In 1908, the Universal Peace Congress in
London was given a reception by the king and a dinner with the prime
minister: can one imagine a similar event taking place today? And yet

one is driven to the conclusion, as A. C. F. Beales wrote much closer to the time, that 'The bitter tragedy of the years that followed the Hague Conference lies in that the idea of World Peace was becoming more practically futile as it grew more theoretically axiomatic. Though the ranks of the world's Peace crusaders had broadened out from the older critics of the War system... the Movement was quite incompatible with the existing system of international relations.'[4] A more recent historian of this period (Sandi Cooper) puts it succinctly: the international movement 'reached its apogee in the same years that the arms race spiralled across Europe (1889–1914)'.[5]

What should we conclude from this 'incompatible' juxtaposition of a blossoming peace movement and a burgeoning arms race. Sceptical commentators such as Michael Howard write off the efforts of the movement as practically futile in the face of the grinding momentum towards war, and as theoretically blind to the true dangers arising from 'the forces inherent in the states-system of the balance of power which they had for so long denounced, and those new forces of militant nationalism which they themselves had done so much to encourage'.[6] In this view, the 'great illusion' of which the British peace advocate Norman Angell wrote in his popular book with that title (1912) was not, as he argued, that war destroys the basis for economic prosperity in an integrated world and is therefore an anachronism.[7] The 'illusion', say the sceptics, was that the driving forces of nationalism and of arms competition could somehow be restrained by rational persuasion and moral appeal. Stated in more moderate terms, there is some truth in the charge of wishful thinking—of which Angell himself was aware. Commenting sarcastically in 1913 on the build-up to war, he observed: 'I have spoken of Pacifists and Bellicists but, of course, we are all Pacifists now....all the Chancelleries of Europe alike declare that their one object is the maintenance of peace. Never were such Pacifists.'[8] (As this suggests, the term 'pacifism', which was first coined only in 1901, did not necessarily imply total or absolutist opposition to violence, and was more of an umbrella term expressing general support for peaceful alternatives and opposition to militarism. It began to acquire its more rigorous meaning of total rejection of war during the First World War, when it was applied to the position of conscientious objectors, but this shift was not completed until the second half of the 1930s, when it applied particularly to those who rejected military preparedness for war even under the threat of fascism.)[9] Bertha von

Suttner had acknowledged in the year before Norman Angell's comment of 1913 that 'We have been mistaken—not in our principles but in our estimate of the level of civilization to which the world in general had attained.'Yet, she went on to argue, this did not mean that the case made by the peace party was false, but that its advocates were not sufficiently powerful to convince the leaders, and sufficient numbers of the peoples, of the European nations.[10] Put simply, their efforts were not enough, and here we encounter a question which the peace movement has had to face up to many times again: does the superiority of the forces with which it is confronted mean that there is no point in opposing them?

These forces in the years leading up to the First World War have been well documented, even if the controversy over who started the war remains (and may always remain) unresolved.[11] They can be summarized under the headings of resurgent nationalism, assertive militarism, and competitive imperialism, all underpinned materially by an industrial revolution which provided the means, and in time became a motive force in its own right, for an escalating arms race. And these forces were driven ideologically by a dangerous mix of ideas, within the framework of free market capitalism, which came to be labelled as Social Darwinism. Darwin's findings on the relationship between natural competition and the development of species appeared to provide a basis for the philosophical belief that war was the driving force behind all human progress. 'The necessity of struggle', Barbara Tuchman has written of this period, 'was voiced by many spokesmen in many guises: in Henri Bergson's *élan vital*, in [Bernard] Shaw's Life Force, in the strange magic jumble of Nietzsche which was then spreading its fascination over Europe.'[12] Much of this ideology should properly be called pseudo-Darwinism, especially when it was entangled with concepts of linguistic nationalism and racial mythology which pre-dated and had nothing to do with Darwin, or presented his ideas in a crude form. (As a recent study has shown, Darwin himself 'viewed violence and altruism as dancing a complex tango in human evolution, and he saw evidence that the cruder forms of human conflict were steadily giving way to a wider sense of sympathy'.)[13] The influence of Social Darwinism was important but diffuse, one of many strands which had made Europe, by the start of the twentieth century, 'a very bellicose, very militarist society' with an 'inflated spirit of patriotism and xenophobia which fuelled an alarmingly intensive arms race'.[14]

The peace societies and their advocates shared the same milieu of intellectual and scientific enquiry, but, while accepting the same premiss that society passed through successive stages of development, reached different conclusions about the driving forces of human progress. Although progressive reformers, in other fields as well as that of peace, rejected the tenets of Social Darwinism, they believed in humanity's ability to advance and to modify its environment, and in the instrumental role played by science and technology. In many respects, they might be described as Progressive Darwinists. The sociologist Jacques Novicow (1849–1912) offered a very different interpretation of the phenomenon of war in his *Les Luttes entre sociétés humaines et leur phases successives* (1893) and shortly before his death published *La Critique du darwinisme social* (1910). War, Novicow argued, far from operating a form of natural selection which favoured the ascendancy of the vigorous and the well endowed (as the Social Darwinists asserted), achieved the reverse, eliminating the most perfect—for those who died in war were generally 'the bravest and fittest'. Novicow also maintained that 'struggle' was not the same as 'war': the economic struggle which was man's principal activity had 'wealth for its object', which was destroyed by war. Those who still believed in the inevitability of war belonged to a retrograde elite trapped in the past.[15] Other perceptive analysts of the role of war in history and of its increasingly anachronistic nature included the French scientist Charles Richet, the Belgian economist Gustave de Molinari, and Jean de Bloch—who as we have seen influenced Tsar Nicholas II in his proposal for what became the first Hague Peace Conference. 'If European society could form a clear idea,' wrote de Bloch, 'not only of the military character, but also of the social and economic consequences of a future war under present conditions, protests against the present state of things would be expressed more often and more determinedly.'[16] It may be concluded that de Bloch, and the Progressive Darwinists generally, overestimated the hold of rationality on modern societies, especially when these were approaching war or engaged in it. They should not be faulted, however, for pressing the case against an irrational descent into world war, and they were entirely right in their predictions of the destruction and misery which it would cause.

High hopes for the League

'It would seem that every great war in history was followed by renewed interest in peace and by the presentation of plans to secure it', observed the peace historian Sylvester Hemleben, writing when new plans were being made for peace in the later years of the Second World War. 'With World War I came the largest number of peace plans occasioned by any war in history.'[17] As on previous occasions, the outbreak of the war in 1914 had emasculated the peace movement. Organizations were hampered by the breaking of their internationalist links, and only three out of the twenty-six national groups in the International Peace Bureau remained active. Many individuals responded to the call of patriotism or were silenced by the weight of pro-war sentiment, while the overt character of German militarism made it relatively easy to support the allied side against Germany. Such pressures and the dilemmas which these caused were understandable: what has been less observed was the reassertion of peace values by a significant minority, long before the war was over, and the variety of plans and ideas which was generated. Early in the field was the International Women's Congress for Peace and Freedom, convened in The Hague in April 1915; more than 1,100 women from twelve countries attended; it resulted in the formation of an international committee led by Jane Addams which would become the Women's International League for Peace and Freedom—an organization still active today. In the British parliament, the Independent Labour Party was a lone voice calling for 'peace not war'. ILP member and Quaker painter Joseph Southall presented their case in a series of acerbic draw-ings, including one that depicted the jingoistic national press threatening the figure of Peace, with its pens sharpened into spears (Plate 11).

Two central themes informed the argument as new groups emerged in Britain, the USA, the Netherlands, France, and half a dozen other countries. (Though peace organizations were suppressed in Germany, three new societies were formed which sometimes managed to evade censorship.)[18] First was the determination to build on previous plans for a form of international organization to establish and maintain peace: just as nations found peaceful means of maintaining peace within their borders, so the community of nations should do the same. As the League to Enforce Peace, set up in the USA in May 1916 (with an opening address from President Wilson), argued:

Always peace has been made and kept, when made and kept at all, by the superior power of superior numbers acting in unity for the common good. Mindful of this teaching of experience, we believe and solemnly urge that the time has come to devise and to create a working union of sovereign nations to establish peace among themselves and to guarantee it by all known and available sanctions at their command, to the end that civilization may be conserved, and the progress of mankind in comfort, enlightenment and happiness may continue.[19]

The second frequently made demand was for an end to the secret diplomacy which in the view of many peace advocates had helped to precipitate the war. The Union of Democratic Control, set up within weeks of the declaration of war, had insisted that the close of hostilities should not be effected by 'a Peace framed in secret by the diplomatists who made the war inevitable'.[20] A few months later, H. G. Wells turned his attention to the form of the eventual congress with which the war was bound to end. Such a congress should be of a world nature, involving neutral nations. It was much more likely to achieve a satisfactory outcome than a peace congress confined to the belligerents, which would be 'tainted with all the traditional policies, aggressions, suspicions, and subterfuges that led up to the war. It will not be the end of the old game, but the readjustment of the old game, the old game which is such an abominable nuisance to the development of modern civilization.'[21]

The Treaty of Versailles, concluded in June 1919 at the Paris Peace Conference, which imposed harsh obligations on the defeated Germany and its allies, was for many a cruel disappointment: 'We arrived determined that a Peace of justice and wisdom should be negotiated: we left it, conscious that the Treaties imposed upon our enemies were neither just nor wise,' wrote the disillusioned young British diplomat Harold Nicolson, and the portrayal of the treaty as a 'Carthaginian peace' by John Maynard Keynes was widely shared.[22] (Though less commented on at the time, the Treaties of Sèvres, 1920, and Lausanne, 1923, between the allies and the defeated Ottoman empire, which established the British and French spheres of influence in a huge swathe of territory from Iraq to Palestine, also imposed a cynical victors' settlement with whose historical consequences we still live painfully today.) The foundation of the League of Nations (in part 1 of the Treaty of Versailles) gave more grounds for optimism. As F. P. Walters, participant and later historian, would observe, the League held out the prospect of 'a new spirit and new methods': while the defeated countries were disarmed, they might hope to see this followed by significant reductions in the armaments of their victors, and the International Labour Organization and other new agencies promised 'a new advance towards social justice and economic prosperity'.[23] 'The tents have been struck, and the great caravan of humanity is once more on the move,' declared General Smuts, in his pamphlet 'League of Nations: A Practical Suggestion', which had a strong influence on President Woodrow Wilson.

The covenant of the League, approved at the Paris Peace Conference, carried forward previous attempts to devise a philosophy of international relations, and to create institutions that would further world peace, in four significant areas: it established the principle of compulsory arbitration; it stipulated that peace must be based on a reduction of armaments; it constituted itself as a permanent organization with its own secretariat; and it provided for sanctions to enforce international peace.[24] While many provisions of the covenant would prove defective in operation, enough progress was made in the 1920s to encourage some degree of optimism that the League could tackle the two dominant challenges of the 1930s—effective measures towards disarmament and the prevention of war through collective League action. Less conspicuous but equally important was the creation of a permanent body which paved the way for a real innovation—an international civil service which could address problems of the day. Half a million refugees and prisoners of war were repatriated by the fledgling High Commission for Refugees, which although regarded as temporary and enjoying minimal support (except from France and Scandinavia) would become the basis for the post-1945 Office of the UN High Commissioner for Refugees (UNHCR). The World Court was also established as the first permanent body to administer international law: by 1939 its authority was recognized in some 600 international agreements. The League's Permanent Mandates Commission imposed some restraints on what would otherwise have been outright colonial rule in seventeen mandated territories in the Middle East, Africa, and the Pacific. The economic and social institutions coordinated international action on a whole range of technical and humanitarian issues such as communications and transport, health, child welfare and trafficking. The concept of what is now referred to as 'positive peace' was put into practice for the first time by the League's agencies, who operated in the spirit of the important principle—set out in the opening words of the constitution of the International Labour Organization—that 'universal and lasting peace can be established only if it is based on social justice'.[25]

None of this would have been possible without the vocal encouragement and organized pressure of millions of supporters of the League in many countries. These national societies had inherited the spirit, and some leading personnel, of the peace societies of the late nineteenth century, whose argument for a new international system to arbitrate disputes and avert conflict had been horribly validated by the bloodshed of the Great War. The International Federation of League of Nations Societies, set up in Brussels in December 1919, would in time number some forty national societies although some national groups were 'hardly more than small gatherings of intellectuals'.[26]

Peace groups in Germany were for obvious reasons highly critical of the Versailles Treaty (as indeed were most of the other national societies) but many campaigned for German admission to the League: by 1928 the German Peace Cartel claimed to represent 100,000 members.[27] The French movement, the Association Française pour la Société des Nations, founded by Léon Bourgeois, suffered from lack of unity but broke new ground in the late 1920s by advocating a regionalization of the League of Nations—in effect an early form of European Union.[28] American participation was weakened from the start by the Senate's rejection of US membership of the League, and part of the US peace movement shared this reluctance to remain involved in Europe. A smaller group of League supporters in the League of Nations Association would adopt the indirect approach of campaigning for US membership of the Permanent Court. Non-governmental international organizations—in particular those which brought together women's and labour movements—would also set up their own peace and disarmament committees which at critical times (especially during the World Disarmament Conference, see below) could mobilize global opinion. In Britain, home of the strongest national movement, the League of Nations Union could by the early 1930s be regarded as expressing 'a broad consensus of all parties and all classes...(and) as representing the mainstream of political opinion'.[29] There was a strong sense that the 'unofficial opinion of the world' (the phrase used by the secretary of the National Peace Council in a letter to the *Manchester Guardian* in 1932) had earned the right, by the sacrifices of the late war, to influence the decisions of governments.[30] As the historian E. H. Carr wrote at the time,

The study of international politics would indeed lose most of its meaning if we were compelled to regard ourselves as the blind victims of some natural law, or of the caprice or self-interest of a governing oligarchy, driving us irresistibly into war. If these conditions existed in the past, they need no longer exist to-day. The responsibility for war and peace rests on every one of us.[31]

Despite the varied objectives and internal disunity of many of the national movements, overall they represented a significant force. Politicians were compelled, and some were voluntarily inclined, to acknowledge the strength of popular pressure as never before (an acknowledgement that would be made more rarely, and more grudgingly, in the cold war decades after the next Great War).

The World Disarmament Conference

The disarming of Germany at Versailles was presented as the first, but essential, step towards a more general process of arms limitation which would reduce the dangers of a future war. According to the preamble to Part V of the treaty, Germany would undertake to 'strictly observe' the clauses governing its military, naval, and air dispositions '*in order to render possible the initiation of a general limitation of the armaments of all nations*' (my italics). An elaboration by French prime minister Georges Clemenceau explained that the limitations on German armaments were not solely aimed at preventing the possibility of renewed aggression: they were 'also the first steps towards the general reduction and limitation of armaments which they seek to bring about as one of the most fruitful preventives of war, and which it will be one of the first duties of the League of Nations to promote'.[32] This was not merely a pious hope. The Great War had been preceded by two decades of rearmament against which not only had the peace societies campaigned, but which many world leaders had acknowledged to be a significant cause of instability. As Edward Grey, British foreign secretary during the war, would conclude famously in retrospect that

… great armaments lead inevitably to war. If there are armaments on one side, there must be armaments on other sides. … Fear begets suspicion and distrust and evil imaginings of all sorts, till each government feels it would be criminal and a betrayal of its own country not to take every precaution, while every government regards every precaution of every other government as evidence of hostile intent…[33]

In effect the great powers had struck a bargain at Versailles, not so much with Germany which had little choice but to accept the terms, but with their own peace-seeking populations, that having defeated and disarmed

Germany, they would deliver—at an unspecified later date—their side of the deal. Pragmatically it was also realized that if the great powers defaulted, Germany could not be held down for ever. As Austen Chamberlain, British delegate to the League's Preparatory (Disarmament) Commission, would tell its first meeting in 1926, 'law or no law, treaty or no treaty, no power on earth could keep Germany at her existing level of armaments indefinitely unless a measure of general disarmament was effected'.[34]

It is not surprising therefore that the issue of disarmament was foremost on the League's agenda and that it dominated public perception throughout the 1920s, or that the World Disarmament Conference (WDC) which finally met at Geneva in 1932 after years of tortuous preparation and delay would be seen as the most significant test to date of the League's credibility. Some progress had already been made with the conclusion of the 1925 Geneva Protocol on banning chemical and biological weapons, and with the five-power naval reduction treaties of Washington (1922) and London (1930)—although the latter were concluded outside the League and in retrospect did little to enhance its authority. Germany had joined the League in 1926, and the Soviet Union (which would join in 1934) took an active part in the disarmament negotiations from 1927 onwards when Maxim Litvinov first attended the Preparatory Commission. His initial proposal for 'general and complete disarmament', clearly designed for propaganda impact, was succeeded the next year by a more realistic plan for the reduction and eventual elimination of offensive weapons such as bombers, tanks, and aircraft carriers: some of these ideas would be revived in the WDC. By 1932 the international climate was again much less favourable, with the world plunged into economic depression and Germany on the path to Nazi rule. Yet there was still a huge demand for concrete results at Geneva to which European leaders had to pay heed, or at least lip-service. Several dozens of non-governmental organizations, representing the interests of peace, Christians, trade unionists, students, women, and ex-servicemen, took part in the International Consultative Group for Peace and Disarmament which pressed for results. Members of the Women's International League for Peace and Freedom collected more than six million signatures for the World Disarmament Petition, presented at Geneva on the opening day of the conference.

In Britain, where the movement was numerically strongest, there were more than 4,000 pro-disarmament demonstrations in the year before the WDC. In one prominently reported example, a rally at the Royal Albert

Hall in July 1931 pledged support for the forthcoming conference in Geneva, and the proceedings were broadcast to more than sixty simultaneous meetings up and down the country. What made this event exceptional was the presence and speeches of Ramsay MacDonald, then prime minister of the Labour minority government, and of Stanley Baldwin and David Lloyd George, leaders of the Conservative and Liberal oppositions. However, all three leaders combined their support for the aims of the conference with a cautious view of the difficulties it faced. 'The sentiment of peace was universal', said MacDonald according to *The Times* report of the meeting (13 July 1931), 'but the practice of peace was circumscribed.' Lloyd George, in the strongest of the three leaders' speeches, warned that 'the victorious powers at Versailles had kept Germany to her promise [to disarm] but they had broken their own'. It is easy to take a cynical view of such peace rallies, yet the strength of feeling for disarmament was shared, in varying degrees, by many contemporary political leaders (though not by their military counterparts—a grave weakness from the start). A careful study of the period shows that the popular voice for peace in Britain did persuade policy-makers and their advisers to take into account the desires of public opinion.[35]

Why then did the World Disarmament Conference fail so signally, and through its failure deal a body blow to the League's credibility and leave the way open for the world to continue marching towards catastrophe? Many modern historians have little doubt that the enterprise was doomed from the start, given the conflicting interests of the major powers, the worsening economic climate, the divisive consequences of Versailles and the rise of Nazism in Germany, and the innate distaste of military establishments for disarmament. Writing in the 1970s, F. S. Northedge in his critical study of the League concluded that responsibility for what he termed 'the disarmament fiasco' was 'widely shared among the leading states in the League', but asked whether the real cause was not that these states were attempting something which they considered impossible—and '*was* in truth impossible, or almost impossible'.[36] In a recent more sympathetic study of the League, Ruth Henig nevertheless concludes that 'the political climate of the early 1930s made the conclusion of a multilateral arms limitation agreement absolutely impossible'.[37]

These negative verdicts carry weight, yet equally categorical judgements in the opposite sense, suggesting that personalities and timing played an important part, have been made by former participants in the conference. The veteran diplomat and peace campaigner Philip Noel-

Baker identified several turning points in the run-up to and course of the conference. The death of the German foreign minister Gustav Stresemann in 1929 had removed someone with 'a burning faith in peace'; the collapse of the Labour minority government (just weeks after the Albert Hall rally) brought a more 'hawkish' turn to British foreign policy with Arthur Henderson replaced as foreign secretary by Sir John Simon. After early setbacks in the conference when it opened in February 1932, the American proposal to reduce offensive weapons (the Hoover Plan) offered the chance of a breakthrough, but was sidetracked by Simon, and by France which disliked its lack of military guarantees for French security.[38] The military historian Basil Liddell Hart regarded the Hoover plan as a missed opportunity, suggesting that if it had been accepted 'as it nearly was' then the Second World War could have been prevented.[39]

There is little dispute that the accession to power of Hitler in January 1933 signified the end of any hope of agreement, even though Germany continued to take part in the Geneva talks and for a while adopted a conciliatory tone. In March MacDonald and Simon presented a new draft disarmament convention: any chance it might have had was promptly undercut by the two British leaders who departed for Rome to talk with Mussolini, instead of lobbying the delegates in Geneva. In October Germany finally withdraw from the WDC: the young Anthony Eden, who had helped prepare the British draft, noted in his diary that the last real opportunity had been lost in the previous year when Germany under the then Chancellor Heinrich Brüning was still willing to negotiate seriously. Simon, as foreign secretary, bore much of the blame for this in Eden's view: 'I should not like Simon's conscience about the earlier part of last year when Bruening was still in power. We missed the bus then, and could never overtake it.' Over thirty years later, writing in his *Memoirs*, Eden would describe this as a 'sweeping and youthful judgement' to which he no longer subscribed. We may wonder whether the chances for peace were not seen by Eden more clearly at the time than with the dubious benefit of hindsight and the Suez War.[40]

The Peace Ballot

Early in 1934, it looked as if the cause of international cooperation were dying. The Disarmament Conference had reached a deadlock, and the possibility of war in Europe was being seriously discussed. The campaign for isolation was being vigorously pressed in certain

quarters. A demonstration of British loyalty to the League and the
collective peace system was urgently needed.

(Adelaide Livingstone, 1935)[41]

The British 'Peace Ballot'—or National Declaration on the League
of Nations and Armaments—of 1934–5 has passed into historical
myth as evidence of a pacifist outlook and reluctance to face up
to fascism, along with the famous resolution of the Oxford Union
'not to fight for King and Country' and the 1933 East Fulham by-
election, widely interpreted as a 'triumph for pacifism'.[42] As the
quotation above from the official history of the ballot shows, it was
in fact organized to demonstrate that the British people supported
the League and its system of collective sanctions to enforce peace—
a very different position from a fully pacifist one. This was well
understood by Lord Beaverbrook as a threat to his own advocacy
of appeasement: indeed he warned readers of the *Daily Express* (25
October 1934) not to sign the 'Ballot of Blood' because it would
'drag you and your children into war on behalf of the League of
Nations'. It was understood correctly by Churchill too, who characterized the final question in the ballot (Q5 to be discussed below)
as indicating 'a positive and courageous policy' which—if answered
in the affirmative—expressed the willingness 'to go to war in a
righteous cause, provided that all the necessary action was taken
under the auspices of the League of Nations'.[43]

It was true, as Churchill also noted, that the popular name of 'Peace
Ballot' could be misinterpreted, but it had been chosen to convey the
belief that support for the League offered the best chance to prevent war. In a letter to all branches of the League of Nations Union
(LNU), its president Lord Cecil, the foremost promoter of the ballot,
argued that a display of British resolution 'for peace, for the league, for
real disarmament, and for collective resistance to aggression' was the
only means of maintaining peace. The national slogan for the ballot
'Britain's Choice: the League or War!' was simplified in some of its
literature to the phrase 'Peace or War'—which the organizers admitted
to be misleading and was later dropped.[44]

What was beyond question was the huge effort made by thousands of
volunteers (the committee claimed half a million) to secure completed
ballot forms from a significant proportion of the British public. Some
thirty-five organizations backed the ballot and supplied many of the volunteers: these ranged from the LNU, the Labour Party, and the Trade Union
Congress to the Association of Headmistresses, the Jewish Peace Society,

the Workers' Educational Association, and the YWCA. The idea for the ballot had come from the initiative of a local newspaper in Ilford whose editor, an LNU member, organized a questionnaire for the borough's residents. Led by Lord Cecil, the LNU leadership, which was concerned by a fall-off in its membership, decided to launch a nationwide movement, believing that ordinary citizens would give clear and intelligent answers to the great problems of world peace if offered the chance. The LNU also hoped to refute the claim of the isolationist press and of prominent right-wing Tories such as Leo Amery that the majority of the British people were opposed to the League, describing it as a 'farce' and as 'likely to become a laughing-stock in a few years'.[45]

The ballot has been criticized for its unscientific approach, but it should be remembered that at the time public opinion sampling was in its infancy. The American Institute of Public Opinion was set up by George Gallup in the same year as the ballot, its British counterpart in 1936. There was also controversy over the notes sent out by the organizing committee to accompany the ballot form—known as the 'rainbow controversy' from the colours of the various papers circulated. Conservative critics on the committee, led by Austen Chamberlain, succeeded in having their own 'blue' note circulated as well as the official 'green' note which they regarded as one-sided.

Yet despite these shortcomings, the total number of completed ballot forms was still impressive at more than 11.5 million, almost a half of the British electorate. While most questions received an overwhelming 'Yes' majority, the response to the last, and most difficult, question suggested that many participants were making a considered judgement. Divided into two parts, it addressed the issues of (a) economic sanctions, and (b) military action, by the League:

Do you consider that, if a nation insists on attacking another, the other nations should combine to compel it to stop by

(a) economic and non-military measures: Yes, 10,027,608. No, 635,074, Doubtful, 27,255, Abstentions, 855,107.

(b) if necessary, military measures: Yes, 6,784,368. No, 2,351,981, Doubtful, 40,893, Abstentions, 2,364,441.[46]

The majority in favour of military action certainly showed that the ballot was not a pacifist exercise (only a few thousands chose a supplementary option, labelled 'Christian Pacifist', for those who objected to such action on conscientious grounds), and Lord Cecil seems justified in concluding that:

In recent years too many people, some of them occupying influential positions, have been ready to suggest that, contrary to all the best traditions of their history, the British people would not be ready to fulfil their obligations under the Covenant; that they would never be ready to risk their money, and still less their lives, in the repression of lawless breaches of international peace. It is satisfactory to know that there is no justification for such a slander on our people. By immense majorities, they have declared themselves ready to restrain an aggressor by economic action and, with more reluctance and by smaller but still important majorities, to follow this up, if it should prove essential, by military measures.[47]

Much has been made in subsequent analyses of an anecdote told by the diplomat and author Harold Nicolson who, during the 1935 general election, received the following letter: 'Dear Sir, Can you assure me that you stand for the League of Nations and Collective Security and will oppose any entanglements in Europe?' Nicolson later claimed that he had read the letter aloud at several meetings and that only in 'rare and isolated cases' did anyone point out that the letter was 'self-contradictory nonsense'.[48] This tale hardly deserves the weight attached to it: Nicolson had not supported the ballot, the wording of the letter was not entirely clear, and most members of an audience were unlikely to respond immediately to a brief text read out from the platform.

The 'failure' of the League

Modern judgements on the League of Nations are generally negative and it is rarely mentioned without its 'failure' being invoked: perhaps that is unsurprising since its aims were not achieved, and the second Great War was even more devastating than the first. However, the fact that the League failed does not justify the blame frequently laid at the door of the campaigns in support of it which, as in the case of the Peace Ballot, are incorrectly characterized as pacifist by nature—a word which, as noted above, had only just fully acquired its more comprehensive meaning of absolute opposition to all war. (In his popular history of the inter-war period, Ronald Blythe claims that the ballot 'marked the pinnacle of thirties pacifism and at the same time revealed the limitations of the League of Nations'.)[49] Certainly, support for military action did not come easily to those who were inclined towards pacifism and distrusted their own military establishments. It was all the more significant, therefore, when the British Labour Party

reversed its policy in 1934 from opposing to supporting military sanctions, and when this was reaffirmed a year later over the Abyssinian
crisis. Notable too was the declaration of the British League of Nations
Union in 1937, under the heading 'Why war can be averted [in Spain]',
which called on all League members 'to take any measures required
for the prevention or repression of aggression, including, if necessary,
military action'.[50] A more balanced judgement would concur with that
expressed in the *Oxford International Encyclopedia of Peace*, that 'there is
no consensus among historians on the success and legacy of the League',
but that it remains 'the first serious and comprehensive attempt to create a peaceful world free from war by developing the machinery to
settle conflict', and that it laid the foundations for future international
cooperation.[51] We may also consider the verdict of Winston Churchill
that 'War could easily have been prevented if the League of Nations
had been used with courage and loyalty by the associated nations.'[52]

In the end, much of the criticism of the League comes down to a
tautological assertion that it was a failure because it did not succeed, and
to criticism not of those who prevented it succeeding, but of those who
worked for its success but ultimately failed. While the former are regarded
as realists, simply behaving in the way that national leaders behave, the latter are portrayed as idealists—and sometimes mocked for proclaiming the
'gospel' of peace. Insufficient attention is paid to the claim of the League
campaigners that vested military interests were doing their best to sabotage
its work for disarmament. Too often, the influential voices of men such as
Maurice Hankey, secretary to the British cabinet throughout this period,
and the senior British diplomat Robert Vansittart are seen as reflecting a
dispassionate, more pragmatic, view of the realities of global power politics (the 'Old Adam' of a famous memorandum by Vansittart), rather than
motivated by prejudice and reaction. One of the few serious studies of the
British role in the World Disarmament Conference has concluded that
Britain must bear a much greater share of responsibility for its failure than
is usually assumed, and that British policy on disarmament may even be
regarded as 'a charade, a public relations exercise masking the fundamental
reality that Britain intended to increase her armaments'.[53]

The League's supporters could sometimes lay themselves open to
ridicule on the grounds of starry-eyed optimism, though more so in
the 1920s, the decade of hope, than in the 1930s, but they were not
wholly unaware of the danger. The British left-wing journalist Henry
Brailsford, in a book which argued for world government, nevertheless

began with a wicked fantasy in which Voltaire's Candide and his mentor Pangloss return to the present day, and continue to assert their belief that we live in the best of all possible worlds.

Pangloss was welcomed with enthusiasm on its [the League's] staff, and from that day to this, though wars have raged and shells, notes, bombs, poison gas, and ultimata have descended in great profusion upon various members and protégés of the League, never did he fail to demonstrate that all is for the best.[54]

Yet as Leonard Woolf, the pacifist writer whose ideas had contributed to the foundation of the League, put it in the same year, the League had failed not because it tried to do too much but because 'the statesmen and governments representing the Members of the League at Geneva never complied with their obligations'.[55] The charge that the alleged 'utopianism' of the inter-war peace movements had led to the appeasement of Germany, and had been a cause of the Second World War, was invoked during the cold war to suggest, by historical analogy, that those calling for nuclear disarmament or for détente with the Soviet Union were also guilty of appeasement (and it would be levelled again at the opponents of the Gulf and Iraq Wars). Yet the advocates of peace are credited with too much influence: as shown in Cecilia Lynch's careful re-evaluation, *Beyond Appeasement*, scholarship on this period, however critical of the peace campaigns, 'does not cite peace movement influence as the primary causal factor for any given economic or strategic decision'.[56] Donald Birn, another historian of the League, has argued that the peace campaigns, predominantly middle-class in composition, showed too much timidity and were easily neutralized by the national leaders who gave them verbal support.[57] Against the charge of idealism levelled at them it may be argued instead, with Noel-Baker, that 'in truth, it has been the internationalists who have been the realists, the men who really faced the facts, the men whose policy would have averted the wars and the disasters that have followed in their train'.[58] And is it really suggested that history would have been better served if the advocates of peace had remained silent?

The non-violent alternative

While it is commonplace to refer to the twentieth century as the bloodiest in history, it is also regarded by peace historians as 'the greatest century for non-violent activism', which shows that 'forms of non-violent action can serve effectively in the place of violence at every level of political affairs'.[59] The growing lethality of war, and the greater publicity given to the efforts of those who sought to resist it, have helped to enlarge the concept of non-violence as an alternative strategy of resistance—a process first brought to public attention by Mahatma Gandhi in the inter-war period. Amid the horrors of twentieth-century war, it has been observed, 'history's most violent era has also seen the dawning of an age of non-violence'.[60] While non-violent resistance has become a more coherent and effective doctrine in the past century, its earlier history should not be overlooked. It has long been the first weapon of the weak against the strong, only turning to violence when harshly repressed, though often labelled by historians as 'rebellion' from the start. The story should also include the pacifist 'heresies' of the Cathars and Waldenses, and early sixteenth-century Anabaptism and seventeenth-century Quakerism which, though historically unrelated, show how under circumstances of acute social tension, non-violence may emerge among the 'churches of the disinherited' as an expression of protest against state and Church orthodoxy and violence.[61]

The ideas and personal examples of two great thinkers and practitioners, Tolstoy and Gandhi, penetrated deeply into the non-violent wing of the peace movement between the two wars, inspiring further development of both theory and practice to bring to bear the individual aspiration for peace upon the reality of state violence. In the next two sections, I shall consider briefly the thought and influence of these two dominating figures.

Tolstoy's thought and influence

When Tolstoy wrote War and Peace (1869), his purpose—he would lightly recall later—was 'simply to amuse his readers'. He had not yet reached the conclusion that it was a human obligation to resist war and not take part in it, although his own early experiences in the Caucasus had already led him to assert that 'War is so unjust and ugly that all who wage it must try to stifle the voice of conscience within themselves.'[62] Tolstoy's exceptional understanding of human behaviour still enabled him to convey in War and Peace the moral complexity of war, its fatal fascination, and its horror—the one sometimes followed the other with terrible speed.

Before the Battle of Austerlitz, Prince Andrei attends the Russian military council which is swayed by those who have convinced the emperor to attack, against the counsel of the wily General Kutuzov. 'Was it really not possible for Kutuzov to state his views plainly to the Emperor?', reflects Andrei. 'Is it possible that on account of court and personal considerations tens of thousands of lives, and my life, *my* life, must be risked?' He manages to dispel his apprehensions by dreaming of possible triumph in the battle. 'Death, wounds, the loss of family—I fear nothing', Andrei convinces himself. 'I would give them all at once for a moment of glory'. Next day he is seriously wounded in the field, and the Russian army is defeated and takes to disorderly flight. Tolstoy describes the scene around the dam and pond banks near the village of Augesd:

It was growing dusk. On the narrow Augesd dam where for so many years the old miller had been accustomed to sit in his tasselled cap peacefully angling, while his grandson, with shirt-sleeves rolled up, handled the floundering silvery fish in the watering-can, on that dam over which for so many years Moravians in shaggy caps and blue jackets had peacefully driven their two-horse carts loaded with wheat and had returned dusty with flour whitening their carts—on that narrow dam amid the wagons and the cannon, under the horses' hooves and between the wagon wheels, men disfigured by fear of death now crowded together, crushing one another, dying, stepping over the dying and killing one another, only to move on a few steps and be killed themselves in the same way.[63]

Passages such as these may lead readers to conclude that Tolstoy already goes well beyond a sympathetic portrayal of human emotion, and of the haphazard way in which war unfolds, to convey an implicit judgement on war as such. Most Tolstoyan scholars would disagree, but the pioneering translator (and friend of Tolstoy) Aylmer Maude had no doubt that 'the result was tantamount to a condemnation'. So did Kropotkin, who remarked that *War and Peace* was a powerful indictment of war.[64]

The British sociologist Ronald Sampson has offered a perceptive analysis of *War and Peace*, in which he sees Tolstoy wrestling with what at the time was for him an irreconcilable dilemma. On the one hand he regards war as a terrible force which 'rules the destiny of men and nations', before which men and women can only 'bow their heads humbly in submission to the awful decrees of Fate'. Yet at the same time Tolstoy believes that war stems from a specific moral defect in humanity, and that since man can overcome evil, then war must be remediable.[65] This is the contradiction with which Tolstoy is strug-gling throughout the book and which he fails to resolve. Tolstoy at this stage accepts the paradox put forward by Proudhon (whose *La Guerre et la paix*, published in 1861, provided him with his title) that 'War is divine: Humanity wants no more war.' This contradiction could not be resolved, it appeared, without denying God, and it would take Tolstoy many more years before he reached the position that a true reading of Christianity requires one to reject violence in all its forms.

However, in *War and Peace* Tolstoy had already come a long way towards his later conviction that war is based upon a confidence trick: that wars are started by individuals with pretensions to exercise power, but that the reality of such power is a fraud, and that, as Sampson argues, 'the actual work of the world which collectively constitutes human history is always undertaken by the common people, the vast majority'.[66] Tolstoy set out his views on the nature of power in the significant final pages of *War and Peace* (the 'second epilogue') on 'The forces that move nations'—often mistakenly regarded as wordy and superfluous to the book. Of course there are men in power who com-mand, and a vast mass who obey, but 'every command executed is always one of an immense number unexecuted'. Wars may appear to be justified by rational argument and decision but this is an illusion:

These justifications release those who produce the events from moral respon-sibility. These temporary aims are like the broom fixed in front of a locomotive to clear the snow from the rails in front: they clear men's moral responsibilities from their path. Without such justifications, there would be no reply to the simplest question that presents itself when examining each historical event. How is it that millions of men commit collective crimes—make war, commit murder, and so on?[67]

More than a decade later, at the age of 50, Tolstoy went through a crisis of belief at the end of which he totally rejected violence and established power—including the power of the Church as well as the state—and returned to the original precepts of Christianity (and of other reli-gions). He set out his process of conversion in a series of essays and books, starting with his *Confession* (1882) in which he explained that while Russia was at war it was impossible not to see that 'killing is an evil repugnant to the first principles of any faith'. His progress towards a philosophy of Christian anarchism continued, at both a personal and a political level: his *The Kingdom of God is Within You* (1894) expressed

a position of passive resistance to violence in its most absolute form,
and his last important novel, *Resurrection* (1899), combined the themes
of personal redemption with commitment to the oppressed minorities
of society. The royalties from this novel were devoted to helping the
pacifist Doukhobor sect flee persecution in the South Caucasus and
migrate to Canada.

Tolstoy drew inspiration from a wide range of sources: in *The Kingdom
of God is Within You* he acknowledged the influence of the fifteenth-
century Bohemian pacifist and leader of the Hussite movement Petr
Chelčický', and particularly his *Net of True Faith* which rejected the
dual authority of pope and emperor. In a letter to an American friend,
Tolstoy also acknowledged a special debt to William Lloyd Garrison,
the US abolitionist and social reformer.[68] In 1838 Garrison had founded
with Adin Ballou the New England Non-Resistance Society, issuing
a 'Declaration of Sentiments' which Tolstoy had read. Garrison would
oppose the 1846–8 war against Mexico, but become less unequivo-
cal about the use of force during the civil war, moving to a position
where he saw a war against slavery as a better choice than peace with
slavery.[69] Tolstoy often referred to Henry Thoreau's writings on civil
disobedience, and included several extracts from them in the *Circle of
Reading*—a collection of 'sayings of the wise' which he began to compile in his last years. Although Tolstoy's thought is often regarded as
idiosyncratic, the extent to which he incorporated ideas from a variety
of outside influences (including Eastern religions) should be recognized. He never developed his thinking into a systematic programme,
and was scornful of the attempts of his followers to formulate what
they called Tolstoyism (as he was of their self-designation as Tolstoyans).
Yet these ideas were not only, as we shall see, an immediate inspiration
to Gandhi but they inspired many in the peace—and particularly the
pacifist—movement in following decades.

In Russia the experimental farm colonies which had been formed
by Tolstoy's followers were expanded after his death, and at least a
hundred Tolstoyan agricultural communes survived into the 1920s. In
January 1919 during the civil war, a United Council of religious groups
led by Tolstoy's former secretary Vladimir Chertkov managed to secure
a decree signed by Lenin granting exemption from military service to
those with genuine religious convictions, and helped many thousands
to benefit from its provision. The Tolstoyan Society in Moscow was
closed down in 1929: the remaining communes gained permission to

resettle in Siberia, establishing the 'Our Life and Labour Commune' with a thousand members, but it was completely destroyed in the Stalinist purges of the late 1930s and many Tolstoyans died in labour camps.[70] More generally, Tolstoy's thought transcended its cultural confines to become a universal resource for those seeking non-violent alternatives. As the peace historian Peter Brock has concluded, 'As an organized movement and as a compact intellectual system, Tolstoyism disappeared. Its influence has remained, helping to produce a healthy fermentation of ideas in twentieth-century pacifism and an increased awareness of the need for individual moral responsibility in regard to social violence and war.'[71]

Gandhi's thought and influence

While the League of Nations was attempting to implement the principle of peaceful settlement of disputes on an international scale, Mahatma Gandhi was putting into practice his principle of *satyagraha* ('searching for truth') coupled with *ahimsa* ('non-violence'), both centred on the responsibility of the individual, against British colonial rule in India. If the League, while failing to prevent the coming war, can be judged to have laid the basis for a new approach to peacemaking among states, Gandhi's philosophy and example would be equally influential, perhaps more so, in offering what for many people was an entirely new method of peaceful protest by individuals within states. His dramatic enactment of non-violent resistance in the Salt March of 1930 brought him to the forefront of the world stage: he became *Time's* Man of the Year and the magazine judged correctly that Gandhi's 'mark on world history will undoubtedly loom largest of all' (5 January 1931). Gandhi's philosophy was elaborated in an influential book by the American Quaker and labour lawyer Richard Gregg (*The Power of Non-violence*, 1935). Non-violent resistance, Gregg wrote, could be 'an effective substitute for war'. It was a skill that could be acquired anywhere in the world, and by men and women of all races, classes, and ages. That women took part was important: indeed, Gregg added, 'they are more effective in it than most men'.[72] Gandhian influence on the peace movement would become more extensive after the Second World War when his techniques were studied and adopted within the US civil rights movement, the civil disobedience wing of the British anti-bomb movement, and among environmental and disarmament groups elsewhere in Europe and in Japan.[73] As well as being used as a protest tool, non-violent action began to be envisaged during the cold war as an alternative basis for a defence policy against occupation or aggression: examples from Scandinavia during the world war and more recently from anti-Soviet resistance in Eastern bloc countries may be cited. (Such examples were particularly relevant when opponents of nuclear deterrence had to face hostile questioning on how they would resist 'communist aggression' by non-violent means.)[74]

Gandhi played a unique role in promoting the concept of non-violent protest, to the extent that he is sometimes credited with having invented it. Yet to assert, as does the Gandhian scholar Raghavan Iyer, that 'Mahatma Gandhi coined the term *non-violence*'[75] is to oversimplify a long and complex history of civil resistance which to varying extents had relied on the use of non-violence. The impulse to respond to violence or the threat of it by passive resistance is as much part of the repertoire of human behaviour as that of responding *with* violence. The historical spectrum ranges from the total pacifism found in early Christianity, Buddhism, and some Hindu sects, where those at the receiving end of violence will refrain from violent response even to the point of martyrdom, to the type of civil disobedience typically displayed in traditional peasant protests which begin non-violently but are provoked by repression into fighting back, with such arms as may be available. Up to the time of Gandhi, total pacifism was more common in the personal realm, while collective civil disobedience was more likely to spill over or escalate into violence. It was Gandhi's genius to translate the personal commitment of non-violent restraint into an effective weapon of mass action, even though at the time this was rejected by significant elements in the Indian anti-colonial struggle. To genuine Gandhians, violence is the enemy and to respond with counter-violence will strengthen that enemy. As Hannah Arendt observed, 'The practice of violence, like all action, changes the world, but the most probable change is to a more violent world.'[76] Or as put more succinctly by Bart de Ligt, the Dutch anti-militarist pastor, 'the more violence, the less revolution'.[77]

Adam Roberts, one of the leading scholars in this field, has summarized the modern view of civil resistance as 'a type of political action that relies on the use of non-violent methods. It is largely synonymous with certain other terms, including "non-violent action", "non-violent resistance", and "people power".'[78] In a less rigorous, pre-Gandhian, sense, civil resistance covered a much wider range of protest. The first practical example of non-violence often cited is the passive resistance of Hungary in the 1860s, led by Ferenc Deák, to taxation and compulsory military service under Austrian rule.[79] However, the conventional story of 'peasant risings' in Europe over many centuries should be reconsidered. Such episodes typically began with passive resistance and attempted negotiation, with 'rebellion' only at the last desperate stage. This can be observed, it is suggested, in events as seemingly different as 'the great French peasant rebellions of the 16th century and the quiet tenacious resistance to taxes in the Holy Roman Empire'.[80] A similar phenomenon occurred in imperial China, where there was often a long process of passive disaffection with the oppressive rule of local mandarins before this broke out in open 'rebellion'. (The tradition survives today in the mainly peaceful protests of deprived rural communities against taxes or local corruption, which may suddenly escalate to violence.) Similarly in Japan under feudal rule, peasants would seek to 'break off the village's relationship to the state, that is, to withhold labour and tribute payments' when local officials failed to act in their interests or exploited them for tax, only turning to violence when this failed.[81]

The record of rural protest in India against British exploitation shows a wide range of actions from the entirely peaceful to those which became violent. In 1830 many villages in Mysore refused to work in the fields and the people fled to the forests in protest against extortion. A British government report concluded that 'the natives understand very well' how best to defend themselves against the abuse of authority: 'The method most in use, and that which gives the best results, is complete non-co-operation in all that concerns the Government, the administration and public life generally.'[82] In the Bengal indigo strike of 1860, tenants refused to grow the crop at very low prices for the British textile industry. They were forced to continue working by the landowners' overseers: some were kidnapped, flogged, or even murdered. The strike spread rapidly when tenants assembled with 'staffs, swords, bows and arrows and matchlocks' to defend their villages. A magistrate's horse was wounded but otherwise there was little violence: a show of weapons had been enough.[83] In 1875 the Mahratta peasants, hard hit by a slump in cotton prices, were told that they could be imprisoned if they refused to pay debts. They raided the houses of moneylenders, destroyed papers relating to their debts, and several moneylenders and their supporters were killed or beaten badly.[84] All three protests achieved a fair measure of success.

Gandhi showed little awareness of the long struggle of the Indian people at the start of his progress towards self-enlightenment and the discovery of non-violence. His own experience began at first hand—vividly described in his autobiography—when in 1893 as a young barrister recently arrived in South Africa he was harassed by railway and coach officials for daring to travel in a first-class carriage, or inside the stage-coach, as if he were a 'white'.[85] Meanwhile his intellectual journey had already begun with his discovery of the *Bhagavad Gita*—the Sanskrit epic to which he was first introduced by members of the Theosophical Society in England during his law course in 1890. Later he read Thoreau's essay *On Civil Disobedience* (1849), and Tolstoy's *The Kingdom of God is Within You*. These works do not appear initially to have made such a deep impression upon Gandhi as his discovery of John Ruskin's essay on social justice *Unto This Last* (1860), which 'captured me and made me transform my life'.[86] However, he came to value Thoreau's advocacy of civil disobedience, and Tolstoy's insistence on absolute non-violence, for the moral and intellectual underpinning they gave to his own campaigns in South Africa and India. Gandhi shared Thoreau's view of the war depicted in the *Bhagavad Gita* as allegorical. Vyasa 'wrote his supremely beautiful epic to depict the futility of war', Gandhi believed, and its war was 'not on an earthly battlefield but between the two natures in us, of good and evil'. And it was through reading Tolstoy's advocacy of 'non-resistance to evil by force' that his 'lack of faith in non-violence vanished'.[87]

Yet Gandhi was very different from Tolstoy in his approach to the existential world. As Cortright has written, 'Gandhi was not a philosopher but a strategist of social and political change' who cared little for grand theory and never organized his thoughts into a coherent philosophy: he was 'a doer more than a thinker'.[88] Gandhi did not advocate withdrawal from the violent world but confrontation with it; neither did he believe that a simple moral precept was sufficient to combat the latent violence within human beings. He wrote in his essay *On Non-violence* (1938) that

Man is by nature non-violent. But he does not owe his origin to non-violence....This [realizing our peaceful potential] can happen only when we voluntarily give up the use of physical force and when we develop the non-violence which lies dormant in our hearts. It can be awakened only through real strength.

Gandhi distinguished between passive resistance, the weapon of the weak, and civil disobedience based upon *satyagraha*, a weapon for which great courage is needed; he says in the same essay: 'just as one must learn the art of killing in the training for violence, so one must learn the art of dying in the training for non-violence'. Non-violence was not the 'mere policy of the coward'. Gandhi, like Garrison and Thoreau—but unlike Tolstoy— took a nuanced view of the relationship of the individual to the state. To practise civil disobedience 'one must have rendered a willing and respectful obedience to the State laws': only after doing so was the individual 'in a position to judge as to which particular rules are good and just and which unjust and iniquitous. Only then does the right accrue to him of the civil disobedience of certain laws in well-defined circumstances.'[89]

Gandhi also saw the individual as participating in the social economy of production, while Tolstoy advocated withdrawal into a separate communal world. In modern terms, we may say that Gandhi advocated local development, self-sufficiency, and appropriate technology which could provide India's poor with the tools, produce, and know-how needed in order to effectively diminish the control exercised over them by the wider state and industrialized world. In his booklet *Constructive Programme: Its Meaning and Place* (1941) Gandhi offered a blueprint for the alternative economy, in which the principle of 'economic equality' was 'the master key to non-violent independence'. It meant 'abolishing the eternal conflict between capital and labour...[and] the levelling down of the few rich in whose hands is concentrated the bulk of the nation's wealth on the one hand, and the levelling up of the semi-starved naked millions on the other. A non-violent system of government is clearly an impossibility so long as the wide gulf between the rich and the hungry millions persists.' Gandhi was well ahead of his time in understanding the threat both to the environment and to the well-being of the poor posed by a modern industrialized world.[90]

Alternatives to war

During the inter-war years there was still a degree of optimism as thoughtful opponents of war searched for alternatives. Tolstoy's legacy and Gandhi's example gave a strong stimulus to new networks of peace activity based upon non-violence. The Fellowship of Reconciliation (FOR), which had supported conscientious objectors in the USA during the First World War, set up the International FOR in 1919. It would mobilize support for the 1932 World Disarmament Conference, leading a Youth Crusade to converge on Geneva. It also organized 'Ambassadors of Reconciliation' to visit world leaders including Hitler and Mussolini as well as Roosevelt and the French prime minister Léon Blum, in the vain hope that they would listen to an appeal for peace. The Women's International League for Peace and Freedom (WILPF), founded during the war (see above p. 154), campaigned for total disarmament: two of its founding members, Jane Addams and Emily Greene Balch, would receive the Nobel Peace Price respectively in 1931 and in 1946. The Quaker American Friends Service Committee (AFSC) fed children in Germany and Austria after the first war, and would negotiate with the Gestapo to aid Jewish refugees. It too was awarded the Nobel Peace Prize, together with the British Friends, in 1947. The War Resisters International (WRI) dated back to an anti-militarist congress held in 1904: in the 1920s and 1930s it would concentrate on conscientious resistance to military service. Its declaration of personal opposition to war was taken up in Britain in 1934 by the Peace Pledge Union (PPU) which sought individual pledges to 'renounce war and never again to support another': the campaign attracted 136,000 signatories. Three of these organizations (FOR, WILPF, and AFSC) remain active to this day while the main legacy of the PPU is the London-based *Peace News* which continues to publish, and is now linked to the WRI as a monthly magazine.

Many inter-war intellectuals also sought solutions to the threat of war in fields such as education, psychology, and social theory, in what was arguably a more extensive and wide-ranging search than the rather restricted questioning which would follow the next world war. The social historian Caroline Playne, for example, wrote in *The Neuroses of the Nations* (1925) that modern war arose from the failure of humans to adjust to 'the ever-increasing strain of life under highly stressed and complicated conditions of existence'. Efforts to restore international peace and security were frustrated by 'a generation of men whose overwrought nerves craved, above all, for some vast excitement'.[91] A famous exchange of letters in 1932 between Albert Einstein and Sigmund Freud, instigated by the League of Nations, was published under the title *Why War?*, in which Einstein posed the question: 'Is it possible to control man's mental evolution so as to make him proof against the psychosis of hate and destructiveness?' In a lengthy reply

Freud sounded a more positive note than is sometimes claimed for it. Certainly, he pointed to the record of history as showing 'an unending series of conflicts' and described the instinct to 'destroy and kill' as being as integral to humanity as the opposite instinct to 'conserve and unify'—roughly the instincts of 'Death' and 'Love'. However, Freud also praised the League of Nations as 'an experiment the like of which has rarely... been attempted in the course of history'. He went on to suggest that the instinct of Death could be tamed: for 'if the propensity for war be due to the destructive instinct, we have always its counter-agent, Eros [Love] to our hand. All that produces ties of sentiment between man and man... must serve us as war's antidote.'[92]

In an address on 'Education and Peace', delivered in 1932, the educational pioneer Maria Montessori drew a powerful analogy between war and the plague. For centuries the plague had appeared at long intervals, had decimated populations, and had been regarded either as an inexplicable scourge or as the punishment of God, against which no measures would prevail. Each time after the plague had gone, the hearts of the survivors filled with hope that it would never return. Was not the contemporary attitude towards war much the same, imagining that the war just ended had been necessary for the final establishment of peace? Yet, Montessori continued, it had eventually been understood that measures could be taken against the plague by personal and public hygiene. Should not the same scientific methods of research which were now available through the modern resources of civilization be used to identify and abolish the primary causes of war?[93] Montessori's hopes, as we know, were not fulfilled: a second world war followed the first, and in 1947 another brilliant thinker, Albert Camus, would again compare war to the plague. In his terrifying, claustrophobic novel *La Peste*, Camus, unlike Montessori, offered no hope of human improvement: instead, in the concluding sentence to the book he predicted that the day would come when 'the plague would again summon its rats and send them out to die in a happy city, for the misery and instruction of mankind'.[94] The optimism of the inter-war period, extinguished by a second world war, had little chance to revive before being dashed again by a new sort of weapon and a new sort of war.

7

The Misappropriation of Peace

From the UN to the Cold War

> But the atom's international, in spite of hysteria
> It flourishes in Utah as well as Siberia,
> And whether you're black, white, red or brown,
> The question is this, when you boil it down,
>   To be or not to be, that is the question.
> The answer to it all ain't military datum,
> Like who gets there fustest with the mostest atoms,
> No, the people of the world must decide their fate,
> They gotta get together or—disintegrate
>   We hold this truth to be self evident—
>   That all men may be cremated equal.
> CHANT: Hiroshima, Nagasaki, Alamogordo, Bikini.
>   (Vern Partlow, 'Old Man Atom' 1945–6)[1]

Long before the mushroom cloud of the atom bomb had appeared on the horizon, the ferocity, devastation, and geographical extent of the conflict which began in 1939 demonstrated that the world now lived in an age of total war. If or when it came to an end, the survivors would be given a second chance for peace which this time they must not lose, less than three decades after the first chance had been offered and thrown away. 'The plain people everywhere', wrote one US advocate of internationalism, were asking, 'what can be done to set humanity on a better course after these terrible wars are over?'[2] In spite of the international failures of the 1930s, the belief that 'world opinion' could be effectively mobilized in favour of peace had not been destroyed but on the contrary was strengthened. US opinion polls showed that in 1937 only 33 per cent were in favour of participation in a League of Nations or other international organization, but by 1942 that had risen to 68 per cent and then climbed even higher. In 1944 more than half believed that such an organization should have a 'permanent military force of its own stronger than any single nation' and as many as 69 per cent agreed that it would have the right to decide 'what military strength each member nation can have'.[3] More than 70 per cent in a poll of British public opinion, surveyed in July 1945, thought that the prospects for world peace were better than after the First World War: over three-quarters believed that the USA would cooperate effectively with the United Nations, and nearly two-thirds believed the same of the Soviet Union.[4]

In the USA, the influential Committee for the Study of the Organization of Peace (CSOP) was given regular air time by the Columbia Broadcasting Service to present its ideas on a 'new world order', and reported personally to President Roosevelt. Impressed by its arguments, Eleanor Roosevelt joined the committee which prepared much of the intellectual groundwork for the security principles to be embodied in the UN.[5] Summarizing its conclusions, its founder James Shotwell warned that 'if the war system persists we have before us the possibility of a new dark age'.[6] The same warning—again made before the Hiroshima bomb—was given by the Philippines leader Carlos Romulo at the San Francisco conference to found the UN: it had been convened, he said, 'to determine whether the human race is going to exist or whether it is to be wiped out in another world holocaust'.[7] As Roosevelt had told Congress on 1 March 1945, 'we cannot fail them [the American servicemen who died in the First World War] again, and expect the world again to survive'.

There was considerable support for arguments in favour of going beyond a world security organization to create a world government. Wendell Willkie, the Republican candidate in the 1940 presidential election, made the case in *One World* (1943), which had sold two million copies by the end of the war. An even more emphatic call for world government would be made by Emery Reves in *The Anatomy of Peace*, published during the San Francisco conference, which topped the US best-seller lists for six months. Regarding the UN as an inadequate solution, Reves argued that world government was not an ultimate goal but an immediate necessity, and that the convulsions of world war had shown that the nation-state belonged to a 'dead and decaying political system'.[8] The cover of his book bore an appeal to the

American people, signed by well-known political figures from both parties including William Fulbright and Claude Pepper, which began:

The first atomic bomb destroyed more than the city of Hiroshima. It also exploded our inherited, outdated political ideas. A few days before the force of Nature was tried out for the first time in history, the San Francisco Charter was ratified in Washington. The dream of a League of Nations, after 26 years, was accepted by the Senate. How long will the United Nations Charter endure? With luck, a generation? A century? There is no one who does not hope for at least that much luck—for the Charter, for himself, for his work, and for his children's children. But is it enough to have Peace by Luck? Peace by Law is what the peoples of the world, beginning with our selves, can have if they want it. And now is the time to get it.

The main thrust of argument, however, in the closing years of the war was directed to the more limited but still ambitious aim of creating an effective successor to the League of Nations: its failure had encouraged both caution and realism which promised a more hopeful outcome. Serious discussion and planning for the UN started at an earlier stage than had been the case for the League; the need for full participation of the main post-war powers was understood from the start; public education to overcome opposition in the USA was seen as a priority; global poverty and under-development were identified as issues to be tackled seriously; and it was widely accepted that the maintenance of peace in a post-war world would require not only agreement but the machinery to, if necessary, enforce it. The question was not whether peace could be maintained on an international basis but how: could it be enforced by the democratic decision of the international community or would it depend entirely on the great powers? The UN was born in the midst of an argument on the nature of international government and democracy reflecting a progressive optimism about the future which would soon be dissipated by the cold war.

The founding of the UN

Planning among the four great powers for the United Nations began in the autumn of 1943 after they had committed themselves in the Moscow Declaration to establishing 'a general international organization, based on the principle of the sovereign equality of all peace-loving states, and open to membership by all such states, large and small, for the maintenance of international peace and security'. From the earliest discussions it was clear that there would be tension between the principle of universality and the need for a pre-eminent role by the great powers.

Roosevelt himself inclined to the first view when discussing disarmament in 1937 with Clark Eichelberger, who would become one of the prime movers behind the CSOP: if most nations agreed on the principle of disarmament, Roosevelt said, 'only a few could hold out against it for very long'. Yet in a subsequent conversation in 1942, Roosevelt expressed a very different, war-hardened view: the approach to post-war disarmament would have to be that of a dictator, and the four great powers would have to 'police and disarm the world'.[9] In his 1943 Christmas Eve message, Roosevelt sought to combine the two views: future peace would depend upon a common determination between Britain, Russia, China, and the United States, but the four powers must 'be united with and cooperate with' the freedom-loving peoples of the whole world and the rights of every nation must be respected. However, in the draft plan for the UN Charter approved at the Dumbarton Oaks conference in October 1944, it was already established that the five permanent great powers in the Security Council (the four and France) would have an effective veto on all decisions except those on procedural matters. According to the draft, the Assembly was not even allowed 'to make recommendations on any matters relating to the maintenance of international peace and security which is being dealt with by the Security Council'. While there would be significant disagreement at Yalta in February 1945 on some issues (such as how to define the 'peace-loving nations' to whom membership was initially confined, and the scope of UN trusteeship which Churchill insisted should not extend to the British colonies liberated from Japan) there was complete harmony between the Soviet Union and the USA on the primary purpose of such an organization—to serve as a tool for the great powers to maintain and if necessary enforce the peace. If the UN was in essence the child nurtured by Roosevelt to bring peace to a troubled world, it was only able to grow because of Stalin's desire to continue the wartime Grand Alliance after the war. Stalin was 'an enthusiastic supporter of Roosevelt's idea that the UN could provide a framework from within which the Great Powers would police a new world order'.[10]

When the San Francisco conference opened on 25 April, a fortnight after the death of Roosevelt, there was still strong pressure from public opinion and among many delegations for a more democratic version of the Charter. The dominant issue, said the *Washington Post* editorially on the eve of the conference, was whether it would result in 'an alliance of the big powers rather than a society embracing all nations'. The *Post* argued for the majority will to be expressed in an international code of justice which would restrain the big powers, and for the Charter itself to be subject to revision every seven years. However, the international climate was darkening: Soviet determination to control Poland cast a long shadow and there were already signs of Truman's shift to a 'get tough' policy with Moscow.[11] In a symbolic shift noted by the *Post*'s correspondent, police had set up road signs proclaiming: 'No Parking, Peace Conference'—but quickly changed this to 'San Francisco Conference'. Peace was being established not at the conference but on the ground where Europe was being divided by the victorious allied armies: within days, the *Washington Post* had changed its editorial line (29 April), acknowledging that 'the overriding fact is that the Big Five will share the power of the world—meaning really the Big Three [Russia, the USA, and Britain]....In other words, they will retain a veto, each one of them, on the use of force.'

Yet that was not the end of the matter: throughout the conference there was a countervailing voice in favour of greater democracy for the larger community of nations, which imposed constraints on the two greatest powers and even achieved some results. The pace-setter for this populist voice calling for a 'genuine society of nations' was at first the Netherlands, in the person of its foreign minister Eelco van Kleffens. In a pre-conference press meeting, Kleffens called for an international code of conduct to be written into the Charter which would constrain the great powers as much as the others (*Washington Post*, 28 April). Amendments tabled by the lesser powers to the Dumbarton Oaks proposals amounted to 700 pages of text: an early concession by the great powers strengthened the authority of the proposed General Assembly, allowing it to recommend measures for the peaceful settlement of any international dispute 'regardless of origin' rather than leaving it entirely to the Security Council. The new clause was judged to be 'generous enough to permit the General Assembly to be a real sounding board for the complaints of all nations' (*Washington Post*, 8 May).

The cause of the smaller nations was then taken up more flamboyantly by Herbert Evatt, foreign minister of Australia's Labour government. By the end of the conference he was being described as 'the

most brilliant and effective voice of the Small Powers, a leading states-
man for the world's conscience'.[12] Evatt in his opening speech warned
that the Dumbarton Oaks proposals bore 'very many characteristics
of a mere prolongation, into the years of peace, of the type of Great
Power leadership that [had] been found necessary in order to win
the war'. He flagged up opposition to the almost unlimited powers
proposed for the Security Council, and especially the veto power, the
highly restricted role of the General Assembly, and other issues relating to the settlement of disputes, social and economic cooperation,
and trusteeship. Energetic and passionate, Evatt sought to outflank the
great powers by holding frequent press conferences to mobilize public
opinion. He worked with some twenty countries, the group varying
in size depending on the issue and the pressure exerted by the great
powers, but including several important South American voices—to
the annoyance of the USA.

On the veto itself, there was little prospect of loosening the great
powers' grip: 'It should be pointed out—because this matter has been
widely misunderstood—' wrote one close observer of the conference,
'that the United States was just as determined as Russia to retain a
veto over enforcement.'[13] The Soviet position initially hardened to the
point where the Soviet delegate Andrei Gromyko appeared to insist on
a veto over procedural matters in the Security Council which meant
that even the discussion of a contentious issue could be blocked. Thus
the Soviet Union was calling for the veto to be stiffened just when
Evatt and his supporters were moving in the opposite direction by
calling for it to be abolished in the case of the peaceful settlement of
disputes. The crisis was only resolved by a direct appeal from President
Truman to Stalin through his personal intermediary Harry Hopkins in
Moscow (won in exchange for a significant concession on the Soviet
role in Poland). The result, as James Reston commented perceptively,
was that the Russians by their tactics had obliged the smaller nations—
relieved that the result was no worse—to accept a sweeping veto in
the Security Council on everything except discussion: their crusade
against the veto had lurched to a halt.[14]

Evatt now staged a last-ditch effort to include decisions on the
peaceful settlement of disputes in the 'procedural' matters exempted
from the veto. 'We don't mind a veto on a shooting match, because
the big powers have to carry the burden of shooting,' he told the press.
'What we object to is a veto on a talking match.' This time he was

slapped down by the USA whose secretary of state Edward Stettinius saw him as behaving like 'a wild steer, doing everything possible he can to break this Conference up'.[15] Even so Evatt's amendment only lost by 10 votes to 20, with a significant number of 15 abstentions including many of the Latin American countries. Evatt's campaign to extend the powers of the General Assembly, during which he entered into direct negotiations with Stettinius and Gromyko, was ultimately more successful. The Assembly won the right to discuss and make recommendations on anything within the scope of the UN Charter or 'relating to the powers and functions of its organs', except for matters actually before the Security Council: this meant that any issue that the Council failed or refused to take up could be discussed by the Assembly.

Summing up the results of San Francisco in liberalizing and making more democratic the original Dumbarton Oaks text, Evatt readily acknowledged that he could not possibly have succeeded without 'the resolution and steadfastness of many nations'. Their collective effort, backed by public opinion, also helped to improve other sections of the Charter, especially in the preamble and chapter 1, which now included provisions on human rights and international justice, and on universal economic and social goals such as full employment, health, and non-discrimination.[16] These provided the legal basis for the wide range of UN specialized agencies which have since then made an incalculable contribution to raising standards of living and promoting development across the world.

However, the UN's relative success in promoting peace in its larger economic and social aspects only underlined the organization's failure to develop similar mechanisms for tackling the problems of war. The Charter established a Military Staff Committee (MSC)—the only subsidiary body of any sort actually named in the document—to 'advise and assist' the Security Council on all questions of a military nature, including both the employment of any armed forces placed at the UN's disposal and any measures of arms control and possible disarmament. All member states were required by the Charter to respond to any call from the Security Council to provide armed forces when needed, and to negotiate special agreements with the Security Council so that such forces would be defined in advance and earmarked for use. The MSC was composed of the chiefs of staff of all five permanent members (or their representatives), but any member which provided military forces could join in the decisions of the Security Council—another unique provision in the Charter. Armed forces employed by the UN would remain under the command (according to a later decision of the MSC) of their own national armed forces but they would also serve under the 'strategic direction' of the MSC, which in turn was responsible to the Security Council.

On paper this demonstrated a robust attitude to the use of force by the UN in order to 'maintain or restore international peace and security', and—again on paper—even the assumption of a measure of authority over national contingents. If properly implemented, it would have meant that the UN had both ready access to military forces and matériel on a significant scale, and a staff structure capable of exercising ultimate control. The MSC began meetings in February 1946 and was soon pressed by the General Assembly through the Security Council for results. It produced a report on 'general principles governing the organisation of the armed forces made available to the Security Council by [UN] members' (MS/265) which showed agreement on many points, but its proceedings then became bogged down in discord. After two years' work the MSC remained deadlocked on the disputed articles and from then on till the end of the cold war it operated (according to one of few academic studies on this body ever published) as 'all but the most empty shell'.[17]

The story of the foundation of the UN, and the struggle to make it a democratic instrument for a more peaceful world, needs to be recalled more often. Nearly seven decades later, it is a reminder both of the magnitude of the task and of the aspirations for universalism which today are much more rarely voiced. The UN diplomat Erskine Childers might put this clearly with characteristic internationalist vision after the end of the cold war—when there were again brief hopes that the ideal might be fully realized. The UN 'was born on a great tide of yearning among ordinary people for democratic multilateral institutions' that would harness humanity's best intellectual and scientific resources 'to tackle problems which must never again result in such hideous conflict'. In spite of the grip on proceedings by the great powers, San Francisco achieved a Charter providing a remarkably sound framework to tackle the whole world's problems. Its wording

reached out all over the globe, lifting people in the hope of saving 'succeeding generations from the scourge of war'... of employing 'international machinery for the promotion of the economic and social advancement of all peoples', and of 'international peace and security with the least diversion for armaments of the world's human and economic resources'. The Charter made the vital connections between political and military, and socio-economic security, stating that 'conditions of stability and well-being [are] necessary for peaceful and friendly relations among nations based on respect [for] equal rights and self-determination...'.[18]

How does the experience of the UN, after the euphoria of its foundation, compare with the experience of the League? The establishment of both organizations was greeted with high hopes and rhetoric, but in the case of the UN these would fade very quickly while the League had retained its popular appeal for much longer. In Britain, the League of Nations Union (LNU) had acquired over 400,000 paying members by 1931 organized into 3,000 branches. Its post-war successor organization the UNA-UK filled the Royal Albert Hall for its inaugural meeting in 1945, but its membership peaked in 1949 at 85,000 with some 200 branches and these figures have never since been matched.[19] As seen by historians of both organizations, the League in 1920 had offered 'almost unlimited prospects of a new spirit and new methods', whereas by contrast the huge enthusiasm evoked by the founding of the UN in 1945 was 'not much longer than a curtain-call'.[20] The League's ideal of internationalism retained a strong appeal for nearly two decades in spite of many setbacks; by the early 1950s supporters of the UN seeking to assert the same ideal were already on the defensive.

Some of the reasons for this came evidently from the failure of the two greatest powers, without whom the UN could not have been set up, to agree to work within its spirit to find solutions to the biggest issues facing the post-war world—control of nuclear weapons, democratic outcomes in Europe (mostly in the Soviet-controlled East but also in some countries of the West under US influence such as Italy and Greece), an agreed programme of economic reconstruction, and a range of Asian problems complicated by revolution and the post-war return of the colonial powers. After 1949 the exclusion of China from the UN, and the outbreak of the Korean War in which the forces of the Western allies served under the flag of the UN, weakened its international appeal further.

Beyond these evident difficulties posed by the cold war, the UN also suffered from hostility and prejudice stirred up by McCarthyism in the USA. Perversely, at a time when the General Assembly was still largely responsive to the wishes of the USA, American public opinion was inflamed to regard the organization as pro-communist and anti-American. The McCarthyite witch-hunt had a disastrous effect on the careers of many loyal UN officials and seriously damaged the work of its specialized agencies. The UN scholar Linda Melvern has highlighted one crucial but forgotten case—that of senior UN economist Alfred Van Tassel who organized the world's first international conference on the environment in 1949. Called to consider 'the wasteful use of the world's natural resources', some 700 international scientists discussed deforestation and its effects on drainage and soil erosion, the problems involved with the control of water pollution, the possibilities of hydro-power, and the conservation of marine life, and proposed ways of achieving more sustainable and equitable growth. One of the most striking presentations was given by the US conservationist Henry Fairfield Osborn, Jr, who had just published *Our Plundered Planet* (1948), a fierce critique of humanity's poor stewardship of the earth's resources. Osborn told the conference:

In considering the problem of organic or life-supporting resources, we are dealing with the economy of nature which in truth is life itself. Consequently, we need to recognize that forests, water resources, productive soils and animal life are interrelated and dependent one upon the other. Our conservation practices, generally speaking, do not even begin as yet to be adapted to this cardinal truth. It is evident that the solution of the renewable resource problem demands a new and enlightened approach...[21]

Van Tassel's career was soon destroyed because of his friendship with one of the thirty-eight UN employees named in 1952 as 'UN Communists' by the McCarran Senate Internal Security Subcommittee. Appearing before the senators, he tried in vain to explain to them that internationalism did not turn people into traitors. He was soon dismissed from the UN after pleading the Fifth Amendment. The significant proceedings of this conference have been wiped from institutional memory, concludes Melvern, and 'the UN's environmental effort officially starts with the UN Conference on the Human Environment in Stockholm in 1972'.[22]

Peace as propaganda

The cold war was an extended period of acute and dangerous conflict, not (as some neo-revisionist historians now regard it) a period of peace, and the possibility that it would escalate into a hot war was never absent from people's minds. To reverse the dictum of Clausewitz, international politics became the continuation of war by other means. Under these circumstances, it is little wonder that the concept of peace suffered: the term was misappropriated for propaganda purposes by both superpowers and their allies, those who sought to use it in a genuine sense were likely to be accused of naivety or subversion, and because of the overwhelming threat of nuclear war its meaning narrowed to focus mainly on opposition to nuclear weapons.

In the official lexis of the superpowers, the term 'peace' was annexed to portray the policies of the user as dedicated to the goal of a peaceful world, while its use by the 'other side' was portrayed as deceptive and designed to conceal its real intentions. When the USA talked of peace and freedom, the Soviet press described this as a 'smokescreen' for the aggressive designs of international capitalism. When the Soviet Union talked of the peace-loving peoples of the world, the US press described this as a 'peace offensive' designed to lull the free world into lowering its guard. Beyond the demands of public propaganda, there was on both sides a less visible 'peace strategy' designed to gain advantage in the cold war contest.

In 1951 Pablo Picasso, then at the height of his reputation, produced a painting titled *Massacre in Korea*, and followed this with a series of works under the heading of 'War and Peace'. *Massacre in Korea* follows the iconographic tradition of works by Goya and Manet in showing the execution of civilians by soldiers, in a starkly bifurcated composition. To the left of the picture, a group of naked women and children stand in front of an empty pit: to the right, a group of naked but helmeted soldiers advance, thrusting grotesque phallic weapons towards the unarmed group, commanded by an officer with massive thighs and outstretched sword. One of the children flees in terror from the soldiers, a smaller one crouches on the ground playing with stones. The picture is comparable in its intensity of emotion with *Guernica*, although designed on a smaller scale. In the eyes of some critics it is a less successful work artistically, but it was criticized on other grounds at the time. Picasso had joined the French Communist Party in 1944 and received the Stalin Peace Prize in 1950, the year when the Korean War broke out. His painting was taken to refer to communist claims of a massacre of Korean civilians by American forces—flatly denied by the USA—in a location known as No Gun Ri.

Unsurprisingly, Picasso's work was evaluated more on political than artistic criteria. The famous Dove of Peace which he had drawn for the Soviet-sponsored World Peace Congress in 1950 was regarded as a pro-Soviet symbol and Picasso was denied a visa to the USA. Until recently Picasso's peace-oriented work of the early 1950s has been among the less well known and discussed parts of his output. However, in 2003 the British artist David Hockney produced a work based on *Massacre in Korea*, with the suggestive title *The Massacre and Problems of Depiction*, and in 2010 an exhibition 'Picasso: Peace and Freedom' at Tate Liverpool gathered together for the first time a significant quantity of his cold war work (see Plate 12). To complete the story we should note that in 1999 the *Associated Press* news agency found eyewitness evidence from US veterans that a massacre did take place, as alleged at the time, at No Gun Ri. In January 2001 a US army review of the evidence conceded that Korean civilians had probably been killed in the area, but maintained that if so it was 'an unfortunate tragedy inherent to war and not a deliberate killing'.[23]

The contested nature of peace was visible during the cold war almost daily, both in routine news coverage and in government statements from the USA, the Soviet Union, and their respective client states or allies. In August 1951 a delegation of British Quakers was received in the Kremlin, shortly after a slight thaw in the cold war as agreement was finally reached to begin the Korean War truce talks. They were told by deputy foreign minister Jacob Malik that Russia was ready 'to enter into negotiations of a most businesslike character and with a view to agreement' with any power and on any issue. This may or may not have been intended as a positive signal: *Time* magazine did not pause to consider the matter. Under the headline 'Peace Offensive' it reported (6 August 1951) that 'Moscow continued to talk peace, peace, peace'. Condemning Malik's 'unctuous tone', it concluded that 'Moscow's purpose was as transparent as vodka: to lure the West into relaxing.' In the febrile mood of McCarthyism, a report published by the House Committee on Un-American Activities in April of the same year was influential. It described the 'Communist "peace" offensive' as 'the most dangerous hoax ever devised by the international Communist conspiracy', warning that 'unless it is completely exposed, many may be deceived and ensnared'.[24] The task of honest reporting by US diplomats abroad, on the defensive as they watched former colleagues denounced in the witch-hunt, became increasingly difficult. Evidence of significant developments—for example, tensions between China and the Soviet Union which might indicate that the relationship between Moscow and Beijing was less than 'monolithic'—was identified by government researchers but failed to reach higher levels or influence policy.

Western governments went to extraordinary lengths to frustrate the activities of Soviet-sponsored peace organizations. Plans to hold the Second World Peace Congress in Sheffield were thwarted by British action which denied entry to most delegates, and the venue was then moved to Warsaw. Harold Holt, the Australian minister of immigration, warned that any Australian citizens who attended would be dealt with severely, and that their passports would be cancelled if they entered Poland. (One of those who defied the ban, the Australian feminist Jessie Street, caused consternation by using a British passport on which she was also entitled to travel: although she had dual nationality she was accused by Holt of obtaining her passport by fraud.) The concept of a worldwide Soviet 'peace offensive', having been established in the early 1950s, became a useful tool until well into the 1980s as a way of discrediting independent peace initiatives, particularly in the nuclear disarmament field, as well as those which really had Soviet backing. Certainly the Soviet Union did sponsor peace campaigns which were transparently one-sided in their opposition to US/Western policies that heightened international tension, while remaining silent about, or actively condoning, similar measures by the Soviet bloc. A resolution passed by the Communist Information Bureau in November 1949 conveys the crude flavour of this activity especially in the early cold war years.

The Defence of Peace and the Struggle Against the Warmongers
During this period the two lines in world policy have been still more clearly and more sharply revealed: the line of the democratic anti-imperialist camp headed by the U.S.S.R., the camp which conducts a persistent and consistent struggle for peace among the peoples and for democracy; and the line of the imperialist anti-democratic camp headed by the ruling circles of the United States, the camp which has as its main aim the forcible establishment of Anglo-American world domination, the enslavement of foreign countries and peoples, the destruction of democracy and the unleashing of a new war.[25]

The resolution went on to say that efforts should be made to 'unite honest supporters of peace' under the leadership of communist and workers' parties in the anti-war movement, while exposing 'Right-Wing Socialist leaders' and 'reactionary trade unionist leaders' in the West as 'the bitterest enemies of peace'. Throughout the next decades, the Soviet-led mobilization of 'international forces for peace' through the World Peace Council and other organizations and forums inflicted real harm on efforts to form a genuinely international peace movement.

The misuse of the term 'peace' in the cold war by both sides would reach a scale which now seems ludicrously Orwellian but was barely questioned at the time. The original motto of the US Strategic Air Command was 'War is our Profession: Peace is our Product'; this was simplified later to 'Peace is our Profession'. In 1972 the popular children's TV serial *Lassie* staged a four-part series under the title 'Peace is our Profession' in which the eponymous dog paid a visit to the Vandenberg Air Force Base in California. In one episode Lassie violated missile range space to rescue a snow goose which he had befriended from an imminent missile launch. In another episode a diabetic poodle stowed away on the SAC's airborne command post: when this was discovered the plane was allowed to land early so the dog could receive his next insulin shot in time. The controversial MX intercontinental range missile deployed by the USA in the 1980s had a multiple (MIRV) capacity, carrying ten re-entry vehicles, each armed with a 300-kiloton warhead (fifteen times as powerful as the Hiroshima bomb). It was originally to be called the Peace-maker, but this was changed to Peace-keeper. Soviet propaganda posters hailed the courage of their MIG fighter pilots in daring to 'fly higher than all others' in the defence of peace. The Soviet armed forces were routinely referred to as fighters for peace, but the greatest 'peace fighter' of all until his death in 1953 was, naturally, Comrade Josef Stalin.

Missed opportunities

Modern historians often suggest a sense of inevitability about the dashing of post-war peace hopes and the onset of the cold war. While the various schools of thought on cold war history do not agree on its causes, they all identify powerful forces at work which could not have been diverted or deterred. In this sense the overwhelming view— a view which I am challenging here—is a crudely determinist one: however dire the consequences may have been, it is allegedly difficult if not impossible to imagine another outcome than the one that actually occurred.

In the orthodox Western view, the root responsibility lay with the Soviet Union, whether it acted as a great power determined to maximize its security and strength, or as the leader of the world communist movement denying the possibility of long-term coexistence—or was driven by both. This resulted in an expansionist policy which threatened post-war Europe and Western interests more widely, and necessarily led to a hostile response. While in theory the Soviet leadership might have been persuaded to adopt in its own interests a less provocative course of action, this was not possible under a system dominated by fear and deference to a supreme leader: hence, the cold war was inevitable.

The revisionist view of cold war history which developed in the 1960s and 1970s appears at first to deny its inevitability. It assigns main responsibility to the hard-line policies of the USA under President Truman, which sought to deny the Soviet Union the sphere of influence it might reasonably have expected to ensure its own security, and was hostile to any progressive forces in Western politics which would have favoured a more consensual relationship. Most versions of this revisionist view also see a fundamental ideological thrust in US policy representing the interests and values of a capitalist system which sought to reproduce itself globally and was innately hostile to the 'socialist' economic alternative offered by the Soviet Union. Some suggest that it is conceivable that if President Roosevelt had not died, the USA and its allies would have continued to accept a 'Yalta model' of post-war arrangement into spheres of influence and that this would have reduced the potential for the cold war. However, the revisionist view is pinned to such an extent on the perceived clash of fundamental values (in an almost mirror image of the orthodox view) that, if accurate, this would have made post-war compromise almost impossible to achieve.[26]

Both approaches began to be supplanted in the later years of the cold war by a new set of interpretations which drew from the earlier analyses and to some extent reconciled them. The new approach, now labelled post-revisionist, placed more emphasis upon mutual misperception and mutual reaction in the superpower relationship: while it might be conceded that the Soviet Union did not actually intend to invade Western Europe after the Second World War, it was natural for Western policy-makers to believe that such a 'Soviet threat' existed, so that the counter-measures then taken easily fed into Soviet suspicions of an aggressive capitalism. On both sides, calculations of national security interest would always be based on the worst-possible-case hypothesis—the presumed enemy could never be given the benefit of the doubt.

Overall, the post-revisionist approach, while attaching much more weight to subjective factors in cold war thinking, views the (mis-) perceptions and (mis-)calculations driving these factors as so powerful that, again, it is hard to envisage any other outcome than that which actually occurred. However regrettable the cold war, there was no way that it could end its course unless and until one of the two rival world views and systems was forced by external pressure or internal weakness, or a combination of both, to concede defeat. (How to evaluate these forces is the main subject of the continuing debate over 'who ended the cold war'.)

In the decade after the ending of the cold war, this relatively balanced post-revisionist view gave way in turn to a less nuanced perspective which has been called neo-orthodox. This, while conceding the mutually reinforcing effects of cold war policies of both superpowers, nevertheless returned to assigning primary responsibility to the Soviet side. (This transition from post-revisionist to neo-orthodox was particularly noticeable in the work of one of the foremost US cold war scholars, John Lewis Gaddis.)[27] However, more recently there has been a revival of interest in the possibility that opportunities were missed to bring the cold war to a conclusion at a much earlier date.[28] It was the failure to grasp these opportunities, it will be argued here, which not only perpetuated and intensified the cold war, but brought back to life, under the most adverse and constricting conditions, the peace movements of the late 1950s onwards (see Chapter 8).

The Soviet 'illusion of peace'

Though Stalin had, in a rare interview at the end of 1952, signalled that he would welcome a meeting with the incoming US president Dwight Eisenhower to discuss easing world tensions, this was dismissed by Eisenhower's advisers as another propaganda gesture. However, his death three months later was followed by a series of conciliatory statements and actions which demanded to be taken more seriously. 'Since the death of Stalin on 5 March 1953', a senior policy planner at the State Department noted, 'there have been more Soviet gestures toward the West than at any other similar period.'[29] Georgy Malenkov, who now succeeded Stalin as chairman of the Council of Ministers, quickly declared that 'there is no litigious or unresolved question which could not be settled by peaceful means on the basis of the mutual agreement of the countries concerned... including the United States of America'. Within days, Moscow had endorsed an exchange of sick and wounded prisoners of war in Korea, and had given other signals of approving a peaceful settlement to the war there: the long-stalled armistice talks resumed on 2 April. Soon, traffic restrictions around Berlin were lifted and Moscow offered to resume quadripartite negotiations on safety in the Berlin air corridors—another long-running cold war sore. It renounced its long-standing claim on military control of the Dardanelles and the Bosphorus; and finally agreed to the appointment of Dag Hammarskjöld as new UN secretary-general. It also put out feelers for a meeting between Malenkov and Eisenhower to discuss disarmament.[30] The Soviet anti-Zionist campaign was curtailed and diplomatic relations opened with Israel, while relations eased with Yugoslavia and ambassadors were exchanged with Belgrade. On the crucial issue of a divided Germany, the post-Stalin leadership repeated long-standing proposals for a peace treaty leading to a unified and neutral Germany: these might be regarded as more credible now in the light of the positive steps taken, as listed above, in other areas of Soviet foreign policy.

The new moves from Moscow were well publicized: on 13 April *Newsweek* published a list with the heading 'Peace Bids: A Calendar of Communist Offers'. By July, the new US ambassador to the Soviet Union, Charles Bohlen, was reporting that recent changes in Soviet policies, both internal and external, could no longer be dismissed simply as another 'peace campaign', and that 'most evidence to date would indicate that the Soviet Government desires a return to diplomacy and a lessening of world tension for an indefinite period of time'.[31] Eisenhower initially wavered, but soon subscribed to the dominant view in Washington that the new Soviet posture was simply designed to weaken Western resolve at a critical time in the negotiations to set up a European defence community. After a month of internal debate, Eisenhower finally responded with his speech, 'A Chance for Peace', on 16 April. Despite its title, this did not engage directly with the Soviet proposals but called for far-reaching concessions by the communist side from Europe to Asia, in effect asking the Soviet leadership

'to alter its entire foreign policy in exchange for American goodwill'.
This was driven home two days later in a speech by John Foster Dulles,
who argued that the Soviet Union was attempting 'to buy off a powerful enemy and gain a respite', to create the 'illusion of peace' based on
the post-war status quo, whereas the USA must make it 'clear to the
captive people [in Eastern Europe] that we do not accept their captivity as a permanent fact of history'.[32]

Winston Churchill was alone among Western leaders in wishing to
explore the possibility of meaningful détente with Moscow. In a correspondence with Eisenhower, he urged that the Western allies should
wait and see where the post-Stalin leadership was heading: 'We do
not know what these men mean. We do not want to deter them from
saying what they mean....'[33] Churchill warned that issues between the
West and the Soviet Union should be solved one by one rather than, as
Eisenhower appeared to demand, in one fell swoop. He privately proposed a summit conference of the Big Three on neutral territory, and
failing that offered to fly to Moscow to meet Malenkov alone. When
Eisenhower showed impatience with Churchill's proposals, the British
prime minister went public with a speech to the House of Commons
(11 May 1953) in which he explored the prospect of offering security
guarantees to the Soviet Union in exchange for a united Germany,
and declared that the time had come for world leaders to confer 'on
the highest level'. The speech was greeted with cautious approval in
Moscow but with horror and anger in Washington. The Republican
Senate majority leader William Knowland accused Churchill of a policy of appeasement. Eisenhower told a news conference that 'the world
happened to be round' and he did not see how one could discuss 'the
great problems of today' piecemeal as Churchill proposed.[34]

Some moves in the direction of détente were successfully carried
out in the next two years, notably the achievement of cease-fires in
Indochina and Korea, the signing of the Austrian State Treaty, and
the holding in Geneva of the first summit conference since 1945 in
Potsdam. Yet a chance to move forward towards solving what was,
together with the division of Germany, the most threatening international issue—the nuclear arms race—was lost almost unnoticed in
1955. On 10 May 1955, the Soviet Union tabled a paper at the UN
Disarmament Subcommittee in Geneva which included the main features of an Anglo-French memorandum for which the USA had previously expressed support. As summarized by the cold war historian

Matthew Evangelista, in one of few studies of this crucial episode, the goals of the memorandum included

the total prohibition of the use and manufacture of nuclear weapons; major reductions in all armed forces and conventional armaments; and the establishment of adequate organs of control and inspection. The USSR's adherence to the plan would have entailed cutting back the Soviet armed forces from 5.7 million soldiers to between 1 and 1.5 million. These figures, proposed originally by the Western powers, would have constituted a significantly disproportionate reduction in Soviet forces, compared with the reduction in French, British and US forces. In return, the Soviets would have benefited from the eventual destruction of stocks of US nuclear weapons, although their own would have been destroyed as well. The USSR seemed willing to accept such a deal.[35]

The initial Western response was favourable: the US delegate expressed his government's gratification; the British delegate expressed satisfaction that the Soviet Union had accepted the West's proposals 'largely, and in some cases, entirely', and that 'we have made an advance that I never dreamed possible', while the French exclaimed that 'the whole thing looks too good to be true'. However, when the subcommittee reconvened in the autumn, the US delegate placed a reservation on his government's previous position and the other Western governments refused to discuss further the Soviet proposal. They did so on the grounds that the proposals for inspection in a nuclear-free world—proposals that they themselves had made—might not prevent a state from cheating and maintaining a secret stock of nuclear weapons. While this was an important technical issue, it had not prevented the West from urging their proposals upon the Soviet Union before, with the argument that an imperfect plan for nuclear disarmament was better than none at all. It was still the case that this possibility would be greatly reduced by a system of UN on-the-ground inspection—which the Soviet Union had at last accepted. In the words of the Nobel Peace Prize winner Philip Noel-Baker, there had been a 'moment of hope', but it had passed. (Significantly, Noel-Baker's analysis, published in 1958, was still 'the classic account of these negotiations' when Evangelista wrote about them more than three decades later.)[36]

Beijing's overture rebuffed

Another opportunity to take a different turning in the cold war was missed in the mid-1950s, when a tentative dialogue between the USA and China at joint ambassadorial talks was rebuffed—an episode which has also received scant attention until recently.[37] Earlier still, in 1945 on the eve of the Chinese civil war, Mao Zedong had sought to open a direct dialogue with President Roosevelt, even offering to fly to Washington. (The offer was blocked by the US embassy in the Chinese Nationalist capital of Chongqing and Roosevelt was probably never aware of it.) At that stage, the Chinese Communist Party was still a junior partner in the wartime united front with Chiang Kai-shek. Ten years later, it was the ruling party of the People's China with whom the USA had just been at war in Korea. Mao and his fellow leaders once more sought to test the possibilities of negotiation with Washington. The time again seemed propitious for some improvement in USA–China relations, following the death of Stalin, the end of the Korean War and the first Vietnam War, and Beijing's adoption of the 'five principles of peaceful coexistence'. Taiwan was the obvious stumbling block: in 1954 Eisenhower announced his intention of signing a Mutual Defence Treaty with the Nationalist regime on the island and Beijing responded by shelling the Nationalist-controlled Offshore Islands. Yet it was this crisis that paved the way for the talks between the US and Chinese ambassadors beginning in Geneva in August 1955. It was significant too that the initiative came from Beijing, which preferred a bilateral dialogue with Washington to a Soviet proposal for an international conference on Taiwan. This was one of several signs at the time of China's desire to emerge from under the shadow of Soviet diplomacy.

The talks were initially promising and resulted in agreement on the first item on the agenda—the mutual exchange of civilians detained on both sides. Negotiations now moved on to the second item, defined as the consideration of 'other practical matters at issue between the two parties'. Here the USA simply stone-walled while China made a number of positive proposals, including one for a meeting of foreign ministers at which, Beijing suggested, 'practical and feasible means' could be found to defuse the Taiwan situation. As Kenneth Young, a former State Department official familiar with the negotiations, later concluded, a hopeful opportunity was missed. If Washington had broken the deadlock by conceding a foreign ministers' conference, this might have led to a high-level negotiation in which China continued to talk about 'easing tensions' in the Taiwan area rather than demand immediate US withdrawal of support for Chiang Kai-shek. Instead the USA 'did not want diplomatic relations or continuing negotiations with Peking. Washington wanted to isolate, not enhance, Peking.'[38]

Young's conclusion is supported in a more recent study of the talks: the aim of Secretary of State Dulles was simply to keep the Chinese talking for as long as possible without seeking any real improvement in relations.[39] Ironically, when Washington finally began to make its own tentative overtures in the early 1960s, it was Beijing which responded at first with an 'all-or-nothing' rejection. Only after the chaos of the Cultural Revolution and the threat of Soviet military action would Mao finally 'seize the hour'. Chinese historians now acknowledge that this was a tragic mistake—but it had been preceded by an equally tragic lost chance on the US side.[40] When Henry Kissinger in October 1971 was paving the way in Beijing for the Nixon visit, he had to find a form of wording to describe the unity of China which would be acceptable to Beijing but would not support either the mainland's or Taipei's claim to be the sole Chinese government. Eventually, as he relates in his memoirs, Kissinger put forward an 'ambiguous formula' which both Beijing and Washington were able to live with. He did not invent this formula himself. It was 'adapted from a State Department planning document for negotiations, which aborted in the Fifties'.[41] We can only speculate how different the course of history might have been if those negotiations had not been 'aborted' by John Foster Dulles.

Obstacles to understanding

The cold war continued unabated with only limited periods of détente, and with an exponential increase in the US and Soviet nuclear arsenals. In spite of the shift in Soviet ideology from the doctrine of inevitable war with capitalism to that of peaceful coexistence, the two blocs coexisted, and on occasion reached agreement, as if under compulsion, and in an atmosphere of hostility and suspicion which more than once—most notably during the 1962 Cuba crisis—nearly precipitated a nuclear war. What then were the reasons for the failure to seize the chance after Stalin's death and in subsequent years?

On the US side, there was little or no political willingness to seek compromise with what was seen, in unvarnished terms, as the enemy, whether this was the Soviet Union with its alleged expansionist territorial aims, or World Communism (with the same aims), or both. As one of the editors of a recent study of this period has concluded, no senior US officials regarded the succession to Stalin as an occasion for the relaxation of tensions or the resolving of differences. 'To the extent that administration officials saw in Stalin's death an opportunity, it was perceived only as a chance for victory in the Cold War.'[42] The historians Joyce and Gabriel Kolko have described post-war US policy as based on 'a strategy of fear'—a concept acknowledged by Dulles who wrote in 1955 that the US-led alliance had been held together till then 'largely by a cement compounded of fear and a sense of moral superiority'. The Eisenhower administration, they argue, while never abandoning its ideological, mystifying view of the world crisis, was also quite capable of perceiving the changed circumstances clearly and of understanding 'the need to sustain a sense of danger even when they knew none existed'. The success of the Soviet peace offensive in convincing a few Western leaders of the value of diplomacy challenged the basis of the alliance, and began a process of erosion of US leadership which was to become 'a defining trend of post-war history'.[43]

Keeping the Western allies in line, and maintaining the cohesion of the US power bloc, was therefore an important consideration: Soviet proposals for a unified neutral Germany were obviously ruled out of court, and the occasional temptation on the part of France and Britain to take an independent diplomatic course caused alarm in Washington. In a revealing comment on the Soviet disarmament proposals of May 1955, Dulles observed that 'the Soviets had actually gone a long way to meet the British and French position on disarmament, without realizing that there was a very wide gap between the United States and the British and French on the issue of disarmament'.[44] Dulles also had a visceral dislike for the Soviet professions of peace, which many other Western officials shared. Emmet John Hughes, a Democrat who had joined the Eisenhower team of speech-writers, complained that 'we are drowning in a sea of [Soviet] honey'. Eisenhower himself told Churchill at the US–Anglo-French summit in Bermuda that 'Russia was a woman of the streets and whether her dress was new, or just the old one patched, it was certainly the same whore underneath. America intended to drive her off her present "beat" into the back streets.'[45] A reverse version of this unpleasant metaphor had been used by one of Churchill's own officials (the Foreign Office was uniformly opposed to his personal quest for détente) who told Foreign Secretary Anthony Eden that they did not believe in 'whoring after the Russians' and that the allies would be incredulous if Eden appeared to be 'gallivanting with Molotov'.[46]

Political judgement took second place, in any case, to perceived military wisdom. At the time of Stalin's death the Soviet Union was believed, according to the inflated estimates of Western intelligence, to have 175 front-line divisions, 'armed to the teeth and ready to attack at a moment's notice', and the assumption was that Moscow was 'capable of the worst'. Western leaders were constrained by their commitment to deterrence: détente would inject uncertainty into the balance of power and in their military advisers' view actually require more, not less, military strength.[47] This calculation prevailed again when the Soviet Union unexpectedly acceded to the Western disarmament proposals in May 1955. Declassified documents show that most American officials 'preferred the risk of an unconstrained arms race' to any conceivable disarmament agreement. They were sceptical about the possibility of adequate verification but believed anyhow 'that US security would be better served by an arms build-up'. This was put clearly by the US joint chiefs of staff in a memorandum commenting on Governor Stassen's report on disarmament policy, which had proposed various compromise measures and was rejected by the administration. 'There is less risk to the security of the United States', the chiefs concluded, 'in the continuation of current armament trends than in entering into an international armaments limitation agreement.'[48]

Maintaining the image of American dominance in East Asia, and therefore its commitment to the Chinese Nationalist government on Taiwan, was also a significant factor behind Washington's lack of interest in exploring the lengths to which the ambassadorial dialogue with China might go. In a study of this important but neglected episode, Steven Goldstein has written that Taiwan was central to administration policy: its existence—or rather the survival of the Chiang Kai-shek regime—was 'essential in maintaining the belief in Asia that the mainland juggernaut could be stopped and that the United States would stand by its anti-communist friends'.[49] (Whether there was any evidence for an expansionist China was another, and mostly undiscussed, matter.) After the agreement in principle had been reached in September 1955 on the mutual repatriation of nationals from each country who wished to return home, the USA reluctantly moved on to the discussion of other, broader, issues raised by the Chinese, but set a condition which they knew Beijing could never agree to: namely, that China must 'renounce the use of force' in the Taiwan Straits—effectively, that China must accept a limitation on its sovereign power.

Moreover, it is clear from internal US documents that even if Beijing had met this demand, the USA would still have refused to consider lifting the trade embargo imposed on China. Dulles's strategy was to spin out the talks without seeking any further agreement: his purpose was to 'beat [China] at their own game by out-sitting and out-talking them'.[50]

On the Soviet side, what were the obstacles to meaningful agreement at this early potential turning point in the cold war? First, foreign policy towards the West too frequently became entangled in intra-Party factional politics, and anyone who proposed relaxation or compromise was vulnerable, unless the policy paid off very quickly, to the accusation of yielding to imperialism. This was the case in the two most important post-war issues—nuclear disarmament and finding a solution to the German question. Georgy Malenkov, whose speech at Stalin's funeral had first signalled a new direction for Soviet policy, openly highlighted the dangers of nuclear war for the future of humanity a year later (12 March 1954). When Malenkov was denounced by Khrushchev in a speech of 8 February 1955, and demoted from his pre-eminent post, he would be blamed for being too pessimistic about the consequences of nuclear war which, Khrushchev insisted, 'would not lead to the end of civilization but to the end of capitalism [and] to an expansion of our borders'. (Khrushchev himself would abandon this line a year later at the 20th Soviet Party Congress—and was then denounced by Mao Zedong for doing so.)

Any substantial progress towards détente would require progress towards a solution of the German question, and the renunciation of the goal of 'building socialism' in that part of Germany under Soviet control. One of the charges against the Soviet intelligence chief Lavrenty Beria, when he was ousted in the first post-Stalin purge, was that he had suggested that a 'peaceful'—i.e. neutral—rather than a 'socialist' Germany would be 'sufficient for our purposes' (if agreement could be reached with the West). As observed in a recent study of Russia and the cold war, 'The uncertain progress of de-Stalinization was continually called into question by active opponents in the leadership. Unrest in Eastern Europe consequent upon further de-Stalinization would play into their hands.'[51] In general, it could be dangerous to suggest that the USA and the Soviet Union had a shared interest in relaxing international tension. By doing so, another scholar of this period has suggested, Malenkov 'was placing the two great enemies on the same footing, calling for compromises from his side as well as the enemy's'.[52]

Russian political leaders recognized the drain on their resources of defence expenditure in the mid-1950s, and wished to divert part of these to raising living standards and satisfying consumer demand, yet again they were vulnerable to the charge of failing to match US strength: only substantial and speedy gains in disarmament would have neutralized the accusation. Instead, as the arms race intensified, the voices of the Soviet military lobby acquired greater strength. As late as 1980–1, there was open controversy in the Soviet media between the defence minister Dmitri Ustinov, appointed by Party general secretary Leonid Brezhnev to keep military spending under control, and the chief of staff Nikolai Ogarkov. In July 1981 Ogarkov published a barely disguised call (in the theoretical journal *Kommunist*) for higher military spending to meet the needs of a nuclear war, in which, he had already maintained, victory remained 'an objective possibility'. This compelled Ustinov to publish what amounted to a riposte (in *Pravda* in November) where he rejected the idea that a nuclear war could be survived, let alone won.[53]

The closed nature of the Soviet system and its resort *in extremis* to punitive military suppression, as in East Germany in 1953 and Hungary in 1956, not only gave opponents of détente in the West ready ammunition for scepticism, but made even the more open-minded hesitate. (The invasion of Czechoslovakia in 1968 would have a similar inhibiting effect.) The judgement of Gabriel Kolko is harsh but justified: Leninism 'possessed no inhibiting ethical criteria to constrain its exercise and abuse of power' and while a communist monopoly of power may have been needed at first to defend against external and internal enemies, 'as Leninists they turned necessity into a virtue and they were immune to their own people'.[54] Dissidents such as the philosopher Roy Medvedev called in vain for 'socialist democratization' which would make foreign policy subject to public scrutiny, so that the Soviet people could exert influence by 'openly expressing views and opinions'.[55] The opaque nature of Soviet foreign policy was acknowledged by Mikhail Gorbachev whose 'new thinking' included the call for a return to 'honest and open politics' in Soviet foreign relations. Writing in the mid-1980s, Gorbachev still found it necessary to make the case against the dogmatic view that peaceful coexistence was simply 'a specific form of class struggle'.[56]

Although most of the above strictures apply also to the Chinese Communist Party, the relative lack of division (at this stage) within its leadership made foreign policy less of a factional issue, and the hand of Premier Zhou Enlai (who as foreign minister personally led the mid-1950s diplomacy) would have been strengthened by a favourable response from the USA. China had an even greater need, after three decades of internal and external war, than the Soviet Union for a reduction of tension to allow faster economic reconstruction. However, although Zhou's initiative had been approved by Mao Zedong, there is some evidence that Mao was not entirely happy from the start. As summarized by Zhang Baijia, a leading Party historian of the Chinese Communist Party, Mao's view in 1958 (when it was clear that the initiative had failed) was that 'China's original policy was good and instead of developing diplomatic relations with the United States, it should have persisted in its struggle against the United States'. Although some Chinese diplomats were criticized, Mao took most of the blame for himself: it was he who had instructed them to make contact with the American officials, but 'this instruction had not been in line with his usual line of thinking', which was that China should 'insist on waging struggle against the United States and refrain from developing relations with the US government'.[57] It remains probable that the radical shift of Mao's last years—from the Great Leap Forward (1958–61) onwards to the Cultural Revolution (1966–76)—would have been softened, at least in some degree, by a successful diplomatic opening to the West. A USA–China thaw might also have slowed Beijing's drive to acquire the bomb, by reducing China's sense of insecurity at a time when its relations with the Soviet Union were deteriorating.[58] These questions remain intriguing but unanswerable, for in Beijing as in Moscow— and in Washington—it was ideologically easier and politically safer to revert to the default mode of cold war discourse:

> They make noises and think they are talking to each other;
> They make faces and think they understand each other;
> And I'm sure that they don't.
>
> (T. S. Eliot, *The Cocktail Party*, 1949, Act 2, Scene 1)[59]

8

Giving Peace a Chance
From the Cold War to Iraq

I like to believe that people, in the long run, are going to do more
to promote peace than our governments. Indeed, I think that people
want peace so much that one of these days governments had better
get out of the way and let them have it…. It's those people that want
these things, and long for them with all their hearts. We have got to
make it possible for them to get them.

(President Eisenhower, London, 31 August 1959)

In the late 1950s, both Western and Soviet leaders professed to pay
more attention to the growing public clamour against nuclear tests
and for a more peaceful world. President Eisenhower's folksy chat in
Downing Street with Prime Minister Harold Macmillan sought to
sound a reassuring note. A lot of the people, young and old, said the
prime minister, were frightened of war. Peace, said the president, was
the imperative of our time and the single objective of their efforts. The
conversation, described as 'historic' by the British press, was broadcast live on radio and television and came to be regarded as breaking
new ground in the effective use of the media. It was considered a
'stunning electoral coup' for Macmillan in the run-up to the October
1959 general election.[1] The Soviet government and press were also
beginning to acknowledge the strength of global protest and to treat
more sympathetically the non-aligned Western activists who favoured
'neither East nor West'. Soviet scientists were allowed to take part in
the international conferences of the Pugwash movement (see below,
p. 208); and there were cautious suggestions that Moscow would not
necessarily disapprove of a Western peace movement which failed to
fully endorse Soviet policy.[2]

However, Khrushchev was no Tsar Alexander, Eisenhower was no Woodrow Wilson, and it would have been inconceivable to imagine Macmillan appearing at an Albert Hall rally for the Campaign for Nuclear Disarmament (CND, founded in 1958). The intermingling of the peace movements with their political establishments had not resumed after the Second World War for several reasons. The belief that peace could be secured through disarmament—if only that might be achieved—was no longer widely shared: the ambitious vision of the peace advocates of the past was now severely constricted. Not only did their idealistic goals appear to be contradicted by the 'lesson of the 1930s', but nuclear weapons now dominated—and narrowed— the agenda. The theory of nuclear deterrence was not open to ques- tion within political and military establishments, and the diplomatic failures of the mid-1950s showed a lack of will to explore seriously a non-nuclear alternative. Furthermore, the cold war had created a much sharper division between the 'free' and the 'communist' worlds than that in the past between the democratic and totalitarian states or, earlier still, between the Central and the Allied powers, with many on both sides believing that, war or no war, 'they' were seeking to overthrow 'us'. Nuclear war might or might not be survivable but there was no alternative to running the risk: for some annihilation was preferable to 'communist domination'. In August 1958, at the height of the Taiwan Straits crisis, the US Senate approved by 82 to 2 the so-called 'Better Dead than Red' amendment banning the appropria- tion of funds to study any circumstances (in the context of the debate, this meant nuclear war) under which the USA might 'surrender to a foreign power'.[3] British willingness to contemplate nuclear war was less openly stated but lay at the heart of defence policy. In the view of Lord Portal of Hungerford (chief of air staff during the Second World War), 'Personally, I think it is worse for a nation to give in to evil and to betray its friends than to run the risk of annihilation....'[4] The British government's Civil Defence programme, launched in 1956, was based on the proposition that while nuclear war would be a catastrophe, knowledge of 'the basic facts and of what to do ... could save countless lives from otherwise certain death'.[5]

In contrast again to the inter-war period, there was little leeway for politicians to take the side—or appear to take the side—of the peace campaigners. By advocating a partial test-ban treaty, Adlai Stevenson, Democratic candidate in the 1956 US presidential elections, provided an opening of which Dwight Eisenhower took full advantage. The policy of unilateral disarmament, adopted in 1960 by the British Labour Party, under pressure from the rank and file, was reversed a year later: it has remained conventional wisdom for the Party's modernizers that advocacy of giving up British nuclear weapons would make it 'unelectable'. Even in non-nuclear West Germany, the Social Democratic Party after its electoral defeats in 1957–8 dropped its opposition to the deployment by NATO of nuclear weapons.[6]

The peace movement revival

The revival of a relatively coherent and international peace movement in the mid-1950s had special characteristics which reflected the nature of the forces to which it was opposed: the division of the world into two blocs; the commitment of governments to the doctrine of nuclear deterrence; the misuse and/or vilification of the actual word 'peace'; and, most important of all, two existential threats presented by nuclear weapons.

First, there was the current and growing threat to human reproduction of nuclear tests. The first mobilizing trigger for the peace movement was the fate of the Japanese fishing vessel the *Lucky Dragon* and the death of its radio engineer Aikichi Kuboyama after the boat strayed into the Bikini Atoll testing area. This tragedy also provided a powerful reminder of the horror of Hiroshima. In Britain Ralph Lapp's account of *The Voyage of the Lucky Dragon* (1957) would be published under the popular Penguin Special imprint simultaneously with a reprint of John Hersey's *Hiroshima* (1946). The implications of nuclear test fallout for our 'children yet unborn' quickly became too powerful an image to be dissolved by any amount of propaganda that fallout was good for you, or at least not bad for you—as in the headline from a 1955 US civil defence pamphlet: 'Radioactivity is nothing new ... the whole world is radioactive.'[7]

Second, there was the future—and for many, increasingly probable— threat to human existence of nuclear war. With the development of the H-bomb by both superpowers, the world now faced a thermonuclear arms race with potential consequences of devastation on a vastly greater scale than that of Hiroshima and Nagasaki. As the leading peace historian of this subject Lawrence Wittner has observed,

'Nuclear testing represented the tip of a potential iceberg, for both the US and Soviet governments showed a clear willingness to use nuclear weapons when it suited their purposes.'[8] While the super-power leaders might have preferred not to alarm their people, the doctrine of deterrence required them to make their intentions clear. The USA declared its adherence to a policy of 'massive retaliation', and Eisenhower stated (16 March 1955) that the USA was prepared to use tactical nuclear weapons 'just exactly as you would use a bullet or any-thing else': the Soviet Union declared that it could survive a nuclear war, and Khrushchev told the Communist Party Congress (February 1956) that their armed forces could deliver a 'smashing rebuff' to any imperialist—and by implication nuclear—attack.

The widespread apprehension that the very future of humanity was now in doubt may be gauged from the titles of such popular works of dissent as *The Causes of World War Three* (C. Wright Mills, 1958); *The Devil's Repertoire* (Victor Gollancz, 1958); *Has Man a Future?* (Bertrand Russell, 1961); *May Man Prevail?* (Erich Fromm, 1961). Nevil Shute's novel *On the Beach* (1957), describing the end of the world as witnessed by the last survivors in Australia, was an instant best-seller. This and other futuristic works such as Mordecai Roshwald's chillingly under-stated *Level 7* (1959) no longer belonged to science fiction. Roshwald portrayed the consequences of a nuclear war as monitored by those who had 'pushed the button' from a military bunker buried deep in the mountainside—and who themselves then died in turn as radiation seeped slowly down.[9]

In the late 1940s a number of largely unrelated groups—scientists, pacifists, supporters of the UN, religious figures, and Japanese survi-vors of the bomb—had spoken out against nuclear weapons. However, their efforts were silenced by the emerging cold war and, before long, the hot war in Korea, which in the USA placed a premium on patriot-ism and put peace advocates at risk of being denounced for supporting the enemy. The new surge of anti-nuclear activity which began in the mid-1950s would by the end of the decade develop effective inter-national links, both between prominent individuals, such as Russell, Albert Einstein, Albert Schweitzer, and Linus Pauling, and between mass organizations such as the Campaign for Nuclear Disarmament (UK) and the National Committee for a Sane Nuclear Policy (USA). It also promoted common action—with some disagree-ments—between the smaller and mainly pacifist groups which had raised a lonely voice in the early 1950s and a much broader movement opposed to nuclear weapons but not necessarily to military action or preparedness under all circumstances. This new popular front of protest was regarded as a serious threat by the governments concerned, but by contrast with the inter-war period no attempt was made to conciliate or co-opt these peace movements. At best, political leaders would claim to 'respect the sincerity' of the majority of protesters, while casting doubt on the motives of their organizers. Both sides recognized the need to win over public opinion which was divided in roughly equal proportions on whether or not to support nuclear testing and the development of the H-bomb.

Russell and Einstein, in their manifesto published in July 1955, appealed to the world's scientists to come together and apply their expert knowledge to find a way of overcoming the divisions of the cold war to achieve 'the abolition of war', towards which the renunciation of nuclear weapons would be a first but important step:

We shall try to say no single word which should appeal to one group rather than to another. All, equally, are in peril, and, if the peril is understood, there is hope that they may collectively avert it. We have to learn to think in a new way. We have to learn to ask ourselves, not what steps can be taken to give military victory to whatever group we prefer, for there no longer are such steps; the question we have to ask ourselves is: what steps can be taken to prevent a military contest of which the issue must be disastrous to all parties?[10]

Their appeal was the stimulus for the Pugwash initiative (launched with a meeting in Pugwash, Nova Scotia, hosted by the American philanthropist Cyrus Eaton in 1957) which would, in a series of conferences over the next decades, bring together scientists, scholars, and public figures 'concerned with reducing the danger of armed conflict and seeking cooperative solutions for global problems'. A notable early achievement was that Khrushchev allowed the participation of Soviet scientists.

Western intellectuals who dissented—sometimes at personal cost—from the prevailing orthodoxies of the cold war produced significant work exploring an alternative approach to the management of international conflict. The concept of a 'non-nuclear club'—intellectual forerunner of the Test-Ban Treaty to which the nuclear powers would eventually agree—was explored by the British Nobel physics laureate Patrick Blackett and others. In one form or another it involved Britain offering to renounce its nuclear weapons as part of an agreement with other nations not to acquire them. Various ideas for disengagement in Europe were proposed following the initiative of Polish foreign minister Adam Rapacki, who in October 1957 presented at the UN his plan for a nuclear-free zone in central Europe (comprising Czechoslovakia, Poland, East and West Germany—known as the 'Rapacki Plan'). Seymour Melman and other US economists looked at ways of ensuring effective inspection systems to police nuclear disarmament, and of converting military industries to civilian use. The purported logic of the cold war was deconstructed by leading social scientists: Wright Mills dissected the 'crack-pot realism' of the arms race, and appealed to Western intellectuals to fill what he called the 'cultural default' in which they 'accept without scrutiny official definitions of world reality'.[11] Fromm characterized the Soviet system, despite its ideological pretences, as a 'conservative state-managerialism' which did not challenge the West and with which an understanding could be reached on the basis of the status quo.[12] Bertrand Russell carried the argument beyond disarmament to propose radical reform to the United Nations which would abolish the veto and in the long term move towards a world government with regional federations and a global armed force.[13]

Yet in spite of these intellectual challenges to conventional cold war thinking, the anti-nuclear movement found it hard to develop a broader alternative approach to the conduct of international relations comparable to those devised in the past by the peace societies and League of Nations Federation. The main impact of the cold war peace movement on public opinion and on governments was the simplicity of its appeal—to 'ban the bomb'. Russell himself appreciated the tactical value of this, writing in 1962 that 'Peace will not be secure until there is an effective world government, but I should not like to see world government added to our programme', because 'some of our supporters might consider [it] irrelevant'. Joseph Rotblat, the main intellectual force behind Pugwash, also regarded the quest for world government as too 'ambitious'.[14]

In the first decade of CND there were periodic efforts to expand the pure message of 'ban the bomb' to address more difficult political and economic questions, such as whether a non-nuclear Britain should remain within NATO, how to convert military production for peaceful purposes, and how to situate the anti-nuclear argument within a general critique of the world economy and society. (There were isolated and unsuccessful attempts to present a broader platform in parliamentary elections, such as the Independent Nuclear Disarmament Election Committee and the Radical Alliance.) But the overwhelming thrust of the nuclear disarmament campaign was based on the immorality of nuclear weapons and their existential threat to civilization, and efforts to offer a more nuanced political approach were open to criticism for appearing to compromise this basic principle. As the historian A. J. P. Taylor, a member of the CND executive, put it bluntly: 'I think people who want to eliminate emotion from their attitude to disarmament are aligning themselves with those American and Russian scientists now planning to blow us up.'[15]

Banning the bomb

The impact of the global anti-nuclear movement, from the late 1950s to the end of the cold war three decades later, was considerable in spite of very large fluctuations in its strength and the sustained hostility of most of the members' governments. The simplicity of its appeal impacted directly upon world leaders, forcing some of them, at some times, to look beyond the dogma of nuclear deterrence towards moral and humanitarian considerations. As Eisenhower observed, thermonuclear weapons were tremendously powerful but not 'as powerful as is world opinion today [1958]'.[16] The political and military establishments of the main nuclear powers sometimes attempted to conciliate their critics by proposals and initiatives which could be seen as steps in a peaceful direction: at other times (or simultaneously) they would seek to discredit the anti-nuclear case and provide counter-propaganda: rarely did they act without regard for public opinion. While polls and other studies often showed that a small majority believed that nuclear weapons made war less likely, opposition to official deterrence theory was substantial and vocal, and large majorities were always registered against nuclear testing. In 1955, 71 per cent of West Germans regarded nuclear tests as dangerous; 87 per cent of the French people approved of a ban on nuclear weapons—44 per cent even if it left Western military forces weaker than communist forces; a secret US official study found that 80 per cent of British opinion supported abolition of nuclear weapons; and a year later that 72 per cent would support a test-ban agreement.[17]

In January 1956, even before the anti-nuclear movement had gained momentum, the British foreign secretary Selwyn Lloyd warned the USA—at a private conference in Washington—that there was a growing body of middle-of-the-road opinion that favoured the regulation of nuclear testing, and that 'the [British] government had to decide whether to be dragged along behind or to take an initiative themselves'. Lloyd proposed a feasibility study which, even if it concluded that limiting nuclear tests was not practical, 'would put the West in a better posture vis-a-vis public opinion'. The United States Information Agency had already launched a major effort to counter the 'widespread fear of nuclear warfare in Western Europe', and made a special effort in Japan to develop favourable 'editorial opinion'.[18] By 1958, as the British negotiator Michael Wright would recall, 'the pressure of public opinion against nuclear testing had...become a serious factor; no British government could afford to appear to drag its feet'. A year later, during the test-ban moratorium (a Soviet initiative to which the USA and Britain had responded) Wright would warn US officials— who were urging Britain to resume testing—that in spite of the election victory of the Conservative Party a resumption of testing 'would cause as much difficulty in the UK as previously'.[19]

While Britain, the USA, and the Soviet Union sought in different ways to neutralize or win over pro-peace opinion, France with its 'independent nuclear deterrent' and China, now moving towards its first nuclear test in October 1964, paid it little attention. However, Canada and the Scandinavian countries were, by the early 1960s, taking an independent line. (In Sweden, the ruling Social Democrats moved towards final rejection of the nuclear option, a decision formalized by legislation in 1968.) New Zealand strongly opposed all nuclear tests in the Pacific, and in 1963 five South American states announced that they would work for a denuclearized zone in Latin America.

The Cuban missile crisis, which brought the world the closest yet to nuclear annihilation, happened too fast, and escalated too rapidly, for the global peace movement to develop a coherent response or influence its course: the overwhelming feeling of many campaigners was shock and numbness at the sudden threat of catastrophe. However, the leaders of both the USA and the Soviet Union occupied a political environment which had been sensitized to the realities of nuclear war by a decade of protest, as well as by their own moral and practical scruples. It is quite possible that in a different context, one in

which the majority of ordinary people had been silent or acquies-
cent to the nuclear arms race, the brink of total war might have been
more easily crossed (as it had been on the eve of the First World War).
Secretary of State Dean Rusk would recall President Kennedy's concern about 'an adverse public reaction': he himself argued against a
surprise attack on Cuba, on the grounds that 'world opinion would
turn against us because we didn't first try diplomatic avenues'.[20] The
views of America's anxious allies were also shaped by anti-nuclear
opinion. In Canada, where the Diefenbaker government was moving
towards a reversal of its earlier decision to acquire nuclear weapons systems, both Howard Green, minister of external affairs, and his deputy,
Norman Robertson, had been strongly influenced in the mid-1950s by
the arguments of the peace movement. During the Cuban crisis the
Canadian cabinet feared that their country would be 'entrapped' by
US brinkmanship and delayed the decision to alert Canadian forces.
Diefenbaker even told one cabinet meeting that 'the Cuba business
was no affair of Canada's'.[21]

Reaction to the Cuban crisis, among both politicians and the public, led within less than a year to the Limited Test-Ban Treaty—the
first effective measure of arms limitation since the war. Public opinion
over the dangers of nuclear war had been revived by the crisis: having
peered into the abyss, the leaders of the two superpowers were even
more aware of those dangers; both were also alarmed (Khrushchev
even more than Kennedy) by the imminent prospect of a Chinese
bomb and further nuclear proliferation. The two sides remained far
apart: the USA insisted on intrusive inspection to guarantee the credibility of a deal, while the Soviet Union refused to exclude underground testing. However, back-channel communications between
Kennedy, Khrushchev, and Macmillan helped to reopen the negotiations; so did the public intervention of Norman Cousins, leader of
the SANE movement in the USA, who had been invited by the pope
to improve relations between the Vatican and the Kremlin. Before his
first visit to Moscow in December 1962, Cousins was entrusted by
Kennedy with the message that he wished to restore friendly relations
and that completion of a test-ban treaty would be a key step. With the
negotiations still deadlocked, Cousins met Kennedy again after a second visit to Moscow. Kennedy observed that both he and the Soviet
leader were under severe pressure from their 'hard-liners', who regarded
every step to prevent a nuclear war as 'appeasement'.[22] Cousins then

suggested that Kennedy should seek to break the deadlock in a presidential address, and worked with the president's aides on the text of
the speech which Kennedy would deliver on 10 June at the American
University in Washington DC. Kennedy called for a reappraisal of the
cold war without assigning blame or pointing the finger of judgement:
peace was not impracticable and war was not inevitable. In a significant
passage, Kennedy also called on the American people to be involved in
the process of rethinking:

Some say that it is useless to speak of world peace or world law or world
disarmament—and that it will be useless until the leaders of the Soviet Union
adopt a more enlightened attitude. I hope they do. I believe we can help them
do it. But I also believe that we must re-examine our own attitude—as individuals and as a Nation—for our attitude is as essential as theirs. And every gradu-
ate of this school, every thoughtful citizen who despairs of war and wishes to
bring peace, should begin by looking inward—by examining his own attitude
toward the possibilities of peace, toward the Soviet Union, toward the course
of the Cold War and toward freedom and peace here at home.

The speech had a favourable impact on Soviet opinion; it was published in full in the Soviet media, and was praised by Khrushchev as the
best US presidential speech since Roosevelt: the way was now clear for
the Test-Ban Treaty to be signed just two months later on 10 August
1963.[23] Full-page advertisements placed by SANE in the US press
called on the public to lobby their senators to ratify the treaty, under
the headline 'Now it's up to the Senate...and You!' Ratification took
place with unusual speed, and by a wide margin, on 24 September.

Public opinion also helped to smooth the way forward for acceptance of the Nuclear Non-Proliferation Treaty (NPT), adopted overwhelmingly by the UN General Assembly in June 1968, and soon
ratified by more than a hundred non-nuclear nations who as a consequence renounced acquiring their own nuclear weapons. By this time
the threat of nuclear proliferation had been given an added edge by
China's entry to the club, and the fear that India might follow suit. The
Soviet Union, the USA, and Britain—France and China only acceded
to the treaty in 1992—were even prepared to concede, under pressure
from the non-nuclear states and domestic public opinion, that they as
nuclear powers would pursue 'negotiations in good faith' towards an
end to the nuclear arms race and nuclear disarmament (Article VI of
the treaty. More than four decades later, they still had not delivered on
this promise.)

However, the Test-Ban Treaty, and later the NPT, also had the consequence of defusing the anti-nuclear movement, even though it could claim a share of the success. This was not only because the world suddenly seemed a safer place (a perception of which the governments concerned took full advantage). Throughout its history, the movement would be vulnerable to sharp fluctuations in appeal, support, and effectiveness. Without a broader agenda, activists were likely to be diverted into other areas which appeared to present more immediate challenges: this was particularly true of the large-scale shift from the anti-bomb to the anti-Vietnam War campaign which now occurred. Lacking a permanent structure capable of adapting to changed circumstances, anti-nuclear cadres were also more likely to suffer from sheer exhaustion and drop out of the movement.

Yet the underlying appeal of peace and the willingness of thousands to campaign for it persisted and under the right conditions would resurface dramatically in the 1980s, when the anti-nuclear movement acquired a remarkable 'second life'. A number of factors came together: the failure of the 1970s 'decade of disarmament' after the hopes raised by the Test-Ban and Non-Proliferation Treaties of the late 1960s; the renewed nuclear arms race and growing overkill power of the superpowers' arsenals; Reaganite belligerence and Brezhnevite stubbornness in the context of new surrogate conflicts in Afghanistan and Africa; the end of the Vietnam War which released activist energies again; and the visible goad of the planned deployment of Cruise and Pershing missiles by the USA to Western Europe, and of SS20 missiles by the Soviet Union to Eastern Europe.

The new cold war of the 1980s was in some respects even more threatening than the old cold war of the 1950s and 1960s. Not only had the size of the nuclear arsenals held by the superpowers vastly increased, but nuclear war had begun to be seen as winnable by strategists on both sides. General David Jones, chairman of the US joint chiefs of staff, warned that the chance of a US–Soviet military confrontation 'will increase significantly' in the first half of the 1980s.[24] Soviet nuclear capability was growing at a rate which the Pentagon claimed was eroding American superiority—and the USA was not willing to concede parity. The number of Soviet strategic warheads had grown from 2,500 in 1970 to 3,650 in 1977, but the corresponding figure for the US had grown from 4,500 to 9,000. Particularly under President Reagan, the assumption (on which 'détente' was based) that Moscow

and Washington could maintain a rough balance had been repudi-
ated. The sheer quantity of nuclear devices, the complexity of their
new technology, and the fallible sophistication of the 'early warning'
methods of detection also increased the possibility of eventual use, by
accident or design. In 1984, the *Bulletin of Atomic Scientists* moved the
hands of its Doomsday Clock to three minutes to midnight.

The anti-nuclear movement was now able to produce a more
sophisticated critique of official doctrine than its predecessor two decades before. Organizations such as the Center for Defense Information
(CDI) and the Institute for Defense and Disarmament Studies (IDDS)
in the USA called on the expertise of former serving officers to spell
out the dangers of nuclear overkill, the missile race, and plans for a neutron bomb and 'Star Wars' technology. Concerned groups of women,
scientists, and physicians, religious bodies, and some trade unions, mobilized support for what became the Nuclear Weapons Freeze Campaign
(Freeze). The original proposal came from Randall Forsberg, IDDS
director: this demanded, simply, that the superpowers should agree 'a
mutual freeze on the testing, production, and deployment of nuclear
weapons and of missiles and new aircraft designed primarily to deliver
nuclear weapons' as an 'essential, verifiable first step towards lessening
the risk of nuclear war and reducing the nuclear arsenals'. A resolution
based on his 'call to halt the nuclear arms race' was narrowly defeated
by the House of Representatives (204–202) in August 1982. A heavily
amended version finally passed in May 1983 but was rejected 58–40 by
the Senate. The Freeze movement was seen by the Reagan administration as a serious threat: particularly (in the view of Eugene Rostow,
the hawkish director of the Arms Control and Disarmament Agency)
because it was supported by churches, Democrats, and 'the unpoliticized
public'. Reagan accused the movement of being manipulated by 'foreign agents'—citing articles in the *Readers' Digest* as his source. Reagan
was prevailed on by his daughter, Patti Davis, to meet Helen Caldicott,
one of the Freeze leaders, but neither was impressed by the other.[25]

In Europe the new focus was provided by the European Nuclear
Disarmament (END) movement, which rallied opposition to the
superpowers' new arms race on a non-aligned basis. END became 'the
very heart and soul of the massive European anti-nuclear campaign'.
END's broader agenda embraced support for independent protest
in Eastern Europe, which led at times to its representatives being
banned from meetings there. 'We must be able to clasp hands with a

non-aligned movement, totally independent of the state, on your side also,' the historian E. P. Thompson, co-founder of END, told a meeting of peace activists in Hungary.[26] END also argued that opposition to European nuclear weapons was only the first step in a campaign for reversal of the arms race. 'We need to campaign against cruise missiles. But we also need to change the military-industrial culture which created them,' wrote the political scientist Mary Kaldor in END's first publication, *Protest and Survive* (a riposte to the British government's pamphlet *Protect and Survive* which purported to advise the public on how best to survive a nuclear attack). 'The conversion from war to peace', Kaldor argued further, 'needs to be seen *not* as *the technical* process of converting swords to ploughshares, but as a *social* process of finding a new mechanism for the allocation of resources.'[27]

Although the anti-nuclear agenda was now broadened vastly by comparison to the 1960s, 'banning the bomb' remained to a large extent a middle-class, Western-based phenomenon, with little appeal to the Third World and anti-colonial (or neo-colonial) struggles, many of which had become entangled with the cold war. The criticism voiced by the Third World scholar activist Eqbal Ahmad in 1985 was overdrawn but to some extent justified: 'The disarmament movement in Western Europe and the United States is, by and large, a-historic, technocentric, nukocentric, ethnocentric, and phobocentric....It is so obsessed with the technology of war, specifically nuclear war, that it ignores the causes of it.'[28] However, in the late 1980s efforts were stepped up to link anti-nuclear agitation to a more complex agenda for détente, in which, as described by Thompson, the peace movement would end its 'single-minded focus on nuclear weaponry'. This wider aim was conveyed in *Prospectus for a Habitable Planet*, END's sequel to *Protest and Survive*. The volume included a call by *Guardian* journalist Jonathan Steele for an explicit linkage between peace and development in which the search for a new set of economic policies for the Third World went hand in hand with the struggle to reduce East–West confrontation in Europe.[29]

As in the 1960s, the efforts of Freeze, END, and related European movements mobilized public opinion as a peace-oriented counterweight to orthodox strategies. While it is difficult to measure their exact effect, we may conclude that they did exercise a restraining influence on the new cold war confrontation, and prepared the ground for more radical change—though not immediately. In Moscow a succession of elderly leaders were incapable of altering course; the last of them, Andropov, is said to have spent his final months morbidly brooding over the possibility of a 'nuclear Armageddon'.[30] In Washington, Reagan warned the supporters of a nuclear freeze not to ignore 'the aggressive impulses of an evil empire': the arms race was not based on misunderstanding, he insisted, but on the 'struggle between right and wrong and good and evil' (speech of 8 March 1983). The check to this dangerous drift finally came from an unexpected source—Mikhail Gorbachev, successor to Andropov as general secretary of the Soviet Communist Party.

The new Soviet leader would recall in his memoirs how he had been influenced in the 1950s by the Russell–Einstein Manifesto and by meeting Indian prime minister Nehru, at that time leader of non-aligned world opinion. Gorbachev's call for 'new thinking' echoed the manifesto's call for 'a new way of thinking' if humanity were to survive. As Thompson observed, 'To our surprise, after 1985 our own words started to come back to us—from Moscow.'[31] Gorbachev soon declared a moratorium on underground testing, in response to a suggestion from the CDI, and in January 1986 proposed a three-stage programme to eliminate all nuclear weapons by 2000. He in effect accepted the argument of the US Freeze movement, telling the Soviet Party Congress in February 1986 that Soviet military doctrine would no longer seek to match US weaponry but would be content with a 'reasonable sufficiency'. Later he released the dissident nuclear scientist Andrei Sakharov, to the displeasure of Soviet conservatives who complained about the spread of 'pacifism'. By the time of the Reykjavik summit in October, Reagan (though not the US national security establishment) had been swayed by Gorbachev to the point of agreeing with him that 'a nuclear war cannot be won and must never be fought'. By now, Gorbachev was consistently outpolling Reagan on disarmament issues among the populations of the USA's European allies. The breakthrough came a few months later when Gorbachev agreed to separate the issue of medium-range missiles in Europe from the Strategic Defence Initiative ('Star Wars') which Reagan insisted on keeping alive: the result was the Intermediate-Range Nuclear Forces (INF) Treaty signed in December 1987. Gorbachev had been encouraged to suggest this compromise, he would say, after listening to foreign anti-nuclear activists who had attended a Forum for a Nuclear-Free World in Moscow.

The 1990s: the missing peace dividend

> In these past months a conviction has grown, among nations large
> and small, that an opportunity has been regained to achieve the great
> objectives of the Charter—a United Nations capable of maintain-
> ing international peace and security, of securing justice and human
> rights and of promoting, in the words of the Charter, 'social progress
> and better standards of life in larger freedom'. This opportunity must
> not be squandered.
>
> (UN, 'Agenda for Peace', 1992)

Peace became the new realism for a brief period after the end of the
cold war. There seemed a fortunate coincidence between the realiza-
tion that humanity urgently needed to tackle its common problems
(with climate change looming on the horizon) and a more relaxed
international environment which would at last allow such a collabora-
tive effort to be made. This effort would be underpinned in material
terms by a 'peace dividend' arising from deep cuts in preparations for
war. The strands of a much broader agenda for global change began to
be drawn together, and the 1990s were often referred to as the 'decade
of decision' (though not the first decade to be labelled in this way).
Events on the ground were acknowledged to have shown up inad-
equacies in the harsh approach of the 'neo-Realist' school which had
come to dominate thinking on international relations and economic
development. With hopes revived for a cooperative approach to the
problems of global poverty and debt, and more respect and optimism
now accorded to the United Nations and its peacekeeping role, the
view that beyond individual states there is nothing but anarchy in the
international arena seemed overly pessimistic.

Higher expectations for real cuts in nuclear weapons, perhaps even
leading towards their abolition, made the argument in favour of a
world where peace depended upon their possession (and which therefore might be safer with more nuclear weapons) appear grotesque.
And the role of popular movements in bringing about the disintegra-
tion of the Soviet bloc, and with it the end of the cold war, simply
did not fit into the narrow structuralist view of the way that states
behave. Yet by the end of the 1990s the integrative enterprise which
the global agenda now required had proved much less than successful,
thrown off course by new and unanticipated shocks and conflicts, and
by the failure of the major international players to rise to the challenge

(though urged to grasp it by public opinion) for new thinking and new policies. 'Neo-Realism' ruled again, claiming that the end of the cold war—rephrased as the 'winning of the cold war'—justified the view that the international system is driven only by competing power and that self-interest is the only ethic. This harsh reductive view of the world—in a new unipolar guise—would reach its peak in the post-11 September policies which led to the 2003 Iraq War. A world which, it was generally agreed, offered enormous challenges as it became more globalized, continued to rely on military, strategic, and diplomatic tools that belonged to an earlier age. After the false optimism of a new internationalist spirit at the start of the 1990s, there was a gloomy return to the defensive postures of nation-state ideology.

Linking peace and development

In an editorial on the Bergen Environmental Conference in 1990, under the headline 'Questions for the Decade of Decision', *The Guardian* said: 'Both sides [North and South] should attach a higher priority to regional stability than to arms sales... Substantial sums could become available as Western arms spending is reduced, if the benefits of our own peace dividend are passed directly South' (24 May 1990). In a similar vein, the second *Human Development Report* produced by the UN Development Programme (UNDP) would devote a large (and generally optimistic) section to the opportunities offered by the peace dividend. It urged that the savings of demilitarization should be devoted to 'the urgent social problems in many industrial nations, from homelessness to drug addiction, and the wide range of development needs in the Third World'. And it heretically advised the World Bank and IMF to fund their adjustment programmes 'by squeezing military—rather than social expenditures'. However, the report also warned that the Gulf War (the first of the decade's many unanticipated shocks) showed 'the real peace dividend may lie in a more distant future than we thought'.[32]

The UNDP attempt at linkage between military and social expenditure reached its highest point in 1994, driven by the tireless concern of Mahbub ul Haq, founder of its annual *Human Development Report*, to capture 'a peace dividend for human development'. The world needed a new transition 'from nuclear security to human security', it argued: it was time to 'capture the peace dividend' and fulfil the prophecy of beating swords into ploughshares. 'The cold war is not over yet—the job is only half-done.' Again it underlined the human development cost of arms imports for developing countries, and sought a targeted reduction in military spending for the decade 1995–2005 of 3 per cent a year to create 'a global fund for human security'.[33]

A year later this broader discourse was central to the call of the Commission on Global Governance (set up in 1992 with the backing of the UN secretary-general) for a new global ethic. The world needed a new system of global governance that 'responds to threats to the security of people and threats to the security of the planet—in short, [threats] to human security'.[34] Yet even as these hopes were being expressed they were already being dashed by events. Armed conflicts within states were increasing, and insofar as the industrial nations had reduced arms expenditure, very little of this was applied to social development. The World Social Summit in 1995 produced in its Copenhagen Declaration only a timid call for 'the appropriate reduction of excessive military expenditures... taking into consideration national security requirements'. Far from this happening, world defence spending began to rise again in the late 1990s.

Initial zeal to tackle conventional weapons and the arms trade also waned very quickly. The Gulf War had thrown embarrassing light on the blind eye turned by Britain and other Western powers to the previous arming of Saddam Hussein: some fine words were then said about curbing the flow of arms to the Middle East. The Paris five-power conference in October 1991 led eventually to the creation of a voluntary UN register for arms sales. Yet no specific transactions were banned, and no regime was instituted to enforce reporting. The end of the cold war did lead at first to an overall decline in the global arms trade. But new nationalist and ethnic struggles across central Europe created new markets which were easily satisfied by a business with excess production capacity and surplus stocks. In East Asia, growing economic power generated new strategic appetites and arms purchases increased there against the global trend. In the Middle East, the arms acquisitions of Israel, Egypt, Saudi Arabia, and several Gulf states, and Iran, all contributed to an unhealthy upward curve. In one area—landmines—international concern was manifested in a more practical way. The legacy of regional conflicts which had been sponsored by both superpowers was appalling. In Afghanistan, Angola, Cambodia,

Mozambique, and elsewhere thousands of civilians were killed and maimed yearly. But the most powerful stimulus to Western consciences came in Bosnia when NATO troops—particularly Americans—began to suffer landmine casualties. Nevertheless the international mines conference in May 1996 did not agree on a total ban.

We may also note the long-running effort, already initiated by the UN General Assembly in 1978, to promote a review of the relationship between disarmament and development. There were two special sessions in 1978 and 1982, the Thorsson Report in 1982, and an international conference in 1987, and the subject was revisited in 2004 with a new report by a group of government experts commissioned by the secretary-general. Regrettably, in spite of the high calibre of those taking part, this last effort—like all the previous ones—had virtually no impact on world media and politicians.[35] The list of failed endeavours in this area should also include the various precursors to the Commission on Global Governance starting with the Brandt Commission in 1980. Indeed, since the 1950s General Assembly resolutions had repeatedly called, with no visible result, for 'reductions in military expenditure and the reallocation of resources to development'.[36]

The follow-up to the Social Summit in 2000, and the ten-year review in 2005, were equally cautious. The eradication of poverty was portrayed as dependent on debt relief, good governance, land reform, education, and health care, but only in parenthesis on the diversion of the huge funds still being expended on armaments. When these sensitive issues were raised there was no consequential action. The UN Millennium Declaration of 2000 set out the brave aim 'to strive for the elimination of weapons of mass destruction, particularly nuclear weapons, and to keep all options open for achieving this aim, including the possibility of convening an international conference to identify ways of eliminating nuclear dangers'. This proposal became the subject of an annual resolution to the UN First Committee. A simpler resolution tabled by Mexico in 2005, although passed overwhelmingly, attracted five negative votes, the USA, UK, France, Israel, and Poland, plus abstentions from many European countries. By 2010 the Europeans had shifted to oppose the resolution, which was passed by a less impressive majority—103 in favour and 48 against, with 14 abstentions. It may safely be predicted that this conference will never be held.

The 'failure' of the UN

In practical terms the UN system, as its persuasive advocate Erskine Childers argued, 'has accomplished vastly more than most of its citizens have ever been told about'.[37] Humanitarian and economic issues are no longer regarded as merely 'technical' but as an integral part of the vision of the Charter and the practical work of its agencies. The first UN conference on the environment was held as early as 1949 (although its proceedings were largely ignored, see above p. 187). The UN soon became regarded—and continues to be regarded—as having primary responsibility for assisting the social and economic development of the less advanced world, and as obliged to act speedily and effectively in cases of man-made or natural disasters. While unable to intervene in conflicts where either superpower was directly involved, the UN was more successful during the cold war in halting or reducing conflict or preventing its spread at various times in the Congo (1960s), Kashmir, Cyprus, and the Middle East. It also provided a forum where cold war tensions could sometimes be restrained by pressure from the general membership. In the most notable example, an informal coalition of non-aligned and moderate Western nations opposed to nuclear testing, which emerged at the UN in the early 1960s, played an important role in forcing the USA, Britain, and the Soviet Union to work towards the Limited Test-Ban Treaty.[38]

Peacekeeping

And yet the greatest failure of the post-cold war 1990s has been in the field of global peacekeeping. In the conventional view, this is because the United Nations 'failed' in Bosnia, Somalia, and Rwanda, while no intervention was even attempted in other areas of severe local conflict such as Chechnya. In truth it was a failure not of the UN organization but of leading member states who denied the organization sufficient authority or the means to act effectively. The Gulf War against Iraq was evidence not of the UN's strength but of its weakness, proving that the organization could not undertake independent action to seek a solution to conflict by peaceful means if the leading powers chose otherwise.

The Bosnia crisis should have provided a better opportunity for the UN to prove itself, yet the challenge posed by the dissolution of the former Yugoslavia was met with reluctance to commit fully to UN intervention. At the start, major powers were too willing to accept the break-up as part of a process in which territorial unities established 'under communism' were dissolved, and their recognition of the need for peacekeeping operations came too late to be effective. Large numbers of peacekeepers were required, at an early date, to contain the spreading conflict. Instead the Security Council sanctioned too few, too late, at first with inadequate powers and then with the responsibility for 'safe areas' but insufficient means to ensure their safety. A misleading lesson was widely drawn: UN peacekeepers, it was said, should not have been placed in a position which required peacemaking. What Bosnia really showed was that ineffective peacekeeping only encouraged the spread of conflict which then made it almost impossible to make effective peace. Even with large-scale commitment on the ground, Bosnia would have presented enormous problems, but the UN never reached the point where these could be seriously faced.

Underlying the Bosnian (and Rwandan and Somalian) failures was a refusal by the main member states to contemplate giving the UN the authority and autonomy which the Charter had envisaged as necessary for effective peacekeeping. Both in Bosnia and in the catastrophe of Somalia, operations were effectively sub-contracted to NATO and the USA respectively. Blue-helmeted efforts undertaken, as in Rwanda, in the name of the international body were weakened by a lack of commitment by member states, but it was the reputation of the UN which suffered. There was only a sluggish debate over the proposals made by Secretary-General Boutros Boutros-Ghali in his 1992 'Agenda for Peace', which followed the Security Council's first summit-level meeting, billed with a fanfare of publicity as a 'unique' opportunity to revitalize the UN. Amazingly, the fiftieth anniversary of the UN passed without serious discussion, far less action, to reform the organization's structures and procedures in the peacekeeping—or indeed any other—field. The secretary-general's request in line with Article 45 of the Charter, long ignored during the cold war, that member states should earmark standing forces which would be ready for use when needed, still elicited no response. Member states such as Britain and France might well be generous in providing peacekeeping troops for an operation such as Bosnia but were unwilling to put this on any permanent basis. Article 47 of the Charter which provides for a properly functioning UN Military Staff Committee (see above pp. 184–5) remained a dead letter (and ten years later, a report on UN reform commissioned by Secretary-General Kofi Annan would recommend that references to it should be removed from the Charter).[39] With the Dayton Agreement in December 1995 which legitimized the replacement of UN peacekeepers by NATO forces in Bosnia, the UN was virtually written out of the script. The downgrading of UN authority continued in the NATO Kosovo operation, while it was ignored altogether in the USA–UK invasion of Iraq in 2003.

Thus hopes that the post-cold war UN would offer a long-term alternative to an international system prone to war, initially as high as those expressed for the League of Nations in 1919, were dashed within a few years. As Linda Melvern has shown, the 'intrigues and manoeuvrings' of the Security Council undermined what was 'an unprecedented chance for UN renaissance', and ensured that 'the future course for the UN was framed by three tragedies shaming the world—Somalia, Bosnia-Hercegovina and Rwanda'.[40] However, the first blow was delivered, though less noted at the time, by the Gulf War, even though this was nominally a collective action undertaken by the UN on behalf of the international community as a whole.

The Gulf War

The speed with which the UN moved to impose economic sanctions on Iraq, after its invasion of Kuwait in August 1990, was initially seen as a good omen for peacekeeping operations. The imposition of economic sanctions under Article 41 of the UN Charter was the appropriate initial response to a clear act of aggression by one member state against another. Sanctions were at first regarded as a 'long haul' operation, in the words of US Secretary of Defence Dick Cheney, while his British counterpart Tom King said that 'it was never going to be a quick fix'.[41] The Charter states that the Security Council, before moving on to institute military sanctions under Article 42, should reach the conclusion that economic sanctions 'would be inadequate or have proved to be inadequate'. No such finding was ever made, The peaceful route was publicly foreclosed when President Bush announced (after the mid-term elections, though the decision had been taken before) the doubling of US troops in the Gulf to half a million. New forecasts that sanctions might produce a withdrawal by spring or summer 1991 were regarded as proving the need for military force. The troops could not wait that long, it was explained, because the coalition might 'crumble' by then. The announcement on 8 November was described as an ultimatum to Saddam Hussein: 'Either withdraw from Kuwait within weeks or face US attack.' In reality the mandates of chapter VI of the UN Charter—to take every possible step to find a 'pacific settlement' of the dispute—were neglected in favour of the military enforcement provisions of chapter VII. While it might have proved impossible to bring about Saddam's withdrawal from Kuwait by diplomatic means, efforts to do so by a number of Western politicians and eventually by UN Secretary-General Javier Perez de Cuellar were undercut by the evident prior commitment of the USA and its allies to go to war.[42] The flawed nature of this intervention, although conducted in the UN's name, was an early sign of the erosion of its authority. Twelve years later the efforts of another UN secretary-general to find a peaceful solution would be totally ignored at the start of another war against Iraq.

The re-evaluation of peace in the optimistic mood of the early 1990s had already ebbed long before 11 September 2001. The failure of the peace dividend to emerge, and the undermining of UN authority, weakened support for genuine internationalism. The new dawn which had been promised was clouded by the increased incidence of civil wars and the persistence of global deprivation and inequality. World military expenditure, which had dipped to a low point of around one thousand billion US dollars in the mid-1990s, was already rising, and would increase by 49 per cent, at constant prices, in the next decade (2000–9).[43] The peace movement had been demobilized by the ending of the cold war and campaigning efforts were diverted to new causes which seemed more urgent—especially those of poverty and the environment.

However, in this more complex world, there was emerging, among governments, international institutions, peace research centres, and NGOs, a clearer understanding of the root causes of instability and a coherent strategy, at least in theory, on how to tackle them. The starting point was the obvious one: conflict is more likely to arise in conditions of poverty and inequality, or where there has been a failure to solve long-standing tensions and injustices. A World Bank study of civil war and development policy showed that low-income countries 'face far higher risks [of civil war]: typically 15 times as high as OECD countries'.[44] If the moral case for tackling the roots of conflict were not sufficient, there was a strong argument based on self-interest. One study of past and prospective conflict zones claimed that 'A spend of

£1 on conflict prevention will, on average, generate savings of £4.1 to the international community (with a range of 1.2 to 7.1).'[45] The UNDP's *Human Development Report* for 1996 spelt out the inverse connection between conflict and development: 'Years of internal warfare undermine standards of human development. And long periods of neglect of human development, especially for particular racial or ethnic groups, can eventually provoke violent conflicts.... Peace opens opportunities for human development....'[46]

The re-focusing of international attention on poverty and inequality during the 1990s reached its highest point in 2000 with the UN Millennium Declaration and its attached eight Human Development Goals. The 1960s had already been proclaimed the first UN Development Decade, but the drive for real change had then stalled, particularly during the 1980s, through a combination of cold war pressures and the dominance of neo-liberal economic orthodoxy. In a new mood of optimism—and urgency—in the early 1990s, the World Bank put poverty reduction back on its agenda, the highly influential *Human Development Report* began publication, and a series of UN summits and conferences began to address the problem, notably the 'Earth Summit' (Rio de Janeiro 1992), the 1992 Cairo Population Conference, and in 1995 the Copenhagen Social Development Summit and the Beijing Women's Summit. (There was also a less noticed negative reason for stepping up anti-poverty advocacy: aid budgets as a proportion of national income in the major developed countries were actually declining.) Over the next years all the international players worked together to produce the framework for *We the Peoples*, the report produced by UN Secretary-General Kofi Annan which became the basis for the Millennium Declaration.[47]

The Declaration, adopted by the General Assembly in September 2000, was rich in content and offered an alternative scenario for the conduct of world affairs in the twenty-first century, which should be regarded almost as an updating of the UN Charter concluded fifty-five years before. Some of its most important statements amounted to an implicit critique of the emerging pattern of great power manipulation of the UN, and of the uneven effects of economic globalization.

- We believe that the central challenge we face today is to ensure that globalization becomes a positive force for all the world's people. For while globalization offers great opportunities, at present its benefits are very unevenly shared, while its costs are unevenly distributed.

- Responsibility for managing worldwide economic and social development, as well as threats to international peace and security, must be shared among the nations of the world and should be exercised multilaterally. As the most universal and most representative organization in the world, the United Nations must play the central role.

- [We resolve] to make the United Nations more effective in maintaining peace and security by giving it the resources and tools it needs for conflict prevention, peaceful resolution of disputes, peacekeeping, post-conflict peace-building and reconstruction.

Towards the Iraq War

For more than a decade before the Iraq War of 2003, the difficult challenge of the Saddam regime had been handled in a way that diminished UN authority and at times infringed international law. One of the provisions of the Millennium Declaration was 'to minimize the adverse effects of United Nations economic sanctions on innocent populations', to subject such sanctions to 'regular reviews', and to 'eliminate the adverse effects of sanctions on third parties'. This was a direct reference to the sanctions imposed upon Iraq since the Gulf War, which although approved by the Security Council were manipulated by two permanent members of the Council (the USA and UK) who opposed their lifting or amelioration. In the judgement of Hans von Sponeck, the UN Humanitarian Coordinator for Iraq from 1998 onwards, 'The pillars of control were carefully guarded by these two governments throughout the years of sanctions.' While not impacting visibly upon the Saddam family and military leadership—the ostensible target of the sanctions—they inflicted dire suffering on the Iraqi people. Equipment for renewing the electricity network, for example, was put in the 'dual-use' category (meaning that it was subject to special restriction on the grounds that it might serve a military purpose). 'For Iraqi households and for public services, including hospitals and schools, such constraints meant long, disabling and not infrequently, life-threatening power cuts.' The Oil for Food programme over 1996–2003 should have generated $43.1 billion (or $284 per person/year) worth of humanitarian supplies: instead, because of delays in arrival, this was reduced to $28.1 billion (or $185 per person/year). Conditions in many schools outside the main cities were so poor that most classrooms lacked blackboards; chalk was often not available; and many children had to sit on the floor. Sponeck complained that the Security Council failed to exercise proper oversight of the programme or to engage in regular dialogue with Iraq as the targeted party. 'The single sanctions strategy for Iraq was to link comprehensive economic sanctions to a military embargo and disarmament. This linkage held the civilian population accountable for the acts of armament of their Government and therefore became a tool for the punishment of innocent people for something they had not done.'[48] This verdict was shared by a report by twelve NGOs led by Save the Children, which said that 'the international community increasingly views the sanctions as illegitimate and punitive, because of well-documented humanitarian suffering in Iraq and widespread doubts about the sanctions' effectiveness and their legal basis under international humanitarian and human rights law'.[49]

The UN suffered another diminution of its authority through the two No Fly Zones imposed by the USA, Britain, and France after the Gulf War, in a 'humanitarian effort' to protect Shia Muslims in the south and Kurds in the north. France later withdrew from the operation, which continued right up to the 2003 war. The connection with the protection of the two minorities became more tenuous, particularly after the allied pilots' rules of engagements were 'enlarged' in 1999, allowing air strikes on a variety of targets and leading to increased numbers of civilian casualties. In a foretaste of the legal arguments used to justify going to war in 2003, the USA claimed that the enforcement of the zones was consistent with a Security Council resolution in April 1991 calling on Iraq to end repression of its civilian population. However, the Council at no stage gave the necessary authorization for the USA–UK action, required under chapter VII of the Charter. In February 2001, the UK attorney-general, in secret advice to the Ministry of Defence, stressed the need to avoid civilian casualties, and warned that 'it is vitally important to keep constantly in view the precarious nature of the legal basis for the UK and US action in the No Fly Zones'.[50]

The approach of the USA and UK to the Iraq problem, as the above indicates, was well established before 11 September 2001: this asserted the right of the two governments to interpret UN resolutions as they saw fit. It embodied the claim that such actions were consistent with the interests of the Iraqi people, and the actual effect upon those people, whether through misapplied sanctions or through bombing, was minimized. The decision taken in 2002 by President George W. Bush to launch a full-scale war was consistent with this approach, the main difference being that reliance upon existing UN resolutions was even more problematic. The essence of the problem for both governments was neatly put by Michael Wood, UK Foreign Office legal adviser, in a memorandum of 4 October 2002: although a Security Council resolution was adopted under chapter VII of the Charter and was therefore mandatory, this 'does not mean that States are thereby authorised to use force to ensure compliance with it. The use of force requires express authorisation.' This was followed by another memorandum of 17 October stating that the conditions which had justified intervention in Kosovo ('an overwhelming humanitarian catastrophe') did not apply in the case of Iraq, and repeating that 'there is currently no express authorisation to use force against Iraq'.[51] Security Council Resolution 1441 of November 2002, on which both belligerent powers would rely when they went to war in the following March, did not authorize military action, and at the time it was passed their ambassadors to the UN had acknowledged that the resolution did not contain any 'automaticity' or 'hidden trigger'. Thus the judgement expressed after the invasion by Secretary-General Kofi Annan that it had been 'illegal', and had been done 'without UN approval',[52] was no more than a statement of fact.

The start of the new millennium had been invested with hopes for a new world environment as high as those which had begun the previous, post-cold war, decade. The events which completed the dashing of these hopes—the rise of Al Qaida and the disaster of the Iraq War—were closely connected to one of the principal failures of that decade. In spite of all the professions of good intent after the Gulf War (they would be repeated with equal earnestness after the 2003 invasion) the Middle East remained the greatest source of instability and a seed-bed for twenty-first-century terrorism, with little change in the backward state systems of the Arab countries of which Saddam Hussein was a typical product; also crictical was the continuing lack of international will-power to find a solution to the chronic tension which the denial of Palestinian rights had stoked for decades. Equally important as a source of disaffection was the lack of job opportunities for young adults: while global youth (aged 15 to 24) unemployment in 2003 was 14.4 per cent, in the Middle East and North Africa it stood at 25.6 per cent—the highest of all world regions—according to the International Labour Organization.

In 2010–11, when unrest finally exploded in Tunisia and Egypt, and elsewhere in the region, the figures for youth unemployment were still almost twice as high in the Middle East and North Africa as the global average.[53]

More generally, by the end of the first post-cold war decade, there had already been a revival of more pessimistic and 'realistic' ways of looking at the world. The failure of the peace dividend to emerge, and the undermining of UN authority, had weakened support for genuine internationalism. The peace movement had been demobilized by the ending of the cold war, and campaigning efforts were fragmented by new causes. While the ending of apartheid in South Africa in the early 1990s had been widely hailed as a hopeful precedent—especially for the Israel–Palestine conflict—the ending of sectarian conflict in Northern Ireland a decade or so later would not be presented in the same terms. The trauma of the terrorist assault of 11 September 2001 reinforced this mood of pessimism, and seemed to validate a new working ideology, already being formulated, which saw the battle against terrorism as defining the age in which we now live. Often an explicit analogy was drawn between the long struggle of the cold war in the past, and the equally long—perhaps even longer—struggle ahead in the new 'war against terror'.[54] The main actors in the USA–UK coalition which led the invasion of Iraq fervently subscribed to what became known as the doctrine of the 'long war'. The relevant section of the US Department of Defence's *Quadrennial Defence Review Report* (2006) was headed 'Fighting the Long War', and the report was endorsed by Secretary of State Donald Rumsfeld with the statement that the USA now faced 'a generational conflict akin to the Cold War'.[55] Looking back on the Iraq War, the former British prime minister Tony Blair has drawn the same parallel. Arguing that the struggle against Islamist terrorism must be continued for 'as long as is necessary'—which might mean decades—he explained: 'If, in the 1950s, when faced with the threat of revolutionary Communism, I had asked you how long you expected us to fight it, you would have answered: As long as the threat exists.'[56]

This approach was supported by a huge body of new strategic thinking on asymmetrical and 'fourth-generational' warfare, while the challenge of Islamic fundamentalism was analysed in epidemiological terms as a contagious virus, akin to the spread of communism in the past.[57] This profoundly pessimistic view of our future has been validated by influential academics such as the historian and writer on military strategy Philip Bobbitt, who saw the attacks of 11 September as the harbingers of a new 'epochal' war waged by 'virtual states'.[58] In this war-oriented environment, those who suggest that more attention should be given to addressing the social and economic environment in which acts of terrorism occur run the risk of being accused of 'making excuses' for terrorism. An enquiry into the causes of terrorism by the prestigious Club de Madrid felt it necessary to stress that it did not want to 'empathise with the terrorists or…give in to their demands'.[59] Social and economic factors behind terrorism are downplayed, sometimes on the grounds that individual terrorists come from less-deprived backgrounds—or, as the *New York Times* columnist put it, 'Osama bin Laden's tricycle was probably gold-plated'.[60] More thoughtful approaches seeking an alternative strategy which addresses the underlying causes of conflict and extremism, such as the Sustainable Security initiative of the Oxford Research Group, have difficulty in getting a hearing in the mainstream media.[61] The lesson of the missed opportunities during the cold war, and of the even greater failures afterwards, is overwhelmingly one of misperception: unless we can see clearly what went wrong in the past, and acknowledge 'our' responsibility as well as 'theirs', we shall simply substitute a new war for an old, and new dangers for those we so narrowly escaped.

Conclusion

Peace in the Twenty-First Century

O Sun of real peace! O hastening light!
O free and extatic! O what I here, preparing, warble for!
O the sun of the world will ascend, dazzling, and take his height—
and you too, O my Ideal, will surely ascend!
O so amazing and broad—up there resplendent, darting and burning!
O vision prophetic, stagger'd with weight of light! with pouring glories!
O lips of my soul, already becoming powerless!
O ample and grand Presidentiads! Now the war, the war is over!

(Walt Whitman, 'Sun of real peace', 1870)[1]

In conclusion, let us seek to strike a balance sheet on matters of peace and war for the world in the second decade of the twenty-first century. There is nothing like the dazzling and 'extatic' display of peace which Walt Whitman believed that he was witnessing after the American Civil War had ended, but there is still much to put on the positive side:

1. War has become almost completely deglamorized: no soldiers fighting today will be, like those described by Tolstoy before the Battle of Austerlitz, in love with 'the glory of the Russian [or American, or British] arms', nor will a modern young Petya rush to join the army because he has caught a glimpse of the tsar—or of the president, or of the prime minister.[2] Bathsheba Everdene, the Hardy heroine in *Far From the Madding Crowd*, will not be seduced a second time by the 'marvellous evolutions' of Sergeant Troy's dazzling sword-blade. The bloodiness and awfulness of war is now a truism from which none will dissent, at least as regards current wars.

By the end of the 1970s the appetite for patriotic war films had been dulled by the Vietnam War, and most such films today make at least some attempt at greater realism. For nearly everyone except a few enthusiasts and neo-Nazis, the collection of military memorabilia now has little more significance than the collection of stamps. One should note, however, that previous wars may still be invested with more glamour than they deserve, while legitimate respect for those soldiers risking injury or death in current engagements— and the obligatory praise of them as 'heroes' when they lose their lives—may inhibit criticism of the wars they are fighting.

2. The United Nations is now in its seventh decade and represents a universally acknowledged international institution attempting to fill the role—though not always succeeding—of which peace thinkers from the Enlightenment onwards have dreamed. It survived the constriction of the cold war: it has been damaged but not rendered redundant by the wars undertaken since then outside its authority; its peacekeeping record is mixed but considerable; a multitude of international agencies on whom we all depend (often without being aware of their existence) operate under its authority; it is the institution of both last and first resort for tackling international emergencies and disasters—and it will be called on even more frequently as climate change worsens. The committees and other UN bodies tasked with promoting disarmament also offer a mechanism for progress even if little has yet been achieved. If the United Nations did not exist, we would want to invent it, but today unlike in 1945 we would be unable to do so from scratch.

3. There has been a parallel growth in international law which now imposes significant constraints upon the use or threat of force and which is underpinned by a growing moral consensus against war. Despite legitimate cynicism, the rule of law 'is arguably the best chance humankind has for learning to live together amicably and abandoning the resort to force and violence to resolve disputes'.[3] Particularly after the disaster of the Iraq War (rightly judged 'illegal' by UN Secretary-General Kofi Annan), there is a new awareness that international law offers 'a more effective way to deal with international problems' in the globalized world.[4] The advisory opinion of the International Court of Justice on the general illegality of the use of nuclear weapons has also provided a measure of legal

backing for the so-called 'nuclear taboo' of world opinion which amounts to 'a normative prohibition against the first use of nuclear weapons'.[5] Another significant advance has been the establishment in 2002 of the International Criminal Court as a permanent tribunal to prosecute individuals for genocide, crimes against humanity, and war crimes, following on from the specific war crimes tribunals for former Yugoslavia and Rwanda. Although subject to the reservations of some states, notably of the USA—which means that its investigations so far have been mainly confined to the most blatant war crimes in Africa (especially in the Democratic Republic of Congo)—it marks a significant step forward in strengthening the principle in international law that such crimes have no immunity.[6]

4. In the face of unremitting hostility during the cold war, those people not content to let the world drift on towards disaster, but who believe that peace has to be worked for to be achieved, have scored significant successes (building on the efforts of previous generations). More generally, the concept of citizens' action, based largely on principles of non-violence, is seen to be capable of achieving political results, particularly since the end of the cold war.

a. The various campaigns against nuclear testing and for nuclear non-proliferation and disarmament exercised a restraining influence on their governments which, at critical times, may have made all the difference between keeping the weapons unused and the launch of global destruction. They also helped create a climate in which international agreements such as the Test-Ban and Nuclear Non-Proliferation Treaties could be reached, and to form a tide of world public opinion which frowns on, and may to some extent restrain, further nuclear proliferation. The anti-nuclear movements should also be seen as part of a wider phenomenon of late twentieth-century activism, including the civil rights, anti-apartheid, and feminist movements. First emerging in the non-governmental organizations that multiplied in the 1970s and 1980s, the international mobilization of civil society became more self-confident in the 1990s, becoming visible at the parallel forums staged alongside the 1992 'Earth Summit' in Rio de Jeneiro, and at subsequent UN conferences, and, more recently, through the World Social Forum from 2001 onwards.[7]

b. While it is commonplace to refer to the twentieth century as the bloodiest in history, the same century has also taught us, as the

US peace scholar Jonathan Schell puts it, that 'forms of non-violent action can serve effectively in the place of violence at every level of political affairs'[8]—or, in the words of his British colleague David Cortright, that 'history's most violent era has also seen the dawning of an age of non-violence'.[9] There has been an impressive list of successful popular interventions (Czechoslovakia, the Philippines, South Africa, etc.) in spite of examples of tragic failure (Tiananmen Square, Burma), and the spread of civil protest in the Middle East and North Africa in 2011 has opened a new stage which will have global consequences. Such protests, we should note, although generally based on the principle of non-violence, may become less peaceful when met by violent repression.

5. The academic pursuit of peace—'peace studies'—has since the 1970s grown remarkably, facing down critics from Margaret Thatcher onwards, to become recognized as an important discipline in the study of international affairs. It has done so without cutting itself off from its activist roots, and continues to be linked to positive action in the fields of development and conflict resolution—as well as being immensely popular with students. More attention is now paid to addressing the underlying causes of violent conflict, particularly in the civil wars and inter-ethnic or communal disputes which have become more common than inter-state war (though less likely to be waged at such high intensity) in recent decades. The dynamics of conflict are seen as complex and shifting: in the words of one contemporary peace scholar they need to be 'tracked through time, identifying patterns, trends and shifting coalitions', so that we can arrive at 'a more realistic analysis of the political economy of war and violence', and devise ways of transforming conflict into peace.[10] The temptation to legitimize 'humanitarian intervention' in the name of peace is also now looked at more critically. In such situations, it has been argued by another scholar, governments and international bodies may impose liberal solutions which create a 'virtual peace', concealing deeper social and economic realities of violence.[11] The concept of a 'peace process' has become more popular since the end of the cold war, but actual peacemaking, it is also suggested, may run the risk of 'freezing conflicts into a negative peace' without tackling the underlying causes.[12]

6. Another important advance has been the general recognition, building especially on the work of the peace pioneer Johan Galtung,

and later on that of the development economist Amartya Sen, that peace and development are indivisible.[13] The need for economic justice which links post-conflict reconstruction, development, and human security[14] has been explored in UN-sponsored reports such as *A More Secure World* (2004) and the *Human Security Report* (2005).[15] The phenomenon of economic globalization has triggered critical efforts to construct an alternative, more 'ethical', vision of a single world community, based on a broader version of the 'reciprocal altruism' (the term is borrowed from evolutionary biology) which already binds families, regions, and nations. This challenging task is described by the international historian Ken Booth, in his ambitious attempt to chart the new territory of 'world security', as that of 'humanising globalisation'. The aim is to create a 'cosmopolitan project' in which violence will be de-legitimized as an instrument of politics, and war can be transcended by creating a 'world security community'.[16] Overall, peace studies has succeeded—perhaps better than war studies—in keeping abreast of a world which continues to change with increasing rapidity, even though 'peace researchers have a more complex and difficult role than the relatively straightforward activities of the Cold War era'.[17]

7. Finally on the positive side of the balance sheet, we may simply say that, in the end, and in the face of huge threats to its existence, the world has continued to survive.

However, there is much to enter on the negative side of our balance sheet for war and peace in the twenty-first century, and consequently much more that needs to be done. In the difficult and dangerous century ahead, a piecemeal approach will never achieve sufficient results, and it is time to put together a comprehensive *Agenda for Peace*.

1. The 'new' wars of the post-cold war era have shown that the resort to war is still too tempting a mechanism, and that the opinions of St Augustine (yes!), Erasmus, Kant, and many more, that it is rarely worth the price paid for it, have not prevailed. This is the real lesson of the Iraq and Afghan Wars, as it was of the Vietnam War, although it took longer to be accepted for Iraq and is still not well understood for Afghanistan. Even when the errors of the past are acknowledged there is no guarantee that, after an interval of time, this will prevent similar disasters being launched in the future. One reason is that—in

spite of the huge advances in peace studies outlined above—there is a still a deep disconnect between the work and arguments of the specialists in war and those of the specialists in peace. This gap needs to be bridged: at times of crisis the professor of peace studies should be invited to give his or her opinions alongside the defence experts, the generals, and the politicians. Specialists in peace should write as frequently for *Foreign Affairs* as specialists in terrorism.

2. The UN as an institution for making and keeping peace is regarded, not unreasonably, as fallible and as having proved deficient in the past, yet the obvious corollary that it cannot be more effective without reforms to increase its effectiveness gains little active support. Such reforms would require above all (a) the expansion of the Security Council and some dilution of the veto powers of the Permanent Five, and (b) measures to institute supervision—completely lacking so far—by the UN as a body, or through its staff, of military operations undertaken in its name. The need for both of these, and the difficulties in achieving them, are set out by Paul Kennedy in his recent study with the Tennysonian title (see above, p. 14) of *The Parliament of Man*.[18] We are entitled to suspect that in their hearts, ruling state establishments of the major powers have scant interest in improving the UN or translating the authority provided for in its Charter into more credible reality—just as they have no real intention of moving towards a world with zero nuclear weapons. We need instead to fulfil the promise of the UN's *Agenda for Peace* (1992) which urged that the new opportunity offered by the end of the cold war should not be 'squandered'. This will require kindling and mobilizing enthusiasm for the UN on a scale which has not been seen since its foundation— a major work of publicity and education.

3. While war as noted above has become less glamorous, it has become more impersonal—except for those immediately affected—when conducted by modern armies, as it is waged with ever more sophisticated and often remote technology. The alienation from the reality of war is compounded by the growing practice of 'embedding' the media within military operations and subjecting them to censorship (though this restriction is often omitted from their reports). The practice was first fully developed in the 1991 Gulf War when, according to a careful study commissioned by the University of Leeds, 'there were essentially two wars going on: the war itself, fought by the coalition's combined military forces against the

regime of Saddam Hussein, and the war as portrayed by the media. The latter did not necessarily reflect the reality of the former.'[19] The new sanitized war can then be contrasted with the technologically less sophisticated forms of combat in 'local' civil wars, particularly in Africa, which are characterized as particularly brutal and savage. The guerrilla techniques of resistance forces which rely on the support—to a large extent, if not always entirely, voluntary—of local populations such as those in Chechnya fighting Russian forces, or those in Afghanistan fighting US forces and their allies, may also be branded as 'cowardly'—a type of warfare in which the enemy refuses to come out and 'fight in the open'. Those working within the media have a responsibility to look more critically at the reporting of war and to explore ways of promoting a more peace-oriented news culture.

4. The rise of terrorism inspired by (although certainly not invented by) an extremist form of Islamism has encouraged the return to default thinking on how to deal with the existence of hostile external forces, which has much in common with default thinking during the cold war, namely that the threat which is posed is global and generational, and that it can only be countered by constant vigilance and deterrence. This new confrontation also shares another characteristic of the cold war, that the extreme depiction of the alleged 'Islamic threat' in the West fosters and nurtures the real Islamist extremists. As the late Fred Halliday, one of the most perceptive scholars of the Arab world, described it:

> At the very core of this supposed challenge or conflict lie confusions: the mere fact of peoples being 'Islamic' in some general religious and cultural sense has been conflated with that of their adhering to beliefs and policies that are strictly described as 'Islamist' or 'fundamentalist'.... As with other political myths, the very fact that these ideas are propagated gives them a certain reality—for those whom they are designed to mobilize, but also for those against whom they are directed.[20]

Worse still, while it was acknowledged that the cold war 'threat' might be removed one day by the 'collapse of communism', those who see the terrorist 'threat' in similar terms hold out no hope that it will go away in our lifetimes. As Halliday also observed, 'the myths of the Islamists and of their opponents often coincide in postulating one single, timeless, all-pervasive "Islam"'.[21] In reality the subject of Islamic attitudes towards peace and war, viewed over more than one millennium, is extremely complex (and would require a book of equal length to this one to deal with properly). Here we may merely note that the concept of jihad or 'struggle' has always had a wide range of meanings: for most Muslims it denotes 'striving to lead a good Muslim life, praying and fasting regularly, being an attentive spouse and parent' and has nothing to do with struggle against an external enemy.[22] Those who present the 'Islamic threat' in generational terms also fail to ask why, if this threat is so pervasive and fundamental, it did not appear before, and they gloss over or dismiss the proximate causes that have created a body of extremists prepared to sacrifice their own lives on a scale never seen previously. A more honest examination is needed of the Western failure to successfully promote peace between Israel and Palestine, and its perverse success in helping, by political and military support, to perpetuate undemocratic regimes in the Middle East—now at last being challenged by the peoples of those countries. It also requires a more self-critical accounting of the way in which terrorism has been fostered when it was in 'our' interests (as during the Soviet occupation of Afghanistan). An equally honest accounting is necessary too of the shortfall of economic programmes of aid and development which, by failing to address fully the issues of poverty, inequality, discrimination, and worsening environment, have created fertile ground for the rise of new terrorism.

5. Although the superpower nuclear arms race ended with the cold war, the major nuclear powers have failed to give convincing evidence at successive Non-Proliferation Treaty conferences of credible movement by them towards nuclear disarmament, which would fulfil the implicit bargain embodied in the treaty between maintaining non-proliferation and making progress towards a non-nuclear world. A new round of proliferation led to India and Pakistan becoming declared nuclear weapons states, while North Korea has more recently also claimed the same status. With Israel long on the scene as an undeclared nuclear power, Iran is suspected of having the same intention, in an unresolved stand-off which carries the threat of pre-emptive war against the presumed Iranian capability, and/or the nuclearization of other states in the region. The nebulous threat of terrorists acquiring nuclear weapons from so-called 'rogue states'

also helps to justify core strategic thinking among major nuclear powers that effectively (though not always openly) rejects even the most distant goal of reducing their possession of such weapons to zero. The British case is instructive: both the Labour prime minister Tony Blair and the Conservative defence spokesman (later defence secretary) Liam Fox argued in 2006–7 that it was impossible to 'predict the future' over the next half-century, and that therefore it was necessary to prepare for the long-term renewal of Britain's Trident force. The logic of this position is that nuclear weapons can never be renounced, because (as Blair argued) 'the one thing that is certain [about the future]...is the unpredictability of it'.[23] Public opinion should be reminded of the double standards of the nuclear haves, and that nuclear weapons and proliferation continue to pose what could be a terminal threat to the world. More than fifty years since the anti-nuclear movement began it is needed as much as ever before.

6. Since the initiation of the annual *Human Development Report* of the UNDP in the 1990s, more effort has been made to unify the (apparently) separate strands of the challenges facing the twenty-first century—the deteriorating environment, the shortfall in development aid and poverty alleviation, and our faulty and increasingly perverse global economic structures—within the framework of sustainable human security. It has also been demonstrated empirically that (as most of us would believe intuitively) there is a direct and dire connection between economic and social deprivation on the one hand, and conflict and the clash of rival ethnicities and/or tribal differences on the other—as in many recent instances of local or internal war.[24] In the case of Afghanistan, the cumulative total of US military-related spending since the start of the war reached $444 billion by 2010, twelve times the $35 billion in non-military aid given to that country by the entire global community over the same period (of which 45 per cent had gone to the security sector, and only 9 per cent to agriculture and rural development).[25] Governments need to understand that they cannot simultaneously maintain a high level of military expenditure (world military expenditure in 2009 totalled $1.53 trillion)[26] and make a significant contribution to poverty reduction. Development and aid packages should not merely patch up the wounds left by conflict and war: they should be targeted to prevent those wounds being created.

7. While the peace movements of the cold war achieved considerable success, this was in a relatively restricted sphere of opposition to nuclear weapons: paradoxically, their activities might have broadened out, as they were beginning to do in the 1980s, if the cold war had lasted longer. In spite of the achievements of the non-governmental and social movements referred to above, these tend to coalesce only for specific occasions, and we miss the grand sweep and design of the seekers for peace from the Enlightenment through to the 1930s. Closer long-term links need to be established between the separate campaigns and movements for combating global warming, for tackling poverty and inequality, for reforming the dominant financial institutions, for promoting real progress towards nuclear disarmament, and for significant reform of the United Nations. Education will play an important part: more needs to be done to address the imbalance between war and peace studies, to seek greater visibility (especially in the media) for the rich contributions of peace research, and to promote peace education particularly in secondary school curricula, building on the international standards for peace education developed by the UN and UNESCO.[27]

8. There is a fatal contradiction between attempting to maintain the status quo through military means, and seeking to resolve the root causes of conflict by peaceful means, which the Oxford Research Group has described as the contradiction between a 'control paradigm' and 'sustainable security'.[28] Political elites who have publicly applauded the use of non-violent methods to achieve change elsewhere—from South Africa to the Ukraine—show a lack of consistency when they resort to violence themselves. They should instead consider adopting non-violent methods as part of their own long-term strategy to deter hypothetical threats such as 'nuclear blackmail', rather than continue to maintain a military capability based on worst-case scenarios. They should lessen reliance on the threat or use of force as an instrument of politics, and foreign policies should be tested by whether or not they contribute to 'the de-legitimation of violence'.[29] Military intervention can only be justified on an international basis with full authority from the UN, and effective supervision by it, to ensure that the limits which have been set are observed—and then only when the 'precautionary principle' has been applied that war is the last resort and that inaction would have been worse.[30]

In conclusion, we should recognize that, as globalization breaks down the confines of the nation-state, a new obligation is imposed on governments to provide human security and good governance not just, or even principally, within states, but across the whole world. This does not mean the rich and powerful telling the poor and weak countries to have democracy: it means shouldering the responsibility for satisfying human needs to ensure a peaceful environment for all. (The majority of rich and developed nations would return much lower scores for 'good governance' if their own failure to meet global obligations were taken into account.) We have reached a new stage in the cosmopolitan view which has its roots deep in ancient Greek and Chinese thinking, which had a strong influence on the humanist approach and was developed further in the writings of the Enlightenment, and which has been expounded in the arguments of peace societies and movements from the nineteenth century to the present day. It is implicit, and often explicit, in the vision of a common identity with common obligations and benefits which is expressed in the modern welfare state, in the United Nations system, in the formulation of universal human rights, and in the commitment to a shared global security.[31] Much has been done but much more remains to be done. Instead of taking refuge in pessimistic 'realism' about the inevitability of war, we need to recognize the essential reality that there is only one world and one future on planet Earth, and, while realizing the need for sustained effort and education, to take an optimistic view of the human potential for peace. We should feel, in the words of the Nobel Peace Prize winner Linus Pauling,

privileged to be alive during this extraordinary age, this unique epoch in the history of the world, the epoch of demarcation between the past millennia of war and suffering, and the future, the great future of peace, justice, morality, and human well-being. We are privileged to have the opportunity of contributing to the achievement of the goal of the abolition of war and its replacement by world law.[32]

River's Rebirth

Rain falls on the ruined city,
wind blows in the ruined city,
and white bones—bones—lie about like sea-shells.
Autumn comes to the ruined city,
plants regain colour,
freshness;
river mirrors blue sky,
heals wounds;
bridges: arcs of steel suspended
over sevenfold river—river.
Peace Bridge, round suns of its handrails
conversing with the sun.
Flowing water mirrors dome;
eternal echo—
the mistake will not be repeated.
'In the twenty years since that day,
he passed on, and so did she.
At dawn I heard the faint sound of insects.'
'Nights by the great river
are beautiful.
I'm glad I'm alive.'
I'm glad I'm alive,
I'm glad I'm alive:
those who sang that tune—
they, too, are now dead.
O sevenfold river
flowing gently, slowly,
through the city of rivers,
O current
creating our future once again.
Carry our joys and sorrows,
flow without cease,
flow forever,
forever, forever
without end.

(Kurihara Sadako, 1966)[33]

Notes

ABBREVIATIONS

OIEP   Nigel Young, ed., *Oxford International Encyclopedia of Peace*, vols. i–iv (New York: Oxford University Press, 2010).

WEP   Linus Pauling, ed., *World Encyclopedia of Peace*, vols. i–iv (Oxford: Pergamon Press, 1986).

INTERNET SOURCES

References for material which has been gathered from online sources give the 'parent' website (for example, the UN *Human Development Report* for various years is sourced to http://hdr.undp.org). The specific url—which may have changed since the document was accessed—can be ascertained by searching within the relevant website, or by using a standard search engine.

TRANSLATIONS

All transactions from Greek and Chinese have been made by the author, unless attributed to another source.

REFERENCES

All references to authors in bold type, e.g., '**Adams (1964)**', indicate a title listed in the Select Bibliography.

INTRODUCTION

1. Aristophanes, *Peace*, 571–81 (my trans.).
2. Hobbes argued in *Leviathan* (13), and earlier in a similar passage in *De Cive* (1. 12), that 'the nature of War, consisteth not in actuall fighting; but in the known disposition thereto, during all the time there is no assurance to the contrary. All other time is Peace.' Only in the Commonwealth, as envisaged by Hobbes, where the 'sovereign power' has the authority and strength to prevent discord, can peace be said to exist. The argument was taken up by Spinoza in his *Tractatus Politicus* (5. 4). Such a situation,

Spinoza argued, where the subjects of the Commonwealth are only 'hindered by terror' from taking arms, cannot be regarded as one of real peace either. For peace is not the 'mere absence of war, but a virtue [*pax enim non belli privatio, sed virtus est*]' that springs from a conscious willingness to carry out what the Commonwealth has decreed should be done. Both Hobbes and Spinoza are making the point that peace requires more than the simple absence of warfare: they are not belittling the significance of peace which is guaranteed (Hobbes) and freely accepted (Spinoza).

3. **Boulding (1978)**, 8.
4. Johan Galtung, 'Violence and Peace', in **Smoker et al. (1990)**, 9–14.
5. Francis Beer, 'The Reduction of War and the Creation of Peace', in **Smoker et al. (1990)**, 15–20.
6. The Global Peace Index is produced by the Institute for Economics and Peace based in Sydney, Australia; the Human Development Index is produced by the UN Development Programme.
7. Thich Nhat Hanh, *Being Peace* (London: Rider, 1992), 80.
8. Mahatma Gandhi, in *Young India*, 11 August 1920, extracted in **Barash (2000)**, 190.
9. Johan Galtung, 'Peace, Negative and Positive', *OIEP* iii. 352–6 (at 355).
10. **Cooper (1991)**, 61.
11. Duane Cady, *From Warism to Pacifism: A Moral Continuum* (Philadelphia: Temple University Press, 1989), 14.
12. Martin Ceadel, 'Pacifism and Pacificism', in Terence Ball and Richard Bellamy, eds., *The Cambridge History of Twentieth-Century Political Thought*, vol. vi (Cambridge: Cambridge University Press, 2003), 473–92. Confusingly, the term 'pacificism' had been used in the nineteenth century by purists who insisted it was the correct English form for 'pacifism'. It was only adopted to describe the 'reformist' wing of the peace movement after a suggestion from the British historian A. J. P. Taylor in 1957 (ibid. 474–5).
13. Thucydides, Book 4.62, in a speech attributed to Hermocrates of Syracuse urging the states of Sicily in 424 BC to make peace among themselves, and arguing that Athens would then be much less likely to intervene. His advice was taken and the Athenian fleet, faced with a united Sicily, sailed back home—though it would return to the island, with disastrous results, nine years later.
14. Gabriel Kolko, *The Age of War: The United States Confronts the World* (London: Lynne Rienner, 2006), 173.
15. Robert Maynard Hutchins, farewell address to the students of the University of Chicago, 1951, *Manas*, 4: 11 (14 March 1951), available online at http://www.manasjournal.org.
16. 'The Arts of Peace' is a lengthy section in Erasmus' *The Education of a Christian Prince:* see further Chapter 4, pp. 105–6.
17. The University of Bradford's Department of Peace Studies was accused by the Thatcher government of being 'the brains behind the Campaign

for Nuclear Disarmament', and was forced to accept an investigation of its activities. School of Social and International Studies, *Peace and Conflict Research at Bradford: Annual Research Report 2010*, 1. See also David Dunn, 'The Peace Studies Debate', *Political Quarterly*, 56: 1 (January 1985), 68–72.

18. The works on which I have relied include particularly **Adams (1962), Bainton (1961), Barash (2000), Beales (1931), Booth (2007), Boulding (1978), Brock (1972), Chatfield** and **Ilukhina (1994), Cooper (1991), Cortright (2008), Fry (2007), Gregor (1996), Roberts and Garton Ash (2009), Wittner (1993–2003)**, and **Zampaglione (1973)**. I should also acknowledge the work of **Michael Howard (1989 and 2000)**, one of very few modern war historians to take the issue of peace seriously—even though I express disagreement with him at various points in this book.

19. The 'Realist' school regards nation-states as the main actors on the international stage and is mostly concerned with the definition and interplay of their national interests and power, while minimizing the role of ideology and morality. The US political scientist Hans Morgenthau, who is seen as one of its intellectual founding fathers, wrote in his *Politics among Nations* (1949) that 'the main signpost that helps political realism to find its way through the landscape of international politics is the concept of interest defined in terms of power'.

20. **Booth (2007)**, 360–78.

21. **Kemp and Fry (2004)**, 185–6.

22. **Boulding (1978)**, 3. The organizers in 1952 of the Research Exchange on the Prevention of War had also judged that the term 'peace' would be 'highly suspect and controversial'; Herbert Kelman, 'Reflections on the History and Status of Peace Research', *Conflict Management and Peace Science*, 5: 2 (1981), 95–110 at 96–7. When the Harry Frank Guggenheim Foundation held a week-long conference on peace in 1990, this was regarded as 'an act of risk-taking on the part of the Foundation, in that peace is a relatively new topic to academic studies'; **Gregor (1996)**, vii.

23. I am indebted to Oliver Taplin's brilliant analysis of the Shield of Achilles, 'The Shield of Achilles within the "Iliad"', *Greece & Rome*, 2nd series, 27: 1 (April 1980), 1–21.

24. Letter No. 189 (AD 418).

25. Fred Halliday, 'Cold War', in **Smoker et al. (1990)**, 51–6 (at 55).

26. The theme of 'Locksley Hall', writes one modern biographer of Tennyson, is 'the still inchoate, somehow painful sense of the future': all that the poet had prophesied early in the reign of Queen Victoria had taken place within ten years of his death or hers: what is lacking tody is 'his sense of freedom, of scarcely tapped resources' (including, I suggest, freedom from war, and the resources for worldwide peace). Peter Levi, *Tennyson* (London: Macmillan, 1993), 147.

I. THE PERCEPTION OF PEACE AND WAR

1. Interview, 16 March 1987, Institute of International Studies, University of California, Berkeley, online at http://conversations.berkeley.edu.

2. Arnold Toynbee, *A Study of History*, abridgement of vols vii–x by D. C. Somervell (London: Oxford University Press, 1957), 323.

3. Lawrence Freedman, ed., *War*, Oxford Readers (Oxford: Oxford University Press, 1994), 6.

4. H. C. Duffin, *Thomas Hardy: A Study of the Wessex Novels, the Poems, and The Dynasts*, 3rd edn, rev. and enlarged (Manchester: Manchester University Press, 1937), 255.

5. William Gay, 'The Language of War and Peace', in Lester Kurtz, ed., *Encyclopedia of Violence, Peace, and Conflict* (San Diego: Academic Press, 1999), ii. 304.

6. Francis Beer, 'Meanings, Metaphors, and Myths of Peace', *OIEP* iii. 4.

7. Napoleon, letter to his brother Joseph, 13 December 1805, *Letters of Napoleon*, ed. J. M. Thompson (Oxford: Blackwell, 1934), 133–4.

8. 'Proclamation to the Soldiers after the Battle of Friedland', 24 June 1807, *Napoleon's Addresses: Selections from the Proclamations, Speeches and Correspondence of Napoleon Bonaparte*, ed. Ida M. Tarbell (Boston: Joseph Knight, 1896).

9. *The Times*, 2 August 1814.

10. *Manchester Guardian*, 2 June 1902.

11. Fragment from Philemon's *Pyrrhus*, text in John Edmonds, ed., *The Fragments of Attic Comedy*, iii: 1 (Leiden: Brill, 1961), 34; translation from **Bainton (1961)**, 17–18. I have translated the last two lines which Bainton omitted.

12. Maurice Davie, *The Evolution of War: A Study of its Rôle in Early Societies* (New Haven: Yale University Press, 1929), 1.

13. Matthew 24: 6 (New International Version, 1984).

14. Paul Fussell, *The Great War and Modern Memory* (New York: Oxford University Press, 2000), 72–4.

15. *Manchester Guardian*, 12 November 1918.

16. National Opinion Research Center, *War and Peace: 1943 Edition, a Nation-Wide Opinion Survey* (Denver: University of Denver, March 1943), 21.

17. Mohammed Bedjaoui et al., *Modern Wars: The Humanitarian Challenge. A Report for the Independent Commission on International Humanitarian Issues* (London: Zed, 1986), 24.

18. *St Louis Post-Dispatch*, 13 December 1953; *Saturday Review*, editorial, 4 April 1954; Norman Cousins, *In Place of Folly* (New York: Harper, 1961).

19. B. Jongman and J. van der Dennen, 'The Great "War Figures" Hoax: An Investigation in Polemomythology', *Bulletin of Peace Proposals*, 19: 2 (1988).

20. Edmund Osmanczyk, *Encyclopedia of the United Nations and International Agreements* 3rd edn, ed. Anthony Mango (London: Routledge, 2003), 1783.

21. See Carl Haub, 'How Many People have ever Lived on Earth?', *Population Today* (November–December 2002), 3–4.

22. **Boulding (1978)**, 28.
23. Pitirim Sorokin, *Social and Cultural Dynamics*, vol. iii (New York: American Book Co., 1937); Lewis F. Richardson, *Statistics of Deadly Quarrels*, ed. Quincy Wright and C. C. Lienau (Pacific Grove, Calif.: Boxwood Press, 1960). See further Brian Hayes, 'Statistics of Deadly Quarrels', *American Scientist*, 90: 1 (January–February 2002), 10–15.
24. **Beer (1974)**, 20.
25. Kenneth Boulding, 'Peace and the Evolutionary Process', in Raimo Vayrynen, ed., *The Quest for Peace: Transcending Collective Violence and War among Societies, Cultures and States* (London: Sage, 1987), 48–59 (at 54).
26. Richard Coudenhove-Kalergi, *From War to Peace* (London: Cape, 1959), 24. However, the author later acknowledges that there have been 'epochs of peace, which also last for generations and centuries', although these are 'less numerous than the great wars', 103.
27. Matthew Melko and Richard Weigel, *Peace in the Ancient World* (Jefferson, NC: McFarland & Co., 1981), 1.
28. Leonard Lewin, ed., *Report from Iron Mountain: On the Possibility and Desirability of Peace* (New York: Dial Press, 1967).
29. Kenneth Boulding, ed., *Peace and the War Industry* (Los Angeles: Aldine Books, 1970), 57.
30. Sombart and Mumford both quoted in Richard Preston and Sydney Wise, *Men in Arms: A History of Warfare and its Interrelationships with Western Society* (New York: Holt, Reinhart & Winston, 1979), 10.
31. Frank Novak, ed., *Lewis Mumford and Patrick Geddes, the Correspondence* (London: Routledge, 1995), 203.
32. **Nef (1968)**, 221.
33. Ibid. 315–16, 325, 352.
34. Toynbee, op. cit. n. 2 above, 392.
35. Clive Trebilcock, 'Spin-Off in British Economic History: Armaments and Industry, 1760–1914', *Economic History Review*, 22: 3 (December 1969), 474–90 (at 474).
36. Vernon Ruttan, *Is War Necessary for Economic Growth? Military Procurement and Technology Development* (New York: Oxford University Press, 2006), 159–62.
37. Thomas Withington, 'The MUAV: Six Inches Long and Deadly', *The Business*, 17 November 2002.
38. Hanan Sher, 'Facets of the Israeli Economy: The Defense Industry', 1 June 2002, Israel Ministry of Foreign Affairs, online at http://www.mfa.gov.il/mfa/archive.
39. Paul Dunne and Derek Braddon, *The Economic Impact of Military R&D* (Bristol: University of the West of England, 2008).
40. Jakob Burckhardt, *Reflections on History* (London: Allen & Unwin, 1943) (lectures given 1868–71), 137–8.
41. Jacob [Jakob] Burckhardt, *The Civilization of the Renaissance in Italy* (Oxford: Phaidon, 1945), 62–4.

42. John Ruskin, 'War' (1865), in *The Crown of Wild Olive: Four Lectures on Industry and War* (London: George Allen, 1890), 115–71. For a discussion of Ruskin's ambiguity on the subject of war, see **Nef (1968)**, 405–6.

43. William James, 'The Moral Equivalent of War', in Harrison Steeves, *Representative Essays in Modern Thought* (New York: American Book Co., 1913), 513–24 (at 524).

44. Martin van Creveld, *The Culture of War* (New York: Ballantine, 2008), xv; 'Why Men Fight', in Freedman, ed., op. cit. n. 3 above, 85–9 (at 87).

45. **Aron (1981)**, 340–1.

46. Julius Fraser, *Time, Conflict, and Human Values* (Champaign, Ill.: University of Illinois Press, 1999), 103.

47. Robert Ardrey, *The Territorial Imperative: A Personal Inquiry into the Animal Origins of Property & Nations* (London: Collins, 1967), 5. 334–7.

48. Konrad Lorenz, *On Aggression* (New York: Harcourt, 1966), 270.

49. Mary Midgley, 'The Pseudo-Darwinist Conspiracy', *RSA Journal* (Winter 2010), online at http://www.theresa.org/fellowship/journal/archive/winter-2010/

50. David Crook, *Darwinism, War, and History: The Debate over the Biology of War from the 'Origin of Species' to the First World War* (Cambridge: Cambridge University Press, 1994), 28.

51. Jane Goodall, *The Chimpanzees of Gombe: Patterns of Behavior* (Cambridge, Mass.: Harvard University Press, 1986), 357.

52. Frans de Waal, 'The Biological Basis of Peaceful Coexistence: A Review of Reconciliation Research on Monkeys and Apes', in **Gregor (1996)**, 37–70 (at 39).

53. Lawrence Keeley, *War before Civilization: The Myth of the Peaceful Savage* (New York: Oxford University Press, 1997), 174; Steven LeBlanc and Katherine Register, *Constant Battles: The Myth of the Peaceful, Noble Savage* (London: St Martin's Press, 2003), 5.

54. Douglas Fry, *The Human Potential for Peace: An Anthropological Challenge to Assumptions about War and Violence* (New York: Oxford University Press, 2005); **Fry (2007)** (quotations), 5, 110, 194.

55. Brian Ferguson, *Yanomami Warfare: A Political History* (Sante Fe, N. Mex.: School of American Research Press, 1995); 'The Birth of War', *Natural History*, 112: 6 (July–August 2003).

56. **Rapoport (1995)**, 9.

57. Friedrich Matz, *Art of the World: Crete and Early Greece* (London: Methuen, 1962), 79. Matz (1890–1974) was a distinguished specialist in the art of ancient Crete, Rome, and the Near East: he was a nephew of the archaeologist Friedrich Matz (1843–74).

58. Walter Burkert, *Greek Religion: Archaic and Classical* (Oxford: Wiley-Blackwell, 1987), 20.

59. Peter Green, *Ancient Greece: A Concise History* (London: Thames & Hudson, 1973), 30.

60. Costis Davaras, *Guide to Cretan Antiquities* (Athens: Eptalofos, 1976), 106–8.
61. Reynold Higgins, *Minoan and Mycenaean Art* (London: Thames & Hudson, 1997), 102.
62. There is an unresolved controversy over the dating of the Linear B tablets at Knossos, ascribed by Arthur Evans to *c.*1400 BC, but apparently identical in writing style to the tablets discovered at Pylos, which are dated more securely *c.*1200 BC. In both cases the firing of the tablets (which allowed their preservation) implies a catastrophic event. If a later date is assigned to the Knossos tablets, this would suggest that the Minoan culture may not have been dominated by the Mycenaeans until the thirteenth century. The case for this alternative view was first argued persuasively by Leonard Palmer, *Mycenaeans and Minoans* (London: Faber, 1961), ch.VI.
63. J. Alexander MacGillivray, *Minotaur: Sir Arthur Evans and the Archaeology of the Minoan Myth* (London: Pimlico, 2000), 195.
64. David Sewell, 'Santorini and its Eruption in the Late Bronze Age', online at http://www.santorini-eruption.org.uk.
65. Martin Nilsson, *The Minoan-Mycenaean Religion and its Survival in Greek Religion*, 2nd rev. edn (Lund: Gleerup, 1950), 19.
66. Azar Gat, *War in Human Civilization* (Oxford: Oxford University Press, 2006), 262–4.
67. See further Nanno Marinatos, *Minoan Religion: Ritual, Image, and Symbol* (Columbia, SC: University of South Carolina Press, 1993), 114; Dennis Hughes, *Human Sacrifice in Ancient Greece* (London: Routledge, 1991), 13–17, 20–2.
68. **Winn (2008)**, 88.
69. Robert Laffineur, ed., *Polemos: Le Contexte guerrier en Égée à l'âge du Bronze*, Aegaeum, 19 (Liège: University of Liège, 1999).
70. Oliver Dickinson, *The Aegean Bronze Age* (Cambridge: Cambridge University Press, 1994), 266.

2. ANCIENT PEACE

1. Homer, *Iliad*, 9. 401–9. I have rendered ψυχη as 'life', except in the last line where 'spirit' seems more appropriate. All translations from Greek and Chinese in this chapter are my own unless otherwise indicated.
2. Zuo Qiuming, *Chronicle of Zuo* (henceforth cited as *Chronicle*), 'Duke Yin', 4th year.
3. *Chapman's Homer: The Iliad and the Odyssey*, ed. Jan Parker (Ware: Wordsworth, 2000), 12.
4. M. M. Sage, *Warfare in Ancient Greece: A Sourcebook* (London: Routledge, 1996), 129.
5. Patricia Buckley Ebrey, *The Cambridge Illustrated History of China* (Cambridge: Cambridge University Press, 1996), 38–9.

6. In Plate 2, the early fifth-century BC Kleophrades Painter portrays Achilles resting his head reflectively. The pose is even more striking in a kylix of the same age (Louvre, G264) attributed to the Tarquinian Painter.

7. E. T. Owen, *The Story of the Iliad* (London: Duckworth, 1989), 95.

8. Herwig Maehler, 'The Singer in the Odyssey', in Irene de Jong, ed., *Homer: Critical Assessments* (London: Routledge, 1999), 6–20 (at 17).

9. Gregory Nagy, *The Best of the Achaeans: Concepts of the Hero in Archaic Greek Poetry* (Baltimore: Johns Hopkins University Press, 1998), ch. 11, online at http://www.press.jhu.edu.

10. *The Iliad*, trans. E.V. Rieu, ed. Peter Jones (London: Penguin Books, 1993), xxxiv.

11. *Iliad*, 14. 493–9; 16. 337–41; 16. 345–50; 17. 520–4.

12. Thomas Seymour, 'Notes on Homeric War', *Transactions and Proceedings of the American Philological Association*, 31 (1900), 82–92.

13. Simone Weil and Rachel Bespaloff, *War and the Iliad* (New York: New York Review Books, 2005), 3, 32.

14. *The Iliad*, trans. E.V. Rieu (Harmondsworth: Penguin Books, 1950), xviii.

15. *The Iliad*, ed. Jones, op. cit. n. 10 above, xxxiv.

16. *The Iliad*, trans. Robert Graves (London: Penguin Books, 2008), 18, 24.

17. *Iliad*, 3. 154–60.

18. Ibid., 11. 32–7. See also the work known as 'The Shield of Herakles', doubtfully attributed to Hesiod and probably composed in the latter half of the seventh century BC, which describes the shield in conventionally awe-inspiring terms, with multiple images of conflict and death. It concludes with a passage describing more peaceful scenes which appears to be an inferior imitation of Homer's 'Shield of Achilles'; see *Hesiod, Homeric Hymns Epic Cycle, Homerica,* trans. Hugh Evelyn-White (Cambridge, Mass.: Harvard University Press, 1943), xxiv.

19. The sixth-century BC jar by the Camtar Painter (Boston Museum of Fine Arts) has a splendidly fierce Gorgon's head. It has been argued that this and similar vases depict the first arming of Achilles at home in Phthia before he set out for Troy, not the second arming described in the *Iliad*. I do not see why this earlier more obscure episode should be celebrated on vases rather than the more dramatic later one. The Phthia hypothesis is discounted in Steven Lowenstam, 'The Arming of Achilleus on Early Greek Vases', *Classical Antiquity*, 12: 2 (October 1993), 199–218. Another vase at Boston, by the Amasis Painter (no. 01.8027) shows a lion devouring an ox. On the front panel of the Monteleone bronze chariot in the Metropolitan Museum of Art in New York, Achilles is also shown receiving a shield with the Gorgon's head from his mother.

20. *Iliad*, 18. 541–9. Here and elsewhere Homer is painting an idyllic picture: no ploughman on such a drinking regime would have kept the plough straight for very long!

21. E. T. Owen, whose account of *The Story of the Iliad* captures so well the artistic logic of Homer's composition, sees this episode as a deliberate interlude before the final act, comparing it to the expedition by Diomedes (Book 10) which provides a similar interlude between the first and second sections of the epic. In the 'Shield of Achilles', says Owen, Homer deepens the poignancy of the tragedy to come by 'lift[ing] our eyes from their concentration on the battlefield to the contemplation of other scenes which remind us of the fullness and variety of life', op. cit. n. 7 above, 107, 187–8.

22. D. H. Porter, 'Violent Juxtaposition in the Similes of the Iliad', *Classical Journal*, 68 (1973), 11–21, reprinted in de Jong, op. cit. n. 8 above, 338–50 (at 339).

23. Oliver Taplin, 'The Shield of Achilles within the "Iliad"', *Greece & Rome*, 2nd series, 27: 1 (April 1980), 1–21 (at 4).

24. W. H. Auden, *The Shield of Achilles* (New York: Random House, 1955).

25. Berenice Geoffroy, 'Homer and the Greek Ideal', *UNESCO Courier*, 45: 9 (September 1992).

26. M. I. Finley, *The World of Odysseus* (Harmondsworth: Penguin, 1967), 138.

27. **Zampaglione (1973)**, 19–21.

28. In a new study, Caroline Alexander suggests that while Homer took care not to betray the epic tradition, his *Iliad* presented war consistently as disastrous rather than heroic; *The War that Killed Achilles: The True Story of the Iliad* (London: Faber, 2011).

29. Peter Green, *Ancient Greece: A Concise History* (London: Thames & Hudson, 1973), 37.

30. Robert Graves, op. cit. n. 16 above, 24.

31. Donald Lateiner, 'The *Iliad*: An Unpredictable Classic', in Robert Fowler, ed., *The Cambridge Companion to Homer* (Cambridge: Cambridge University Press, 2004), 11–30 (at 14).

32. Jean Giraudoux, *La Guerre de Troie n'aura pas lieu,* ed. H. J. G. Godin (London: University of London Press, 1958), Act 2, Scene 14. The play was first performed in Paris in 1935. It was translated by Christopher Fry under the title *Tiger at the Gates* (London: Methuen, 1955).

33. Mark Edward Lewis, *Sanctioned Violence in Early China* (Albany, NY: State University of New York Press, 1989), 15.

34. Yuri Pines, *Foundations of Confucian Thought: Intellectual Life in the Chunqiu Period, 722–453 B.C.E.* (Honolulu: University of Hawaii Press, 2002), 53–4.

35. *Chronicle*, (a) 'Duke Xi', 22nd year; (b) 'Duke Cheng', 15th year; (c) 'Duke Xi', 13th year.

36. Ibid., 'Duke Xiang', 27th year.

37. Cho-yun Hsu, 'The Spring and Autumn Period', in Michael Loewe and Edward Shaughnessy, eds., *The Cambridge History of Ancient China: From the Origins of Civilization to 221 BC* (Cambridge: Cambridge University Press, 1999), 561–3.

38. Pines, op. cit. n. 34 above, 54.
39. *Chronicle*, 'Duke Wen', 3rd year.
40. Ibid., 'Duke Zhao', 14th year.
41. Ibid., 'Duke Xi', 5th year.
42. Ibid., 'Duke Huan', 6th year.
43. *Book of Songs*, No. 66 (100). In this and other references to the *Book of Songs*, the first figure refers to the traditional numbering, and the second (in brackets) to the number as published in *The Book of Songs*, trans. Arthur Waley (London: Allen & Unwin, 1937).
44. Kuang-yu Chen, 'The Book of Odes: A Case Study in the Chinese Hermeneutic Tradition', in Tu Ching-i, *Interpretation and Intellectual Change: Chinese Hermeneutics in Historical Perspective* (New Brunswick, NJ: Transaction, 2005), 52.
45. Waley, op. cit. n. 43 above, 336.
46. *Book of Songs*, No. 192 (292). This song is one of a dozen odes assigned a number by Waley but omitted from his translation (see preface to his first edition).
47. *Book of Songs*, Nos. 68 (150), 79–80 (118–19), 121 (151), 167–8 (131–2), 169 (145), 232 (129), 234 (130).
48. Ibid., No. 156 (125).
49. Ibid., No. 110 (124).
50. See further Eric Wan-hsiang Wang, 'The Frontier Poems of Chang Chi', *Journal of National Taitung Teachers College*, 9 (1998), 365–406.
51. Frank Adcock and D. J. Mosley, *Diplomacy in Ancient Greece* (London: Thames & Hudson, 1975). 12. See also Simon Hornblower, 'Warfare in Ancient Literature: The Paradox of War', in Philip Sabin and Hans van Wees, eds., *The Cambridge History of Greek and Roman Warfare*, vol. i (Cambridge: Cambridge University Press, 2007).
52. The statue by Kephisodotos was noted by the Greek traveller Pausanias (*c.* second century AD) as still standing next to the Prytaneion (town hall): it only survives now in Roman copies. It celebrated either the peace treaty with Persia of 375 BC or the common peace between all the Greeks of 371 BC. For a discussion of the peace festival and of the Greeks' 'general antipathy to war', see **Hunt** (2010), 240–4. 'Sweet Eirene' is invoked in an anonymous lyric: David Campbell, *Greek Lyric*, vol. v (Cambridge, Mass.: Harvard University Press, 1993), p. 421.
53. Henk Singor, 'War and International Relations', in Kurt Raaflaub and Hans van Wees, eds., *A Companion to Archaic Greece* (Oxford: Blackwell, 2009), 585.
54. David Pritchard, 'The Symbiosis between Democracy and War: The Case of Ancient Athens', in Pritchard, ed., *War, Democracy and Culture in Classical Athens* (Cambridge: Cambridge University Press, 2010), 8.
55. Victor Alonso, 'War, Peace, and International Law in Ancient Greece', in **Raaflaub (2007)**, 206–25 (at 221).

56. See further Green, op. cit. n. 29 above, 49 ff.

57. Hornblower, op. cit. n. 51 above, 22–53 (at 25).

58. Van Wees, 'War and Peace in Ancient Greece', in **Hartmann and Heuser (2001)**, 45–6.

59. Thucydides, *History of the Peloponnesian War*, trans. Rex Warner (London: Penguin, 1972), 3. 81–2; see also his description of the 'butchering' of the entire population of Mycalessus, 7. 29–30.

60. For the view that we need to take into account 'the horrific experience of the battlefield' in assessing Thucydides as a historian, see **Tritle (2000)**, 125–7.

61. Hans van Wees, 'War and Society', in Sabin and van Wees, op. cit. n. 51 above, 299.

62. Lawrence Tritle, '"Laughing for Joy": War and Peace among the Greeks', in **Raaflaub (2007)**, 181–2. W. S. Ferguson, *Greek Imperialism* (New York: Biblo & Tannen, 1981).

63. Ferguson, op. cit. n. 62 above, 22.

64. Xenophon, *Hellenica, I*, ed. Carleton Brownson (Cambridge, Mass.: Harvard University Press, 1918), Book 6, 3. 6.

65. See further Adcock and Mosley, op. cit. n. 51 above, 136–9; P. J. Rhodes, 'Making and Breaking Treaties in the Greek World', in **De Souza and France (2008)**.

66. Thucydides, op. cit. n. 59 above, 82–6; Donald Kagan, *The Peloponnesian War* (London: HarperCollins, 2003), 47.

67. Plutarch, *Greek Lives*, trans. Robin Waterfield (Oxford: Oxford University Press, 1998), 'Nicias', 193. The 'spiders' webs' quotation comes from the *Erechtheus*, a lost play by Euripides. There is a similar expression in an ode to peace by Bacchylides (No. 310 in *The Oxford Book of Greek Verse*). The prediction that the war would last for twenty-seven years was recorded by Thucydides (5. 26) as something 'put about by many people from the beginning [i.e. 431 BC] to the end of the [Peloponnesian] war'. Though attributed to an oracle, this sounds suspiciously like pro-war propaganda.

68. Andocides, 'On the Peace', 3. 30, in *Minor Attic Orators*, vol. i, trans. K. J. Maidment (Cambridge: Cambridge University Press, 1968).

69. Isocrates, 'On the Peace', in *Isocrates*, vol. ii, trans. George Norlin (London: William Heinemann, 1980), 8. 14.

70. **Hunt (2010)**, 245–7.

71. Isocrates, op. cit. n. 69 above, 8. 20.

72. Euripides, *Orestes and Other Plays*, trans. Philip Vellacott (Harmondsworth: Penguin, 1972), 8–9. See also Vellacott's introduction to *The Bacchae and Other Plays* (Harmondsworth: Penguin, 1973), 17.

73. Aristophanes, *Aristophanes: Lysistrata and Other Plays*, trans. Alan H. Sommerstein (London: Penguin, 2002), 5.

74. The slaughter in Sicily is only mentioned once and indirectly. How noisy these women are, complains the magistrate who attempts

unsuccessfully to evict them from the Akropolis. Did not they make enough noise when the assembly was voting to send the troops to Sicily, and the women went onto the rooftops crying 'Weep, weep for Adonis'?

75. Patric Dickinson, *Aristophanes against War* (London: Oxford University Press, 1957), xv.

76. Aeschylus had taken part in the defeat of Persia at Salamis, and in the earlier Greek victory at Marathon (the latter recalled with pride in his own epitaph). Sophocles also had war experience: he had been given an important post in the Athenian campaign against the island of Samos in the Samian War (441–439 BC), which paved the way for the outbreak of the Peloponnesian War ten years later. Euripides wrote most of his plays after passing the age for military service: we may assume, with Gilbert Murray, that he too had witnessed considerable fighting in the previous wars by which Athens established its supremacy, *Euripides and his Age* (London: Williams & Norgate, 1913), 99.

77. Gerardo Zampaglione regards *The Persians* as showing 'the impact of war on a defeated people', and comments that while the pride of the victorious Greeks might seem legitimate to Aeschylus, 'nothing could induce him to forget the tears this success had cost', **Zampaglione (1973)**, 72–3; More recently, Thomas Harrison has described it as essentially a patriotic play not intended to arouse sympathy for the defeated; *The Emptiness of Asia: Aeschylus' Persians and the History of the Fifth Century* (London: Duckworth, 2000).

78. **Tritle (2000)**, 44–5.

79. Aeschylus, *Seven against Thebes*, trans. Anthony Hecht and Helen Bacon (London: Oxford University Press, 1974), 61. The chorus's lament occupies lines 915–40 of the original text.

80. Sophocles, *Ajax*, lines 679–83, in *Sophocles: Electra and Other Plays*, trans. David Raeburn (London: Penguin, 2008), 97.

81. **Tritle (2000)**, 96.

82. **Vellacott (1975)**, ch. 6, 'Comment on War', 153.

83. Melos had simply sought to remain neutral in the war between Sparta and Athens. The episode was famously presented by Thucydides in his 'Melian Dialogue'—Book 5 of his *History*—a probably imagined dialogue between the magistrates of Melos and the envoys of Athens, who justify their intended action unless Melos capitulates.

84. Neil Croally, *Euripidean Polemic: The Trojan Women and the Function of Tragedy* (Cambridge: Cambridge University Press, 1994), 264.

85. Cassandra learns that she has been allocated as a concubine (in the context of war, an intended rape victim) to the supreme Greek leader Agamemnon who—the audience knows very well—will be murdered by his own wife on his return home. In the play's most powerful speech, Cassandra declares that conquered Troy is more to be envied than the

victorious Greeks. The Trojans at least died defending their country and were buried at home, while the Greeks came far from home to die in a pointless cause. Prophesying death for her 'bridegroom' (Agamemnon), she warns that the outcome of the war will be disastrous for the other Greek leaders, envisaging 'horrors too shameful' for a prophetess to utter in words.

86. Robert Meagher, *Herakles Gone Mad: Rethinking Heroism in an Age of Endless War* (Northampton, Mass.: Olive Branch Press, 2006). Other Euripidean plays which denounce the futility and horror of war include his *Suppliant Women, Helen, The Phoenician Women,* and *Iphigenia in Aulis.*

87. *Mengzi,* 4A. 14 (Harvard–Yenching concordance number).

88. Shang Yang, 'The Book of Lord Shang', trans. in Robert Wilkinson, ed., *The Art of War* (Ware: Wordsworth, 1998), 214.

89. Tao Hanzhang, 'Commentary on *The Art of War*', in Wilkinson, ibid., 130.

90. Laozi, *Daodejing,* ch. 30.

91. *Mengzi,* 4A. 14.

92. *Mozi,* Book 5, 2. 2.

93. **Pines (2009)**, 201.

94. *Chronicle,* 'Duke Ai', 11th Year.

95. Confucius, *The Analects,* trans. D. C. Lau (Harmondsworth: Penguin, 1979), 26.

96. Kongzi [Confucius], *Lunyu (Analects),* 12. 7.

97. Ibid., 16. 1.

98. *Mengzi,* 6B. 9.

99. Ibid., 1B. 11, 7B. 4.

100. W. A. C. H. Dobson, *Mencius: A New Translation* (London: Oxford University Press, 1963), 124.

101. *Mengzi,* 7B. 2. Inconsistencies in Mengzi's position would probably be clarified if we had his own writings rather than a collection of episodes, anecdotes, and sayings recorded by his disciples and compiled later.

102. Burton Watson, *Hsun Tzu: Basic Writings* (New York: Columbia University Press, 1963), 4–5.

103. *Xunzi,* 15. 5, 7. I have amended Xunzi's comment on military matters to follow the same wording as when he refers back to it in 15. 21, i.e. *fan zai yu jun* (everything to do with the army), instead of *fan zai da wang* (everything to do with the ruler).

104. *Xunzi,* 15. 5.

105. Ibid., 15. 16. I have translated this more than usually terse passage quite loosely.

106. The word *ru* may originally have had the derogatory meaning of a 'weakling' who did not take up arms: **Needham (1956)**, 31. The Confucians belonged mainly to the class of functionaries and specialists whose positions became less secure during the break-up of the feudal courts. Mozi

may have begun life as a wheelwright, and the original meaning of *mo* was a captive engaged in hard labour.

107. *Mozi*, 4, 1. 4.

108. Ibid., 5, 3. 6.

109. The Confucian Gongsun Hong in the Han dynasty would define *ren* as 'extending benefit and eliminating harm, inclusively caring without partiality': Chris Fraser, 'Mohism', section 9 (revised March 2010) in the online *Stanford Encyclopedia of Philosophy* at http://plato.stanford.edu.

110. Laozi, op. cit. n. 90 above, ch. 46.

111. Roger Ames, *The Art of Rulership: A Study in Ancient Chinese Political Thought* (Honolulu: University of Hawaii Press, 1983), 39.

112. Laozi, op. cit. n. 90 above, ch. 31, ch. 68.

113. Ibid., ch. 80.

114. *Zhuangzi*, 33. Fragments of both scholars have been collected by John Knoblock at http://www.as.miami.edu/phi/bio/Buddha/songx1.htm. The Logician Gongsun Long (best known for his sophistry in defending the proposition that 'a white horse is not a horse') also advocated the peaceful settlement of disputes. The *Annals of Lu Buwei* contains an anecdote in which his clever use of logic undermines the Qin ruler's attempt to persuade the state of Zhao to join him in an aggressive war. See the entry on Gongsun Long at http://www.newworldencyclopedia.org.

115. See further Paul Gregor, 'War and Peace in Classical Chinese Thought, with Particular Regard to Chinese Religion', in Perry Schmidt-Leukel, ed., *War and Peace in World Religions* (London: SCM Press, 2004), 72–5.

116. James Stroble, 'Justification of War in Ancient China', *Asian Philosophy*, 8: 3 (1998), 165–90.

117. Thomas Kane, 'Inauspicious Tools: Chinese Thought on the Morality of Warfare', in Paul Robinson, ed., *Just War in Comparative Perspective* (Aldershot: Ashgate, 2003), ch. 9, 151–2.

118. John King Fairbank, 'Introduction: Varieties of the Chinese Military Experience', in Fairbank and Frank A. Kierman, eds., *Chinese Ways in Warfare* (Cambridge, Mass.: Harvard University Press, 1974), 4, 25. Fairbank's approach is shared by Joseph Needham in his introduction to *Science and Civilisation in China*, vol. v, pt 6 (Cambridge: Cambridge University Press, 1995).

119. Christopher Rand, 'The Role of Military Thought in Early Chinese Intellectual History' (Harvard University, unpublished PhD, 1977), 23.

120. Pines, op. cit. n. 34 above, 65–6, 78.

121. Emily Kearns, 'The Gods in the Homeric Epics', in Fowler, op. cit. n. 31 above, 59–73 at 70.

122. **Zampaglione (1973)**, 50–4.

123. **Reichberg et al. (2006)**, 19–20.

124. Ibid., 31–2.

125. Jonathan Shay, *Achilles in Vietnam: Combat Trauma and the Undoing of Character* (New York: Scribner, 1994). See also David McCann and Barry Strauss, eds.,

War and Democracy: A Comparative Study of the Korean War and the Peloponnesian War (Armonk, NY: M. E. Sharpe, 2001) for many interesting insights.

126. For some contrary views, see Ralph Sawyer, 'Chinese Warfare: The Paradox of the Unlearned Lesson', *American Diplomacy*, 4: 4 (1999); Andrew Scobell, *China and Strategic Culture* (Carlisle, Pa.: US Army War College Strategic Studies Institute, May 2002).

127. Li Shijia, 'Harmonious World: China's Ancient Philosophy for New International Order', *People's Daily Online*, 2 October 2007. Also 'China Supports Buddhism in Building a Harmonious World', *People's Daily Online*, 13 April 2006.

128. Kurt Raaflaub, 'Searching for Peace in the Ancient World', in **Raaflaub (2007)**, 1–33 (at 12).

129. Hans van Wees, 'Peace and the Society of States in Antiquity', in Jost Dülffer and Robert Frank, eds., *Peace, War and Gender from Antiquity to the Present: Cross-Cultural Perspectives* (Essen: Klartext Verlag, 2009), 25–43 (at 26).

3. THE MORALITY OF PEACE

1. *The Letters and Poems of Fulbert of Chartres*, ed. Frederick Behrends (Oxford: Clarendon Press, 1976), 263 (slightly adapted). Fulbert was bishop of Chartres, 1006–28.

2. *Works of Sulpitius Severus*, trans. Alexander Roberts in *Nicene and Post-Nicene Fathers of the Christian Church*, 2nd series, vol. xi (Oxford: James Parker, 1894), chs. 2–4.

3. **Cadoux (1940)**, 259–61, cites a number of examples.

4. See the version of St Martin's life published in the monumental *Catholic Encyclopedia* (1907–14), available online at http://www.newadvent.org, which merely states that Martin 'soon received baptism, and was a little later finally freed from military service'.

5. **Brock (1972)**, 4.

6. M. K. Gandhi, 'Swadeshi', 14 February 1916, in *Third Class in Indian Railways* (Lahore: Gandhi Publications League, n.d.), 13.

7. **Bainton (1961)**, 66.

8. Justin Martyr, 'Dialogue with Trypho', ch. cx, in Alexander Roberts and James Donaldson, eds., *Ante-Nicene Fathers: The Writings of the Fathers down to A.D. 325*, vol. i (New York: Christian Literature Publishing Co., 1885), 254.

9. Translations from the *New English Bible* (Oxford: Oxford University Press, 1970).

10. Tertullian, *On Idolatry*, ch. xix, 'Concerning Military Service', in Allan Menzies, ed., *Ante-Nicene Fathers: The Writings of the Fathers down to A.D. 325*, vol. iii (New York: Christian Literature Publishing Co., 1885). This volume, and those cited in other notes containing the works of the Ante-Nicene, Nicene, and Post-Nicene Fathers, have been edited and electronically transcribed on the New Advent website (http://www1000.newadvent.

org), and on the Christian Classics Ethereal Library website (http://www. ccel.org/fathers.html).

11. For a recent discussion of the 'two swords' argument, see James Arlandson, 'Pacifism and the Sword in the Gospels', *American Thinker*, online at http://www.americanthinker.com. See also Gerard Caspary, *Politics and Exegesis: Origen and the Two Swords* (Berkeley and Los Angeles: University of California Press, 1979). In spite of his title, Caspary (at 2) says that it is unlikely that Origen ever referred to 'the two swords of Luke'.

12. **Cadoux (1940)**, III.

13. Ibid., 152–3.

14. Ibid., 131–2.

15. **Bainton (1961)**, 68–70.

16. Peter Brock, 'Why Did St Maximilian Refuse to Serve in the Roman Army?', *Journal of Ecclesiastical History*, 45 (1994), 195–209.

17. Louis Swift, 'Early Christian Views on Violence, War, and Peace', in **Raaflaub (2007)**, 279–96 (at 279–80).

18. Cited in Andrew Holt, 'Early Christian Views of War: A Bibliographical Essay', in *Crusades Encyclopaedia*, online at http://www.crusades-encyclopedia.com. Holt provides a good summary of the conflicting views.

19. Henry Chadwick, 'The Early Christian Community', in John McManners, ed., *Oxford Illustrated History of Christianity* (Oxford: Oxford University Press, 1990), 21–61; Adrian Hastings, *A World History of Christianity* (London: Cassell, 1999); Carter Lindberg, *A Brief History of Christianity* (Oxford: Wiley-Blackwell, 2005).

20. Michael Walzer, *Just and Unjust Wars*, 2nd edn (New York: Basic Books, 1992), 269.

21. James O'Donnell, 'Augustine: *City of God*', 1983, online at http://www9. georgetown.edu/faculty/jod/augustine/civ.html. In his biography of Augustine, O'Donnell observes that while 'we are right to attach these notions [including the Just War] to him, yet we misrepresent him when we do', *Augustine, Sinner and Saint* (London: Profile, 2005), 4.

22. John Mattox, *Saint Augustine and the Theory of Just War* (New York: Continuum, 2006), 44–5.

23. Paula Fredriksen, 'Christians in the Roman Empire in the First Three Centuries CE', in David Potter, ed., *A Companion to the Roman Empire* (Oxford: Blackwell Publishing, 2006), 587–606 (at 587).

24. **Bainton (1961)**, 85–7.

25. Eusebius, 'Oratio Constantini', 16. 4, 7, trans. Ernest Cushing Richardson in *Nicene and Post-Nicene Fathers of the Christian Church*, 2nd series, vol. i (Buffalo, NY: Christian Literature Publishing Co., 1890).

26. H.A. Drake, *Constantine and the Bishops: The Politics of Intolerance* (Baltimore: Johns Hopkins University Press, 2000), 73.

27. Ambrose, *De Fide Christiana*, 2. 16, trans. H. de Romestic in *Nicene and Post-Nicene Fathers of the Christian Church*, 2nd series, vol. x (Buffalo, NY: Christian Literature Publishing Co., 1896).

28. Bruce Duncan, 'The Struggle to Develop a Just War Tradition in the West', n.d., online at http://www.socialjustice.catholic.org.au.

29. **Johnson (1987)**, 58.

30. Mattox, op. cit. n. 22 above, 82.

31. Augustine, *City of God*, 19. 13. All translations from the *Letters* and *City of God* are by Marcus Dods from *Nicene and Post-Nicene Fathers of the Christian Church*, 1st series, vols. i and ii (Buffalo, NY: Christian Literature Publishing Co., 1887).

32. My translation from a French version of Augustine's *Questions on the Heptateuch*, online at http://www.abbaye-saint-benoit.ch/saints/augustin/questions/josue.htm.

33. Mattox, op. cit. n. 22 above, 51–4.

34. Letter No. 189 (AD 418); see further Peter Brown, *Augustine of Hippo* (London: Faber, 2000), 425–8.

35. Letter No. 229 (AD 429).

36. Augustine, *City of God*, Book 19. 7.

37. N. Ben-Aryeh Debby, 'War and Peace: The Description of Ambrogio Lorenzetti's Frescoes in Saint Bernardino's 1425 Siena Sermons', *Renaissance Studies*, 15: 3 (2001), 272–86.

38. See further William Bowsky, *A Medieval Italian Commune: Siena under the Nine, 1287–1355* (Berkeley and Los Angeles: University of California Press, 1982), 299–314.

39. Thomas Bulfinch, *Bulfinch's Mythology: The Age of Chivalry* (Teddington: Echo, 2006), 1. This work was first published in Boston in 1858.

40. Maurice Keen, *The Penguin History of Medieval Europe* (Harmondsworth: Penguin, 1991), 274.

41. Barbara Tuchman, *A Distant Mirror: The Calamitous 14th Century* (Harmondsworth: Penguin, 1978), 141.

42. Thomas Asbridge, *The First Crusade: A New History* (London: Free Press, 2004), 316–19.

43. See further the introduction to Andrew Ayton and J. L. Price, *The Medieval Military Revolution: State, Society and Military Change in Medieval and Early Modern Europe* (London: Tauris, 1995).

44. J. H. Plumb, *The Penguin Book of the Renaissance* (London: Penguin, 1991), 36.

45. J. R. Hale, *Renaissance War Studies* (London: Continuum, 1983), 362, 367.

46. Thomas Renna, 'The Idea of Peace in the West, 500–1500', *Journal of Medieval History*, 6 (1980), 143–67 (at 143).

47. See further Georges Duby, *The Three Orders: Feudal Society Imagined* (Chicago: University of Chicago Press, 1980), 134–9.

48. Oliver Thatcher and E. H. McNeal, eds., *A Source Book for Medieval History* (New York: Scribners, 1905), 412.

49. Ibid., 417–18.

50. Ralph Glaber, *Historiarum Libri Quinque*, Lib. 4. 5, 'De pace et abundantia anni millesimi a passione Domini', trans. in C. G. Coulton, ed., *Life in the Middle Ages* (New York: Macmillan, 1930), i. 1–7.

51. Richard Landes, 'Peace of God: Pax Dei', n.d., online at http://www. bu.edu/mille/people/rlpages/paxdei.html.

52. Loren MacKinney, 'The People and Public Opinion in the Eleventh-Century Peace Movement', *Speculum*, 5: 2 (April 1930), 181–206 (at 185, 196).

53. Thomas Head, 'Peace and Power in France around the Year 1000', *Essays in Medieval Studies*, 23 (2006), 1–17 (at 10–11).

54. **Wood (1916)**, 19–20.

55. Helen Cooper, 'Speaking for the Victim', in Corinne Saunders et al., eds., *Writing War: Medieval Literary Responses to Warfare* (Cambridge: Brewer, 2004), 213–32 (at 213). This essay offers significant new insight into an under-researched area.

56. **Heyn (1997)**, 31.

57. Asbridge, op. cit. n. 42 above, 26.

58. MacKinney, op. cit. n. 52 above, 202.

59. Thatcher and McNeal, op. cit. n. 48 above, 516.

60. Keith Haines, 'Attitudes and Impediments to Pacifism in Medieval Europe', *Journal of Medieval History*, 7 (1981), 369–88 (at 379).

61. Asbridge, op. cit. n. 42 above, 65.

62. Josiah Russell, 'The Population of the Crusader States', in N. P. Zacour and H. W. Hazard, eds., *A History of the Crusades*, v: *The Impact of the Crusades on the Near East* (Madison: University of Wisconsin Press, 1985), 295.

63. Jonathan Riley-Smith, 'Religious Warriors: Reinterpreting the Crusades', *The Economist*, 23 December 1995.

64. Thomas Madden, 'The Real History of the Crusades', *Crisis*, 20: 4 (April 2002).

65. Asbridge, op. cit. n. 42 above, 40–1.

66. **Brock (1972)**, 27.

67. Stanley Kahrl, 'Introduction', in Thomas Murphy, ed., *The Holy War* (Columbus, Oh.: Ohio State University Press, 1976), 1–8 (at 7).

68. James Brundage, 'Holy War and the Medieval Lawyers', in Murphy, op. cit. n. 67 above, 99–140 (at 121).

69. Palmer Throop, *Criticism of the Crusade: A Study of Public Opinion and Crusade Propaganda* (Amsterdam: Swets & Zeitlinger, 1940). Norman Housley, *Contesting the Crusades* (Oxford: Wiley-Blackwell, 2006), 59, has a useful discussion of the value of Throop's work. More recent major works include Elizabeth Siberry, *Criticism of Crusading, 1095–1274* (Oxford:

Clarendon Press, 1985), and Tomaz Mastnak, *Crusading Peace: Christendom, the Muslim World, and Western Political Order* (Berkeley and Los Angeles: University of California Press, 2002).

70. Throop, op. cit. n. 69 above, 1, 23.

71. Ibid., 40.

72. Ibid., 69, 94, 99–101.

73. *St Francis of Assisi: Writings and Early Biographies, English Omnibus of the Sources for the Life of St Francis of Assisi*, ed. Marion Habig (Chicago: Franciscan Herald Press, 1973), 388. The controversy is summed up by Brad Pardue, 'Francis of Assisi among the Saracens', *2005 Proceedings of the Florida Conference of Historians*, 13 (April 2006), 96–104.

74. Throop, op. cit. n. 69 above, 133.

75. Ibid., 162–8.

76. John Derksen, 'Peacemaking Principles Drawn from Opposition to the Crusades, 1095–1276', *Peace Research*, 36: 2 (November 2004), 41–58.

77. Siberry, op. cit. n. 69 above, 217.

78. Haines, op. cit. n. 60 above, 370.

4. THE HUMANIST APPROACH

1. Pierre de Ronsard, *Exhortation pour la paix* (Paris: Wechel, 1558), published online by the Bibliothèque Nationale de France (my translation). This is not the same poem as Ronsard's better-known 'Ode de la paix'. See further James Hutton, *Themes of Peace in Renaissance Poetry* (Ithaca, NY: Cornell University Press, 1984), 186, 198–219.

2. Kristin Lohse Belkin, *Rubens* (London: Phaidon, 1998), 288–9.

3. Rubens's optimism for peace during his time in London can also be seen in the personification of Peace and Plenty in his ceiling painting for the Banqueting House in Whitehall, completed in 1634.

4. Desiderius Erasmus, *The Education of a Christian Prince* (1516), trans. Lester Born (New York: Octagon, 1963), section 3, 'The Arts of Peace', 205, online at http://www.stoics.com.

5. J. W. Mackail, ed., *Erasmus against War* (Boston: Merrymount Press, 1907), ix.

6. Ronald Bainton, *Erasmus of Christendom* (Tring: Lion Publishing, 1969), 13–16.

7. Jean-Claude Margolin, 'Erasmus (1467?–1536)', *Prospects: The Quarterly Review of Comparative Education* (Paris: UNESCO), 23: 1/2 (1993), 333–52.

8. Desiderius Erasmus, *Praise of Folly*, trans. Betty Radice (London: Penguin, 1993). Other translations include *The Praise of Folly and Other Writings*, trans. Robert Adams (New York: Norton, 1989), and *Praise of Folly*, trans. Roger Clarke (Richmond: OneWorld, 2008).

9. **Howard (1989)**, 16. In his later book, **Howard (2000)**, Erasmus is not mentioned.

10. Johan Huizinga, *Erasmus of Rotterdam* (London: Phaidon, 1952).

11. Peter van den Dungen,'Erasmus: 16th Century Pioneer of Peace Education and a Culture of Peace', *Civilisation 3000,* online at http://civilisation3000. wordpress.com.

12. Lucius Annaeus Seneca, *Moral Epistles*, vol. iii, trans. Richard M. Gummere (Cambridge, Mass.: Harvard University Press, 1925), Epistle 95.

13. **Adams (1962),** 7.

14. Bainton, op. cit. n. 6 above, 41.

15. Cicero, *De Officiis*, 3. 5, trans. Michael Grant in *Cicero: Selected Works* (Harmondsworth: Penguin, 1971), 175–6.

16. Susan Bruce, ed., *Three Early Modern Utopias* (New York: Oxford University Press, 1999), ix–xi. It has been suggested that More was influenced by reading a plan for a utopian community submitted to King Charles of Spain by the friar and social reformer Bartolomé de las Casas, who was one of the first settlers in the New World; Victor Baptiste, *Bartolomé de las Casas and Thomas More's Utopia: Connections and Similarities* (Culver City, Calif.: Labyrinthos, 1990).

17. **Adams (1962),** 122–5, 144–57.Van den Dungen, op. cit. n. 11 above, comments that 'Peace... would have had grounds to complain bitterly that she was not welcome even in the allegedly perfect human society that [Erasmus'] friend More had sketched in his *Utopia.*'

18. The resonance between Bosch's work and More's *Utopia* is discussed in Hans Belting, *Hieronymus Bosch: Garden of Earthly Delights* (Munich: Prestel, 2005), 107–20.

19. See further Barbara Deimling, *Botticelli* (Cologne: Taschen, 2007), 78–86.

20. For example, in the works of the Flemish Roelant Savery. See further Gerd-Helge Vogel: 'The Vision of Peace in Landscape Painting', *Hiroshima Journal of International Studies,* 9 (2003), 163–76.

21. **Adams (1962),** 164–5.

22. Ibid., 166–71.

23. Bainton, op. cit. n. 6 above, 38.

24. Erasmus, *Antipolemus*, trans. in *The Works of Vicesimus Knox* (London: J. Mawman, 1824), vol. v, extracts at 435, 451–2, available on the Online Library of Liberty, http://oll.libertyfund.org/.

25. Bainton, op. cit. n. 6 above, 41–2.

26. **Adams (1962),** 165.

27. Adams, op. cit. n. 8 above, 105–6, 108.

28. Ricardo Marín Ibáñez,'Juan Luis Vives', *Prospects: The Quarterly Review of Comparative Education* (Paris, UNESCO), 24: 3/4 (1994), 743–59.

29. **Adams (1962),** 241 ff.

30. Josef Trueta, *The Spirit of Catalonia* (London: Oxford University Press, 1946), 131.Although usually described as 'Spanish',Vives was a Catalonian, and never wrote in Spanish except for a few letters which show clearly that it was not his native language; ibid., 135.

31. Quoted in Ibáñez, op. cit. n. 28 above.

32. Ibid., 120. A copy of *De Concordia* was once owned by Henry VIII's first wife, Catherine of Aragon, and can still be found in the Chapter Library of Windsor Castle.

33. Juan Luis Vives, 'De concordia et discordia in humano genere (Sobre la concordia y la discordia en el género humano)', text and Spanish trans. in *Collección J. L. Vives*, vol. viiia (Valencia: Ajuntament de Valencia, 1997), 49–315 (my translation from the Spanish version).

34. **Adams (1962)**, 173.

35. John Hale, *War and Society in Renaissance Europe, 1450–1620* (London: Fontana, 1985), 15.

36. Stefan Zweig, *Erasmus* (London: Cassell, 1934), 221.

37. Paul Jorgensen, 'Shakespeare's Use of War and Peace', *Huntington Library Quarterly*, 4 (August 1953), 319–52.

38. e.g. Anthony Holden, *William Shakespeare: His Life and Work* (London: Abacus, 1999), 264.

39. Harold Jenkins, 'Shakespeare's History Plays: 1900–1951', in Allardyce Nicoll, ed., *Shakespeare Survey*, vi: *The Histories* (Cambridge: Cambridge University Press, 1953), 1, 7.

40. G. Blakemore Evans, ed., *The Riverside Shakespeare*, vol. i (New York: Houghton Mifflin, 1997), 53.

41. Michael Coveney, 'How *Troilus and Cressida* was Saved by the March of History and the Modern Theatre', in Edinburgh International Festival, *Troilus and Cressida* (Edinburgh, 2006).

42. Text in Simonds D'Ewes, *The Journals of all the Parliaments during the Reign of Queen Elizabeth* (1682), available at British History Online, http://www.british-history.ac.uk.

43. Theodor Meron, *Bloody Constraint: War and Chivalry in Shakespeare* (Oxford: Oxford University Press, 1998), 30.

44. *All's Well That Ends Well, Measure for Measure*, and *Troilus and Cressida* are conventionally regarded as Shakespeare's 'problem plays' as first defined by the critic F. S. Boas. In them, Boas wrote, 'we move along dim untrodden paths, and at the close our feeling is neither of simple joy nor pain....we are left to interpret their enigmas as best we may.' *Shakespere and his Predecessors* (London: John Murray, 1896), 345.

45. John Dover Wilson, ed., *Henry V* (Cambridge: Cambridge University Press, 1947), xxi.

46. Cited in Kevin Ewart, 'Henry V, the Gulf War, and Cultural Materialism', *Academic Exchange Quarterly*, 6: 4 (Winter 2002), online at http://rapidintellect.com.

47. A. R. Humphreys, ed., *Henry V (William Shakespeare)* (Harmondsworth: Penguin, 1968), 32.

48. J. H. Walter, ed., *King Henry V* (London: Methuen, 1954), xxix.

49. Lily Campbell, *Shakespeare's Histories* (London: Routledge, 1964), 281–6.

50. William Hazlitt, *Characters of Shakespeare's Plays* (London: Reynell, 1817; Oxford: Oxford University Press World's Classics, 1931), 170.

51. Annalisa Castaldo, ed., *The Life of Henry V*', New Kittredge Shakespeare (Newburyport: Focus, 2007), xi–xii.

52. John Sutherland and Cedric Watts, *Henry V, War Criminal? & Other Shakespeare Puzzles* (Oxford: Oxford University Press, 2000). My discussion of this episode, and the quotations from Johnson and Holinshed, come from this source.

53. Cedric Watts, ed., *Henry V* (Ware: Wordsworth Classics, 2000), 11.

54. Norman Rabkin, 'Rabbits, Ducks and *Henry V*', *Shakespeare Quarterly*, 28: 3 (Summer 1977), 279–96 (at 279).

55. Steven Marx, 'Shakespeare's Pacifism', *Renaissance Quarterly*, 45: 1 (1992), 49–98 (at 70).

56. J. M. Nosworthy, ed., *Cymbeline*, The Arden Shakespeare (London: Methuen, 1995), lxxxiii.

57. Paul Jorgensen, *Shakespeare's Military World* (Berkeley and Los Angeles: University of California Press, 1956), 200.

58. See the note on Prospero's Epilogue in Frank Kermode, ed., *The Tempest*, The Arden Shakespeare (London: Routledge, 1988), 133–4.

59. Holden, op. cit. n. 38 above, 293, suggests that Shakespeare quickly wearied of the Puritan atmosphere in his home town of Stratford which banned theatrical performances.

60. R. A. Foakes, ed., *King Henry VIII*, The Arden Shakespeare (London: Routledge, 1991), xxv.

61. Marx, op. cit. n. 55 above, 83.

62. Holden, op. cit. n. 38 above, 297, dismisses Cranmer's speech as 'sickeningly fulsome'. Frank Kermode is kinder to its 'quasi-liturgical grandeur, which is after all in character [with an archbishop's speech]'; *Shakespeare's Language* (London: Penguin, 2000), 307.

5. THE GROWTH OF PEACE CONSCIOUSNESS

1. 'Jeannette's Song, You are going far away', words by Charles Jefferys, music by Charles William Glover, *c.* 1848. This is the first song in a set of four published as *The Conscript's Vow*: its second verse is reproduced here. The songs were widely performed, and circulated in broadsheet form. A musical drama based upon them, written by W. H. Eburne, was staged in London in 1850. The last four lines of this verse were quoted by peace advocates.

2. Ronda Kasl and Suzanne Stratton, eds., *Painting in Spain in the Age of Enlightenment: Goya and his Contemporaries* (Indianapolis: Indianapolis Museum of Art, 1997), 158–9.

3. Larry Addington, *The Patterns of War since the Eighteenth Century* (Bloomington, Ind.: Indiana University Press, 1994), 1.

4. Jeremy Black, 'The Military Revolution, II: Eighteenth-Century War', in Charles Townshend, ed., *The Oxford History of Modern War* (Oxford: Oxford University Press, 2005), 54.

5. Denis Diderot and Jean Le Rond d'Alembert, *Encyclopédie, ou Dictionnaire raisonné des sciences, des arts et des métiers* (1751–72), vol. xi, online at http://fr.wikisource.org/wiki/L'Encyclopédie (my translation).

6. **Bainton (1961)**, 177.

7. **Penn (1993)**, 5–22.

8. See further Roderick Pace, 'Saint-Pierre, Abbé de', *OIEP* iv. 3–4.

9. John Mason, *The Indispensable Rousseau* (London: Quartet, 1979), 104–6; Garrett McAinsh, 'Jean-Jacques Rousseau', *WEP*, ii. 347–8.

10. In fact the title to Kant's essay comes not from an inn-sign but from the Abbé de Saint-Pierre's *Project*. The text used here is that reproduced in Immanuel Kant, *Perpetual Peace* (Minneapolis: Filiquarian, 2007).

11. Bertrand Russell, *History of Western Philosophy* (London: Allen & Unwin, 1946), 738; W. B. Gallie, *Philosophers of Peace and War* (Cambridge: Cambridge University Press, 1978), 5–6.

12. The classic work by Michael Walzer, *Just and Unjust Wars* (New York: Basic Books, 1977), cites Karl von Clausewitz at length but makes no mention of Kant. Robert Kagan describes Kant's ideas as a utopian quest for a 'paradise of peace and relative prosperity'; *Paradise and Power: America and Europe in the New World Order* (New York: Knopf, 2003), 3. F. H. Hinsley presents a very different view of Kant (and also Rousseau) as breaking with traditional internationalist theory. Kant was 'at pains to demonstrate why the goal of international integration was unattainable and undesirable and ought to be abandoned'; *Power and the Pursuit of Peace* (Cambridge: Cambridge University Press, 1963), 81.

13. **Cortright (2008)**, 249; **Barash (2000)**, 123; Jochen Rauber, 'The United Nations: A Kantian Dream Come True?', *Hanse Law Review*, 5: 1 (2009), 52.

14. We are fortunate to have several major works of modern peace research on this period, notably by **Cooper (1991)** and **Ceadel (2000)**, on which I have drawn for the following account.

15. Philo Pacificus (Noah Worcester), *A Solemn Review of the Custom of War, showing that War is the Effect of Popular Delusion and proposing a Remedy*, 11th rev. edn (Boston: Simpkins, 1833), online at http://www.nonresistance.org.

16. **Cooper (1991)**, 18.

17. Ibid., 24.

18. Henry Richard and Elihu Burritt, *Report of the Proceedings of the Second General Peace Congress held in Paris on the 22nd, 23rd and 24th of August, 1849* (London: Gilpin, 1849), 12.

19. **Beales (1931)**, 81.

20. **Cooper (1991)**, 28.

21. **Ceadel (2000)**, 32.

22. Trevor Royle, *Crimea* (London: Abacus, 2000), 64, 81.

23. **Ceadel (2000)**, 46.

24. **Beales (1931)**, 97.

25. Ibid., 105–6.

26. Eugène Labaume, *A Circumstantial Narrative of the Campaign in Russia*, trans. Edmund Boyce (London: Samuel Leigh, 1815), online at http://openlibrary.org, 217, 373–4.

27. Stefanie Markovits, *The Crimean War in the British Imagination* (New York: Cambridge University Press, 2009), introduction.

28. W. H. Russell, *The War: From the Landing at Gallipoli to the Death of Lord Raglan* (London: Routledge, 1855), 134, 323–35, online at http://www.archive.org.

29. Donald Mackenzie Wallace, *Russia* (London: Cassell, 1905), i. 371.

30. Henri Dunant, *A Memory of Solferino* (Geneva: International Committee of the Red Cross, 1986), 5.

31. See further Hans Rothe, ed., *Daumier on War* (New York: Da Capo, 1977).

32. Sandi Cooper, 'Peace Movements of the Nineteenth Century', *WEP* ii (1986), 230–4.

33. At the LPL's meeting in Lausanne (1869) Victor Hugo stressed the connection between national liberation and peace: Yes, war was bad, even glorious death in war was infamous, and life was sacred, and yet...'Qu'une dernière guerre soit nécessaire, hélas! je ne suis, certes, pas de ceux qui le nient. Que sera cette guerre? Une guerre de conquête. Quelle est la conquête à faire? La liberté.' Hugo, *Actes et paroles*, ii: *Pendant l'exil 1852–1870* (Paris: Nelson, n.d.).

34. **Cooper (1991)**, 43–4.

35. **Beales (1931)**, 145–9.

36. See further **Cortright (2008)**, 38–44.

37. Merze Tate, *The Disarmament Illusion: The Movement for a Limitation of Armaments to 1907* (New York: Macmillan, 1942), 190.

38. Arthur Eyffinger, *The 1899 Hague Peace Conference: 'The parliament of man, the federation of the world'* (Dordrecht: Nijhoff, 1999), 55–6. See also Eyffinger, *The 1907 Hague Peace Conference: The Conscience of the Civilized World* (The Hague: JudiCap, 2007), 56.

39. Tolstoy, 'Thou Shalt Not Kill', *Last Steps: The Late Writings of Leo Tolstoy*, ed. J. Parini (London: Penguin, 2009), 116.

40. Tate, op. cit. n. 37 above, 198.

41. Speech of 15 April 1907, *Addresses on International Subjects by Elihu Root*, ed. Robert Bacon and James Scott (Cambridge, Mass.: Harvard University Press, 1916), 144.

42. Tate, op. cit. n. 37 above, 293.

43. Eyffinger, *1899 Hague Peace Conference*, op. cit. n. 38 above, 438.

44. The first comment from Lenin and those from Luxemburg are quoted in **Cortright (2008)**, 267; Lenin remarks on 'sentimental liberals' in his 'Letter to Shlyapnikov', 14 November 1914.

45. Martin Shaw, 'War, Peace and British Marxism, 1895–1945', in **Taylor and Young (1987)**, 49–72 (at 50).
46. See further **Cortright (2008)**, 264–6.
47. Jean Jaurès, *L'Armée nouvelle* (Paris: L'Humanité, 1915), 4 (first published in 1910; my translation).
48. Nigel Young, 'Stuttgart Resolution', *OIEP* iv. 126–9. Text of Stuttgart Resolution ibid., 501–2.
49. James Joll, *The Second International 1889–1914* (London: Weidenfeld, 1955), 139.

6. ALTERNATIVES TO WAR

1. M. S. Anderson, *The Ascendancy of Europe, 1815–1914* (New York: Longman, 1985), 228.
2. **Howard (1989)**, 53.
3. **Cortright (2008)**, 43.
4. **Beales (1931)**, 243.
5. Sandi Cooper, 'Peace Movements of the Nineteenth Century', *WEP* ii (1986), 230–4.
6. **Howard (1989)**, 72.
7. Norman Angell, *The Great Illusion: A Study of the Relation of Military Power in Nations to their Economic and Social Advantage* (London: Heinemann, 1912).
8. Quoted in **Cooper (1991)**, 185.
9. Martin Ceadel, 'Pacifism and Pacificism', in Terence Ball and Richard Bellamy, eds., *The Cambridge History of Twentieth-Century Political Thought*, vol. vi (Cambridge: Cambridge University Press, 2003), 473–92. Also Ceadel, 'Pacifism versus Pacificism', *OIEP* iii. 323–5.
10. **Cooper (1991)**, 184.
11. See further John Langdon, *July 1914: The Long Debate 1918–1990* (New York: Berg, 1991); Annika Mombauer, *The Origins of the First World War: Controversies and Consensus* (London: Longman, 2002).
12. Barbara Tuchman, *The Proud Tower: A Portrait of the World before the War, 1890–1914* (London: Macmillan, 1966), 250.
13. David Crook, *Darwinism, War, and History: The Debate over the Biology of War from the 'Origin of Species' to the First World War* (Cambridge: Cambridge University Press, 1994), 20.
14. **Howard (1989)**, 61.
15. J. Novikow [Novicow], *War and its Alleged Benefits* (London: Heinemann, 1912), 23, 125; see also **Cooper (1991)**, 141–5.
16. Jan Bloch [Jean de Bloch], *The Future of War in its Technical, Economic and Political Relations* (Boston: The World Peace Foundation, 1914), 347; **Cooper (1991)**, 146–53.
17. Sylvester John Hemleben, *Plans for World Peace through Six Centuries* (Chicago: University of Chicago Press, 1943; repr. New York: Garland, 1972), 182.
18. **Beales (1931)**, 295–7.

19. Hemleben, op. cit. n. 17 above, 149.

20. Ibid., 165.

21. H. G. Wells, 'Peace of the World' (second instalment), *New York Times*, 28 February 1915.

22. Harold Nicolson, *Peacemaking 1919* (London: Constable, 1933), 153–4; John Maynard Keynes, *The Economic Consequences of the Peace* (London: Macmillan, 1919), 35, 56.

23. F. P. Walters, *A History of the League of Nations* (Oxford: Oxford University Press, 1952), 82.

24. **Beales (1931)**, 310–11.

25. See further **Chatfield and Ilukhina (1994)**, 207–11.

26. **Beales (1931)**, 322.

27. **Cortright (2008)**, 60.

28. Jean-Michel Guieu, 'L'Europe des militants français pour la Société des Nations, d'un après-guerre à l'autre (1918–1950)', 5, online at http:// jmguieu.free.fr.

29. **Howard (1989)**, 86.

30. Catherine Krull and B. J. McKercher, 'The Press, Public Opinion, Arms Limitation, and Government Policy in Britain, 1932–34: Some Preliminary Observations', *Diplomacy & Statecraft*, 13: 3 (2002), 103–36 (at 103).

31. E. H. Carr, 'Public Opinion as a Safeguard of Peace', *International Affairs*, 15: 6 (November–December 1936), 846–62 (at 847).

32. F. S. Northedge, *The League of Nations: Its Life and Times 1920–1946* (Leicester: Leicester University Press, 1986), 114.

33. Edward Grey, *Twenty-Five Years 1892–1916* (London: Hodder & Stoughton, 1925), 91–2. Grey was an early example of those distinguished statesmen who, in retirement, finally acknowledge the obvious truth from which they averted their gaze when in office. Recent examples include Robert McNamara on the Cuban crisis and Henry Kissinger on nuclear proliferation.

34. Ruth Henig, *The League of Nations* (London: Haus, 2010), 122.

35. Krull and McKercher, op. cit. n. 30 above, 104–5.

36. Northedge, op. cit. n. 32 above, 136.

37. Henig, op. cit. n. 34 above, 133.

38. Philip Noel-Baker, *The First World Disarmament Conference 1932–33, and Why it Failed* (Oxford: Pergamon, 1979).

39. Basil Liddell Hart, *Deterrent or Defence: A Fresh Look at the West's Military Position* (London: Stevens, 1960), 256–7.

40. Anthony Eden, *The Eden Memoirs: Facing the Dictators* (London: Cassell, 1962), 47.

41. Adelaide Livingstone, *The Peace Ballot: The Official History* (London: Gollancz, 1935), 6.

42. Charles Arnold-Baker, *The Companion to British History* (London: Routledge, 2001), 448.

43. Beaverbrook and Churchill quoted in Terry Charman, 'The Peace Ballot' (Peace History Conference, Imperial War Museum, London, 17 April 2010), online at http://www.abolishwar.org.uk.

44. J. A. Thompson, 'The "Peace Ballot" and the "Rainbow" Controversy', *Journal of British Studies*, 20: 2 (Spring 1981), 150–70 (at 151).

45. Leo Amery, *My Political Life*, ii: *War and Peace 1914–1929* (London: Hutchinson, 1953), 162–3.

46. Figures from the statistical survey of the results published with Livingstone, op. cit. n. 41 above.

47. Ibid., 62–3.

48. Quoted in J. A. Thompson, 'The Peace Ballot and the Public', *Albion: A Quarterly Journal Concerned with British Studies*, 13: 4 (Winter 1981), 381–92 (at 388).

49. Ronald Blythe, *The Age of Illusion* (London: Hamish Hamilton, 1963), 251.

50. League of Nations Union, *Year Book 1938* (London: League of Nations Union, 1938), 12.

51. Lucian Ashworth, 'League of Nations', *OIEP* ii. 612–14.

52. Quoted in Donald Birn, *The League of Nations Union 1918–1945* (Oxford: Clarendon Press, 1981), 228.

53. Dick Richardson and Carolyn Kitching, 'Britain and the World Disarmament Conference', in Peter Catterall and C. J. Morris, eds., *Britain and the Threat to Stability in Europe, 1918–45* (London: Leicester University Press, 1993), 35–56 (at 45).

54. Henry Brailsford, *Olives of Endless Age* (New York: Harper, 1928), 29.

55. Leonard Woolf, 'The Ideal of the League Remains', *Political Quarterly*, 7 (1936), 330–45 (at 333).

56. Cecilia Lynch, *Beyond Appeasement: Interpreting Interwar Peace Movements in World Politics* (Ithaca, NY: Cornell University Press, 1999), 4. Lynch also credits the peace movements with laying the groundwork for the United Nations by articulating a vision 'that did not rely solely on Great Power machinations', 172. In a similar balanced judgement, three British scholars conclude that we may see the League 'not as having failed but simply as having made a start, if not an especially promising one': David Armstrong, Lorna Lloyd, and John Redmond, *From Versailles to Maastricht: International Organisation in the Twentieth Century* (Basingstoke: Palgrave, 1996), 61.

57. Donald Birn, 'What of Peace History? Lessons from World War I', in Linda Forcey, ed., *Peace: Meanings, Politics, Strategies* (New York: Praeger, 1989), 189–95 (at 193).

58. Noel-Baker, op. cit. n. 38 above, 5.

59. Mark Kurlansky, *Non-violence: The History of a Dangerous Idea* (London: Vintage, 2007), 145; Schell (2004), 8.

60. Cortright (2008), 20–1.

61. Brock (1972), 479–80.

62. Henri Troyat, *Tolstoy* (Harmondsworth: Penguin, 1970), 141.
63. Leo Tolstoy, *War and Peace*, trans. Louise and Aylmer Maude (London: Macmillan and Oxford University Press, 1943), 281–2, 309.
64. Aylmer Maude, *The Life of Tolstoy* (Oxford: Oxford University Press, 1953), 420–1.
65. **Sampson (1973)**, 121–2. I am indebted to this analysis for much of my own account.
66. Ibid., 164.
67. Tolstoy, op. cit. n. 63 above, 1326.
68. Leo Tolstoy, letter to Ernest Howard Crosby, in **Holmes (1990)**, 45–50.
69. Horace Seldon, 'Garrison on Violence, Non-violence and the Use of Force', online at http://www.theliberatorfiles.com.
70. Cory Bushman, 'A Brief History of Peasant Tolstoyans', online at http://www.themormonworker.org.
71. **Brock (1972)**, 470.
72. Richard Gregg, *The Power of Non-violence* (London: Routledge, 1935), 101–2.
73. See further Thomas Weber, 'Gandhian Influence on Peace Movement', *OIEP* ii. 197–200.
74. See further Adam Roberts, ed., *Civilian Resistance as a National Defence* (Harmondsworth: Pelican, 1969); Gene Sharp, *The Politics of Non-violent Action, Part One: Power and Struggle* (Boston: Porter Sargent, 1973).
75. 'Foreword' in Rashmi-Sudha Puri, *Gandhi on War and Peace* (Westport, Conn.: Praeger, 1986), i.
76. Hannah Arendt, 'Reflections on Violence', *New York Review of Books*, 27 February 1969.
77. Bart de Ligt, *The Conquest of Violence: An Essay on War and Revolution* (London: Routledge, 1937; repr. London: Pluto, 1989), xxix.
78. **Roberts and Garton Ash (2009)**, 2.
79. For early examples of non-violent action, see de Ligt, op. cit. n. 77 above, ch. 7; Gregg, op. cit. n. 72 above, ch. 1.
80. Thomas Brady et al., eds., *Handbook of European History, 1400–1600* (Leiden: Brill, 1994), 101.
81. Herbert Bix, *Peasant Protest in Japan, 1590–1884* (New Haven: Yale University Press, 1986), xxxii.
82. De Ligt, op. cit. n. 77 above, 89.
83. Kathleen Gough, 'Indian Peasant Uprisings', in A. R. Desai, ed., *Peasant Struggles in India* (Bombay: Oxford University Press, 1979), 85–126 (at 110).
84. N. G. Ranga, 'Agrarian Revolts', in Desai, op. cit. n. 83 above, 47–65 (at 51).
85. M. K. Gandhi, *An Autobiography, or The Story of my Experiments with Truth*, vol. i (Ahmedabad: Navajivan, 1927), 91–8.
86. Ibid., 250.
87. Puri, op. cit. n. 75 above, 4–6, 17.
88. **Cortright (2008)**, 216.

89. M. K. Gandhi, 'On *Satyagraha*', in **Holmes (1990)**, 51.
90. Joseph Prabhu, 'Gandhi's Economics of Peace', *Peace Review*, 7: 1 (1995), 107–12.
91. **Chatfield and Ilukhina (1994)**, 238, 240.
92. Albert Einstein and Sigmund Freud, *Why War?* (Paris: League of Nations, International Institute of Intellectual Cooperation, 1933).
93. Maria Montessori, 'Peace' (1932), in *Education and Peace*, trans. Helen Lane (Oxford: Clio, 1992), 5–23.
94. See discussion of *La Peste* in A. D. Harvey, *A Muse of Fire: Literature, Art and War* (London: Hambledon, 1998), 293–4.

7. THE MISAPPROPRIATION OF PEACE

1. Vern Partlow, folk singer, union activist, and freelance journalist in California, wrote this song after interviewing various atomic scientists for the *Los Angeles Daily News* in 1945. Published in 1947 under the title 'Talking Atomic Blues', it quickly became popular and was widely recorded, but in 1950 it was banned by two record labels and several radio stations after being denounced for promoting 'communistic ideas'. There are several versions of the lyrics. The version used here comes from *Old Man Atom (A Talking Atomic Blues)* (Beverly Hills, Calif.: Alamo Music Inc., 1950). See further Ronald D. Cohen and Dave Samuelson, liner notes for *Songs for Political Action*, Bear Family Records, BCD 15 720 JL (1996), 134.
2. Eugene Harley, 'The Coming Revival of the League of Nations', in Julia Johnsen, ed., *Reconstituting the League of Nations* (New York: H. W. Wilson, 1943), 7–13 (at 7).
3. Gardner Murphy, ed., *Human Nature and Enduring Peace: Third Yearbook of the Society for the Psychological Study of Social Issues* (Boston: Houghton Mifflin, 1945), 387–8.
4. British Institute of Public Opinion, *(Gallup) Polls, 1938–1946*, online at the Economic and Social Data Service website, http://www.esds.ac.uk.
5. Robert Hillmann, 'Quincy Wright and the Commission to Study the Organization of Peace', *Global Governance*, 4 (1998), 485–99 (at 485).
6. James Shotwell, *The Great Decision* (New York: Macmillan, 1944), 219.
7. Hans-Martin Jaeger, '"World Opinion" and the Founding of the UN: Governmentalizing International Politics', *European Journal of International Relations*, 14 (2008), 589–618 (598).
8. Emery Reves, *The Anatomy of Peace* (New York: Harper, 1945), 284.
9. Clark Eichelberger, *Organizing for Peace* (New York: Harper & Row, 1977), 228–9, 236–7.
10. Geoffrey Roberts, 'Why Roosevelt was Right about Stalin', *History News Network*, 19 March 2007, online at http://hnn.us.
11. **Yergin (1977)**, 84, 99.
12. *New York Times*, 27 June 1945, quoted in Moreen Dee, 'Dr H. V. Evatt and the Negotiation of the United Nations Charter', in Gabriel Robin, ed.,

8e Conférence des éditeurs de documents diplomatiques: Des états et de l'ONU (Brussels: Peter Lang, 2008), 137–49 (at 137).

13. Vera Micheles Dean, *The Four Cornerstones of Peace* (New York: Whittlesey House, 1946), 72.

14. **Schlesinger (2003)**, 218–21.

15. *San Francisco Chronicle*, 31 May 1945, quoted in Dee, op. cit. n. 12 above, 142; **Schlesinger (2003)**, 222–3.

16. Dean, op. cit. n. 13 above, 76.

17. Eric Grove, 'UN Armed Forces and the Military Staff Committee: A Look Back', *International Security*, 17: 4 (1993), 172–82 (at 172).

18. Erskine Childers, ed., *Challenges to the United Nations: Building a Safer World* (London: Catholic Institute for International Relations, 1994), 2–3.

19. Frank Field, *60 Years of UNA-UK* (London: United Nations Association, 2006), 3–4.

20. F. P. Walters, *A History of the League of Nations* (Oxford: Oxford University Press, 1952), 82; **Melvern (1995)**, 27.

21. UN Department of Economic Affairs, *Proceedings of the United Nations Scientific Conference on the Conservation and Utilisation of Resources* (New York: United Nations Publications, 1950), i. 15.

22. **Melvern (1995)**, 60–1, 69, 74.

23. Sang-hun Choe and Charles Hanley, 'Ex-GIs Tell AP of Korea Killings', *Associated Press*, 30 September 1999; Department of [US] Army Inspector General, *Report of the No Gun Ri Review* (January 2001).

24. United States Congress, House Committee on Un-American Activities, *Report on the Communist 'Peace' Offensive: A Campaign to Disarm and Defeat the United States* (Washington: USGPO, 1951).

25. Communist Party of Great Britain, *Communist Information Bureau Resolutions (November 1949)* (London: Communist Party of Great Britain, 1949), 4–22.

26. Christoph Bluth, 'Three Theses on the Cold War', *Global Dialogue*, 3: 4 (Autumn 2001).

27. Geir Lundestad, 'The Cold War According to John Gaddis', *Cold War History*, 6: 4 (2006), 535–42.

28. See especially **Larres and Osgood (2006)**; **Ross and Jiang (2002)**.

29. Jeffrey Brooks, *When the Cold War did not End: The Soviet Peace Offensive of 1953 and the American Response*, Kennan Institute Occasional Papers, no. 278 (Washington: Woodrow Wilson International Center for Scholars, 2000).

30. Klaus Larres, *Churchill's Cold War: The Politics of Personal Diplomacy* (New Haven: Yale University Press, 2002), 205–6.

31. Quoted in Brooks, op. cit. n. 29 above.

32. Larres, op. cit. n. 30 above, 212–13.

33. Ibid., 210.

34. Walter LaFeber, *America, Russia, and the Cold War 1945–1966* (New York: Wiley, 1967), 150.

35. Matthew Evangelista, 'Cooperation Theory and Disarmament Negotiations in the 1950s', *World Politics*, 42: 4 (1990), 502–28 (at 502).

36. Philip Noel-Baker, *The Arms Race* (London: John Calder, 1958), ch. 2, 'The Moment of Hope'.

37. See further **Ross and Jiang (2002)** for serious discussion of this period of USA–China relations, based on a conference in which scholars from both countries took part. However, the suggestion that an opportunity might have been missed was made as far back as 1968 by Kenneth Young, *Negotiating with the Chinese Communists* (New York: Council on Foreign Relations, 1968). I also examined this issue in *The World and China 1922–1972* (London: Eyre-Methuen, 1974), 201–8.

38. Young, op. cit. n. 37 above, 112–13.

39. Steven Goldstein, 'Dialogue of the Deaf? The Sino-American Ambassadorial Level Talks, 1955–1970', in **Ross and Jiang (2002)**, 200–37.

40. See further Zhang Baijia and Jia Qingguo, 'Steering Wheel, Shock Absorber, and Diplomatic Probe in Confrontation: Sino-American Ambassadorial Talks Seen from the Chinese Perspective', in **Ross and Jiang (2002)**, 173–99.

41. Henry Kissinger, *The White House Years* (London: Weidenfeld & Nicolson, 1979), 783.

42. Kenneth Osgood, 'The Perils of Co-existence: Peace and Propaganda in Eisenhower's Foreign Policy', in **Larres and Osgood (2006)**, 27–48 (at 27).

43. Joyce and Gabriel Kolko, *The Limits of Power: The World and United States Foreign Policy, 1945–1954* (New York: Harper & Row, 1972), 705.

44. Evangelista, op. cit. n. 35 above, 521.

45. Lloyd Gardner, 'Poisoned Apples: John Foster Dulles and the "Peace Offensive"', in **Larres and Osgood (2006)**, 73–92 (at 84, 89).

46. Larres, op. cit. n. 30 above, 197.

47. Vojtech Mastny, 'The Elusive Détente: Stalin's Successors and the West', in **Larres and Osgood (2006)**, 3–26 (at 3, 26).

48. Evangelista, op. cit. n. 35 above, 514, 518–19.

49. Goldstein, op. cit. n. 39 above, 201.

50. Ibid., 217.

51. Jonathan Haslam, *Russia's Cold War: From the October Revolution to the Fall of the Wall* (New Haven: Yale University Press, 2011), 164–5.

52. Ira Chernus, 'Meanings of Peace: The Rhetorical Cold War after Stalin', in **Larres and Osgood (2006)**, 95–113 (at 105).

53. Martin Walker, *The Waking Giant: The Soviet Union under Gorbachev* (London: Abacus, 1986), 127–30.

54. Gabriel Kolko, *After Socialism* (Abingdon: Routledge, 2006), 62.

55. Roy Medvedev, *On Socialist Democracy* (New York: Knopf, 1975), 284.

56. Mikhail Gorbachev, *Perestroika: New Thinking for our Country and the World* (London: Collins, 1987), 148, 158.

57. **Ross and Jiang (2002)**, 56, 188.

58. See further John Gittings, 'What if Mao had Met Roosevelt?', in Duncan Brack, ed., *President Gore and Other Things that Never Happened* (London: Politico, 2006), 171–87.

59. This quotation from *The Cocktail Party* (1949) appeared on the title page of the annual 'Survey' volume of the Royal Institute of International Affairs which covered the early years of the cold war. Peter Calvocoressi, *Survey of International Affairs 1947–1948* (London: Oxford University Press, 1952), iii.

8. GIVING PEACE A CHANCE

1. Richard Aldous, *Macmillan, Eisenhower and the Cold War* (Dublin: Four Courts, 2005), 97.

2. **Wittner (1997)**, 104–6.

3. Jerry Sweeney, 'The Better Dead than Red Amendment', *American Diplomacy* (July 2004), online at http://americandiplomacy.org.

4. Philip Toynbee, *The Fearful Choice: A Debate on Nuclear Policy* (London: Gollancz, 1958), 26.

5. Home Office (UK), *Nuclear Weapons: Manual of Civil Defence*, vol. i, pamphlet no. 1 (London: Her Majesty's Stationery Office, 1959), 1.

6. **Wittner (1997)**, 185–6, 219.

7. Ibid., 153.

8. Ibid., 3.

9. Mordecai Roshwald, *Level 7* (London: Heinemann, 1959).

10. See further Sandra Butcher, *The Origins of the Russell–Einstein Manifesto*, Pugwash History Series No. 1 (Fredericksburg, Va., 1995), 25–6.

11. C. Wright Mills, *The Causes of World War Three* (New York: Simon & Schuster, 1958; New York: Ballantine, 1960), 145.

12. Erich Fromm, *May Man Prevail?* (New York: Anchor Books, 1961), publisher's blurb.

13. Bertrand Russell, *Common Sense and Nuclear Warfare* (London: Allen & Unwin, 1959), 59–71; Russell, *Has Man a Future?* (Harmondsworth: Penguin, 1961), 69–77.

14. **Wittner (1997)**, 465.

15. Personal communication, A. J. P. Taylor to John Gittings, 1960.

16. **Wittner (1997)**, 182.

17. Ibid., 17–19.

18. Ibid., 109, 120, 154.

19. Michael Wright, *Disarm & Verify* (London: Chatto & Windus, 1964), 135; **Wittner (1997)**, 393.

20. **Wittner (1997)**, 404; Dean Rusk, *As I Saw It* (New York: Norton, 1990), 231–2.

21. Erika Simpson, 'New Ways of Thinking about Nuclear Weapons and Canada's Defence Policy', in D. C. Story and R. Bruce Shepard, eds., *Diefenbaker's Legacy* (Regina: Canadian Plains Research Centre, 1998), 27–41 (at 32).

22. Norman Cousins, *The Improbable Triumvirate* (New York: Norton, 1972), 113–14.
23. William Burr and Hector Montford, *The Making of the Limited Test Ban Treaty, 1958–1963* (Washington: National Security Archive, online publication, 8 August 2003), at http://www.gwu.edu.
24. *The Guardian*, 30 January 1980.
25. **Wittner (2003)**, 75–6, 253–60; see further David Meyer, *A Winter of Discontent: The Nuclear Freeze and American Politics* (New York: ABC-Clio, 1990), 160.
26. **Wittner (2003)**, 234–5.
27. E. P. Thompson and Dan Smith, eds., *Protest and Survive* (Harmondsworth: Penguin, 1980), 215.
28. Eqbal Ahmad, 'Cracks in the Western World View', *The Selected Writings of Eqbal Ahmad*, ed. Carollee Bengelsdorf et al. (New York: Columbia University Press, 2006), 232–41 (at 235); originally published in *END Journal* (April–May 1985).
29. Dan Smith and E. P. Thompson, eds., *Prospectus for a Habitable Planet* (Harmondsworth: Penguin, 1987), 12, 145.
30. **Wittner (2003)**, 308.
31. Ibid., 371–2.
32. United Nations Development Programme [UNDP], *Human Development Report 1991: Financing Human Development* (New York: Oxford University Press, 1991), ch. 6, online at http://hdr.undp.org.
33. UNDP, *Human Development Report 1994: New Dimensions of Human Security* (New York: Oxford University Press, 1994), chs. 3 and 4, online at http://hdr.undp.org.
34. Shridash Ramphal, 'Peace in our Global Neighbourhood', *Peace and Conflict Studies*, 3: 1 (1996), 1.
35. United Nations Department for Disarmament Affairs, *Symposium on the Relationship between Disarmament and Development*, UNDDA Occasional Paper 9 (New York: UNDDA, 2004), v–vi.
36. Kerstin Vignard, 'Beyond the Peace Dividend—Disarmament, Development and Security', *Disarmament, Development and Mine Action* (Geneva: United Nations Institute for Disarmament Research, 2003), 6.
37. Erskine Childers, ed., *Challenges to the United Nations: Building a Safer World* (London: Catholic Institute for International Relations, 1994), 3.
38. **Wittner (1997)**, 385–91.
39. United Nations, *A More Secure World: Our Shared Responsibility. Report of the Secretary-General's High-level Panel on Threats, Challenges and Change* (New York: UN Secretariat, 2004), para. 300, online at http://www.un.org.secureworld.
40. **Melvern (1995)**, 353.
41. *Associated Press*, 15 October 1990.

42. According to the transcript of the secretary-general's meeting with Saddam on 13 January 1991, the Iraqi leader professed to be willing to discuss withdrawal. At one point he produced a map of Kuwait and asked Mr Perez de Cuellar: 'Where should Iraq withdraw to?' See further, John Gittings, ed., *Beyond the Gulf War: The Middle East and the New World Order* (London: Catholic Institute for International Relations, 1991), introduction, 1–10.

43. *SIPRI Yearbook 2010: Summary* (Oxford: Oxford University Press, 2010), 9–10.

44. Paul Collier et al., *Breaking the Conflict Trap: Civil War and Development Policy* (Oxford: World Bank and Oxford University Press, 2003), 5.

45. Malcolm Chalmers and Susan Willett, *Spending to Save: An Analysis of the Cost Effectiveness of Conflict Prevention versus Intervention after the Onset of Violent Conflict* (Bradford: Department of Peace Studies, 2003), 2.

46. UNDP, *Human Development Report 1996: Economic Growth and Human Development* (New York: Oxford University Press, 1996), 26, online at http://hdr.undp.org.

47. See further David Hulme, *The Millennium Development Goals (MDGs): A Short History of the World's Biggest Promise* (Manchester: Brooks World Poverty Institute, 2009).

48. Hans von Sponeck, *A Different Kind of War: The UN Sanctions Regime in Iraq* (Oxford: Berghahn Books, 2006), 61, 75–6, 95, 145, 273.

49. Save the Children (and others), *Iraq Sanctions: Humanitarian Implications and Options for the Future* (New York: Global Policy Forum, 2002), 1, online at http://www.globalpolicy.org.

50. David Brummell to Tom McKane, 12 February 2001, document available on the Chilcot Inquiry website, http://www.iraqinquiry.org.uk, in the 'Declassified Documents' section.

51. Ibid. The 4 October 2002 memo is in 'Declassified Documents', and the 17 October 2002 memo in 'Written Evidence by Date'.

52. BBC News (online), 'Iraq war illegal, says Annan', 16 September 2004.

53. 'Youth unemployment at all time high, new ILO report says half the world's jobless are under 24', *ILO News* (Geneva), 11 August 2004; 'Global Employment Trends for Youth', *ILO Report* (August 2010). Youth unemployment was highest of all in Algeria (45%) at the end of the decade, with Gaza and the West Bank ranking second (37.5%); 'Taking Stock of the Youth Challenge in the Middle East: New Data and New Questions', *Brookings Newsletter* (online), 7 March 2011.

54. See further James Carafano and Paul Rosenzweig, *Winning the Long War: Lessons from the Cold War for Defeating Terrorism and Preserving Freedom* (New York: Heritage, 2005).

55. Department of Defence, *Quadrennial Defence Review Report* (Washington, DC: DoD, 2006).

56. 'Tony Blair Takes on the World', *Wall Street Journal*, 4 September 2010. Blair's successor, Gordon Brown, also described the war ahead as 'generational' on his first visit to Washington in July 2007.

57. Mona Yacoubian and Paul Stares, 'Rethinking the War on Terror', *USI Peace Briefing*, September 2005 (Washington: United States Institute of Peace, 2005), online at http://www.usip.org.

58. Philip Bobbitt, 'Get Ready for the Next Long War', *Time Magazine*, 9 September 2002.

59. Club de Madrid, *The Causes and Underlying Factors of Terrorism* (Madrid, 11 January 2005), online at http://submit.clubmadrid.org.

60. Nicholas Kristof, 'Behind the Terrorists', *New York Times*, 7 May 2002.

61. Chris Abbott, Paul Rogers, and John Sloboda, *Beyond Terror: The Truth about the Real Threats to our World* (London: Rider, 2006), 80–90.

CONCLUSION

1. An earlier version of what would become Whitman's poem 'Sun of Real Peace' formed part of his much longer 'Apostroph' (1860). He revised the section beginning with these lines in 1870, adding the references to peace and the end of war, and published it under its new title in the 1871–2 edition of *Leaves of Grass*.

2. Leo Tolstoy, *War and Peace*, trans. Louise and Aylmer Maude (London: Macmillan and Oxford University Press, 1943), 273–4, 739–44.

3. David Kinsella and Craig Carr, eds., *The Morality of War: A Reader* (Boulder, Colo.: Lynne Rienner, 2007), 6.

4. Thomas Schoenbaum, *International Relations: The Path not Taken* (Cambridge: Cambridge University Press, 2006), 11.

5. Nina Tannenwald, *The Nuclear Taboo: The United States and the Non-use of Nuclear Weapons since 1945* (Cambridge: Cambridge University Press, 2007), 3.

6. See further Gerry Simpson, *Law, War and Crime: War Crime Trials and the Reinvention of International Law* (Cambridge: Polity, 2007).

7. Mario Pianta and Raffaele Marchetti, 'The Global Justice Movements: The Transnational Dimension', in Donatella Della Porta, ed., *The Global Justice Movement: Cross-national and Transnational Perspectives* (Boulder, Colo.: Paradigm, 2006), 29–51.

8. Schell (2004), 8.

9. Cortright (2008), 20–7.

10. Kevin Clements, 'Towards Conflict Transformation and a Just Peace', *Berghof Handbook for Conflict Transformation* (Berlin: Berghof, 2004), 18, online at http://www.berghof-handbook.net.

11. Oliver Richmond, *The Transformation of Peace: Peace as Governance in Contemporary Conflict Endings* (Basingstoke: Palgrave, 2006), 227–30. See also Vivienne Jabri, *War and the Transformation of Global Politics* (Basingstoke: Palgrave, 2007).

12. John Darby and Roger MacGinty, eds., *Contemporary Peacemaking: Conflict, Violence and Peace Processes* (Basingstoke: Palgrave, 2003), 5.

13. See further Frances Stewart and Valpy Fitzgerald, eds., *War and Underdevelopment*, i: *The Economic and Social Consequences of Conflict* (Oxford: Oxford University Press, 2001).

14. Michael Pugh, 'The Political Economy of Peace-Building: A Critical Theory Perspective', *International Journal of Peace Studies*, 10: 2 (2005), 23–42.

15. United Nations, *A More Secure World: Our Shared Responsibility. Report of the Secretary-General's High level Panel on Threats, Challenges and Change* (New York: UN Secretariat, 2004), online at http://www.un.org/secureworld; Human Security Centre, *Human Security Report 2005: War and Peace in the 21st Century* (New York: Oxford University Press, 2005).

16. **Booth (2007)**, 360–78, 428–31.

17. Paul Rogers and Oliver Ramsbotham, 'Then and Now: Peace Research— Past and Future', *Political Studies*, 47 (1999), 740–54 (at 753).

18. **Kennedy (2006)**, ch. 8.

19. Philip Taylor, *War and the Media: Propaganda and Persuasion in the Gulf War* (Manchester: Manchester University Press, 1992), 8. See also Graham Spencer, *The Media and Peace: From Vietnam to the 'War on Terror'* (Basingstoke: Palgrave, 2008), 7–22.

20. Fred Halliday, *Islam and the Myth of Confrontation* (London: Tauris, 1996), 107.

21. Ibid., 132.

22. John Esposito, *Unholy War: Terror in the Name of Islam* (Oxford: Oxford University Press, 2002), 26–8. The concept of 'Islamic fundamentalism' was raised early on by the Arabist scholar Bernard Lewis in an influential article, 'The Roots of Muslim Rage', *Atlantic Monthly*, 266: 3 (September 1990), 47–60. Lewis is also credited with having been one of the first to put forward, in this article, the emotive image of 'the clash of civilizations'. However, he also believed that 'At no point do the basic texts of Islam enjoin terrorism and murder. At no point—as far as I am aware—do they even consider the random slaughter of uninvolved bystanders.' *The Crisis of Islam: Holy War and Unholy Terror* (London: Phoenix, 2003), 34.

23. Tony Blair, *Hansard*, 4 December 2006, col. 21; ibid., 14 March 2007, col. 277; Liam Fox, ibid., col. 395.

24. There is abundant material on the economic basis of contemporary conflict in the *Economics of Peace and Security Journal* (2006–), which focuses on 'economic analysis of causes, consequences, and possible solutions to mitigate conflict and violence'. See also Frances Stewart, ed., *Horizontal Inequalities and Conflict: Understanding Group Violence in Multiethnic Societies* (Basingstoke: Palgrave, 2008).

25. Amy Belasco, *The Cost of Iraq, Afghanistan, and Other Global War on Terror Operations since 9/11* (Washington, DC: Congressional Research Service, March 2011), 1; 'International Aid to Afghanistan', *Middle East Progress* (blog archive), 18 May 2010.

26. *SIPRI Yearbook 2010* (Oxford: Oxford University Press, 2010), 177–8.
27. Werner Wintersteiner, 'Education', *OIEP* ii. 39–42. See also the special issue on peace education of *Peace and Change*, 34: 4 (October 2009).
28. Chris Abbott, Paul Rogers, and John Sloboda, *Global Responses to Global Threats: Sustainable Security for the 21st Century* (London: Oxford Research Group, 2006), 26–30.
29. **Booth (2007)**, 429.
30. See further the thoughtful discussion of this issue in **Cortright (2008)**, 279–301.
31. See further Jerry Sanders, 'Cosmopolitanism as a Peace Theory', *OIEP* i. 497–501.
32. Linus Pauling, Nobel Lecture on receiving the 1962 Peace Prize, 11 December 1963.
33. Kurihara Sadako, 'River's Rebirth' (part 6 of 'River'), trans. Richard H. Minear, *Black Eggs*, Michigan Monograph Series in Japanese Studies, no. 12 (Ann Arbor: Center for Japanese Studies, University of Michigan, 1994), 199–203. Kurihara (1913–2005) was born in Hiroshima, was in the city on 6 August 1945 when the bomb fell, and continued to live there until her death. She has been described as the 'poet of the atomic bomb', ibid., 1.

Select Bibliography

Adams, Robert, *The Better Part of Valor: More, Erasmus, Colet, and Vives, on Humanism, War, and Peace, 1496–1535* (Seattle: University of Washington Press, 1962).

Adolf, Antony, *Peace: A World History* (Cambridge: Polity, 2009).

Aron, Raymond, *Peace and War: A Theory of International Relations* (Malabar, Fla.: Krieger, 1981).

Bainton, Roland, *Christian Attitudes toward War and Peace* (London: Hodder & Stoughton, 1961).

Barash, David, ed., *Approaches to Peace: A Reader in Peace Studies* (Oxford: Oxford University Press, 2000).

Beales, A. C. F., *The History of Peace: A Short Account of the Organised Movements for International Peace* (London: Dial Press, 1931).

Beer, Francis, *How Much War in History: Definitions, Estimates, Extrapolations, and Trends* (Beverly Hills, Calif.: Sage, 1974).

Booth, Ken, *Theory of World Security* (Cambridge: Cambridge University Press, 2007).

Boulding, Kenneth, *Stable Peace* (Austin, Tex.: University of Texas, 1978).

Brock, Peter, *Pacifism in Europe to 1914* (Princeton: Princeton University Press, 1972).

Cadoux, John Cecil, *The Early Christian Attitude to War: A Contribution to the History of Christian Ethics* (London: Allen & Unwin, 1940).

Carter, April, Clark, Howard, and Randle, Michael, *People Power and Protest since 1945: A Bibliography of Nonviolent Action* (London: Housmans, 2006).

Ceadel, Martin, *The Origins of War Prevention: The British Peace Movement and International Relations 1730–1854* (Oxford: Clarendon, 1996).

—— *Semi-detached Idealists: The British Peace Movement and International Relations, 1854–1945* (Oxford: Oxford University Press, 2000).

Chatfield, Charles, and Ilukhina, Ruzanne, *Peace/Mir: An Anthology of Historic Alternatives to War* (Syracuse, NY: Syracuse University Press, 1994).

—— and Van den Dungen, Peter, eds., *Peace Movements and Political Cultures* (Knoxville, Tenn.: University of Tennessee Press, 1988).

Cooper, Sandi, *Patriotic Pacifism: Waging War on War in Europe, 1815–1914* (New York: Oxford University Press, 1991).

Cortright, David, *Peace: A History of Movements and Ideas* (Cambridge: Cambridge University Press, 2008).

De Souza, Philip, and France, John, *War and Peace in Ancient and Medieval History* (Cambridge: Cambridge University Press, 2008).

Dolan, John, *The Essential Erasmus* (New York: Mentor-Omega, 1964).

Fry, Douglas, *Beyond War: The Human Potential for Peace* (New York: Oxford University Press, 2007).

Gregor, Thomas, ed., *A Natural History of Peace* (Nashville: Vanderbilt, 1996).

Hartmann, Anja, and Heuser, Beatrice, *War, Peace and World Orders in European History* (London: Routledge, 2001).

Heyn, Udo, *Peacemaking in Medieval Europe: A Historical and Bibliographical Guide* (Claremont, Calif.: Regina Books, 1997).

Holmes, Robert, *Nonviolence in Theory and Practice* (Prospect Heights, Ill.: Waveland, 1990).

Howard, Michael, *War and the Liberal Conscience*, updated edn with new postscript (Oxford: Oxford University Press, 1989).

—— *The Invention of Peace: Reflections on War and International Order* (London: Profile, 2000).

Hunt, Peter, *War, Peace, and Alliance in Demosthenes' Athens* (Cambridge: Cambridge University Press, 2010).

Johnson, James Turner, *The Quest for Peace: Three Moral Traditions in Western Cultural History* (Princeton: Princeton University Press, 1987).

Kemp, Graham, and Fry, Douglas, eds., *Keeping the Peace: Conflict Resolution and Peaceful Societies around the World* (London: Routledge, 2004).

Kennedy, Paul, *The Parliament of Man: The United Nations and the Quest for World Government* (London: Allen Lane, 2006).

Larres, Klaus, and Osgood, Kenneth, eds., *The Cold War after Stalin's Death: A Missed Opportunity for Peace?* (Lanham, Md.: Rowman & Littlefield, 2006).

Melvern, Linda, *The Ultimate Crime: Who Betrayed the UN and Why* (London: Allison & Busby, 1995).

Needham, Joseph, *Science and Civilisation in China*, vol. ii (Cambridge: Cambridge University Press, 1956).

Nef, John, *War and Human Progress: An Essay on the Rise of Industrial Civilization* (Cambridge, Mass.: Harvard University Press, 1950; New York: Russell & Russell, 1968).

Pauling, Linus, ed., *World Encyclopedia of Peace*, vols. i–iv (Oxford: Pergamon Press, 1986).

Penn, William, *The Peace of Europe, The Fruits of Solitude and Other Writings*, ed. Edwin Bronner (London: Everyman, 1993).

Pick, Daniel, *War Machine: The Rationalisation of Slaughter in the Modern Age* (New Haven: Yale University Press, 1993).

Pines, Yuri, *Envisioning Eternal Empire: Chinese Political Thought of the Warring States Era* (Honolulu: University of Hawaii Press, 2009).

Raaflaub, Kurt A., ed., *War and Peace in the Ancient World* (Oxford: Blackwell, 2007).

Rapoport, Anatol, *The Origins of Violence: Approaches to the Study of Conflict (with a New Introduction by the Author)* (New Brunswick, NJ: Transaction Publishers, 1995).

Reichberg, Gregory, Syse, Henrik, and Begby, Endre, eds., *The Ethics of War: Classic and Contemporary Readings* (Oxford: Blackwell, 2006).

Roberts, Adam, and Garton Ash, Timothy, eds., *Civil Resistance and Power Politics: The Experience of Non-violent Action from Gandhi to the Present* (Oxford: Oxford University Press, 2009).

Ross, Robert, and Jiang Changbin, eds., *Re-examining the Cold War: US–China Diplomacy, 1954–1973* (Cambridge, Mass.: Harvard University Press, 2002).

Sampson, R.V., *Tolstoy: The Discovery of Peace* (London: Heinemann, 1973).

Schell, Jonathan, *The Unconquerable World: Power, Non-violence and the Will of the People* (London: Allen Lane, 2004).

Schlesinger, Stephen, *Act of Creation: The Founding of the United Nations* (Boulder, Colo.: Westview Press, 2003).

Singer, Peter, *One World: The Ethics of Globalization* (New Haven: Yale University Press, 2004).

Smoker, Paul, Davies, Ruth, and Munske, Barbara, eds., *A Reader in Peace Studies* (Oxford: Pergamon, 1990).

Spiegel, Nathan, *War and Peace in Classical Greek Literature* (Jerusalem: Mount Scopus Publications, 1990).

Taylor, Richard, and Young, Nigel, eds., *Campaigns for Peace: British Peace Movements in the Twentieth Century* (Manchester: Manchester University Press, 1987).

Tritle, Lawrence, *From Melos to My Lai: War and Survival* (London: Routledge, 2000).

Vellacott, Philip, *Ironic Drama: A Study of Euripides' Method and Meaning* (London: Cambridge University Press, 1975).

Winn, James, *The Poetry of War* (Cambridge: Cambridge University Press, 2008).

Wittner, Lawrence, *The Struggle against the Bomb*, vols. i–iii (Stanford, Calif.: Stanford University Press, 1993–2003): vol. i: *One World or None: A History of the World Nuclear Disarmament Movement through 1953* (1993): vol. ii: *Resisting the Bomb: A History of the World Nuclear Disarmament Movement, 1954–1970* (1997); vol. iii: *Toward Nuclear Abolition: A History of the World Nuclear Disarmament Movement, 1971 to the Present* (2003).

——*Confronting the Bomb* (Stanford, Calif.: Stanford University Press, 2009).

Wood, Mary Morton, *The Spirit of Protest in Old French Literature* (New York: Columbia University Press, 1916).

Yergin, Daniel, *Shattered Peace: The Origins of the Cold War and the National Security State* (Boston: Houghton Mifflin, 1977).

Young, Nigel, ed., *Oxford International Encyclopedia of Peace*, vols. i–iv (New York: Oxford University Press, 2010).

Zampaglione, Gerardo, *The Idea of Peace in Antiquity*, trans. Richard Dunn (Notre Dame, Ind.: University of Notre Dame Press, 1973).

Index

Aberdeen, earl of 145
Aberdeen, Lord 138
Abyssinian crisis (1935) 165
Acharnians, The (Aristophanes) 58
Achilles:
  in the Iliad 40, 43–4, 60
  in Shakespeare 119–20
Achilles' Shield 44–6, 47, 251 n.19,
  251 n.19, 252 n.21
Adams, Robert 102, 103
Adcock, Frank 53
Addams, Jane 154, 176
Aeneid (Virgil) 38
Aeschylus 59–60, 255 n.76
Afghanistan conflict 79, 214, 236,
  238, 240
  civilian deaths from land mines
  220–1
Agamemnon in the Iliad 40, 42, 44
Agenda for Peace initiative (1992),
  UN 223
ahimsa concept 2, 3
Ahmed, Eqbal 216
Ajax:
  in the Iliad 43, 47, 70
  in Sophocles 60, 61
Al Qaida 13, 229
Albigensian Crusades 94–5
Alexander the Great 41, 71
Alexander II, Tsar 139, 205
Altar of Peace, Athens 53
'Ambassadors of Reconciliation' 176
Ambrose, St 80–1
American Civil War (1861–5) 232
  and the American Peace
  Society 136, 143

American Peace Society 132, 136,
  143, 147
Amery, Leo 163
Anabaptism 167
Anatomy of Peace, The (Reves) 179–80
Anderson, M. S. 150
Andicides 57
Andropov, Yuri 217
Anemosphilia 37
Angell, Norman 151, 152
Angola, civilian deaths from land
  mines 220–1
animal behaviour and aggression 31
Annan, Kofi 224, 226, 229, 233
anti–colonialism 130, 216
Antipolemus (Erasmus) 104
apartheid, in South Africa 230
Apollo 70
Aquinas, St Thomas 87
Arab Spring democracy movement
  (2010–11) 13, 230, 235
arbitration:
  and the Boer War 147
  compulsory 156
  Erasmus on 101, 106
  and the Hague Peace Conference
  (1899) 146
  on an international scale 133, 142,
  143, 145
Archidamus 56
Ardrey, Robert 30
Arendt, Hannah 172
Ares 41
Argos, treaties with Sparta 56
Ariadne 38
Aristophanes 1, 9, 58–9

Aristotle 71
Armada, Spanish 116, 117
arms industry 27–8, 220
  civilian 'spin-off' arguments
    27, 28
  as proportion of national GDP 23
  'smart' technology 28
arms race (1889–1914) 151, 152, 153
  and the Hague Peace Conference
    (1899) 144–5
  see also nuclear arms race
Aron, Raymond 29–30
Art of War (attrib. Sunzi) 6, 63, 68–9
Association Française pour la
    Société des Nations 157
Athena 70
Athens 53, 54, 55, 56
  theatre and public opinion and
    instruction 58
  treaties and alliances 56–7, 58
  see also Greek theatre
atomic bomb see nuclear weapons
Auden, W. H. 45
Augustine, St 9, 79–80, 81–4, 87, 90,
    105, 236
  on peace 82–4
Austerlitz, Battle of (1805) 18,
    168, 232
Australia, and the UN Charter
    182–3
Austrian State Treaty (1955) 195

Bacon, Nicholas 110–11
Bacon, Roger 96
Bainton, Roland 75, 77, 100
Balaclava, Battle of (1854) 138
'balance of power' concept 124
Balch, Emily Greene 176
Baldwin, Stanley 160
Baldwin of Hainault, Count 89
Balfour, Arthur 145–6
Ballou, Adin 170
Balzac, Honoré de 137
Ban Gu 52
Barash, David 6
Barot, Odysse 22

Barton, Clara 141
Basel, Treaty of (1499) 127
Battle of Britain (1940) 116
Beales, A. C. F. 151
Beaverbrook, Lord 162
Beer, Francis 2, 16
Beijing Women's Summit
    (1995) 226
Bellini, Giovanni 103
Bengal indigo strike (1860) 173
Bergen Environmental Conference
    (1990) 219
Bergson, Henri 152
Beria, Laventry 201
Berlin air corridors 194
Bernard of Clairvaux 92
Bhagavad Gita 174
Bikini Atoll nuclear testing area 206
bin Laden, Osama 231
Birn, Donald 166
Bismarck, Otto von 109
Black Death, the 85
Blackett, Patrick 208
Blair, Tony 230, 240
Blenheim, Battle of (1704) 124
Bloch, Jean de 144, 153
Blum, Léon 176
Blunden, Edmund 20
Blythe, Ronald 164
Bobbitt, Philip 231
Bodel, Jean 91
Boer War (1902) 19, 147
Bohlen, Charles 194
Boniface, Count 84
Book of Songs (Shijing) 9, 51–3
  and the reality of military
    service 52–3
  Song of Solomon compared 52
Booth, Ken 8, 236
Borodino, Battle of (1812) 137
Bosch, Hieronymus 103
Bosnia 21
  and UN peacekeeping failures
    222, 223
Botticelli, Sandro 103
Boulding, Kenneth 2, 8, 15, 22–3

Bourgeois, Léon 157
Boutros-Ghali, Boutros 223
Boxer Rebellion (1899–1901) 147
Brailsford, Henry 165–6
Branagh, Kenneth 110, 116, 118
Brandt Commission (UN, 1980) 221
Brezhnev, Leonid 202, 214
Bright, John 136
British Aerospace 27–8
British (originally, London) Peace
    Society 132, 133, 134, 136, 143,
    145, 147
British Red Cross 141
Brock, Peter 74, 93, 171
Brüning, Chancellor Heinrich 161
Buddhism:
    Chinese 72
    concepts of shanti and ahimsa 2, 3
Bull Games, Minoan Crete 34
Burckhardt, Jacob 28
Burkert, Walter 34–5
Burritt, Elihu 133, 134
Bush, George 116, 224
Bush, George W. 229

Cady, Duane 3
Cairo Population Conference
    (1992) 226
Caldicott, Helen 215
Cambodia, civilian deaths from land
    mines 220–1
Campaign for Nuclear Disarmament
    (CND), UK 205, 207, 209–10
Camus, Albert 177
Canada, opposition to nuclear
    testing 211
capitalism and the free market
    152, 198
    and war 148
Carr, E. H. 157–8
Cathar sect 93, 167
Ceadel, Martin 3–4, 245 n.12
Cecil, Lord 162, 163–4
Celsus 76
Center for Defense Information
    (CDI) 215

Center for Research on Conflict
    Resolution, Michigan 8
Chagnon, Napoleon 32–3
Chamberlain, Austen 159, 163
'Chance for Peace, A', US
    initiative 194–5
Charge of the Light Brigade
    (1854) 137
Charlemagne 88
Charles, Prince of Castile 105
Charles I of England 17
Charles III of Spain 124
Charles V, Holy Roman Emperor 107
Chechnya 238
Chelčický, Petr 170
chemical and biological weapons, and
    the Geneva protocol 146, 159
Cheney, Dick 224
Cheney, Thomas 138
Chertkov, Vladimir 170
Chiang Kai-shek 197, 200
Childers, Erskine 185, 222
China, ancient
    changing attitudes to war and
        conflict 69–72
    civil wars 63
    'pacifist bias' tradition in
        government 71
    periods of peace 24
    rural protest 173
    see also Book of Songs; Chronicles of
        Zou; 'Hundred Schools of
        Thought'; individual schools;
        Warring States Period
China, Peoples Republic of:
    Cold War foreign policy 202–3
    Cold War relations with
        USA 196–8, 200–1, 203
    Communist Party 197
    Cultural Revolution 198, 203
    excluded from the UN 186
    Great Leap Forward 203
    and nuclear deterrents 211, 212, 213
    tensions with Soviet Union 189–90
    tensions with US over
        Taiwan 197–8

Chinese Buddhism 72
chivalric values 85–6, 112
Christian Church
  and pacifism 9, 74, 75–9
  and the Peace of God movement
    88–91
  relationship with the Roman
    Empire 80
  and the Truce of God movement
    88, 89
Christian evangelists, and the early
  peace movement 132–3
Christian morality, and nuclear
  deterrent policy 78, 79
Chronicle of Zuo (Zuo Zhuan) 47–51
  and military service 50–1
  peace initiatives 49–50
Chu state, China 49, 50
Churchill, Sir Winston 11, 116,
    181, 199
  and détente with Moscow 195
  and the League of Nations
    162, 165
Cicero 81, 101, 102
Civil Defence programme (1956),
  UK 205
civil disobedience/resistance 172–5
civil rights movement, US, and
  non-violent activism 171
civil wars 225–6, 238
  in ancient China 63
  see also individual wars
Clarendon, earl of 135
Clausewitz, Carl von 6, 187–8
Clemenceau, Georges 158
climate change 233
Club de Madrid 231
Cobden, Richard 133, 134, 135, 136
Cold War 12–13, 25, 29, 186, 205,
    207, 233, 234, 236, 239
  Anglo-French position on
    disarmament 199
  and colonialism 216
  disarmament 194
  and the morality of nuclear
    deterrents 78, 79

neo-orthodox view of 193
and non-violent activism 172
peace as propaganda 187–91
post-revisionist view of 192–3
and the prevailing political
  mindset 208, 209, 213
and the Soviet 'illusion of
  peace' 193–6
US/China dialogue 196–8,
  200–1, 203
US policy representing
  capitalism 192
US/Soviet relations 198–203
see also nuclear arms race; nuclear
  deterrents; nuclear testing
Colet, John 101, 103
Collectio de Scandalis Ecclesiae 95
Collins, Colonel Tim 116
colonialism:
  and British colonial rule in
    India 171–5
  Kant's opposition to 130
Commission on Global Governance
  220, 221
Committee for the study of the
  Organization of Peace
  (CSOP) 179, 181
'common peace' treaties, Greece
  54, 57
communism, revolutionary 25,
  198, 230
Communist Information
  Bureau 190
Complaint of Peace, The (Erasmus)
  100, 103, 104, 106
Confucian School 64–6, 67, 72
  anti-war sentiments 63–4
  and humanitarian intervention
    65, 66
  and pacifist principles 67
Confucius (Kongzi) 9, 48, 64, 66, 67
Congo conflict 222
Congress of Vienna (1814–15) 132
conscientious objectors 151
  USA 175–6
Constantine, Emperor 73, 74, 75, 80

Cooper, Sandi 151
cooperation and human
     behaviour 30
Copenhagen Declaration (1995) 220
Copenhagen Social Development
     Summit (1995) 226
Corinthian War 54
Coriolanus (Shakespeare) 109,
     112, 113
Corn Laws 133
Cortright, David 6, 150, 174, 235
Council of Ambassadors proposal, by
     Crucé 125
Council of Montriond (1041) 90
Council of Nicaea (325/787) 80
Cousins, Norman 21–2, 23, 212
Cranmer, Archbishop Thomas 122
Crimean War (1853–56) 135, 137–9
   Charge of the Light Brigade 137
   newspaper coverage 137–8
Crook, David 31
Crucé, Émeric 125, 126
Cruise missiles 214, 216
Crusades 10
   First 86, 92
   as Just War 87
   motivation of crusaders 93
   opposition to 91–7
   Second 92
Cuban missile crisis (1962) 198,
     211–12
Cuellar, Javier Perez de 225
Cultural Revolution (1966–76),
     China 198, 203
Cyprus conflict 222
Cyrus the Great 54

Dalai Lama 72
Damietta, Battle of (1250) 96
Daoist School, China 63–4, 67–8
Darius, Count 84
Darwin, Charles 30–1, 152
Darwinism
   and competition 30–1
   and Kant 130
   Progressive 153

   pseudo 30–1
Daumier, Honoré 131, 140–1
Davie, M. R. 20
Davis, Patti 215
Dayton Agreement (1995) 224
de Ligt, Bart 172
de Sellon, Jean-Jaques 133
De Statu Saracenorum (William of
     Tripoli) 95
de Waal, Frans 31
Deák, Ferenc 173
Decretists 87
'democratic peace theory' 127
Derksen, John 96
development and peace linkage 13,
     216, 219–21, 236
   and the UN 221
Dickinson, Oliver 38
Diderot, Denis 124–5
Diefenbaker administration,
     Canada 212
Diogenes 71
disarmament:
   and the Frankfurt Peace
      Congress 135
   and the Hague Peace Conference
      (1899) 146
   and the League of Nations
      156, 165
   see also nuclear disarmament
Dobson, W. A. C. H. 65
Doukhobor sect 170
Dover Wilson, J. 116
Drogo, Bishop of Terouanne 89
Dulles, John Foster 195, 198,
     199, 201
Dumbarton Oaks conference
     (1944) 181, 182, 183, 184
Dunant, Henri 139–40, 145
Dynasts, The (Hardy) 16

'Earth Summit' (1992), Rio de
     Janeiro 226, 234
East Germany, 1953 uprising 202
Eastern Zhou dynasty, China 47–8
Eaton, Cyril 208

economic irrationality of war
    argument 133
Eden, Anthony 11, 161, 199
Edinburgh Peace Congress
    (1853) 135
Education of a Christian Prince
    (Erasmus) 100, 105–6, 108–9
Edward III 86
Egypt
    Arab Spring (2010–11) 230
    arms acquisitions 220
Egypt, ancient
    Middle Kingdom, and periods of
        peace 24
Eichelberger, Clark 181
Einstein, Albert 207, 208
    correspondence with Sigmund
        Freud 176–7
Eirene, goddess of peace 53–4
Eisenhower, Dwight D. 193,
        194–5, 197, 199, 204, 205, 206,
        207, 210
Elgar, Sir Edward 114
Elizabeth I 110–11, 117, 121, 122
Encyclopédie (Diderot) 124–5
Enlightenment 101, 242
    influence of Erasmus 109
    and Peace 125–31
Erasmus 6, 99, 110, 122, 125, 236
    on arbitration 106
    influence on the
        Enlightenment 109
    Machiavelli contrasted 108–9
    as peace pioneer 99–106
*Essay Towards the Present and Future
    Peace of Europe* (Penn) 125–6
Étiennes de Fougères 90–1
Euripides 58, 59, 61–2
European Nuclear Disarmament
    (END) campaign 215–16
European Union 132
Eusebius, Bishop of Caesarea 80
Evangelista, Matthew 195–6
Evans, Sir Arthur 36
Evatt, Herbert 182–3, 183–4
Eyffinger, Arthur 147

Fairbank, John King 69, 71
fascism 4
Fellowship of Reconciliation
    175–6
Ferdinand VI 123–4
Ferguson, Brian 33
Field of the Cloth of Gold 103
First World War 20, 142, 150, 154,
        158, 179
Fletcher, John 122
Florence 85, 87
Foakes, R. A. 122
Forsberg, Randall 215
Forum for a Nuclear-Free World,
    Moscow 217
Fourier, Charles 133
Fox, Liam 240
Fox, Richard, Bishop of
    Winchester 107
France
    No Fly Zones, Iraq 228
    and nuclear deterrents 211
    opposition to nuclear testing 210
    position on Cold War
        disarmament 199
Francis, St 95–6
Franco-Austrian War (1859) 137
François I 100, 103
Franco-Prussian War (1870–1)
        137, 140
    and the peace society
        movement 142–3
    and Red Cross societies 141
Frankfurt Peace Congress (1850) 135
Franz Josef I 139
Fraser, Julius 30
Frederick Hendrik, Prince of
    Orange 146
Freedman, Lawrence 6, 16
Freeze movement, US 215, 216, 217
Freud, Sigmund, correspondence
    with Albert Einstein 176–7
Friedland, Battle of (1807) 18
Friends of Peace, First International
    Congress(1848), Brussels
    133–4

Fromm, Erich 209
Fry, Douglas 8, 32
Fulbert of Chartres 73, 92
Fulbright, William 180
Fussell, Paul 20

Gaddis, John Lewis 193
Gallup, George 163
Galtung, Johan 2, 3, 235–6
Gandhi, Mohandas 'Mahatma' 3,
    11–12, 75, 167, 170
  thought and influence 171–5
Garibaldi, Giuseppe 142
Garland Library of War and Peace 6
Garrison, William Lloyd 170, 175
Gat, Azar 6, 36–7
Gay, William 16
Geddes, Patrick 26, 27
Geneva, association with peace
    movements 133
Geneva Convention, First (1864)
    10, 140
Geneva Protocol (1925) on chemical
    and biological weapons 46, 159
Geneva Society for Public
    Welfare 140
Geneva summit (1955) 195
George I 17
German Peace Cartel 157
Germany:
  appeasement with 166
  joins the League of Nations
    (1926) 159
  militarism 154
  peace movement and the Versailles
    Treaty 157
  unification question during the
    cold war 194, 195, 199, 201
  Versailles Treaty and
    disarmament 158–9
Gestapo, Nazi 176
Giap, General 63
Giaquito, Corrado 123
Gibbon, Edward 18
Giraudoux, Jean 47
Glaber, Ralph 89–90

Gladstone, William 143
Global Peace Index 2
globalization 8, 236, 242
  and world citizenship 129–30
Goldstein, Steven 200
Goodall, Jane 31
Gorbachev, Mikhail 13, 202, 217
Gorgias 55
Gospel of Matthew 20, 75
Gospels 75
Goya, Francisco 188
Grand Design plan of 'perpetual
    peace' 125–6
Gratian, Emperor 81
Gratian, jurist 81, 87
Graves, Robert 41–2, 47
Great Exhibition (1851),
    London 135
Great Leap Forward (1958–61),
    China 203
Greek city states, peace and war
    in 53–5
  changing attitudes to war and
    conflict 69–72
  and the decision to go to
    war 70–1
  diplomacy and debate 56–8
  heralds and envoys 56
  and Thucydides' history 55
  see also Athens
Greek theatre 71
  and peace advocacy 58–62,
    59–62
Green, Howard 212
Gregg, Richard 171
Gregory X, Pope 94, 95
Grey, Edward 158, 269 n.33
Gromyko, Andrei 183, 184
Grotius, Hugo 101
Guan Yin 72
Gueroult, M. De 135
guerrilla techniques 238
Guillaume de Clerc 91
Gulf War (1991) 63, 116, 219, 220,
    222, 224–5, 227, 229, 237,
    277 n.44

H–bomb development 206, 208
Hague Peace Conference
  (1899) 142–9, 151, 153
  and the arms race 144–5
  and disarmament 146
  establishing a uniform practice of
    arbitration 146
  and the laws of war 146
  Muraviev Circular 146
Haig, General Douglas 20
Haines, Keith 97
Halliday, Fred 238
Hammarskjöld, Dag 194
Han dynasty, China 53, 62, 68
Hankey, Maurice 165
Haq, Mahbub ul 219
Hardy, Thomas 16, 113, 232
Hazlitt, William 10, 117
Hector:
  in the Iliad 43–4, 47, 70
  in Shakespeare 119–20, 120–1
Helen of Troy in the Iliad 42, 43,
  46, 47
Hemleben, Sylvester 154
Henderson, Arthur 161
Henig, Ruth 160
Henry III, Emperor 90
Henry IV (Shakespeare) 122, 125
Henry V (Shakespeare) 10, 109,
  110, 112, 113, 115, 116–19, 117,
  120, 122
Henry VII 101, 112
Henry VIII 100, 101, 103, 107, 122
Hephaestus 45
Hera 43
Herakles (Euripides) 61–2
Herodotus 36, 54
Hersey, John 206
High Commission for Refugees
  (UNHCR) 156
Hindu concepts of shanti and
  ahimsa 2, 3
Hiroshima atomic bomb attack 179,
  180, 206
Hispanic-Roman era, and periods of
  peace 24

Hitler, Adolf 161, 176
Hobbes, Thomas 30, 244 n.2
Hockney, David 189
Holinshed, Raphael 118
Holt, Harold 190
Holy Roman Empire 173
Homer 8–9, 10, 35, 39, 40–7, 56, 70, 71
  'countra–factual hypotheticals' in
    the Iliad 47
  description of the Shield of
    Achilles in the Iliad 9, 44–6, 47,
    251 n.19, 252 n.21
  depictions of war in the Iliad 8–9,
    40–2
  'process of refinement' in the
    Iliad 46–7
Hoover Plan, US 161
Hopkins, Harry 183
Hornblower, Simon 55
Howard, Michael 100, 150, 151
Hudson Institute 25
Hughes, Emmet John 199
Hugo, Victor 131–2, 134, 142, 267 n.33
Huizinga, Johan 100
Human Development Goals, UN 226
Human Development Reports
  (UNDP) 2, 219–20, 226, 240
human nature, and war/
  aggression 29–34
human rights:
  dawning of 148
  and the UN Charter 184
Human Security Report (2005),
  UN 236
humanism, and the Utopians 102
humanist approaches to war and
  peace 98–122
humanitarianism:
  and Confucian thought 65, 66
  and nineteenth century
    Europe 136–41
Humbert of Romans
  94, 96
'Hundred Schools of Thought',
  Warring States period, China
  9, 63, 69, 70

Hungary:
  civil disobedience/resistance to
    Austrian rule 173
  1956 uprising 202
Hunt, Peter 58
Hussein, Saddam 220, 225
Hussite movement 170
Hutchins, Robert Maynard 5

Iliad (Homer) 8–9, 35, 39, 40–7, 70, 71
  'countra–factual hypotheticals' 47
  depictions of war in the *Iliad* 8–9,
    40–2
  peace thread 42–4
  'process of refinement' 46–7
  and the shield of Achilles 9, 44–6,
    47, 251 n.19, 251 n.19, 252 n.21
imperialism 152
Independent Nuclear Disarmament
    Committee 210
India:
  and British colonial rule 171–5
  Mahratta peasant protests
    (1875) 173–4
  Mysore rural protest (1830) 173
  and nuclear weapons 213, 239
  and rural protest 173–4
  Salt March (1930) 171
Indochina, cease-fires 195
Innocent III, Pope 94
Inquisition 101
Institute for Defense and
    Disarmament Studies
    (IDDS) 215
Intermediate-Range Nuclear Forces
    (INF) Treaty (1987) 217
International Consultative Group
    for Peace and
    Disarmament 159
International Court of Justice, The
    Hague 233–4
International Criminal Court, The
    Hague 234
International Crusade of Peace 145
International Federation of League
    of Nations Societies 157

International Fellowship of
    Reconciliation 176
International Labour Organization
    (ILO) 11, 156, 229
international law 129
  Grotius on 101
  growth in 233–4
  humanitarian 137, 142
  Kant on 130
  and nuclear weapons 233–4
  and the UN Charter 184
International Monetary Fund
    (IMF) 219
International Peace Bureau,
    Berne 143–4, 154
International Women's Congress for
    Peace and Freedom (1915), The
    Hague 154
Inter-Parliamentary Conference
    (IPC), Paris (1889) 143, 144–5
Iran, and nuclear weapons 239
Iraq:
  arms acquisitions 220
  and the Gulf War 63, 116, 219,
    220, 222, 224–5, 227, 229, 237
  Oil for Food programme 227–8
  UN economic sanctions
    against 227–8
Iraq invasion (2003) 4, 13, 79, 116,
    219, 224, 229, 230, 233, 236
  No Fly Zones 228
Islam, attitudes to war and peace 239
Islamic fundamentalism 230, 238,
    279 n.22
Isocrates 57, 58
Israel 194
  arms acquisitions 220
  defence industry 28
  Jewish refugees 176
  and nuclear weapons 239
Israel-Palestine conflict 229, 230, 239
Italian unification 139
Iyer, Raghavan 172

James I 121, 122
James, William 28–9

Japan, and rural protest 173
Jaurès, Jean 148–9
Jean, King of France 86
Jenkins, Harold 110
Jerusalem:
    Latin Kingdom of 94
    sack of 86
Jesus and pacifism 74, 75–6
Jewish refugees 176
Jin state, China 49, 50
Jixia Academy, Qi state, China 63
Johnson, James Turner 81
Johnson, Dr Samuel 118
Jones, General David 214
Jones, Peter 41
Jorgensen, Paul 109–10
Joshua, Book of 83
journalism, and war reporting
    137–8
Judas 75
Julian, Emperor 73–4, 80
Julius, Pope 108
'Just War' doctrine and theory 4,
    79–84, 87
    Crusades as 87
    and the Old Testament 81
    and Shakespeare 112
Justin Martyr 75

Kahn, Herman 25
Kaldor, Mary 216
Kant, Immanuel 10–11, 101, 127–31,
    236, 266 n.12
    and Darwinism 130
    on international law 130
    League of Nations proposal 127
    opposition to colonialism 130
Kashmir conflict 222
Keeley, Lawrence 31–2
Kennedy, President John F. 212–13
Kennedy, Paul 237
Kephisodotos 53
Keynes, John Maynard 155
Khrushchev, Nikita 201, 205, 207,
    208, 212, 213
King, Tom 224

'King's Peace', Greece 54
Kissinger, Henry 198
Kleffens, Eelco van 182
Knossos palace, Minoan Crete 34,
    36, 37
Knowland, William 195
Kolko, Gabriel 5, 199, 202
Kolko, Joyce 199
Korean War 186, 194, 195, 197, 207
    ceasefires 195
    truce talks 189
Kosovo, NATO operation 224, 229
Kropotkin, Peter 168
Kuboyama, Aikichi 206
Kurds, Iraqi 228
Kutuzov, General Mikhail 168
Kuwait 224

Labaume, Eugène 136
land mines, and civilian
    casualties 220–1
    international conference on
    (1996) 220
Landes, Richard 90
Laozi 63, 67–8
Lapp, Ralph 206
Lassie, TV serial 191
Last Supper 75–6
Lau, D. C. 64
Lausanne, Treaty of (1923) 155
Le Sauvage, Jean 105
League of European States proposal
    (1712) 126–7
League of Nations 11, 12, 154–8,
    164, 176, 177, 178, 180, 224
    and British colonial rule in
    India 171
    and Churchill 162, 165
    and disarmament 156, 159, 165
    establishment of World
    Court 156, 157
    failure of the World Disarmament
    Conference 160
    foundation and covenant 155–6
    modern judgement on its 'failure'
    164–6

Permanent Mandates
    Commission 156
popular support in Britain 162
and 'positive peace' 156
UN compared 186
US Senate's rejection of 157
League of Nations Association 157
League of Nations Federation 209
League of Nations Union
    (LNU) 162, 163
British branch 157, 165, 186
League to Enforce Peace, USA 154
LeBlanc, Steven 31–2
Legalist (fajia) School, China 63,
    66, 71
endorsement of war 69
Leipzig, Battle of (Battle of
    Nations, 1813) 137
Lenin, Vladimir 148, 170
Lewin, Leonard 25, 26
Liddell Hart, Basil 161
Ligue Internationale de la Paix ed
    de la Liberté (LPL), Geneva
    (1867) 142
Ligue Internationale et Permanente
    de la Paix (LPP), Paris
    (1867) 142
Linear B tablets, from the Minoan
    civilization 35, 250 n.62
Litvinov, Maxim 159
Lloyd, Selwyn 211
Lloyd George, David 160
Locke, John 109
London, Treaty of (1518) 103
London Naval Treaty (1930) 159
London Peace Congress (1851) 135–6
Lorenz, Konrad 30
Lorenzetti, Ambrogio 84–5
Loyd-Lindsay, Colonel Robert 141
Lucky Dragon, fishing vessel 206
Luxemburg, Rosa 148, 149
Lynch, Cecilia 166, 270 n.56
Lysistrata (Aristophanes) 59

MacDonald, Ramsay 160, 161
Machiavelli 6, 10, 87, 99, 100

Erasmus contrasted 108–9
on statecraft 111
Mackail, J. W. 99–100
MacKinney, Loren 90, 92
Macmillan, Harold 204, 205, 212
Mahratta, peasant protests
    (1875) 173–4
Malenkov, Georgy 194, 195, 201
Malik, Jacob 189
Mallia palace, Minoan Crete 34
'man the warrior' outlook 32–3
Manchester Peace Congress
    (1853) 135
Manet, Édouard 188
Mantinea treaties with Sparta 56
Mao Zedong 63, 71–2, 196, 198,
    201, 203
Marcellus 76
Marlowe, Christopher 111
Martin, St 7, 3–4
Martini, Simone 73–4
Marvell, Andrew 17–18
Marx, Steven 120
Mary, Princess 106–7
Mattox, John 81
Matz, Friedrich 34, 249 n.57
Maude, Aylmer 168
Maupassant, Guy de 141
Maximilian, Roman legionary 77
McCarran Senate Internal Security
    Subcommittee, US 187
McCarthyism 189
and the UN 186–7
McKinley, President William 147
Meagher, Robert 62, 71
Medvedev, Roy 202
Melko, Matthew 23–4
Melman, Seymour 209
Melos massacre 61
Melvern, Linda 187, 224
Menelaus 42–3
Mengzi (Mencius) 63–4, 64–5, 66, 67
Meron, Theodor 112
Mexico-US war (1846–8) 170
'Micro Uninhabited Aerial Vehicle'
    (MUAV, miniature drone) 27–8

Middle Ages 84–97
    and the development of
        warfare 87
MIG fighter pilots 191
militarism 152
    German 154
military expenditure, global 225
military technology, at the time of
        the Seven Years War 124
millennialism 89, 90
Minoan civilization 34–8
    comparison with Victorian
        Britain 36
    and fortifications 34–6
    and human sacrifice 37
    Linear B tablets 35, 250 n.62
Minos, King 37–8
Mohist School, China 66–7, 68
    anti-war sentiments 63–4
    and pacifism 68
Molinari, Gustave de 153
Molotov, Vyacheslav 199
Montessori, Maria 177
More, Sir Thomas 10, 101, 100,
        102–3, 108, 263 n.16
Moscow, 1812 136–7
Moscow Declaration (1943) 180–1
Mozambique, civilian deaths from
        land mines 221
Mozi (Mo Tzu) 64, 66–7
Mumford, Lewis 26
Munster, Peace of (1648) 146
Muraviev, Count Mikhail 144, 145
Muraviev Circular 146
Mussolini, Benito 161, 176
MX intercontinental missile 191
Mycenaean civilization 34, 35, 36,
        37, 38, 70
    and militarism 39–40
Mysore, rural protest (1830) 173

Nagasaki atomic bomb attack 206
Napoleon Bonaparte 18, 41, 63, 127,
        136–7
Napoleon III, Emperor 134,
        139, 140

Napoleonic Wars 11, 124, 132,
        136–7
    and economic progress 27
nation–states:
    and the capacity to wage war
        16, 25
    internal structure and external
        behaviour 101
nationalism 151, 152
NATO 209, 221
    deployment of nuclear
        weapons 206
    Kosovo operation 224, 229
    Somalia mission 223
Nazism 76, 159
    rise of, in Germany 160
    neo-Nazis 233
Needham, Joseph 71
Nef, John 26
Nehru, Jawaharlal 217
neo-Nazis 233
'neo-Realist' school of international
        relations 218, 219
Nesselrode, Count 135
Netherlands, and the UN
        Charter 182
neutron bomb 215
New England Non-Resistance
        Society, USA 170
New Testament 75
New Zealand, opposition to nuclear
        testing 211
newspaper and media war
        reporting 137–8, 237–8
Nicholas II, Tsar 153
    and the Hague Peace Conference
        (1899) 144, 145, 146
Nicias, Peace of (421 BC) 56–7, 59
Nicolson, Harold 155, 164
Nietzsche, Friedrich 152
Niger, Ralph 94
Nightingale, Florence 137
Nilsson, Martin 36
9/11 terrorist attack 25, 79, 219, 225,
        228, 231
Nixon, President Richard 198

No Gun Ri allegations, Vietnam War 188, 189
Nobel Peace Prize 142, 176, 196, 241
Noel-Baker, Philip 160–1, 166, 196
non-violent activism 3, 166–75, 234–5
women's effectiveness 171
North Korea, and nuclear weapons 239
Northedge, F. S. 160
Northern Ireland sectarian conflict 230
Noveschi (Council of Nine) 85
Novicow, Jacques 153
Noyen, Treaty of (1516) 103
nuclear arms race 195–6, 213, 214, 239–40
nuclear deterrents
and Christian morality 78, 79
theory of 205
nuclear disarmament 166, 181, 194, 201, 234
Anglo-French memorandum 195–6
Western proposals (1955) 200, 209
nuclear disarmament campaigns 210–17, 234
Campaign for Nuclear Disarmament (CND), UK 205, 207, 209–10
European Nuclear Disarmament (END) 215–16
Forum for a Nuclear-Free World, Moscow 217
Freeze movement, USA 215, 216, 217
Independent Nuclear Disarmament Committee 210
National Committee for a SANE Nuclear Policy (USA) 207, 212, 213
Pugwash movement 204, 208, 209
Nuclear Non-Proliferation Treaty (NPT) (1968) 13, 213, 214, 234, 239

nuclear power, as spin-off technology 27
Nuclear Test-Ban Treaty (1963) 13, 208, 212, 213, 214, 222, 234
nuclear testing 204, 208
campaigns against 210–11, 234
and the threat to human reproduction 206–7
nuclear weapons 12–13, 178, 179, 186
and international law 233–4
Nuclear Weapons Freeze Campaign (Freeze), USA 215, 216, 217

O'Donnell, James 79
Odysseus in the Iliad 40, 42, 47, 60
Odyssey (Homer) 45
Ogarkov, Nikolai 202
Oil for Food programme, Iraq 227–8
Old Testament and 'just war' 81
Olivier, Laurence 110, 118
Organization for Economic Co-operation and Development (OECD) 225
Origen 76, 77, 78
Osborn, Henry Fairfield Jr. 187
Othello (Shakespeare) 17, 114
Oxford Research Group 241
Oxford Union debate, on fighting for 'King and country' 162

pacificism 4, 132, 245 n.12
pacifism 29, 171, 172, 245 n.12
contradictions with socialism 148–9
and the early Christian Church 9, 74, 75–9
first usage of the term 3–4, 151
Jacobean 121
in medieval Europe 97
in 1930's Britain 162
and the Peace Ballot (1934–5) 164
scientific 148
Pakistan, and nuclear weapons 239
Palestine-Israel conflict 229, 230, 239

Palestinian rights 229
Palmerston, Lord 136
Paris, Peace of (1515) 103
Paris Peace Conference (1919)
    155, 156
Paris Peace Congress (1849)
    131–2, 134
Paris Peace Treaty (1783) 19
'Parisienne, La' fresco 35
Partlow, Vern 178
Passy, Frederic 142
Patroclus in the *Iliad* 43–4
Pauling, Linus 207, 242
pax romana 102
Peace (Aristophanes) 59
peace and development linkage 13,
    216, 219–21, 236
  and the UN 221
peace as propaganda, Cold War
    187–91
Peace Ballot (1934–5) 161–4
  and pacifism 164
Peace Congresses (1848–51) 144
'peace dividend' 218, 219, 225, 230
  and the Third World 219
peace movements:
  and the American Civil war
    136, 143
  association with Geneva 133
  before the outbreak of First World
    War 150–2, 153
  birth of 131–6
  campaigns against nuclear
    testing 234
  campaigns for nuclear
    disarmament 210–17, 234
  and Christian evangelists 132–3
  demobilized by the ending of the
    Cold War 225, 230, 241
  and the Franco-Prussian
    War 142–3
  inter-war period 175–7
  from the late 1860s 142,
    143–4, 157
  at the outbreak of the First World
    War 154

  and the Quakers 132–3
  resurgence in the mid-1950's
    204–31
  in the US 157
  see also individual movements
Peace of God (*pax dei*)
    movement 88–91 *see also* Truce
    of God movement
'Peace Offensive', Soviet 189–91, 199
Peace Pledge Union 176
peace studies, academic 6, 235, 236,
    241, 245–6 n.17
peace treaties, numbers of 22
peacekeeping, international 132
  UN missions 218, 222–4
Peloponnesian War (431–404 BC) 54,
    55, 56, 61
Penn, William 125–6
Pepper, Claude 180
Pericles 56, 57, 58
Permanent Court of Arbitration,
    The Hague 146
Perpetual Peace (Russell) 127–31
Pershing missiles 214
Persian empire 54
Persian Wars 54
Peter, St 75
Phaistos palace, Minoan Crete 34
Philemon 19–20
Philip of Macedon 57
Philip II of Spain 111
Picasso, Pablo 188–9
Pines, Yuri 70
Plato 71
Playne, Caroline 176
Ploutos 53
Plutarch 56–7, 101
Portal, Charles, Lord
    Hungerford 205
Portsmouth, Treaty of (1905) 19
'positive peace' and the League of
    Nations 156
poverty reduction, global 240
Predator drone 27–8
Priam, King 70
Prince, The (Machiavelli) 108

prisoners of war 156
Proudhon, Pierre-Joseph 169
Pugwash movement 204, 208, 209

Qi state, China 49, 50
Qin state, China 9, 49, 50, 62
Quakerism 167
    American Friends Service
        Committee (AFSC) 176
    and the early peace
        movement 132–3
    *Qunqiu (Spring and Autumn
        Annals)* 48

Rabkin, Norman 118
Radical Alliance, UK 210
Raimon Gaucelm de Béziers 95
Rapacki, Adam 209
'Rapacki Plan' 209
Rapaport, Anatol 33–4
Reagan, President Ronald 214,
    215, 217
'reciprocal altruism' 236
Red Cross 140, 142
    and the Franco-Prussian War 141
Reformation 101
refugees 156, 176
Register, Katherine 31–2
Renaissance period 110
    and the military ethos 87
    view of Ancient Rome 101–2
Report from Iron Mountain, US 25–6
republican forms of government,
    Kant on 128
Reston, James 183
Reves, Emery 179–80
Reykjavik summit (1986) 217
Richard II 112
Richard, Henry 134, 143
Richardson, Lewis Fry 23
Richet, Charles 153
Rieu, E.V. 41
Robert the Monk 93
Roberts, Adam 172
Robertson, Norman 212
'rogue states' 239–40

Roman Empire's relationship with
    the Christian Church 80
Romulu, Carlos 179
Ronsard, Pierre 98
Roosevelt, Eleanor 179
Roosevelt, President Franklin D.
    176, 179, 181, 192, 196, 213
Roosevelt, President Theodore 147
Root, Elihu 147, 148
Roshwald, Mordecai 207
Rotblat, Joseph 209
Rousseau, Jean-Jacques 31, 127
Royal Albert Hall disarmament rally
    (1931) 159–60
Rubens, Peter Paul 98–9, 262 n.3
Rumsfeld, Donald 230
Runciman, Steven 93
Rusk, Dean 212
Ruskin, John 28, 174
Russell, Bertrand 131, 207, 208, 209
    Russell-Einstein Manifesto 217
Russell, William Howard 137, 138
Russo-Japanese War (1904–5)
    63, 147
Ruttan, Vernon 27
Rwanda:
    and UN peacekeeping
        failures 222, 223
    war crime tribunals 234

Saddam Hussein 227, 229, 238,
    277 n.42
Saint-Pierre, Abbé de 126–7, 140
Saint-Simon, Henri de 133
Sakharov, Andrei 217
Salamis, Battle of (306 BC) 60
Salt March (1930), India 171
Sampson, Ronald 168–9
samurai warriors 86
San Francisco conference
    (1945) 181–4, 185
SANE nuclear disarmament
    movement, USA 207, 212, 213
Saudi Arabia, and arms
    acquisitions 220
Save the Children 228

Savonarola, Girolamo 103
Say, Jean-Paul 133
Schell, Jonathan 235
School of Strategists (*bingjia*),
    China 63
Schweitzer, Albert 207
Sebastopol, Crimea 137, 138
Second Opium War (1856–60) 136
Second World Peace Congress,
    Warsaw 190
Second World War 20, 29,
    63, 171
'security, sustainable' 241
Sedan, Battle of (1870) 140
Seljuk Turks 92
Sen, Amartya 236
Seneca 101
Seven Years War (1756–63) 124
Sèvres, Treaty of (1920) 155
Shakespeare, William 10, 17, 99
    and the doctrine of Just War 112
    and pacifism 120
    on peace and war 109–22
    and Renaissance thinking 110
    see also individual plays
Shang dynasty, China 52, 70
    and militarism 39–40
shanti concept 2
Shaw, George Bernard 20, 152
Shay, Jonathan 71
Shen Shushi 49
Shia Muslims, Iraq 228
Shotwell, James 179
Shute, Nevil 207
Siberry, Elizabeth 94, 96–7
siege warfare 87
Siena 84–5
Sima Qian 62, 63
Simon, Sir John 161
Simon de Montfort 95
slavery, opposition to 130, 132, 133
Smuts, General Jan 156
socialism 148–9
Société de la Paix de Genève
    (1830) 133
Solferino, Battle of (1859) 139–40

Somalia, UN peacekeeping
    failures 222–4
Sombart, Werner 26
Song of Solomon 52
Song state, China 49–50
Song Xing 68
Song Xu 49–50
Sophocles 59–60
Sorokin, Pitirim 23
Southall, Joseph 154
Southey, Robert 124
Soviet Union:
    anti-Zionist campaign 194
    China tensions 189–90
    Churchill's détente
        approaches 195
    Cold War foreign policy
        202, 203
    Cold War 'Peace Offensive'
        189–91, 199
    Cold War relations with US
        198–203
    control of Poland 182
    de-Stalinization 201
    defence spending 1980–1 202
    disintegration of 25, 218
    German unification proposals 199
    joins the League of Nations
        (1934) 159
    military capability at the time of
        Stalin's death 200
    military control of the
        Dardanelles and the
        Bosphorous 194
    nuclear deterrence doctrine
        207–9
    Party Congresses 201, 207
    post-Stalinist 'illusion of
        peace' 193–6
    and the UN 181
Spanish Armada 111
Sparta 54, 56, 57
    treaties with Argos and
        Mantinea 56
Spinoza, Baruch 244–5 n.2
Sponeck, Hans von 227, 228

Spring and Autumn (*Qunqui*) period, China 9, 47–8, 51, 62, 64, 69, 70

Spring and Autumn Annals 65

Stalin, Joseph 181, 183, 191, 193, 197, 198, 201

Stalinist purges 171

'Star Wars' initiative and technology 215, 217

Stassen, Harold 200

Stead, William 147

Steele, Jonathan 216

Stendhal 137

Stettinius, Edward 184

Stevenson, Adlai 205–6

Stockholm Conference on the Human Environment (1972), UN 187

Stoics 101, 102

Strategist School, China 65–6, 68–9

Street, Jessie 190

Stresemann, Gustav 161

Stuttgart Congress of the Second Socialist International (1907) 149

Suez Canal 133, 161

Sully, duc de 125–6

Sulpicius Severus 74

Sunzi 6, 63, 68–9

Sustainable Security initiative, Oxford Research Group 231

Suttner, Bertha von 145, 151–2

Sweden, rejecting the nuclear option 211

Synod of Charroux (989) 88

Syracuse 57

Taiwan 197–8, 200

Taiwan straits crisis 205

Tang dynasty, China 53

Tate, Merze 147

Tate Liverpool gallery 189

Taylor, A. J. P. 147, 210

Temple of Concorde, Green Park 18

Tennyson, Alfred, Lord 14, 137, 246 n.26

terrorism 237

Islamist 13, 229, 230–1, 238–9

Tertullian 75–6, 77, 78

Test-Ban Treaty, Nuclear (1963) 13, 208, 212, 213, 214, 222, 234

Thackeray, William Makepeace 137

Thatcher, Margaret 6, 235, 245 n.17

Thebes 54, 57

Thersites 47

Theseus and the Minotaur 37–8

Thetis 44

Thich Nhat Hanh 2–3

Third Coalition (1805) 127

Thomas Aquinas, St 81

Thomas of Celano 96

Thompson, E. P. 216, 217

Thoreau, Henry 170, 174, 175

Thorsson Report (1982) 221

Throop, Palmer 94, 95, 96

Thucydides 4, 36, 54, 55, 56, 58, 245 n.13

Tibet 72

Tolstoy, Leo 11, 137, 138–9, 145, 174, 175, 232

thought and influence 167–71

Toynbee, Arnold 15, 27

Treaty of Universal Peace (1520) 103

Trident missile force 240

Tritle, Lawrence 60, 71

Troilus and Cressida (Shakespeare) 10, 109, 110, 112–13, 115–16, 119–22

Trojan War 60, 70, 109

and the *Iliad* 40–7

Trojan Women (Euripides) 61

Truce of God (*treuga dei*) movement 88, 89 *see also* Peace of God movement

Truman, President Harry S. 182, 183, 192

Tuchman, Barbara 86, 152

Tunisia, and the Arab Spring movement (2010–11) 230

Turkey-Serbia War (1876) 141

United Kingdom:
  Civil Defence programme
    (1956) 205
  contemporary thinking on atomic
    weapons 240
  and the invasion of Iraq 4, 13,
    79, 116, 219, 224, 229, 230,
    233, 236
  Labour Party policy on nuclear
    deterrents 206
  No Fly Zones, Iraq 228
  nuclear testing and public opinion
    210–11
  nuclear war policy 205
  policy on Iraq after the Gulf War
    227–9
  position on Cold War
    disarmament 199
  UN Association 186
United Nations (UN) 2, 11, 12, 13,
    128, 131, 230, 233, 241
  Conference on the Human
    Environment, Stockholm
    (1972) 187
  Disarmament Subcommittee
    (1955), Geneva 195–6
  and economic sanctions against
    Iraq 227–8
  founding of 179, 180–1
  General Assembly 182, 183,
    184, 185
  and the Gulf War 224–5
  Human Development Goals 226
  Human Development Reports 2,
    219–20, 226, 240
  Human Security Report
    (2005) 236
  and the humanitarian
    challenge 21
  internal reform agenda 237
  Iraq resolutions 229
  Kosovo intervention 224, 229
  League of Nations compared 186
  and McCarthyism 186–7
  Military Staff Committee
    (MSC) 184–5, 223–4

Millennium Declaration 221,
    226–7
  peace and development
    linkage 221
  peacekeeping missions 218,
    222–4
  provision for armed forces 184–5
  register for arms sales 220
  Security Council 181, 182, 183,
    184–5
  sponsored environmental
    conference (1949) 187
  veto issue 183
United Nations Charter 181, 182–6
  Article 41 224
  Article 42 224
  Article 45 223
  Article 47 223–4
  chapter VI 225
  chapter VII 225, 228
  human rights 184
  and international law 184
United Nations Development
    Programme (UNDP) 219–20
United Nations Educational,
    Scientific and Cultural
    Organization (UNESCO)
    6, 241
United Nations High Commissioner
    for Refugees (UNHCR) 156
Union of Democratic Control
    (1914) 155
Universal Peace Conference (1889),
    Paris 143, 144–5
Universal Peace Congress (1908),
    London 150
Universal Peace Union, America
    (1866) 136
Urban II, Pope 92, 93
United States of America:
  'Better Dead than Red' Senate
    amendment 205
  'A Chance for Peace'
    initiative 194–5
  Cold War disarmament
    policy 200

Cold War hostility to the socialist
economic alternative 192
Cold War policy representing the
capitalist system 192
Cold War relations with
China 196–8, 200–1, 203
Cold War relations with Soviet
Union 198–203
and the Gulf War 63, 116, 219,
220, 222, 224–5, 227, 229, 237
Hoover Plan 161
and the invasion of Iraq 4, 13, 79,
116, 119, 224, 229, 230, 233, 236
McCarran Senate Internal
Security Subcommittee,
US 187
McCarthism 186–7, 189
Mutual Defence Treaty with
Taiwan 197
No Fly Zones, Iraq 228
nuclear deterrence doctrine
207–9
nuclear testing and public
opinion 211
policy towards Iraq after Gulf
War 227–9
reaction to Churchill's détente
approaches to Moscow 195
reaction to the Soviet 'Peace
Offensive' 190–1
Senate's rejection of the League of
Nations 157
and the Soviet post-Stalinist
'illusion of peace' 193–6
Strategic Air Command
motto 191
tensions with China over
Taiwan 197–8
and the UN 181
US-Mexico War (1846–8) 170
Ustinov, Dmitri 202
Utopians and humanism 102

van Creveld, Martin 29
van den Dungen, Peter 100–1
Van Tassel, Alfred 187

van Wees, Hans 55
Vandenberg Air Force Base,
California 191
Vansittart, Robert 165
Vellacott, Philip 58, 61
Versailles, Treaty of (1919) 155, 160
and German disarmament 158–9
and peace groups in
Germany 157
Vespucci, Amerigo 102
Victor Emmanual II 139
Vietnam War 4, 60, 63, 71, 79,
233, 236
campaign against 214
No Gun Ri allegations 188, 189
Vitricius, St 74
Vives, Juan Luis 101, 106–8
and concepts anticipating the
League of Nations 107–8
Voltaire 109, 166

Waldensian sect 93, 167
Waley, Arthur 52
Walpole, Robert 17
Walter, J. H. 116–17
Walters, F. P. 155
Walzer, Michael 79
war and peace:
anthropology of 29–34
benefits of 24–9
cost–benefit analysis of 25
language of 16–20
statistics of 20–4
War and Peace (Tolstoy) 167–9
War of the Spanish Succession
(1701–14) 124, 126
'war on terror' 25
War Resisters International
(WRI) 176
war/aggression, and animal
behaviour 31
warfare:
development in the Middle
Ages 87
and the Renaissance ethos 87
and sieges 87

Warring States period, China 9, 39, 40, 53, 62–4, 65
and the decision to go to war 70–1
and the Strategist School 69
'Wars of Italy' period 108
Wars of the Roses (1455–87) 101
Washington, Treaty of (1871) 143
Washington Naval Treaty (1922) 159
Watson, Burton 65
Weigel, Richard 24
Weil, Simone 41
Wells, H. G. 155
West Germany, opposition to nuclear testing 210
Whitman, Walt 232, 278 n.1
William of Tripoli 95
Wilson Knight, G. 110
Wilson, President Woodrow 154–5, 156, 205, 206–7
Willkie, Wendell 179
Wolsey, Cardinal 103, 107
women, and non-violent activism 171
Women's International League for Peace and Freedom (WILPF) 154, 159, 176
Wood, Mary Morton 90
Wood, Michael 229
Woolf, Leonard 166
Worcester, Noah 132
World Anti-Slavery Convention (1840) 133
World Bank 219, 225, 226
world citizenship 129–30
World Court, established by the League of Nations 156, 157
World Disarmament Conference (1932), Geneva 11, 158–61, 176
British role in 165
World Disarmament Petition 159

World Fair (1867), Paris 140
world government concept 179
World Peace Congress (1950) 189
World Peace Council 191
World Social Forum (2001) 234
World Social Summit (1995) 220
World Social Summit (2000) 221
Wright, Michael 211
Wright, Quincy 23
Wright Mills, Charles 209
Wuzi 69

Xenophon 54, 55
Xerxes 60
Xuan of Qi, King 62–3, 65
Xunzi (Hsun Tzu) 65–6, 67

Yalta conference (1945) 181
'Yalta model' 192
Yan state, China 65
Yanomami people 32–3
Yin Wen 68
Yoder, John Howard 78
Young, Edward 17
Young, Kenneth 197, 198
Yugoslavia 194
war crime tribunals 234

Zakros palace, Minoan Crete 34
Zampaglione, Gerardo 46, 255 n.77
Zeus 42, 43
Zhang Baijia 203
Zhong Zhong 35
Zhou dynasty and kingdoms, China 64, 70
Zhou Enlai 203
Zhuangzi 68, 257 n.114
Zifan 49
Zola, Émile 141
Zweig, Stefan 108